B.L. Ullmann and N. E. Henry

ELEMENTARY LATIN

Simon Publications

2000

About the Authors

When this book was written in the
early 1920s

B.L. Ullman, Ph.D., was Professor of
Latin at the University of Chicago

Norman E. Henry, M.A., taught at the
Peabody High School in Pittsburgh

Requiescunt in Pace

If elegancy still preceedeth, and English pens
maintain that stream [of new words] we have
of late observed to flow from many, we shall
within a few years be fain to learn Latin to
understand English.

– Sir Thomas Browne, 1646

TO THE TEACHER

ATTENTION is here called to the chief features of this book in order that teachers may use it most effectively.[1]

1. Latin for English. — First among the new features is the attention given to the correlation of Latin and English, for it is generally admitted that the chief value of first year Latin for most students is in the increased knowledge of English which it affords. Latin and English are correlated throughout as follows:

(a) *Vocabulary.* — The vocabulary of the lessons was taken chiefly from an unpublished list of those Latin words which have the largest number of English derivatives in ordinary prose. This list is the result of exhaustive research. The total vocabulary consists of only six hundred three words. Three hundred eighty-six of these words are primitives and two hundred seventeen are derivatives. The authors have made it a practice not to introduce Latin derivatives until after the primitive has been encountered, so that the task of mastering the lesson vocabularies may be simplified and the student taught to associate words according to their root meaning. By reference to Lodge's *Vocabulary of High School Latin*, it will be found that five hundred eight of these words are used five or more times in Caesar, although they

---

[1] In the preparation of this book careful consideration was given to the unpublished recommendations of the Committee on Classical Languages, appointed by the National Education Association, and to the *Latin Sylla bus for Secondary Schools*, published by the University of the State of New York. Teachers will also find that the book meets the suggestions and requirements of the latest syllabi issued by various other state departments of public instruction.

are of a general rather than of a strictly military character. Many more Caesarean words occur in the reading selections.

For the benefit of New York teachers, it is pointed out that approximately ninety per cent of the words required by the New York Syllabus for the first and second half-years have been used in the lessons; the remaining are included in the general vocabulary at the end of the book. It will require little time for the teacher to dictate the Syllabus list by half-years and have the class check these words in the general vocabulary for special study for efficiency tests.

(*b*) *Word Study*. — Every lesson contains Latin and English Word Studies covering such topics as prefixes, suffixes, loan words, phonetic changes, spelling, interesting words, abbreviations, phrases and quotations, etc. Topics are introduced in the order of their importance and *grow out of the material presented in the lessons;* they are not relegated to the appendix.

(*c*) *Laboratory Method*. — The arrangement of a notebook giving English derivatives is explained and its use urged. Encouragement in its use is furnished by giving after each word in the lesson vocabularies one English derivative or related Latin word previously studied.

(*d*) *Correlation of Latin and English Grammar*. — A section of the Appendix is devoted to the elementary principles of grammar usually studied before the seventh grade. These are illustrated by English and Latin examples. The material is based upon that in use in the elementary schools. In the lessons themselves the topics treated in Elementary Grammar are assigned for review at the appropriate points. Some teachers may prefer to review this material at the outset.

In discussing matters of form and syntax, constant reference is made to English usage, and many difficult points in English grammar are elucidated (*e.g.* the relative and interrogative pronouns, Lesson XLIII). Difficult matters are developed slowly and with constant reference to English (cf. the infinitive, including indirect statement, Lessons XVIII, XXXVI, LXVI, and the participle, Lessons XLVII, L, LXIV).

2. Simplification: (*a*) *Forms.* — In accordance with certain special investigations as to relative frequency, many unimportant forms commonly found in beginners' books have been omitted.

(*b*) *Syntax.* — Byrne's *Syntax of High School Latin* and the latest state syllabi have been consulted in an attempt to introduce the minimum of syntax consistent with sound teaching. *The Report of the N. E. A. Committee on Uniform Grammatical Nomenclature* has been followed with few exceptions.

3. Lessons: (*a*) Most of the lessons are short enough to be covered in one class period by high school students and even at times by junior high school classes; hence the large number of lessons.

(*b*) The vocabularies are put first to show their importance and to have them learned as such. They are uniformly short.

(*c*) All words are repeated at frequent intervals in the exercises.

(*d*) Words are introduced in the vocabularies to a large extent in the order of their importance for English word derivation. Primitives are regularly introduced before derivatives.

(*e*) Constructions are introduced as far as possible in the order of their importance, and only one new construction, as a rule, is developed in a lesson.

(*f*) The translation of English into Latin is subordinated to the translation of Latin into English.

4. Reviews. — Systematic reviews recur at intervals of nine or ten lessons throughout the book and are intended not only to furnish drill material for oral work but also to serve as the basis for written tests. It is expected, of course, that the teacher will conduct additional reviews, for which the material in the review lessons will prove suggestive.

5. Connected Reading. — In the body of the book there is a considerable amount of graded reading dealing with Roman life, private and public, forming a continued story of interest to boys and girls. In this way the student is given an introduction to Roman civilization *through Latin*. Many of the passages are intended for rapid reading at sight, without the use of the vocabulary. A few new words are introduced in each to teach the student to rely upon himself. In addition, simplified material from *Viri Romae*, Eutropius, Nepos, etc. is given.

6. Oral Work, Plays, etc. — In the earlier part of the book conversational material is introduced as a sample of what may be done by the teacher. The pictures also may be made the basis for conversation. In the Appendix a list of classroom phrases is given. A special feature is the inclusion of two Latin plays for reading or presentation. These plays were written expressly for this book and therefore afford an excellent review of forms and vocabulary.

7. French and Spanish. — A supplement is devoted to correlating French and Spanish with Latin and shows the student how he may get the maximum profit from his Latin while studying these Romance languages.

8. Teaching Devices. — An effort has been made to furnish a number of aids for the teacher, *e.g. A Color Scheme for Learning Verb Forms* (Lesson XXXIX), *Vocabulary Matches* (Lesson LXVIII), drills, etc.

The Junior High School. — It is the belief of the authors that it is a mistake to use different beginning Latin books in the junior and the senior high school, since such use tends to make articulation difficult, as experience shows. Yet the current high school texts are not altogether suitable for the lower school. The changes which the four-year high school regards as desirable, the junior high school demands as necessary. Most of the features mentioned above are in this class: the emphasis upon English derivation and grammar, simplification of forms and syntax, the short lessons, the introduction of interesting material in the form of readings, conversations, and plays, the French and Spanish supplement, the use of graphic teaching devices, etc. The numerous illustrations with helpful explanations are likewise intended to make the book particularly attractive to younger students.

The statue of Marcus Aurelius on the cover symbolizes for us the unbroken continuity of the Roman civilization, since this is said to be the only ancient statue in Rome that was never overthrown.

Acknowledgments. — The authors wish to acknowledge their indebtedness to Miss Louise M. Weller of the Dilworth School, Pittsburgh, for helpful suggestions with regard to the sections dealing with seventh and eighth grade English; to Miss Lillian B. Lawler of the University of Iowa, who wrote the two Latin plays expressly for this book and assisted in numerous other ways; to Mr. Charles R. Fisher of the Allegheny High School, Pittsburgh, Professor Charles H. Beeson of the University of Chicago, and Miss Helen M. Eddy of the University High School, Iowa City, who read the manuscript and offered many helpful suggestions for its improvement; and to Mr. George Kleine for the unique scenes from the motion picture " Julius Caesar."

B. L. U.
N. E. H.

CONTENTS

CONTENTS

xiii

CONTENTS

CONTENTS

XV

VOCABULARY NOTEBOOK

Many teachers have found vocabulary and derivative notebooks helpful. A large notebook of the loose-leaf variety is preferable, with page ruled in three columns for (1) Latin Words, (2) Related Words, (3) English Derivatives (see illustration). The words of the advance vocabulary should be distributed by the student according to the part of speech, a page being reserved for each of the five declensions of nouns, one for each of the four conjugations, etc. In the second and third columns respectively he should record as many related Latin words and English derivatives as are readily suggested. Others should be added from time to time as encountered.

It will be found helpful to have the student compile a separate list of the prefixes and suffixes given in this book, together with numerous examples of their use in English words.

pōnō, -ere, posuī, positus (put, place)	prōpōnō	position, positive, proposition
mittō, -ere, mīsī, missus (let go, send)	committō, āmittō, dimittō, permittō, submittō	commit, committal, commissary, missive, mission, permission, submit
dūcō, -ere, dūxī, ductus (lead).	redūcō, prōdūcō, ēdūcō, addūcō, trādūcō, sed	ductile, reduction, educe, traduce, duke

Other Types of Notebooks

Type 1 (with definitions)

vocō, vocāre, vocāvī, vocātus,
   call

vocation — a *calling*, occupation
convoke — *call* together
invocation — a *calling* upon, a prayer, etc.

Type 2 (with examples of use in English)

mittō, mittere, mīsī, missus,
   send

mission — He was sent on a *mission* to Europe
missive — The letter was a formidable *missive*
transmit — They will *transmit* the message to us, etc.

ELEMENTARY LATIN

ELEMENTARY LATIN

TO THE STUDENT

1. You are about to begin the study of a new language. Perhaps you are a little curious and eager about it because it is something new, different from anything you have studied; or perhaps you are a little afraid of it because you think of it as something strange and difficult. Let us see what we know about it already.

Twenty-five hundred years ago Rome was one of many little towns in Italy. Its language, Latin, got its name from the district of Latium in which the town was situated. As the power of Rome spread, first over Italy and then over most of the civilized world of that day, its language came to be used everywhere. The modern civilization of Europe and America is largely the outgrowth of the Roman. American boys and girls play many games that Roman children played, American students read literature that was greatly influenced by the Roman, American citizens deal with political and legal ideas that are largely a Roman inheritance. To get acquainted with this Roman civilization is an important reason for studying Latin.

The Romans, however, have handed down not only their ideas but also their language. The Romance languages are the various forms which the Roman (Latin) language has taken in the course of centuries in the various parts of the Roman Empire. They are Italian, French, Spanish, Portuguese, Rumanian, and even, to a large extent, English, since about seventy per cent of our English words are derived from Latin. French, Spanish, and Italian become very easy after a study of Latin. But the chief reason why you are going to study Latin is to get a better knowledge of English. The study of Latin will make English grammar much easier to understand. Then again, there are Latin words, phrases, and mottoes used in English, such as *radius, per annum*, and *e pluribus unum*. Many Latin phrases are used in law, such as *habeas corpus;* therefore lawyers must know Latin. Many abbreviations used in English are Latin, such as *i.e.* for *id est.*

You see then that this Latin of the Romans is not so remote a thing after all and that a knowledge of it will be very useful to you.

2.   Exercise

1. *How many events of Roman history can you think of?*
2. *What famous Romans do you remember?*
3. *What Roman gods can you recall?*
4. *What do you know about Rome as it is to-day?*
5. *How many Latin words, phrases, legal terms, scientific terms, mottoes, proverbs, and abbreviations can you give?*

Exercises in Pronunciation (see 603–611)

3. Pronounce nā′vēs, Rū′fus, Marī′a, nau′tae, īn′sula, eō′rum, exer′citus, appellā′tur, vīdis′set, cognō′vit, Mīran′da, tenē′bant, proe′liō, Colum′bus, Clā′ra, Iū′lius, Augus′tus.

4. Read the following translation of a part of Lincoln's Gettysburg Address (by James A. Kleist):

Octā′vus iam et octōgē′simus an′nus est hic, cum maiō′rēs nos′trī no′vam in hāc ter′rae par′te rem pū′blicam peperē′- runt, quam lībertā′tis in condiciō′ne concep′tam in il′lam cōnsecrā′runt senten′tiam: ae′quō nās′cī iū′re ho′minēs ūniver′sōs. Nunc vē′rō ingen′tī bel′lō cīvī′lī in′itō nōs experī′mur, haec′ne rēs pū′blica vel a′lia, sīc nā′ta, sīc cōnsecrā′ta, per lon′gum tem′poris spa′tium pos′sit stā′re.

LESSON I

FIRST DECLENSION: THE NOMINATIVE CASE

ELEMENTARY GRAMMAR: Review *Number*, **623**; *Gender*, **624**; *Case*, **625**; *Nouns*, **614**; *Inflection*, **622**.

Inflection or Declension of Nouns

5. Number. — In English, nearly all nouns undergo change to indicate plural number. Most nouns add –s or –es: way, ways; bush, bushes. A few form their plurals irregularly: pony, ponies; knife, knives; ox, oxen; man, men.

In Latin, most nouns undergo change of ending to indicate number.

6. Gender. — In English, masculine or feminine gender is assigned to nouns according to sex, nouns denoting sexless objects being classified as neuter. This use is known as **natural gender.**

In Latin, however, many nouns are regarded as masculine or feminine which are neuter in English: **via** (f.), *way;* **numerus** (m.), *number.* This use is known as **grammatical gender.** It is determined, not by the meaning of the word, but largely by its ending.

7. Case. — In English, with the exception of the genitive (or possessive) case, change of case does not involve change of ending: nominative (denoting the subject), " The *man* sees "; accusative (denoting the object), " I see the *man* "; but genitive (denoting possession), "the *man's* hat."

In Latin, however, change of case regularly requires change of ending. The hundreds of nouns in the Latin language are divided by **case endings** into five classes called **declensions.**

8.   First Declension: Nominative Case Endings

The case endings for the **nominative**, singular and plural,
of the **first declension** are as follows:

	SINGULAR	PLURAL
	–a	–ae
Examples:	via	viae

These endings are preserved in many English words, as,
singular, **alumna**, plural, **alumnae**. Other examples will be
given later.

9. Rule. — *Nouns of the first declension are feminine (except a few which refer to males).*

10.   English Word Studies

The following are English words, borrowed from the Latin
first declension, which have never lost their Latin nominative
endings. Consult the dictionary for the English pronunciation and meaning of these **loan words**. (Observe that in
English **–ae** is pronounced $\bar{e}$, as in *me*.)

alumna, alumnae; antenna, antennae; larva, larvae · minutiae
(singular rare).

FIG. 2. CUPIDS AS DYERS AND CLEANERS

From a Pompeian wall painting. One of a series of similar pictures (cf. Fig. 54).

LESSON II

USE OF THE NOMINATIVE. AGREEMENT OF ADJECTIVES

ELEMENTARY GRAMMAR: Review *Subject, Predicate,* **612**; *Nominative,* **627**, *a*; *Linking verb,* **617**, *b*; *Adjectives,* **616**; *Modifiers,* **612**.

11. English Derivatives

An English word formed from a Latin word is called a **derivative**. In this book derivatives are given in parentheses after the words in vocabularies; for their meanings see the dictionary whenever necessary. Write additional derivatives in your notebook.

12. Vocabulary

Nouns		Adjectives	
fā′ma, *report, fame*	(famous)	**bo′na,** *good*	(bonus)
fortū′na, *fortune*	(fortunate)	**lon′ga,** *long*	(longitude)
īn′sula, *island*	(insulate)	**mag′na,** *large, great*	(magnify)
vi′a, *way, road, street*	(viaduct)	**no′va,** *new, strange*	(novice)

Linking (or Copula) Verb

est, is   sunt, are

13. Nominative as Subject and Predicate

The nominative case in Latin has the same uses as in English:

(*a*) The subject of a verb is in the nominative case. This is called **subject nominative.**

(*b*) A noun or adjective used in the predicate after a linking verb (*is, are, seem,* etc.) to complete its meaning is in the nominative case. This is called **predicate nominative.**

   (*a*) (*b*) (*a*) (*b*)
1. **Īnsula est magna,** *The island is large.*
2. **Sicilia est īnsula,** *Sicily is an island.*
   (*a*) (*b*) (*a*) (*b*)

14.   **Adjectives**

In English, an adjective does not undergo change to indicate number, gender, and case. *This* and *that*, however, change in the plural to *these* and *those.*

In Latin, an adjective indicates by its ending the number, gender, and case of the noun which it modifies. Compare the adjectives in the following Latin and English sentences:

    1. **Via longa est bona,** *A long street is good.*
    2. **Viae longae sunt bonae,** *The long streets are good.*

15. Rule. — *An adjective agrees in number, gender, and case with the noun which it modifies.*

16. Observe in the above sentences:

(*a*) There is no word in Latin for *a*, *an*, or *the*.
(*b*) The Latin adjective regularly follows its noun.
(*c*) The adjective may modify its noun directly or in the predicate.

17.   **Exercises**

Oral. (*Read in Latin and translate into English.*)

1. Īnsula est magna. 2. Via est nova. 3. Viae sunt longae. 4. Viae longae sunt bonae. 5. Fortūna est bona. 6. Via bona est longa. 7. Fāma est bona. 8. Īnsulae novae sunt magnae. 9. Īnsula nova est longa. 10. Viae bonae sunt novae.

Written. 1. Long Island is large. 2. Great fortune is good. 3. The islands are long. 4. A new road is good. 5. New roads are good. 6. The new island is large. 7. Great is fame.

LESSON III

FIRST CONJUGATION: PRESENT INDICATIVE ACTIVE

ELEMENTARY GRAMMAR: Review *Verbs,* **617;** *Common, progressive, and emphatic forms,* **631.**

18.   **Vocabulary**

NOUN

cau'sa, *cause, reason*   (causal)

ADJECTIVES

par'va, *small*

vĕ'ra, *true*   (verify)

VERBS

accū'sō, *blame, accuse* (accusation)

pa'rō, *get, get ready, prepare* (prepare)

por'tō, *carry* (porter)

ADVERB

u'bi, *where*

Note. — Enter the above words in your notebook and find additional derivatives.

19.   **English Word Studies**

The following are additional **loan words,** borrowed from the Latin first declension, often found in high school textbooks of science:

     nebula, nebulae; papilla, papillae; vertebra, vertebrae

Can you find others?

FIG. 3. ROMAN BUCKETS OF BRONZE

20.   Formation of the Present Indicative Active

In English, verbs sometimes change to indicate person:
I have, he has; sometimes also to indicate number: *I am,
we are;* but usually the distinction of person and number is
made only by use of the personal pronouns (*I, you, he, we,
they*).

In Latin, the personal pronoun subjects are usually
omitted, and sets of endings called **personal endings** serve
to indicate the person and number of all verbs.   The following are used in forming five of the six tenses of the **indicative active** of all verbs:

	SINGULAR	PLURAL
1st person	–ō (or –**m**) = *I*	–**mus** = *we*
2nd "	–**s** = *you*	–**tis** = *you*
3rd "	–**t** = *he, she, it*	–**nt** = *they*

Present Stem. — The **present infinitive active** of all regular verbs ends in –**re**: accūsā*re*, parā*re*.

The present tense of any verb is formed by adding the
personal endings directly to the **present stem**, obtained from
the infinitive by dropping the ending –**re**. The hundreds
of regular verbs in Latin are divided, according to the present
stem, into four classes called **conjugations**. The present
stem of verbs of the **first conjugation** ends in –**ā**. Thus
parō, parāre (present stem **parā**–) is conjugated in the present
indicative active as follows:

SINGULAR	PLURAL
pa′rō, *I prepare, am preparing, do prepare*	parā′**mus**, *we prepare, are pre- paring, do prepare*
pa′rās, *you prepare, are prepar- ing, do prepare*	parā′**tis**, *you prepare, are pre- paring, do prepare*
pa′rat, *he prepares, is prepar- ing, does prepare*	pa′rant, *they prepare, are pre- paring, do prepare*

a. **Remember** that all vowels are shortened before –nt and final –m or –t, and that –ā– disappears entirely before final ō in the first singular.

b. **Observe** the three ways to translate each Latin verb form — **common**, **progressive**, and **emphatic**. In English, when *am* and *do* are used as auxiliary verbs, they have no Latin equivalent.

21. Drill. — Give the present indicative active of **accūsō** and **portō**, translating each form in three ways.

22.   **Exercises**

Oral. 1. Accūsō; parās; portat. 2. Portāmus; accūsātis; parant. 3. Ubi est Longa Īnsula? 4. Causae sunt vērae. 5. Īnsula nova est parva. 6. Via parva est nova. 7. Ubi sunt viae longae?

Written. 1. The reason is true. 2. The new islands are small. 3. Where are the islands? 4. He does accuse; they prepare; he is carrying.

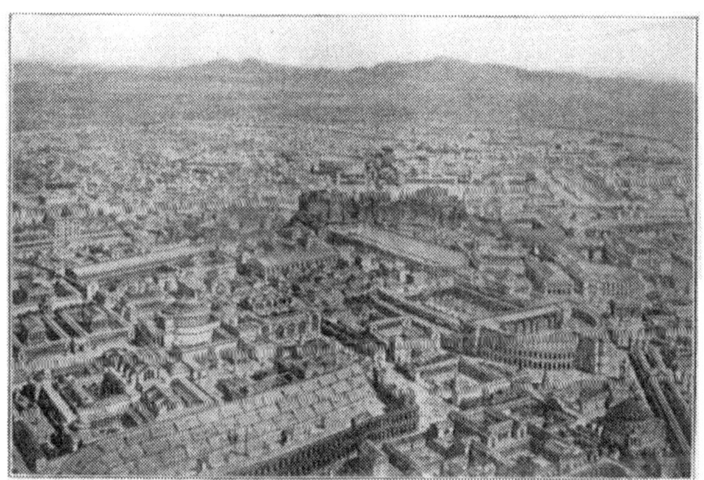

FIG. 4. ROME IN ANCIENT TIMES

LESSON IV

FIRST DECLENSION: THE ACCUSATIVE CASE

ELEMENTARY GRAMMAR: Review *Direct object,* **626,** *b* ; *Accusative,* **627,** *b* ; *Transitive and intransitive verbs,* **617,** *a.*

23. **Vocabulary**

NOUNS

VERB

a'qua, *water*   (aqueous)   **pro'bō, probā're,** *test, prove, approve*
māte'ria, *matter, timber*   (material)   (probation)
nau'ta, m., *sailor*   (nautical)

ADJECTIVE

CONJUNCTION

mul'ta, *much;* plur., *many*

et, *and*   (multitude)

Dictionary drill. Consult a large dictionary to see how many interesting facts you can discover about the derivatives of words in this vocabulary. How does a *nautical* mile differ from an ordinary mile? Why is the " chambered nautilus " so called? One of Oliver Wendell Holmes' finest poems bears this title.

24. **Latin Phrases in English**

Magna Charta, the *Great Paper,* or document, which is the corner stone of English liberty.
māteria medica, *material,* such as herbs, used in making *medicines.*
Fortūna caeca est, *Fortune is blind.*

25. **Accusative : Direct Object**

The endings of the **accusative** in the **first declension** are :

SINGULAR   PLURAL

–am   –ās

Examples :   viam   viās

1. **Anna nautam accūsat,** *Anna blames the sailor.*
2. **Nauta Annam accūsat,** *The sailor blames Anna.*
3. (*a*) *I saw* **him**.   (*b*) **He** *saw* **me**.

Observe in the preceding sentences :

(*a*) In 1 and 2 a noun in English does not undergo change to indicate the direct object in the accusative (objective) case, but difference in case depends solely upon word order and sense.

(*b*) In 3 (*a*) and (*b*) personal pronouns do have different forms for the accusative.

(*c*) In Latin the accusative of a noun is distinguished from the nominative by its ending.

26. Rule. — *The direct object of a transitive verb is in the accusative.*

Caution. — A noun is not necessarily in the accusative because it is used with or after a verb. **Est** and **sunt** serve as an equation sign (=) and take the same case after them as before them :

Italy is a country, **Italia est terra**.

Query. — Why is it incorrect to say in English, *It is **him?***

27. Drill. — Give the Latin nominative and accusative, singular and plural, of *island, fortune, matter, water*.

28.   Agreement

1. **Nauta aquam portat,** *The sailor carries water.*
2. **Viam parāmus,** *We are preparing a way.*
3. **Anna et nauta causās probant,** *Anna and the sailor approve the reasons.*

Observe the following points :

(*a*) The verb in each sentence shows the person and number of its subject by means of personal endings.

(*b*) The personal endings are not translated by pronoun subjects when a noun subject occurs.

(*c*) The verb stands last.

(*d*) Two singular subjects connected by **et** require a plural verb.

29. Rule. — *A verb agrees with its subject in person and number.*

30.   **Exercises**

Oral. 1. Nautās accūsō. 2. Causās bonās probātis.
3. Multam māteriam parātis. 4. Fāmam et fortūnam
probās. 5. Nautae multās causās probant. 6. Anna et
nauta multam aquam portant. 7. Causae sunt multae
et vērae. 8. Nautae aquam et māteriam portant.

Written. 1. You (*sing.*) approve; you (*plur.*) are carrying; we do prepare. 2. We are carrying water. 3. The
sailor approves many reasons. 4. Where are the small
islands?

FIG. 5. IN A ROMAN PARK

LESSON V

FIRST CONJUGATION: IMPERFECT INDICATIVE ACTIVE

ELEMENTARY GRAMMAR: Review *Progressive verb forms*, **631**, *a*.

31. Vocabulary

NOUN

ter'ra, *land, earth* (territory)

VERBS

a'mō, amā're, *love* (amiable)

vǎs'tō, vāstā're, *lay waste* (devastate)

ADJECTIVE

plā'na, *level* (plane)

LINKING VERB

e'rat, *he, she, it was* e'rant, *they were*

32. English Word Studies

The following, now regarded as English words, have been adopted from the Latin without change in the nominative singular. Their plurals sometimes end in –ae, but usually in –s, like most English nouns:

amoeba, arena, aurora, **camera**, copula, formula

FIG. 0. TEMPLE OF NEPTUNE, PAESTUM

One of the best preserved Greek temples, built in the sixth century B.C. Southern Italy, in which Paestum is situated, was inhabited by Greeks at an early period.

33.   **Imperfect Indicative Active**

A regular verb forms its imperfect tense by adding the tense sign –bā– to the present stem and then attaching the personal endings : [1]

<table>
<tr><td align="center">SINGULAR</td><td align="center">PLURAL</td></tr>
<tr><td>parā′bam, I was preparing, did prepare, prepared</td><td>parābā′mus, we were preparing, etc.</td></tr>
<tr><td>parā′bās, you were preparing, etc.</td><td>parābā′tis, you were preparing, etc.</td></tr>
<tr><td>parā′bat, he, she, it was preparing, etc.</td><td>parā′bant, they were preparing, etc.</td></tr>
</table>

Note that the personal ending for the first person singular is –m (not –ō as in the present tense). Observe that the Latin imperfect, like the English progressive past, denotes *continuous* or *repeated* action (or being) in past time.

34. Drill. — Give the imperfect indicative active of **amō, accūsō, vāstō**, with meanings.

35.   **Exercises**

Oral. 1. Ubi erat Anna? 2. Nautam accūsābāmus. 3. Causās bonās probātis. 4. Ubi est terra nova? 5. Viae erant longae et plānae. 6. Nauta Annam amābat et Anna nautam amābat. 7. Terrās multās vāstābātis. 8. Nautae aquam et māteriam portābant.

Written. 1. He accused; we were preparing; they did love. 2. We love; you (*sing.*) carried; they are getting. 3. They laid waste the land. 4. The little street was new. 5. Where are the good streets?

---

[1] A similar formation is seen in the English solemn style : **accūsā-bā-s,** (thou) *accuse-d-st.*

LESSON VI

FIRST DECLENSION: GENITIVE CASE

Elementary Grammar: Review *Genitive (possessive) case*, **627**, *d.*

36.   Vocabulary

Nouns		Verb	
cŏ′pia, *supply, abundance;* plur.,		**spec′tŏ**, **spectā′re**, *look at, face*	
forces, troops	(copious)		(spectacle)
cū′ra, *care, concern*	(curator)	Adjective	
fŏr′ma, *shape*	(form)	**clā′ra**, *clear, famous*	(clarify)

37.   English Word Studies

The following words have been borrowed without change from the Latin. Each has an English plural in –s (wherever used):

inertia, insomnia, militia, nausea, saliva

38.   Genitive

In English, possession is indicated by the genitive (or possessive) case ending in –'*s*, or by the accusative (objective) with *of: the boy'***s*** *father* or *the father **of** the boy.*

In Latin, we have already seen that a noun undergoes change in case ending to show a change in case relation. Possession is expressed by the **genitive** case. The genitive endings of the first declension are:

	Singular	Plural
	–ae	**–ārum**
Examples:	viae	viārum

    1. **īnsulae viae**, *the roads of the island.*
    2. **īnsulārum viae**, *the roads of the islands.*

39. Drill. — Write the Latin nominative, genitive, and accusative, singular and plural, of *water, supply, sailor, land.*

40.   Exercises

Oral. 1. Nautās amāmus. 2. Multae erant nautārum causae. 3. Magnam cōpiam aquae portat. 4. Magnās cōpiās īnsulae clārae spectābāmus. 5. Est [1] cōpia aquae. 6. Cūrae Annae erant multae et magnae. 7. Nautae cōpiam aquae clārae portābant. 8. Fōrma īnsulae erat nova.

Written. 1. The sailors accused Anna. 2. Anna looked at the sailors. 3. Where did they get the water supply[2]? 4. The sailor's reasons were true. 5. We are carrying an abundance of good water.

FIG. 7. THE AMPHITHEATER AT POMPEII

Mt. Vesuvius, the eruption of which destroyed Pompeii in 79 A.D., is shown in the background, with smoke issuing from it. Amphitheaters were used for gladiatorial contests — duels between professionals. Beast fights — similar to the modern bull fights — were also held there.

---

[1] Supply *there*, which is omitted in Latin when it does not refer to place.
[2] Cf. Oral 3.

LESSON VII

FIRST CONJUGATION: FUTURE INDICATIVE ACTIVE

ELEMENTARY GRAMMAR: Review *Future tense,* **630,** *c.*

41. Vocabulary

NOUNS

fami′lia, –ae, f.,[1] *household, family* (familiar)

pecū′nia, –ae, f., *money* (pecuniary)

prae′da, –ae, f., *booty, prey* (predatory)

sil′va, –ae, f., *forest, woods* (Pennsylvania)

un′da, –ae, f., *wave* (undulate)

VERB

nā′vigō, –ā′re, *sail* (navigation)

PREPOSITION

ad, with acc., *to, toward* (with verbs of motion); *near* (with verbs of rest)

What other derivatives are suggested by these words?

FIG. 8. PECŪNIA

In early times the Romans did their trading with sheep and oxen (**pecus**). Then bars of bronze bearing the figure of an ox, as above, were used for money. Each piece weighed a pound and was worth only sixteen cents. But the cost of living was very low then.

42. English Word Studies

The following are additional loan words of the first declension with an English plural in –s:

area, corolla, dementia, toga, villa

---

[1] Memorize the nominative, genitive, and gender of each noun as printed in all vocabularies.

43.   **Future Indicative Active**

The **future active** is formed by adding the tense sign –bi–
(corresponding to *shall* and *will* in English) to the present
stem before attaching the personal endings:

SINGULAR	PLURAL
parā′**bō**, *I shall prepare*	parā′**bimus**, *we shall prepare*
parā′**bis**, *you will prepare*	parā′**bitis**, *you will prepare*
parā′**bit**, *he, she, it will prepare*	parā′**bunt**, *they will prepare*

Note that the future sign –bi– loses i before –ō in the 1st sing. and
changes to –bu– before –nt in the 3rd plur.

44. Drill. — Give the future indicative active, with meanings, of **spectō, probō, nāvigō.**

45.   **Exercises**

FIG. 9. A ROMAN LANTERN

Oral. 1. Ubi magnam cōpiam pecūniae parābis? 2. Ad terram novam nāvigābimus. 3. Pecūnia est vēra causa cūrārum. 4. Magnae undae sunt ad īnsulam. 5. Nautae ad īnsulam nāvigābunt. 6. Nautae erant ad terram. 7. Praedam ad silvam portābunt. 8. Anna cōpiam aquae ad familiam portābit.

Written. 1. We shall sail to the new land. 2. They will look-at the large waves. 3. I shall carry the money to the large family. 4. Many are the cares of the sailors. 5. The roads of the large island were level and good.

LESSON VIII

FIRST DECLENSION: DATIVE CASE. INDIRECT OBJECT

ELEMENTARY GRAMMAR: Review *Dative*, **627**, *c*; *Prepositions*, **619**

46. Vocabulary

NOUNS	VERBS
lit′tera, –ae, f., *letter* (of the alpha-bet); plur., *letter, epistle* (literary)	dō′nō, –ā′re, *give, present* (donation)
poe′na, –ae, f., *penalty, punish-ment* (penal)	man′dō, –ā′re, *intrust* (mandate)
victō′ria, –ae, f., *victory* (victorious)	mōns′trō, –ā′re, *point out, show* (demonstration)
	nūn′tiō, –ā′re, *report, announce* (denunciation)

ADJECTIVE

grằ′ta, *pleasing, grateful* (gratify)

47. English Word Studies

Always try to see the relation between the meaning of the English derivative and the Latin word from which it comes, and then use the derivative in a sentence.

(*a*) A thing is "familiar" when it is well known, like a member of the *family.*

(*b*) An author is a man of "letters," or a "literary" man; a "literal" translation is one that is almost *letter for letter.*

(*c*) An "undulating" motion is like that of the *waves.*

(*d*) A "mandate" is something *intrusted* to a person or a group, as the government of a weak nation.

(*e*) A "navigable" river is one on which *sailing* is possible.

(*f*) A "novelty" is something *new.*

(*g*) A person who is placed on "probation" is being *tested.*

48.   Dative: Indirect Object

The endings of the **dative** in the **first declension** are:

	SINGULAR	PLURAL
	–ae	–īs
Examples:	viae	viīs

Nautae pecūniam dōnō, *I give money to the sailor,* or *I give the sailor money.*

a. **Observe** the following points:

(1) In addition to the direct object (**pecūniam,** *money*) in the accusative, an indirect object (**nautae,** *sailor*) may be used to indicate the receiver.

(2) In Latin the indirect object is expressed by the dative, but in English it may be expressed either by the dative, as in the second translation, or by the accusative with *to* (or *for*).

(3) In English there is no separate form for the dative.

(4) In Latin and English the dative is placed before the accusative.

(5) The genitive and dative singular have the same ending.

b. **Note.** — The dative is used with verbs of *giving, reporting, telling, showing,* etc.

49. Rule. — *The indirect object of a verb is in the dative.*

Caution. — After verbs of motion like "come" and "go" *to* is expressed in Latin, as in English, by a preposition (**ad** with the acc.).

1. He reported the case *to the officer* (dative of indirect object).
2. He went *to the city* (accusative with **ad**).

50. Drill. — Give the Latin nominative, genitive, dative, and accusative, singular and plural, of *family, money, care, reason.*

FIG. 10. ANCIENT SPINNING TOPS

51. Exercises

Oral. 1. Nautīs poenam nūntiābimus. 2. Familiae pecūniam dōnābit. 3. Fortūnam bonam et fāmam magnam amāmus. 4. Nautae litterās mandābimus. 5. Nautīs victōriam grātam nūntiābō. 6. Aquam clāram et bonam ad īnsulam parvam portābant. 7. Annae viās silvae mōnstrābō. 8. Nautae Annae magnam pecūniam dōnābunt.

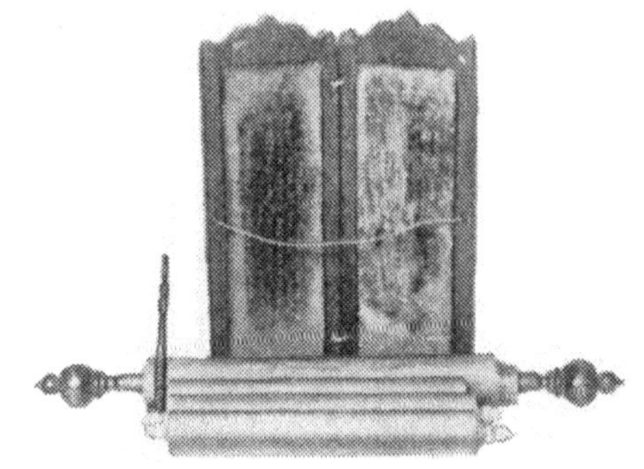

FIG. 11. WAX TABLET AND PAPYRUS ROLLS

Wax tablets, used for letters, accounts, etc., were of wood, covered with a thin layer of wax on which the letters were scratched with a bone or metal stylus. The rolls were used for books. Ink was used on them. (Photographed from models.)

Written. 1. We shall intrust the money to Anna. 2. He is giving money to many families. 3. He will report the punishment to Anna. 4. I shall intrust the letter to the sailor. 5. They point-out the road for the sailors.

52. COLUMBUS

Columbus nauta ad Hispāniam nāvigat. Isabellae, rēgīnae (*queen*) Hispāniae, nūntiat: " Terra nōn (*not*) plāna est; probābō!" Isabella nautae pecūniam dōnat. Columbus nauta nāvigat et probat; terram novam Americam mōnstrat. Nunc (*now*) fāma nautae magna est.

LESSON IX

FIRST DECLENSION: ABLATIVE CASE. ABLATIVE OF MEANS

53.   Vocabulary

NOUNS	VERBS
iniū'ria, –ae, f., *wrong, injustice* (injurious)	in'citō, –ā're, *urge on, arouse* (excitement)
memo'ria, –ae, f., *memory* (memorial)	oc'cupō, –ā're, *seize* (occupation)
pug'na, –ae, f., *battle* (pugnacious)	pug'nō, –ā're, *fight* (pugnacity)
vī'ta, –ae, f., *life* (vital)	ser'vō, –ā're, *save, guard* (conservation)

54.   Latin Phrases in English

Nova Scōtia, *New Scotland*, a province in Canada.
aqua vītae, *water of life*, formerly applied to alcohol.
ad nauseam, *to* (the point of) *seasickness* or *disgust*.

55.   Ablative

In English, the object of any preposition is in the accusative (objective).

In Latin, the object of some prepositions is in the accusative; of others, in a special case called the **ablative**, the endings of which are:

	SINGULAR	PLURAL
	–ā	–īs
Examples:	viā	viīs

56.   Ablative of Means

Many thought relations expressed by prepositional phrases in English are expressed in Latin by the ablative with or without a preposition.

Litterīs victōriam nūntiant, *They report the victory by-means-of a letter.*

Observe that litterīs (abl.) shows *by-what-means* they report and that no preposition is used.

57. Rule. — *Means or instrument is expressed by the ablative without a preposition.*

58. Sentence Analysis. — Before writing an English sentence in Latin, make it your practice to place above every noun the case and number required in the Latin sentence, as follows:

Nom. S. Acc. S. Dat. S.

1. The *man* gave a *book* to the *boy*.

Gen. S. Nom. S. Acc. S. Abl. S.

2. My *friend's son* saved his *life* by *flight*.

59.   **Exercises**

Oral. 1. Pugnīs īnsulam vāstābātis. 2. Aquā vītam Annae servābō. 3. Pugnābimus et terram novam occupābimus. 4. Litterīs familiae magnam victōriam nūntiābit. 5. Viae silvārum grātae sunt. 6. Memoria iniūriae nautās incitābit. 7. Victōriīs vītam et terram et pecūniam servābant. 8. Magnā pecūniā multās familiās servābitis. 9. Columbus nautīs īnsulam parvam mōnstrābat.

Written. 1. By-the-victory we shall save the island. 2. We urged the sailors on to battle with-money. 3. The memory of (their) wrongs will arouse the sailors. 4. I shall announce the victory to the family. 5. They saved the timber of the forest with-water.

LESSON X

REVIEW

60.   **English Word Studies**

Give the nominative, genitive, gender, and meaning of the Latin noun suggested by each of the following English derivatives:

aqueduct, causal, copious, curate, fortunate, injure, insulation, literature, memorable, nautical, pecuniary, penalize, pugnacity, viaduct, vitality

61.   **Present System: A Summary**

The present system comprises the present, imperfect, and future tenses of a verb, which are built upon the present stem **(20)**.

62. Drill. — Give the infinitive and present stem, and conjugate in the present system **probō, spectō, nūntiō.**

63.

First Declension: A Summary				
ENDINGS		ENGLISH FORCE	**via longa,** *a long way*	
SING.	PLUR.		SING.	PLUR.
Nom. –a –ae		Subject	vi′a lon′ga	vi′ae lon′gae
Gen. –ae –ārum		Possessive (*of*)	vi′ae lon′gae	viā′rum lon-gā′rum
Dat. –ae –īs		Indir. obj. (*to* or *for*)	vi′ae lon′gae	vi′īs lon′gīs
Acc. –am –ās		Direct obj.	vi′am lon′gam	vi′ās lon′gās
Abl. –ā –īs		*from, by, with, in*	vi′ā lon′gā	vi′īs lon′gīs

a. **Note.** — That part of a word to which endings are attached is called the **base.** The base of a noun or adjective is obtained by dropping the genitive singular ending: gen. sing. **viae,** base, **vi–.**

24

b. **Observe** the following points:

(1) The nominative and ablative singular both end in –a, but the –a is long in the ablative.

(2) The genitive and dative singular and the nominative plural have the same ending (–**ae**).

(3) The dative and ablative plural have the same ending (–īs).

(4) Most of the endings contain –a, for this is the **A-Declension.**

FIG. 12. A HOUSE IN POMPEII

The main room (*atrium*) at the front of the house. The basin in the foreground caught the rain water which fell through the skylight. In the background are the columns of the rear of the house (*peristyle*) with its garden (cf. Figs 71, 80).

64. Drill. — (*a*) Like **via longa** (see **63**) decline together in all cases, singular and plural, **cōpia magna, silva grāta, victōria parva.**

(*b*) Give the singular and plural of the following nouns in the cases required:

(1) **victōria** in the dative; (2) **poena** in the genitive; (3) **unda** in the ablative; (4) **īnsula** in the accusative; (5) **littera** in the nominative.

(*c*) Translate into Latin:

(1) *a large island* in the nom., sing. and plur.
(2) *the true reason* in the gen., sing. and plur.
(3) *a new letter* in the dat., sing. and plur.
(4) *a long battle* in the acc., sing. and plur.
(5) *great wrong* in the abl., sing. and plur.

65. Blackboard Exercise (*To the teacher*). — Write a number of miscellaneous forms in columns and ask for the possibilities of each with regard to case and number.

66. Perception Cards for Word Reviews. — An excellent way to review vocabularies is by the use of "flash" cards. The Latin word should be printed on one side and the English meaning on the other. The lettering should be large enough to be seen clearly when held before the class.

Fig. 13. Aetna

67.   Sicily

Sicilia est īnsula ad Italiam. Multae colōniae (*colonies*) Graeciae erant in Siciliā. Magna erat fāma īnsulae. In Siciliā est Aetna clāra. Aetna saepe (*often*) terram "lavā" vāstat.

LESSON XI

SECOND CONJUGATION: PRESENT SYSTEM ACTIVE

68.   **Vocabulary**

Nouns	Verbs
disciplī'na, –ae, f., *training, learn-*	**au'geō**, –ē're, *increase* (augment)
ing (disciplinary)	**do'ceō**, –ē're, *teach* (docile)
lin'gua, –ae, f., *tongue, language*	**ha'beō**, –ē're, *have, hold* (habit)
(linguistic)	**ter'reō**, –ē're, *terrify* (terrific)
pa'tria, –ae, f., *fatherland, country*	

. Adverb

nōn, *not*   (nonconductor)

69. Second Conjugation: Present System Active

The verbs that have occurred in previous lessons contain the stem vowel –ā– and belong to the **first conjugation.** All verbs which show the stem vowel –ē– in the **present system** (present, imperfect, and future tenses) belong to the **second conjugation.**

<table>
<tr><td colspan="2" align="center">Present</td></tr>
<tr><td>ha'beō, I have, am having, do have</td><td>habē'mus, we have, are having, do have</td></tr>
<tr><td>ha'bēs, you have, etc.</td><td>habē'tis, you have, etc.</td></tr>
<tr><td>ha'bet, he, she, it has, etc.</td><td>ha'bent, they have, etc.</td></tr>
<tr><td colspan="2" align="center">Imperfect</td></tr>
<tr><td>habē'bam, I was having, did have, had</td><td>habēbā'mus, we were having, did have, had</td></tr>
<tr><td>habē'bās, you were having, etc.</td><td>habēbā'tis, you were having, etc.</td></tr>
<tr><td>habē'bat, he, she, it was having, etc.</td><td>habē'bant, they were having, etc.</td></tr>
<tr><td colspan="2" align="center">Future</td></tr>
<tr><td>habō'bō, I shall have</td><td>habē'bimus, we shall have</td></tr>
<tr><td>habē'bis, you will have</td><td>habē'bitis, you will have</td></tr>
<tr><td>habē'bit, he, she, it will have</td><td>habē'bunt, they will have</td></tr>
</table>

70. Drill. — Conjugate **doceō** in the present tense, **terreō** in the imperfect tense, and **augeō** in the future tense.

71. **Exercises**

Fig. 14. Ruins of a Bakery

The bakers ground their own flour in stone mills and baked the bread in large brick ovens.

Oral. 1. Magnae undae Annam terrēbant. 2. Linguam patriae amāmus. 3. Multās linguās nōn docēbō. 4. Familiīs patriae magnam victōriam nūntiābimus. 5. Magnae undae cūrās nautārum augent. 6. Anna linguās docet et multam disciplīnam habet. 7. Victōria cōpiārum cōpiam pecūniae nōn augēbit. 8. Magnam pecūniam et parvam disciplīnam habēbat.

Written. 1. He will teach; they increased; you (*sing.*) terrified; we have. 2. The sailors were frightening Anna. 3. We gave much money to the country. 4. He is teaching languages. 5. We are reporting the victory by letter.

72. **English Word Studies**

A number of Latin verb forms are preserved as English words. First conjugation: **veto, habitat, ignoramus, mandamus.** Second conjugation: **tenet.** For their meanings, see the dictionary.

LESSON XII

ABLATIVE OF PLACE WHERE

73.   Vocabulary

NOUNS

amīci′tia, –ae, f., *friendship* [**amō**] [1]
glō′ria, –ae, f., *glory*   (glorious)
grā′tia, –ae, f., *gratitude, favor, influence*   [**grāta**]
vigi′lia, –ae, f., *watchfulness, guard*   (vigilant)

VERBS

ma′neō, –ē′re, *remain*   (manse)
vi′deō, –ē′re, *see*   (provide)

PREPOSITION

in, with abl., *in* or *on*

74. Drill. — (*a*) Decline **magna grātia, vīta longa,** and **lingua nova.**

(*b*) Give in Latin:

(1) *true friendship*   in the accusative, singular and plural.
(2) *good memory*   in the genitive, singular and plural.
(3) *a great country*   in the ablative, singular and plural.
(4) *a famous language* in the dative, singular and plural.

75.   Prepositions of Place

In the preceding lessons the various relations of the English accusative with *of, to, for, by,* and *with* have been expressed in Latin by means of case endings without the use of prepositions. But certain constructions of the English accusative with prepositions require corresponding prepositions in Latin. Chief among these constructions in Latin are the three constructions of place — answering the questions (*a*) *Where?* (*b*) *Where from?* (*c*) *Where to?* — which will be discussed in this and the following lessons.

---

[1] When a new word in the vocabulary is related to a word previously studied, the latter is given in brackets instead of an English derivative.

a. **Place Where.** **In** with the ablative = *in* or *on.*

Examples: **in silvā,** *in a forest.*
in viīs, *on the streets.*

76. **Exercises**

Oral. 1. Magnam pecūniam in patriā habēmus. 2. Magna erat grātia nautārum. 3. Nautae in terrā nōn manēbunt. 4. Vēra amīcitia est grāta. 5. Cōpiae fāmam et glōriam patriae augēbunt. 6. Multās vigiliās in viīs videō. 7. Multam māteriam in silvīs vidēbitis.

Written. 1. We saw guards on the streets. 2. (There) is much timber in the forest. 3. The troops did not remain on the island. 4. We shall see many forests. 5. Great is the glory of true friendship.

77. **English Word Studies**

The Latin ablative of the first declension is preserved in English in the word **via** : " I am going to New York *via* (by way of) Pittsburgh." The ablative plural is found in **gratis** : " He is giving this *gratis* " (out of favor, *i.e.* for nothing). *Gratis* is a contracted form of **grātiīs**.

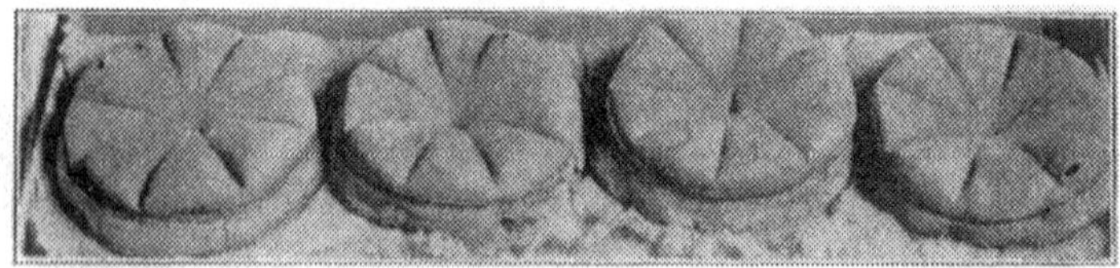

FIG. 15. ROMAN BREAD

Charred loaves of bread found at Pompeii and now in the Museum at Naples. They are marked with lines so that they may be broken into pieces easily, as is still the custom in Italy. (Other foods were found intact at Pompeii, even uncracked eggs.)

SECOND DECLENSION: NOUNS AND ADJECTIVES IN *-US*

78.   Vocabulary

NOUNS

car'rus, –ī, m., *cart, wagon*   (car)
nu'merus, –ī, m., *number* (numerical)
ser'vus, –ī, m., *slave*   (servile)
so'cius, so'cī, m., *comrade, ally*
              (associate)

ADJECTIVES

al'tus, –a, *high, deep* (altitude)
me'us, –a, *my, mine*
pū'blicus, –a, *public*   (publish)

VERBS

me'reō, –ē're, *deserve, earn*   (merit)
te'neō, –ē're, *hold, keep*   (retention)

79. Second Declension: Nouns and Adjectives in *-us*

All nouns studied thus far have the genitive singular ending –ae and belong to the **first declension**. Nouns of the **second declension** have the genitive singular ending –ī; the endings of the other cases also are different. Nouns ending in –us in the nominative are masculine.

Adjectives of the first and second declensions are declined in the feminine like nouns of the first declension and in the masculine like those of the second declension.

ENDINGS		ENGLISH FORCE	ser'vus bo'nus, *a good slave* (base, **serv– bon–**)	
SING.	PLUR.		SINGULAR	PLURAL
Nom. –us (ius)	–ī	Subject	ser'vus bo'nus	ser'vī bo'nī
Gen. –ī	–ōrum	Possessive	ser'vī bo'nī	servō'rum bo-nō'rum
Dat. –ō	–īs	Indir. obj.	ser'vō bo'nō	ser'vīs bo'nīs
Acc. –um	–ōs	Direct obj.	ser'vum bo'num	ser'vōs bo'nōs
Abl. –ō	–īs	With prep-ositions	ser'vō bo'nō	ser'vīs bo'nīs

Observe that :

(*a*) The genitive singular and the nominative plural have the same ending (–ī), just as these cases have the same ending (–ae) in the first declension.

(*b*) The dative and ablative singular have the same ending (–ŏ), likewise the dative and ablative plural (–īs) ; the latter is the same as in the first declension.

(*c*) Several of the endings include an –o, for this is the **O–Declension**.

(*d*) Nouns and adjectives ending in –ius contract –iī to –ī in the genitive singular : **so'ciī** becomes **so'cī**. The accent is not changed. The –i–, being a part of the base, appears in every form : dat. **so'ciŏ**, etc.

Caution. the nominative plural does not contract.

(*e*) The nominative singular and plural are preserved in many English words : **alumnus, alumni**. Other examples are given in **82**.

80. Drill. — (*a*) Decline **carrus parvus, socius meus**.

(*b*) Give in Latin :

(1) *a good cart*   in the nominative, singular and plural.
(2) *a new comrade*   in the genitive, singular and plural.
(3) *a small number* in the dative, singular and plural.
(4) *a large forest*   in the accusative, singular and plural.
(5) *a public slave*   in the ablative, singular and plural.

81.   Exercises

Oral.   1. Amīcitiam sociōrum merēmus.   2. Magnus numerus servōrum est in viā.   3. Sociō meō carrum novum mōnstrābō.   4. Magnum numerum carrōrum altōrum in viā pūblicā vidēbam.   5. Anna magnam grātiam et amīcitiam servōrum meret.   6. Sociī pugnant in terrā et in aquā ; victōriīs magnīs patriam servābunt.   7. Parvam cōpiam aquae bonae in īnsulā tenēbāmus.

Written.   1. Where did you see the allies' carts?   2. The slaves did not remain on the streets.   3. The strange language terrified the slaves.   4. We shall keep a large number of good wagons.

82. English Word Studies

The following are some words of the –**us** type preserved in English in their original form. Note that in English –**ī** is pronounced like –*i* in mile:

SINGULAR	PLURAL
alumnus	alumni
bacillus	bacilli
genius	genii (or **geniuses**, with different meaning)
radius	radii (or **radiuses**)
	literati (singular rare)

Other –**us** nouns without plurals or with plurals in –**es**: **campus, circus, discus.** Adjectives: **bonus, quietus** (both nouns in English).

© *International*

FIG. 16. POMPEII FROM AN AIRPLANE

LESSON XIV

ABLATIVE OF PLACE FROM WHICH

83.   Vocabulary

NOUNS

amī′cus, –ī, m., *friend*   [*amō*]
captī′vus, –ī, m., *prisoner*
        (captivate)

VERBS

mo′veŏ, –ē′re, *move* (movement)
vo′cŏ, –ā′re, *call, summon*
        (vocation)

ADJECTIVES

ma′lus, –a, *bad*   (malice)
sin′gulī, –ae, plur., *one at a time*
        (singular)

PREPOSITIONS

ā, ab,[1] with abl., *from, by*
dē, with abl., *down from, from, concerning*
ē, ex,[1] with abl., *out of, from*

84.   **Prepositions of Place: Place from Which**

$$\left.\begin{array}{l}\textbf{ā, ab}\\\textbf{dē}\\\textbf{ē, ex}\end{array}\right\}\ \text{used with the ablative} = from.$$

Examples: **ā viā,** *(away) from the road.*
           dē silvā, *(down) from the forest.*
           ex aquā, *(out) from the water.*

Note. — While all three prepositions convey the general idea of separation (*from*), **ab** means *away from the outside,* **ex** *out from the inside,* **dē** merely *from* when it is not important to distinguish between *away from* and *out from.* Sometimes **dē** means *down from.* See diagram:

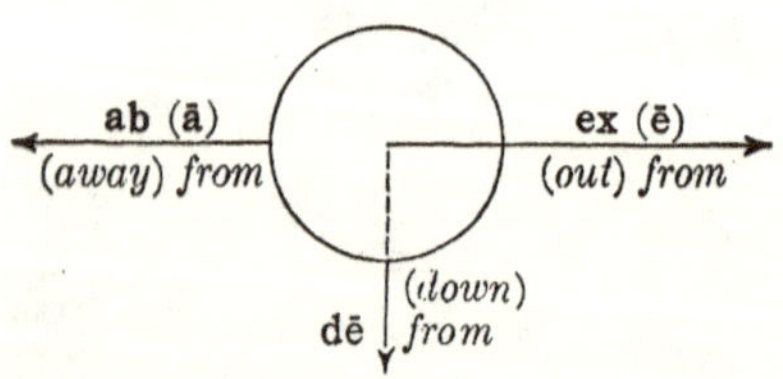

---

[1] The shorter forms **ā** and **ē** are used only before words beginning with a consonant (except *h*).

Fig. 17. A Roman House

Note the **arca**, or safe, at the right.   (From " Julius Caesar.")

85. **Blackboard Drill** (*To the teacher*). — Select fifteen or twenty nouns of the first and second declensions in various cases, singular and plural, place them on the board without reference to order of cases, and exhaust the possibilities of case and meaning. This will afford an excellent drill for the rapid recognition of forms.

86.   Exercises

Oral. 1. Servī malī magnam pecūniam et praedam ab īnsulīs portābant. 2. Carrōs singulōs dē silvā altā movēbunt. 3. Servōs ē silvā vocābimus et ab īnsulā nāvigābimus. 4. Sociī captīvōs ē viā pūblicā movēbunt. 5. In malā fortūnā vērōs amīcōs habēbāmus. 6. Māteriam dē silvīs ad aquam portābimus. 7. Magnus numerus carrōrum erat in viīs plānīs.

Written. 1. Anna had a large number of true friends. 2. We moved many prisoners from the island. 3. My friends carried the timber out-of the woods. 4. The allies are summoning forces from many lands. 5. One-at-a-time they sailed from the island to the new land.

87.   Latin and English Word Formation

A great many Latin words are formed by joining prefixes (**prae** = *in front;* **fīxus** = *attached*) to *root* words. These same prefixes, most of which are prepositions, are those chiefly used in English, and by their use many new words are continually being formed. Thus through them English *lives* and grows — without them it would be *dead*.

The following are examples of the prefixes **ab-, dē-**, and **ex-**:

(a) **ab- (abs-, ā-)** : *a-vocation, ab-undance, abs-tain.*
(b) **dē-** : *de-fame, de-form, de-ter, de-viate.*
(c) **ex-(ē-, ef-)** : *ex-alt, ex-port, ex-pect* (from **spectō**), *e-voke.*

Define the above words according to prefix and root. For root words, see previous vocabularies.

The following are other examples of the prefix **ex-** in English: *ex-cuse, e-dict, ex-empt, ef-fect, e-gress, ex-it, e-ject, e-mit, ex-quisite.*

88. Slaves

Servī Rōmānī erant captīvī. Rōmānī pugnīs multās terrās vāstābant et magnus erat numerus captīvōrum. Servōs ē Graeciā, ē Galliā, ex Asiā, ex Āfricā parābant. In familiā Rōmānā erant multī servī. Aquam portābant, litterās Graecās docēbant, vigiliae erant, medicī (*doctors*) erant. Multī clārī Graecī erant servī Rōmānōrum. Amīcitiam et grātiam Rōmānōrum merēbant. Litterae Rōmānōrum memoriam servōrum bonōrum et malōrum servant. Poena servī malī magna erat.

Fig. 18. A Pompeian House Wall

Our chief knowledge of Roman houses comes from Pompeii, because the lower portions of them were well preserved by the ashes thrown out by Mt. Vesuvius (cf. Fig. 7). Most of the walls were handsomely painted in bright colors.

SECOND DECLENSION: NOUNS AND ADJECTIVES IN *–ER* AND *–R*

89.   Vocabulary

Nouns	Adjectives
a′ger, a′grī, m., *field* (agrarian)	**lī′ber, lī′bera,** *free* (liberty)
e′quus, –ī, m., *horse* (equine)	**nos′ter, nos′tra,** *our* (nostrum)
magis′ter, magis′trī, m., *teacher* (Mr.)	**sa′cer, sa′cra,** *sacred* (desecrate)
pu′er, pu′erī, m., *boy* (puerile)	
vir, vi′rī, m., *man, hero* (virile)	

FIG. 19. PUER RŌMĀNUS

This Roman boy looks like a
bright, modern schoolboy.

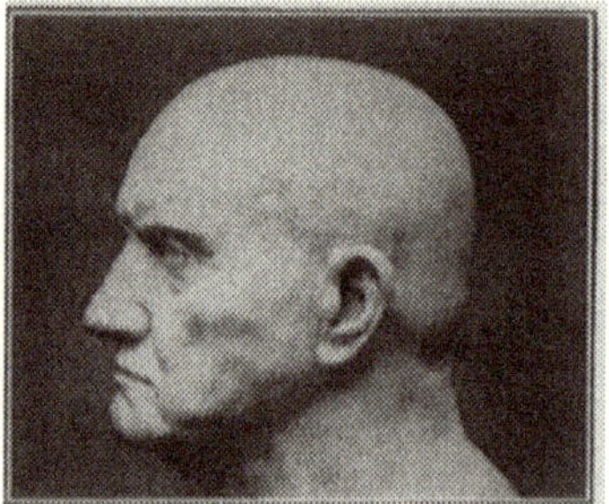

FIG. 20. VIR RŌMĀNUS

This ancient Roman looks like a
modern business man or lawyer.

90. Second Declension: Nouns and Adjectives in *–r*

Masculine nouns and adjectives whose base ends in –r
omit the ending in **–us** in the nominative singular. Such
words accordingly end in **–er** or –r in the nominative. The
genitive singular shows whether –e– is retained before –r
in the other forms. In memorizing vocabularies, always
note carefully (*a*) the *nominative*, (*b*) the *genitive*, (*c*) the
gender of every noun.

a'ger nos'ter, *our field* (base, **agr- nostr-**)		pu'er lĭ'ber, *a free boy* (base, **puer- lĭber-**)	
SINGULAR	PLURAL	SINGULAR	PLURAL
Nom. a'ger nos'ter	a'grī nos'trī	pu'er lĭ'ber	pu'erī lĭ'berī
Gen. a'grī nos'trī	agrō'**rum** nos-trō'**rum**	pu'erī lĭ'berī	puerō'**rum** lī-berō'**rum**
Dat. a'grō nos'trō	a'grīs nos'trīs	pu'erō lĭ'berō	pu'erīs lĭ'berīs
Acc. a'**grum** nos'-**trum**	a'grōs nos'-trōs	pu'er**um** lĭ'be-**rum**	pu'erōs lĭ'be-rōs
Abl. a'grō nos'trō	a'grīs nos'trīs	pu'erō lĭ'berō	pu'erīs lĭ'berīs

Note. — (1) Nouns and adjectives like **puer** and **līber** retain the -e- throughout; those like **ager** and **noster** retain it only in the nominative singular, while **vir** drops it entirely. Most **-er** words are like **ager**; no others are like **vir**.

(2) The English derivative will usually help determine whether the -e- is retained or not; *e.g. puerile, liberal, miserable; agriculture, sacred, magistrate.*

91. Drill. — Decline **magister līber, ager malus, vir bonus.**

92.   **Exercises**

Oral. 1. Puer equum ad aquam incitābat. 2. Magister noster linguam clāram docet. 3. Magister puerō malō pecūniam nōn dōnābit. 4. Magnōs agrōs et viās bonās et virōs līberōs in Americā vidēbitis. 5. Memoria clārōrum nostrōrum virōrum sacra est. 6. Virī nostrī agrōs sociōrum nōn vāstābant. 7. Equōs nostrōs magistrō et puerīs mōnstrābimus.

Written. 1. I shall give Anna the boy's money. 2. Our country is free and sacred. 3. They were moving the timber out-of the forest to the water with horses. 4. I see many horses in our friends' fields. 5. The teacher is showing the shapes of the letters to the boys.

93.   **English Word Studies**

Several Latin words of the –**er** type are in common use in English :

Nouns : **arbiter, cancer, minister, vesper.**

Adjectives : **integer, miser, neuter, sinister** (the first two are used as nouns in English).

Assimilation. — Some prefixes change their final consonants to make them like the initial consonants of the words to which they are attached. This is called **assimilation** (**ad** = *to ;* **similis** = *like*).

When used as a prefix **ad-** is assimilated. Define the following — all formed from words in the previous vocabularies : *ac-curate, al-literation, an-nounce, ap-paratus, a-spect, as-sociate, ad-vocate.*

Additional examples of assimilation of **ad-** are : *ab-breviate, af-fect, ag-gressive, ac-quire, ar-rogant, at-tend.*

FIG. 21. A ROMAN WEDDING. (From " Julius Caesar.")

LESSON XVI

PRESENT INDICATIVE OF *SUM*. ACCUSATIVE OF PLACE TO WHICH

94.   **Vocabulary**

NOUNS

a′nimus, –ī, m., *mind, courage* (animated)
colō′nus, –ī, m., *settler* (colonize)
nūn′tius, nūn′tī, m., *messenger* [*nūntiō*]

VERBS

ha′bitō, –ā′re, *live* (habitation)
labō′rō, –ā′re, *labor, suffer* (laborious)
mi′grō, –ā′re, *depart* (migratory)

PREPOSITION

in, with acc., *into;* with abl., *in, on*

95.   **Present Indicative of *Sum***

The verb *to be* is irregular in both English and Latin:

sum, *I am*	su′**mus**, *we are*
es, *you are*	es′**tis**, *you are*
est, *he, she, it is*	**sunt**, *they are*

96.   **Prepositions of Place : Place to Which**

ad with acc. = *(up) to*   **in** with acc. = *into*

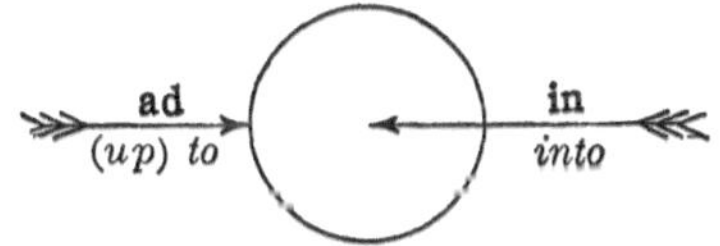

Carrōs ⎰**ad**⎱ aquam movent, *They move the carts* ⎰*to*⎱ *the water.*
     ⎰**in**⎱   ⎰*into*⎱

Compare a like difference between **ab** and **ex** (84).

97.   Exercises

FIG. 22. CARICATURE OF AN OFFICER

Drawn in red chalk by a Roman soldier on the wall of the barracks in Pompeii. Many interesting things are found scratched, drawn, or painted on the walls of Pompeii: notices of elections, games, etc., schoolboys' nonsense, poetry.

Oral. 1. Servī multī in agrīs labōrant. 2. Bonus servus labōrat iniūriā[1] malī servī. 3. Animus magnus virōrum nautās terrēbat. 4. Māteriam equīs et carrīs dē silvīs ad aquam portābitis. 5. Multī līberī virī in īnsulā magnā habitant. 6. Sociī nostrī numerum magnum captīvōrum in īnsulam movēbant. 7. Colōnī ex Eurōpā migrant et ad līberam Americam nāvigant. 8. Servī equōs nūntī in silvās incitābant.

Written. 1. We are messengers of a great victory. 2. The messenger's horse is in our field. 3. The prisoners will carry the timber from the woods into the fields with horses. 4. We shall give the booty to the settlers of the island. 5. The boys are in the woods.

98.   English Word Formation

The prefix **in-** is often assimilated. Define the following, formed from words found in recent vocabularies: *in-gratiate, in-habit, im-migrant, im-port, in-spect, in-undate.* Additional examples of assimilation of **in-** are: *im-bibe, il-lusion.* Words that have come in through the French often have **en-** or **em-** for **in-** or **im-**: *enchant, inquire* or *enquire.*

---

[1] The **ablative of cause** is used chiefly with verbs and adjectives expressing feeling: **Labōrāre iniūriā,** *To suffer because of the wrong.*

LESSON XVII

SECOND DECLENSION: NOUNS AND ADJECTIVES IN *-UM*

99.   Vocabulary

Nouns

cas'tra, -ō'rum, n., plur., *camp*
         (Lancaster)

cōnsi'lium, -ī, n., *plan, prudence,*
  advice   (counsel)

sig'num, -ī, n., *sign, standard, signal*
         (sign)

frūmen'tum, -ī, n., *grain*
         (fruition)

prae'mium, -ī, n., *reward*
         (premium)

Verb

ē'vocō, -ā're, *call out, summon*
         [**vocō**]

Watch for other English derivatives in your daily reading.

100.   Second Declension: Neuter Nouns and
Adjectives in *-um*

The second declension, in addition to the masculine nouns
ending in **-us**, **-er**, and **-r**, contains a large group of neuter
nouns ending in **-um**. The only difference between them
and the **-us** nouns is in the nominative and accusative, singular and plural.

Case Endings		sig'num par'vum, *a small sign* (base, **sign-** **parv-**)	
Singular	Plural	Singular	Plural
Nom. **-um** -a		sig'num par'vum	sig'na par'va
Gen. -ī -ōrum		sig'nī par'vī	signō'rum parvō'rum
Dat. -ō -īs		sig'nō par'vō	sig'nīs par'vīs
Acc. **-um** -a		sig'num par'vum	sig'na par'va
Abl. -ō -īs		sig'nō par'vō	sig'nīs par'vīs

Note. — (*a*) Neuter nouns and adjectives of all declensions have the
same form in the accusative singular as in the nominative.

(*b*) Neuter nouns and adjectives of all declensions end in -ă in
the nominative and accusative plural.

(*c*) Neuter nouns and adjectives of the second declension ending in –ium contract –iī to –ī in the genitive singular: **cōnsi'liī** becomes **cōnsi'lī**. The accent is not changed. The –i–, being a part of the base, appears in every form: (dat.) **cōnsiliō**, etc.

101. Drill. — (*a*) Decline **frūmentum bonum** and **praemium grātum**.

(*b*)   Give in Latin:

(1) *a new standard*   in the accusative, singular and plural.
(2) *a famous reward* in the ablative, singular and plural.
(3) *a great plan*   in the genitive, singular and plural.
(4) *a small camp*   in the dative.

102.   **Exercises**

Oral.   1. Amīcus meus multa praemia meret.   2. Cōnsiliō bonō vītam amīcī nostrī servābō.   3. Litterīs virōs ad castra ēvocābat.   4. Servī frūmentum ex agrīs in castra portābant.   5. Captīvī singulī nostrīs virīs cōnsilium nūntiābant.   6. Castra sociōrum nostrōrum sunt in magnā īnsulā.   7. Signō amīcīs victōriam nūntiābimus.

Written.   1. We shall give our friends great rewards. 2. The men were moving the grain from the camp with horse and wagon.   3. We saw much grain (*plur.*) in our friends' fields.   4. The colonists will sail from Europe to America and live in a free land.

103.   **English Word Studies**

(*a*) The following are Latin words of the –um and –ium type preserved in their original form in English:

Singular	Plural		Singular	Plural
bacterium	bacteria		curriculum	curricula (or –ums)
candelabrum	candelabra (or –ums)		spectrum	spectra

(*b*) Latin adjectives and participles used as nouns in English :

Singular	Plural	Singular	Plural
addendum	addenda	memorandum	memoranda
datum	data (remember to		(or –ums)
	say *these* data)	minimum	minima
dictum	dicta (or –ums)	stratum	strata (or –ums)
maximum	maxima (or –ums)		

Fig. 23. Roman Amphitheater at Nîmes, France

The amphitheater in accord with its past is used to-day for bull fights.

LESSON XVIII

IMPERFECT AND FUTURE INDICATIVE OF *SUM*. INFINITIVE USED AS SUBJECT AND OBJECT

104.   **Vocabulary**

NOUNS

ar'ma, –ō'rum, n., plur., *arms, weapons*   (armor)

auxi'lium, –ī, n., *help, aid;* plur., *reinforcements*   (auxiliary)

bel'lum, –ī, n., *war* (belligerent)

concor'dia, –ae, f., *harmony*   (concord)

VERBS

dē'beō, –ē're, *owe, ought, be obliged to*   (debt)

mātū'rō, –ā're, *hasten* (maturity)

105.   **Imperfect and Future Indicative of *Sum***

Review the present tense of the verb **sum** (**95**). The imperfect and future tenses of **sum** are likewise irregularly formed:

<table>
<tr><td colspan="2" align="center">IMPERFECT</td></tr>
<tr><td>e'ram, I was</td><td>erā'mus, we were</td></tr>
<tr><td>e'rās, you were</td><td>erā'tis, you were</td></tr>
<tr><td>e'rat, he, she, it was</td><td>e'rant, they were</td></tr>
<tr><td colspan="2" align="center">FUTURE</td></tr>
<tr><td>e'rō, I shall be</td><td>e'rimus, we shall be</td></tr>
<tr><td>e'ris, you will be</td><td>e'ritis, you will be</td></tr>
<tr><td>e'rit, he, she, it will be</td><td>e'runt, they will be</td></tr>
</table>

Caution. — Do not say *You **was**.*

106.   **Infinitive Used as Subject**

In English, a verb preceded by *to* (as *to see, to hear,* etc.) is called an *infinitive.* The English infinitive sign, therefore, is *to.*[1] The corresponding sign of the present active infinitive in Latin is **-re**, which is added directly to the present stem; as **portā-re**, *to carry;* **vidē-re**, *to see.*

(*a*) The infinitive is a verbal noun, and as such it may be used as the subject of a verb; as,

> **Habēre amīcōs est grātum,** *To have friends is pleasing.*
> (Cf. **Errāre hūmānum est,** *To err is human.*)

Note. — While Latin nouns are declined and represent different genders, the infinitive when used as subject is indeclinable and is always *neuter* (see **grātum** in the example above).

(*b*) An infinitive may be used as a predicate nominative; as, **Vidēre est crēdere,** *To see is to believe.*

107.   Infinitive Used as Object

With many verbs the infinitive may be used as direct object, like other nouns; as,

> **Parat cōpiās movēre,** *He prepares to move the troops.*

Note. — This is sometimes called the **complementary infinitive,** because it *completes* the meaning of the main verb.

108.   Exercises

Oral. 1. Grātum erat vidēre magnum numerum equōrum in agrīs. 2. Magnum est vītam amīcī servāre. 3. Puerō praemium nostrum mōnstrāre mātūrāmus. 4. Nūntiī pecūniā et praemiīs animōs nautārum incitāre parābant. 5. Cōpiae signa et arma ad terram novam portāre mātūrant. 6. Patriae nostrae pecūniam mandāre dēbēmus. 7. Sociī nostrī arma et frūmentum habēre dēbent. 8. Bonum erit habēre concordiam et auxilium in bellō.

---

[1] The preposition *to* introducing the infinitive is omitted, however, after the verbs *bid, dare, feel, hear, let, make, need, see,* and the auxiliary verbs *can, may, must, shall,* and *will.*

Written. 1. It was pleasing to see the courage and harmony of the troops. 2. The free men are preparing to fight with new weapons on land and water. 3. The slaves will hasten to increase the supply of grain. 4. The messenger ought to report the plan of war to the men. 5. It will be pleasing to see tall grain (*plur.*) in the fields.

109. English Word Studies

English words borrowed from the Latin which have preserved the original case forms of the second declension are:

Gen. *agri*-culture, *horti*-culture
Abl. *quarto, limbo, No.* (= *Numero*)

a, **Latin Phrases in English**

multum in parvō, *much in little.*
dē novō, *anew,* literally, *from a new (start).*
in memoriam, *to the memory (of)* — the title of a poem by Tennyson.

110. Spartacus to the Gladiators

Spartacus erat clārus servus, captīvus Rōmānōrum. Sociōs ēvocābat et incitābat: "O sociī, Rōmānī nōn sunt amīcī nostrī; sunt malī! Puer eram in patriā meā et vīta grāta erat. Silvās et agrōs amābam; līber eram. Vērum amīcum habēbam, puerum bonum et grātum. Sed (*but*) Rōmānī patriam meam vāstant: mē et amīcum meum ex patriā portant: nunc (*now*) captīvus sum et servus! Vir sum et in arēnā pugnō. Hodiē (*to-day*) virum necāre (*kill*) dē-bēbam — et erat amīcus meus! Virī estis; Rōmam nōn amātis! Pugnābimus! Līberī erimus et ad patriam migrāre mātūrābimus!"

LESSON XIX

REVIEW

111. Review the nominative, genitive, gender, and meaning of every noun in Lessons XI–XVIII.

112. Declension and Agreement of Adjectives and Nouns

We have noted (**14**) that an adjective in Latin must agree with its noun in gender, number, and case. This agreement is indicated by endings. In order, therefore, to modify nouns of different genders, every adjective thus far studied has a threefold declension as follows:

	SINGULAR			PLURAL		
	M.	F.	N.	M.	F.	N.
Nom.	mag′nus	mag′na	mag′num	mag′nī	mag′nae	mag′na
Gen.	mag′nī	mag′nae	mag′nī	magnō′-rum	magnā′-rum	magnō′-rum
Dat.	mag′nō	mag′nae	mag′nō	mag′nīs	mag′nīs	mag′nīs
Acc.	mag′num	mag′nam	mag′num	mag′nōs	mag′nās	mag′na
Abl.	mag′nō	mag′nā	mag′nō	mag′nīs	mag′nīs	mag′nīs

113. Drill. — (*a*) Decline in full **līber, lībera, līberum** and **novus, nova, novum.**

(*b*) Decline the adjective **sacer, sacra, sacrum** in turn with **nūntius, via,** and **bellum.**

114. A Study in Agreement

Inasmuch as **nauta** is masculine and belongs to the first declension, an adjective, when made to agree with it in gender, number, and case, must assume the masculine endings of the second declension, as follows: **nauta bonus, nautae bonī,** etc. Decline in full.

115. Drill. —Decline together *a bad boy, pleasing harmony,* and *public aid.*

49

116.   Review of Verbs

(1) Give the present stems of the following verbs: **habitō, terreō, vocō, moveō, dēbeō, mātūrō, augeō.**

(2) Conjugate in full, with meanings, (*a*) **migrō** in the present, (*b*) **maneō** in the imperfect, (*c*) **doceō** in the future.

(3) Give in Latin: *they were, he will be, I am, you* (sing.) *are, she is, you* (plur.) *were, we shall be, I was, they are.*

117.   Rapid-fire Drills

(1) *Translate:* we were; **habēbis; māteriā; probāmus;** to the small waves; **manent;** she did intrust; of our gratitude; **bonōs amīcōs;** you were laying waste.

(2) What forms are: **tenent, socī, amābāmus, vigiliīs, nūntiī, nūntiābimus, docēbitis, mōnstrās, auxiliōrum?**

118.   English Word Studies — Review

(1) Give and define three English nouns which retain Latin nominative forms, singular and plural, of the first declension.

(2) Give and define three English words which preserve Latin verb forms.

(3) Give and define three English nouns which retain Latin nominative forms, singular and plural, of the second declension, masculine.

(4) Give and define three English nouns which retain Latin nominative forms, singular and plural, of the second declension, neuter.

(5) Give prefix and root word from which the following are derived, and define:

defame, approve, advocate, invocation, immigrant, emigrant, avocation, vocation, deter.

(6) What is the original form of the prefix in the following?

affect, effect, defect, aspect, improve, alliteration, affront, abstain, illusion.

LESSON XX

CONNECTED READING: WAR AND VICTORY.
CONVERSATION

119.   WAR AND VICTORY

Colōnī in īnsulā manēbant et sociīs arma et frūmentum dōnābant. Equīs et carrīs frūmentum ad castra portābant. Virī pugnāre et augēre numerum captīvōrum mātūrābant. Longum erat bellum, magna victōria. Cōpiae sociōrum multōs agrōs vāstābant et colōnīs praedam multam dōnābant. Castra movēre et nāvigāre parābant. Multōs nautās et nūntiōs singulōs in viā vidēbāmus. Erat novum vidēre multōs virōs, equōs, et carrōs. Multōs captīvōs et arma habēbant. Cōpiae ad patriam nāvigābant. Patria pugnās et victōriās memoriā tenēbit.

120.   **Questions**

In Latin a question is regularly introduced by an interrogative word — either a pronoun or adverb (*who? where?* etc.), or the particle **-ne**. The latter is never used alone but is always attached to the first word in the sentence. Such attached words are called **enclitics**. As the enclitic becomes part of the preceding word, the word accent may shift: **īnsulam'ne, Corsi'cane**. When **nōn** is used in a question, it is put first and the enclitic **-ne** is attached to it.

121.   **Conversation: A Geography Lesson**

M. = **Magister**, *teacher*   **D.** = **Discipulī**, *pupils*

    M. Spectātisne?   **D.** Spectāmus.

    M. Ubi est Italia?   **D.** In Eurōpā Italia est.

    M. Īnsulamne vidētis?   **D.** Corsicam vidēmus.

    M. Corsicane est magna īnsula?   **D.** Parva, nōn magna īnsula est Corsica.

    M. Magnam īnsulam mōnstrō; Britannia est. Colōnī ex Britanniā ad Americam migrābant.

M. Ubi magna victōria erat?   **D.** In Galliā magna victōria erat.

M. Nōnne magna erat glōria Galliae?   **D.** Magna erat et est et erit glōria Galliae.

Note. — Ask questions and make statements similar to the above, using the accompanying map or preferably a large wall map.

Questions to Be Answered in Latin

1. Eurōpane est in Italiā?   2. Īnsulane est Italia?   3. Ubi est Rōma?

FIG. 24. THE TOMB OF HADRIAN AND THE TIBER

The emperor Hadrian (117–138 A.D.) built this tomb for members of the imperial family. It was so used for eighty years. During the Middle Ages it was used as a fortress and its handsome exterior was destroyed.

LESSON XXI

THIRD CONJUGATION: PRESENT AND IMPERFECT INDICATIVE ACTIVE

122.   **Vocabulary**

a'gō, –ere, *drive, do, discuss,* live *or* spend (time)   (agent)
cē'dō, –ere, *move, retreat*   (accede)
  accē'dō, –ere, *approach*
  excē'dō, –ere, *go away, depart*
dēfen'dō, –ere, *defend*   (defendant)
op'pidum, –ī, n., *town*
pō'nō, –ere, *put, place*   (postpone)
sem'per, adv., *always*   (sempiternal)

123.   **Third Conjugation**

(*a*) Verbs of the **third conjugation** have the stem vowel –ĕ–.
Note the difference of stem vowel in:

1st Conj. (*Long-A Verbs*): Pres. stem **parā–** (from infin. **parāre**)
2nd Conj. (*Long-E Verbs*): Pres. stem **vidē–** (from infin. **vidēre**)
3rd Conj. (*Short-E Verbs*): Pres. stem **pōnĕ–** (from infin. **pōnĕre**)

(*b*) The short vowel –e– of the third conjugation changes
to –i– in forming the present tense, except in the third person
plural, where it becomes –u–. In the first person singular
it disappears before –ō. Short –e– is lengthened in the
imperfect tense.

PRESENT (*I place,* etc.)		IMPERFECT (*I was placing,* etc.)	
pō'nō	pō'nimus	pōnē'bam	pōnēbā'mus
pō'nis	pō'nitis	pōnē'bās	pōnēbā'tis
pō'nit	pō'nunt	pōnē'bat	pōnē'bant

124. Drill. — Memorize the model verb **pōnō** and conjugate **agō**, **dēfendō**, and **cēdō** in the present and imperfect tenses.

125. **Exercises**

Oral. 1. Vītam bonam semper agēbat. 2. Colōnī ex agrīs in oppida excēdēbant. 3. Equōsne in aquam agis? 4. Memoria poenae nōn grāta est. 5. Ubi praedam pōnitis? In viā praedam pōnimus. 6. Sociī ad castra accēdunt et pugnāre parant. 7. Ad īnsulam cēdēbāmus et castra dēfendere parābāmus.

Written. 1. He was living a good life. 2. They are defending the camp with arms. 3. The slave is-getting-ready to put the grain into the wagon. 4. We ought to increase the number of our forces in the land of our allies. 5. Is he not living a long life?

126. **English Word Studies**

We have seen that many English nouns have preserved their original Latin forms. A great many more have preserved the base of the Latin noun. Others again consist of the Latin base plus silent –**e**. Some adjectives also preserve the Latin base or the base plus –**e**. The following are examples:

(a) *form, public, long, sign;* (b) *cause, fortune, fame, cure, plane.*

The same rule is illustrated in the following words, which have undergone changes in the base:

(a) *letter* (**littera**), *number* (**numerus**), *car* (**carrus**), *clear* (**clārus**); (b) *single* (**singulī**).

Give other examples of this rule from nouns and adjectives already studied.

LESSON XXII

APPOSITION

127.   Vocabulary

ae′quus, –a, –um, *even, equal, fair, just*   (equality)
exspec′tō, –ā′re, *look out for, await*   [*spectō*]
mit′tō, –ere, *let go, send*   (intermittent)
offi′cium, –ī, n., *duty*   (office)
po′pulus, –ī, m., *people*   (popular)
re′gō, –ere, *guide, rule*   (regent)
sed, conj., *but*

128.   English Word Study

Many English verbs preserve the Latin base with or without silent –**e** : (*a*) *cede, probe, accuse, evoke;* (*b*) *defend, labor.*

Give other examples of this rule from verbs that you have studied.

129.   Apposition

1. **Multī virī, amīcī captīvōrum, in castrīs sunt,** *Many men, friends of the prisoners, are in the camp.*
2. **Nautīs, amīcīs nostrīs, pecūniam dōnāmus,** *We give money to the sailors, our friends.*

Observe that **amīcī** (1) describes the subject **virī** and stands in direct relation to it and is therefore in the nominative, while **amīcīs** (2) limits or refers directly to **nautīs**, the indirect object, and is accordingly in the dative. No verb intervenes. This construction is called **apposition.**

130. Rule. — *A noun in apposition with another noun (or pronoun) is in the same case.*

131. Drill. — (*a*) Decline **officium nostrum** and **populus aequus.**

(*b*) Conjugate **exspectō, mittō,** and **regō** in the present and imperfect tenses.

132.   **Exercises**

Oral. 1. Puerōs malōs, cūram familiārum, nōn amāmus. 2. In Americā, patriā nostrā, semper habitābimus. 3. Vir bonus et aequus populum patriae nostrae regit. 4. Dēfendere patriam est officium virōrum. 5. Cōpiae in castrīs nōn manent sed ad oppidum cēdunt et nūntium exspectant. 6. Auxilia ad Rōmānōs, sociōs nostrōs, nōn mittēbat. 7. Magna erat et semper erit glōria populī Rōmānī.

Written. 1. Did the boys see our friend, the sailor, on the street? 2. It is the duty of the slave to drive the horses to water. 3. Are you sending aid to our allies, the Roman people? 4. The sailors, our allies and friends, were departing from the town.

FIG. 25. VIA RŌMĀNA IN ĀFRICĀ

This street is in Timgad, Algeria. Under Roman rule all northern Africa was rich and prosperous.

LESSON XXIII

THIRD CONJUGATION –*IŌ* VERBS, FOURTH CONJUGATION VERBS: PRESENT AND IMPERFECT INDICATIVE ACTIVE

133.   Vocabulary

ca'piŏ, –ere, *take, seize*   (captive)
   acci'piŏ, –ere, *receive*
fa'ciŏ, –ere, *do, make*   (efficient)
mū'niŏ, –ī're, *fortify*   (munitions)
quod, conj., *because*
ve'niŏ, –ī're, *come*   (convene)
   inve'niŏ, –ī're, *come upon, find*

134. Latin and English Word Formation: Vowel Changes

When a Latin word is compounded with a prefix, short **a** or short **e** in the root is usually "weakened" to short **i** before a single consonant except **r**. The English derivatives show the same change. Long vowels are not affected; for example:

From **agō**, Latin **ex-igō, ab-igō, red-igō**, etc.; English *exigency,* etc.

From **capiō**, Latin **ac-cipiō, in-cipiō**, etc.; English *incipient, recipe,* etc.

From **faciō**, Latin **ef-ficiō, dē-ficiō**, etc.; English *efficient, deficient,* etc.

From **habeō**, Latin **pro-hibeō, ex-hibeō**, etc.; English *prohibit, exhibit,* etc.

From **teneō**, Latin **con-tineō, re-tineō**, etc.; English *continent, retinue,* etc.

Exercise. — Illustrate the rule further with English derivatives of the Latin verbs which you have studied in previous lessons.

135. Third Conjugation Verbs in –*iō* : Present and Imperfect Indicative Active

A small but important group of verbs of the third conjugation ends in –**iō** instead of –**ŏ**. While their present stems end in –**ĕ**, –**i**– is inserted before the lengthened stem vowel in forming the imperfect and future tenses, as well as in the first person singular and the third person plural of the present tense. Compare the following model of an –**iō** verb with **pōnŏ** (**123**, *b*) :

PRESENT (*I take*, etc.)		IMPERFECT (*I was taking*, etc.)	
ca′piŏ	ca′pimus	capiē′bam	capiēbā′mus
ca′pis	ca′pitis	capiē′bās	capiēbā′tis
ca′pit	ca′piunt	capiē′bat	capiē′bant

136.   Fourth Conjugation

Most verbs ending in –**iō**, however, belong to the **fourth conjugation** and are distinguished by the stem vowel –**ī**–.

Verbs of the fourth conjugation are called Long-I Verbs, because they retain long –**ī** throughout their conjugation except where long vowels are regularly shortened (**20**, *a*). Note by contrast that –**iō** verbs of the third conjugation have short –**i**– throughout.

PRESENT (*I fortify*, etc.)		IMPERFECT (*I was fortifying*, etc.)	
mū′niŏ	mūnī′mus	mūniē′bam	mūniēbā′mus
mū′nīs	mūnī′tis	mūniē′bās	mūniēbā′tis
mū′nit	mū′niunt	mūniē′bat	mūniē′bant

137. Drill. — Conjugate and give all possible meanings of the present and imperfect tenses of **accēdō, inveniō, faciō.**

138.   **Exercises**

Oral.   1. Magnam pecūniam in viā invenit.   2. Ubi estis? Venīmus.   3. Magnam poenam merent puerī malī sed bonī multa praemia merent.   4. Nōnne aequum est semper dēfendere amīcōs?   5. Castra mūniēbant et virōs ēvocābant, quod pugnāre parābant.   6. In castrīs captīvōs inveniunt et multam praedam capiunt.   7. Magna praemia virī accipiunt, quod officium faciunt et armīs patriam dēfendunt.

Written.   1. We do not find good timber in the forest. 2. We were fortifying the camp and defending the island with arms.   3. It is pleasing to find money.   4. We shall sail to the island and lay waste the fields.   5. Marcus is not receiving a reward because he was a bad boy.

FIG. 26. WATCHING THE BULLETIN BOARDS

The Romans had no newspapers like ours and depended on bulletin boards
for news. (From " Julius Caesar.")

LESSON XXIV

WORD ORDER

139.   **Vocabulary**

dū′cō, –ere, *lead*   (reduce)
effi′ciō, –ere, *make out, bring about*   [*faciō*]
lo′cus, –ī, m., *place;* plur., lo′ca[1]   (local)
pre′tium, –ī, n., *price*   (precious)
ter′minus, –ī, m., *end, boundary*   (terminal)

140.   **Latin Phrases in English**

ad īnfinītum, *to infinity, i.e.* without limit.
ad astra per aspera, *to the stars through difficulties.*
ex animō, *from the heart* (sincerely).
Experientia docet, *Experience teaches.*

141.   **Word Order**

We have observed from the beginning (**7**) that the words
in a Latin sentence show their connection with one another
by means of endings, regardless of position (unlike English).
They may therefore be shifted rather freely without obscuring
the relationship.   The normal order is:

SUBJECT

NOUN — *adjective,* (*genitive, appositive*)

PREDICATE

ablative — indir. obj. — dir. obj. — *adverb* — **VERB**

(*a*) **Remember**, therefore, that the normal order of words
is as follows:

1. Adjectives usually follow their nouns, but adjectives of quantity precede: **virī bonī; multī virī.**
2. A genitive follows its noun.
3. An indirect object stands before a direct object.

---

[1] When used in this original sense, **locus** changes gender in the plural.

60

4. A word used to ask a question usually stands first, as in English.

5. The verb stands last. Forms of the linking verb are often placed in the middle of a sentence, as in English.

6. For **nōnne**, see **120**.

(*b*) But this normal order is far less regular in Latin than the normal order is in English. The shifted order serves to bring out varying shades of emphasis. This is done also in English, though to a less extent, largely in imitation of the Latin. Emphasis is gained particularly by:

1. Putting the emphatic word *first* in the sentence.
2. *Separating* the emphatic word from the word to which it belongs.

The former is common in English: *Great is the glory of the Lord!*

142.   **Exercises**

Oral. 1. Arma nova capiunt et locum dēfendunt. 2. Ad terram sociōrum cōpiās dūcēbāmus. 3. Multōs equōs habēre dēbēmus, sed magnum est pretium. 4. Magister concordiam nōn efficit, quod puerī sunt malī. 5. Ad arma virōs vocāmus et loca plāna mūnīmus. 6. Ubi est terminus agrōrum Mārcī, amīcī nostrī? 7. Ad oppidum auxilia mittimus, sed locum nōn mūnīmus.

Written. 1. The price of instruction is small, but the rewards are great. 2. Great is the fame of our teacher. 3. The sailors were seizing and fortifying many places on the island. 4. We are coming to the boundaries of our friends' fields. 5. They are hastening to lead a large number of prisoners to the small camp.

FIG. 27. A BUTCHER SHOP

LESSON XXV

THIRD CONJUGATION: FUTURE INDICATIVE ACTIVE

143. **Vocabulary**

com'modus, –a, –um, *suitable, convenient*	(commodity)
fu'giŏ, –ere, *flee*	(fugitive)
ŏ'tium, –ī, n., *leisure, rest*	(otiose)
puel'la, –ae, f., *girl*	[*puer*]
stu'dium, –ī, n., *eagerness, interest;* plur., *studies*	(studious)
va'leŏ, –ē're, *be strong, be well, be powerful*	• (valid)
va'rius, –a, –um, *changing, varying*	(variety)

144. **Latin Phrases in English**

victŏria, nŏn praeda, *victory, not booty.*

auxiliŏ ab altŏ, *by aid from (on) high.*

Montānī semper līberī, *Mountaineers (are) always free* (motto of West Virginia).

ex officiŏ, *out of (as a result of) one's duty or office;* e.g. a president of an organization may be a member of a committee *ex officio,* as a result of his office as president (pronounced " offishio ").

145. **Third Conjugation: Future Active**

The future sign of verbs of the first and second conjugations is –bi– (**43**). The future sign of verbs of the third and fourth conjugations, however, is –ē–. The –ŏ verbs of the third conjugation, in forming the future, substitute –ē– for the stem vowel –ĕ–, except in the first singular (–am).[1]

pŏ'nam, *I shall place*	pŏnē'mus, *we shall place*
pŏ'nēs, *you will place*	pŏnē'tis, *you will place*
pŏ'net, *he will place*	pŏ'nent, *they will place*

146. Drill. — Give the present of **mittŏ**, the imperfect of **cēdŏ**, and the future of **dūcŏ**, **dēfendŏ**, and **agŏ**.

---

[1] The third singular and plural have –ĕ, according to rule (**20**, *a*).

147.   **Exercises**

Oral.   1. Valēsne?   Valeō.   2. Puerī bonī magnam fāmam ex studiīs accipiunt.   3. Varia est fortūna bellī, sed
victōria erit nostra.   4. Vītam in ōtiō nōn agēmus sed
semper labōrābimus.   5. Puerī nōn excēdent sed puellās
dēfendent.   6. Cōpiae nostrae ē castrīs nōn fugiunt sed
ad locum commodum excēdunt.   7. Litterās ad Mārcum,
amīcum meum, mittam.

Written.   1. They will be powerful; we are fleeing; he
will lead; they were fortifying.   2. Where were the girls?
Did they remain in a suitable place?   3. We shall remain
in the town and send a messenger to our slaves.   4. They
fortify the camp and summon reinforcements from the
town.

Fig. 28. Roman Ruins in Palmyra, Syria

LESSON XXVI

ABLATIVE OF ACCOMPANIMENT

148.   Vocabulary

affi'ciō, –ere, *affect, visit with, afflict with*	[*faciō*]
cum, prep. with abl., *with*	
dū'rus, –a, –um, *hard, harsh*	(durable)
fir'mus, –a, –um, *strong, steadfast, firm*	(firmness)
ge'rō, –ere, *carry on, manage*	(belligerent)
inci'piō, –ere, *take to, begin*	[*capiō*]
perpe'tuus, –a, –um, *constant*	(perpetuity)

149.   Latin and English Word Formation

The preposition **cum** is often used as a prefix in Latin and English but always in the assimilated forms **com-, con-, col-, cor-, co-.** It usually means *together* rather than *with.*

Define the following words, all formed from verbs which you have studied: *convoke, collaborate, commotion, convene.*

Give some other English words formed by attaching this prefix to Latin verbs, nouns, or adjectives already studied.

150.   Ablative of Accompaniment

The means or instrument *with which* something is done is expressed by the ablative without a preposition (**57**): *They fought with arms,* **Armīs pugnābant.** When, however, *with* means *together with* or *along with,* the preposition **cum** with the ablative is used. This expresses **accompaniment: Cum servō venit,** *He is coming with the slave.*

Caution. — When tempted to use **cum** (*with*), be sure that *with* means accompaniment or association. In the following English sentences determine when **cum** should be used and when it should be omitted:

(a) *Anna is* **with the sailor.**

(b) *Soldiers fight* **with weapons;** *generals fight* **with armies;** *both soldiers and generals fight* **with their enemies.**

151. Rule. — *The ablative is used with* **cum** *to express accompaniment.*

152. **Exercises**

Oral. 1. Amīcus noster cum familiā ad Eurōpam nāvigābit. 2. Cum cōpiīs īnsulārum bellum dūrum et perpetuum gerēmus. 3. Armīs oppida dēfendent et cum sociīs pugnābunt. 4. Magister dūrus sed aequus puerōs malōs et puellās malās poenā afficit. 5. Nautae terram firmam vidēre incipiēbant. 6. Grātum est amīcitiam cum multīs virīs bonīs gerere. 7. Servus cum magnā cōpiā pecūniae ē patriā fugit; nōn ōtium sed dūrās cūrās invenit. 8. In amīcitiā firmā et perpetuā cum sociīs nostrīs manēbimus.

Written. 1. It is not just to carry on war with friends. 2. They fortify the camp and begin to fight with our allies. 3. A bad boy afflicts the family with constant care. 4. The settlers began to flee to the town with (their) families. 5. We shall send reinforcements with grain and defend the island with our troops.

153. BROTHERS

Rōmānī et Aquītānī, sociī Rōmānōrum, cum Germānīs pugnābant. Lūcius, clārus Aquītānus, ex equō virōs Rōmānōs et Aquītānōs in Germānōs incitābat. Servus Lūciō nūntiat: "Germānī frātrem (*brother*) tuum (*your*) Mārcum capiunt!" Lūcius frātrem amābat. Equum incitat, Germānōs terret, frātrem servat, fugit, sed equus nōn valēbat: Lūcius frātrem sōlum (*alone*) in equō pōnit, et ad castra Aquītānōrum et Rōmānōrum equum incitat. Tum (*then*) sōlus Germānōs exspectat. Multī Germānī accēdunt. Lūcius cēdere incipit, auxilium exspectat — sed auxilium nōn venit — ē vītā excēdit. Mārcus videt et equum in Germānōs incitat — et vītam āmittit (*loses*).

LESSON XXVII

FOURTH CONJUGATION: FUTURE INDICATIVE ACTIVE. FUTURE OF *–IŌ* VERBS OF THE THIRD CONJUGATION

154. **Vocabulary**

au'diō, –ī're, *hear*	(auditory)
conti'neō, –ē're, *hold together, detain, contain*	[*teneō*]
tar'dus, –a, –um, *slow, late*	(retard)
tra'hō, –ere, *draw, drag*	(traction)
ver'bum, –ī, n., *word*	(verbal)

155. Future Active of Fourth Conjugation and Third Conjugation *–iō* Verbs

Verbs of the fourth conjugation form the future by adding –ē– directly to the present stem (long –ī– of the stem is shortened, however, since it precedes another vowel). Verbs of the third conjugation ending in –iō resemble fourth conjugation verbs in the future tense, owing to the insertion of –i– (**135**):

mū'niam	mūniē'mus	ca'piam	capiē'mus
mū'niēs	mūniē'tis	ca'piēs	capiē'tis
mū'niet	mū'nient	ca'piet	ca'pient

156. Drill. — Give the future of **portō, contineō, trahō, incipiō, audiō.**

157. **Exercises**

Oral. 1. Grātum est audīre vēra verba amīcōrum. 2. Captīvōs in locō commodō continēbimus. 3. Nauta ex aquā puerum trahit et vītam servat. 4. Armīsne oppidum dēfendere incipiēmus? 5. Magister tardōs puerōs poenā afficiet sed puellās bonās verbīs dūrīs nōn terrēbit.

6. Colōnī ex agrīs ad oppidum carrīs frūmentum portābunt et magnam pecūniam accipient.   7. Magnus numerus equōrum multōs carrōs trahēbat.   Carrī frūmentum continēbant. Frūmentum ad sociōs mittere mātūrābāmus.

Written.   1. Anna, a good girl, will receive a large reward.   2. We shall fortify the camp and defend (it) with arms.   3. The men are dragging the prisoner to the water. 4. The boys will not receive the reward, because they are late.   5. The late boys and girls will not hear the words of the famous man.

158.   Latin and English Word Formation

Most prefixes are prepositions, but a few are not. **Re-** is used only as a prefix in Latin and English : it means *back* or *again*.   It sometimes has the form **red-**, especially before vowels.   Examples : **retineō**, *hold **back**;* **reficiō**, *make **again**;* **redigō**, *drive **back**.*

In English, **re-** is freely used with all sorts of words : *reduce, revisit, rehash, refill.*

Exercise. — Give other examples of the prefix **re-** in Latin and English words.

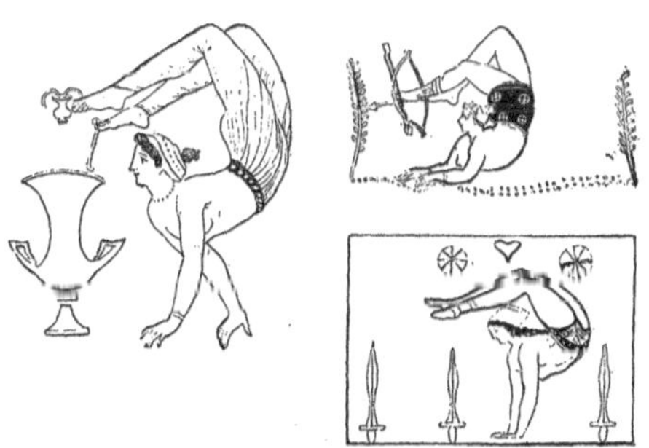

FIG. 29. ACROBATS

LESSON XXVIII

IDIOMS

159.   **Vocabulary**

conve′niō, –ī′re, *come together, assemble*	[**veniō**]
con′vocō, –ā′re, *call together*	[**vocō**]
i′bi, adv., *there*	
me′dius, –a, –um, *middle, middle of*	(mediator)
redū′cō, –ere, *lead back*	[**dūcō**]
senten′tia, –ae, f., *feeling, opinion, motto*	(sentence)

160.   **English Word Study**

A friend is a person whom you know well, love dearly, and treat familiarly. How many English words can you call friends, according to this definition? If you will trace English words back to their Latin roots, you will gain many new friends. For example: A " sentence " in grammar is a single, complete *opinion* or expression. A judicial " sentence " is a judge's *opinion*. A " convention " *comes together* in an " auditorium " to *hear* the speaker. A " mediator " settles disputes by taking a *middle* position. A spiritualistic "medium" is supposed to take a *middle* position between the unseen spirit and the " audience " who *hear*. A " studious " person is one who is *eager* to learn. An " alarm " is a call *to arms* (**ad arma**). To " repatriate " a person is to bring him *back* to his *fatherland*. Learn to look carefully at the *make-up* of every strange English word and you will often detect an old Latin friend *in disguise*.

Fig. 30. A Roman Lamp

161. Idioms

Every language contains set phrases or fixed expressions with meanings which can not be translated literally. For example, we say, *How are you?* when we really mean, *How do you feel?*

Certain set phrases occur in Latin which are peculiar to it and can not be translated literally into English. These fixed expressions are said to be **idiomatic.** The following should be memorized and entered in the notebook under the general heading " Idioms " :

1. **grātiās agere,** *to thank,* with dat. (literally, *to act gratitude*)
2. **grātiam habēre,** *to feel grateful,* with dat. (lit., *to have gratitude*)
3. **vītam agere,** *to live a life* (lit., *to act life*)
4. **bellum gerere,** *to wage* or *carry on war*
5. **castra pōnere,** *to pitch camp* (lit., *to place camp*)
6. **castra movēre,** *to break camp* (lit., *to move camp*)
7. **viam mūnīre,** *to build a road* (lit., *to fortify a road;* roads were built like walls)
8. **verba facere,** *to speak, make a speech* (lit., *to make words*)
9. **memoriā tenēre,** *to remember* (lit., *to hold in memory*)

162. Exercises

Oral. 1. In agrīs castra pōnēmus et ibi līberam vītam agēmus. 2. Magistrō nostrō grātiam habēmus et grātiās agēmus. 3. Cōpiās ex mediā silvā redūcam et pugnāre incipiam. 4. Rōmānī multās longās viās in Italiā mūniēbant. 5. Puerōs singulōs convocābimus et sententiās audiēmus. 6. Virī ex multīs terrīs convenient et verba facient. 7. Magister verba faciet et puellīs grātiās aget.

Written. 1. We shall break camp and come to town with our friends. 2. The boys and girls feel grateful and will thank the teacher. 3. We ought to feel grateful to our friends. 4. The boys will find water and pitch camp. 5. We shall remember the teacher's words concerning duty.

LESSON XXIX

REVIEW

163.   Nouns and Adjectives

Drill Exercises. — 1. Decline (*a*) **oppidum commodum,** (*b*) **puella bona,** (*c*) **vir aequus,** (*d*) **officium magnum.**

2. Decline in Latin (*a*) *a small word,* (*b*) *harsh opinion,* (*c*) *a sacred place,* (*d*) *a famous people.*

3. Give the nominative, singular and plural, of *great interest.*

Give the genitive, singular and plural, of *a constant duty.*
Give the dative, singular and plural, of *a good price.*
Give the accusative, singular and plural, of *varying opinion.*
Give the ablative, singular and plural, of *a firm man.*

164. Verbs: Present System of the Four Conjugations

Drill Exercises. — 1. Conjugate in the present indicative active: **sum, exspectō, dēbeō, mittō, efficiō, veniō.**

2. Conjugate in the imperfect indicative active: **sum, convocō, mereō, cēdō, afficiō, inveniō.**

3. Conjugate in the future indicative active: **sum, mātūrō, videō, dēfendō, accipiō, audiō.**

165. Recognition of Verb Forms — Rapid-fire Drills

I. *Give tense, person, and number, and translate:* Vident, mittent, dūcent, pōnit, pōnet, terrent, mittunt, incipient, erunt, valēbō, erās, fugiēbās, es, audiētis, exspectābimus, eris, dūcēbant, capiēmus, inveniēmus, erimus, veniam, accēdunt, erant, exspectāmus.

II. *Give in Latin:* We shall send; he will be; I fortified; they approached; you (*sing.*) await; we are strong; we were; they will flee; they receive; you (*plur.*) did come; they were; he is managing; he is; they will begin; they will be.

166. Conundrum. — Why is the future tense of the third and fourth conjugations like a horse without a bridle?   (Answer: It has no " –bit.")

167.   **English and Latin Word Studies**

1. Give prefix and Latin root word from which the following are derived : **redigō, concipiō, attrahō, corrigō, committō**; *respect, allocation, depopulate, exigency, deficient.*

2. Define according to derivation: *inspect, exponent, fugitive, verbose, incipient.*

3. Make Latin words out of **ad-** and **capiō, in-** and **pōnō, con-** and **labōrō, ad-** and **teneō, dē-** and **mereō.**

Fɪɢ. 31. Vɪᴀ Aᴘᴘɪᴀ

The first and most famous of Roman roads, built by Appius Claudius in 312 B.C. to connect Rome with southern Italy.   Portions of it are still used.   In many places the ancient surface blocks may be seen.   Roman roads compare favorably with the best modern highways.

FIG. 32. FORUM RŌMĀNUM

A view of the Forum as it is to-day, facing west (cf. Figs. 34, 36). At the left are three columns of the temple of Castor. The rostra is to the left of the arch shown at the extreme right.

LESSON XXX

SUBSTANTIVES. CONNECTED READING: FORUM RŌMĀNUM

168.   Substantives

When any part of speech, other than a noun or pronoun, is used like a noun or pronoun, it is called a **substantive**. We have already noted the substantive use of the infinitive (**106, 107**). Likewise, an adjective which agrees with an *omitted* noun in gender, number, and case is said to be used substantively:

    (*a*) **Nostrī (virī) veniunt,** *Our (men) are coming.*

    (*b*) **Multa audiēs,** *You will hear many (things).*

169.   **Hints for Reading and Translating**

The first step in translating Latin is to follow the order of words, separating them into groups according to their agreement. Such word groups or phrases should be read and translated as units, with proper attention to emphasis and expression.

After translating **Forum Rōmānum** with due regard to the word groups in each sentence, practice reading the entire passage aloud in the Latin with as much expression as you can.

170.   THE STORY OF LUCIUS

Forum Rōmānum

Quondam (*once upon a time*) puer parvus Lūcius in Italiā habitābat. Dē glōriā patriae multa audiēbat. Magister Lūciō et cēteris (*the other*) puerīs loca clāra Rōmae mōnstrābat. In Forum Rōmānum puerōs dūcēbat. In hunc (*this*) locum populus Rōmānus conveniēbat. Ibi virī amīcōs vidēbant et aedificia (*buildings*) pūblica spectābant. Ibi

73

nūntiī magnās victōriās nūntiābant.　Ibi virī clārī in rōstrīs[1]
verba faciēbant.　Magister multa dē patriā in Forō docēbat.
Puerī magistrō magnam grātiam habēbant, quod Forum
amābant.　Ē Forō puerī cum magistrō in Sacram Viam
ambulābant (*walked*) et tabernās (*shops*) spectābant.　Cupi-
tisne (*desire*) plūra (*more*) dē Lūciō audīre?

171.　　　　　Conversation

(See *Color Map of the Roman World* between pp. 52 and 53.)

M. = **Magister**　　　**D.** = **Discipulī**

M. Spectātisne, puerī et puellae?　**D.** Spectāmus.

M. Ubi oppida vidētis?　**D.** In Āfricā et in Asiā et in
Eurōpā multa oppida vidēmus.

M. In mediā terrā aquam vidētis.　Illam aquam "Medi-
terrā-neum Mare" (*Sea*) vocāmus.

M. Ibi est Lūsitānia — vidētisne?　**D.** Vidēmus.

M. Ubi est Hibernia?　**D.** Hibernia est īnsula in Ōceanō
Atlanticō.

M. Multī virī multōrum populōrum in Eurōpā habitant.

M. Ubi pugnābant Sociī in Bellō Magnō?　**D.** Sociī
in Galliā et in Italiā pugnābant.

Questions to Be Answered in Latin

1. Ubi habitāmus?　2. Nōnne officium nostrum erat
virōs et arma in Galliam mittere?　3. Ubi Germānī agrōs
vāstābant?　4. Reguntne Germānī in Galliā?

---

[1] *The rostra* (speakers' platform).

LESSON XXXI

PRESENT SYSTEM PASSIVE OF THE FOUR CONJUGATIONS

ELEMENTARY GRAMMAR: Review *Voice*, **632**; *Progressive verb forms*, **631**; *Participles*, **635**.

172. Vocabulary

commit′tō, –ere, *join together, commit, intrust;* proe′lium
    commit′tere, *to begin battle*   [*mittō*]

fīni′timus, –a, –um, *neighboring;* fīni′timus, –ī, m., *neighbor*

pau′cī, –ae, –a, *few*   (paucity)

proe′lium, –ī, n., *battle*

–que, conj., *and* (translated before the word to which it is
    joined)

re′liquus, –a, –um, *remaining, rest of*   (relic)

173. English and Latin Word Formation

We have seen how Latin and English words are formed from others by the use of prefixes. There are other ways of forming new words. These we shall discuss later. For the present it is sufficient to recognize the roots that words have in common. Note the relationship and review the meanings of the following words which have occurred in the preceding vocabularies:

(*a*) **amīcus** and **amīcitia**, (*b*) **nāvigō** and **nauta**, (*c*) **nūntiō** and **nūntius**, (*d*) **capiō** and **captīvus** (a " captive " is one who is *taken*), (*e*) **pugna** and **pugnō**, (*f*) **puer** and **puella**, (*g*) **habeō** and **habitō** (to " inhabit " a place is to keep on *having* it).

From now on try to associate new Latin words with those you have already had, as well as with English derivatives which you find.

174. Voice: Active and Passive

1. **Vir accūsābit,** *The man will accuse.*
2. **Vir accūsābitur,** *The man will be accused.*

Observe (*a*) that in 1 the verb shows that the subject *acts* (**active voice**), and in 2 it is *acted upon* (**passive voice**); (*b*) that voice is indicated by endings in Latin.

Note. — The linking verb **sum** has no voice, for it indicates merely existence.

175. Progressive and Passive Verb Forms Distinguished in English

Be careful to distinguish between active progressive forms and true passive verb phrases, both of which employ the verb *to be*.

FIG. 33. CUPIDS FISHING

The cupids *are catching* fish (active).
The fish *are being caught* (passive).

ACTIVE (progressive): The present participle combined with any tense of the verb *to be* is active: *He is seeing* (**videt**); *They were calling* (**vocābant**).

PASSIVE: The past participle combined with any tense of the verb *to be* is passive: *He is seen* (**vidētur**); *They were called* (**vocābantur**).

Summary: 1. *to be* + present participle = active
2. *to be* + past participle = passive

176. Passive Voice of the Four Conjugations in Present System

The passive personal endings, which are substituted for the active,[1] are:

---

[1] But in forms ending in −ō in the active (as **parō** and **parābō**), the passive ending −**r** is *added to*, not *substituted for*, the active ending. The −**o**− becomes short.

PERSONAL ENDINGS		PRESENT	
-r	-mur	parʹror, *I am prepared*	parā'mur, *we are pre-pared*
-ris	-minī	parā'ris, *you are pre-pared*	parā'minī, *you are pre-pared*
-tur	-ntur	parā'tur, *he is prepared*	paran'tur,[1] *they are pre-pared*
		Similarly **habeor, pōnor, capior, mūnior** (see **661, 662, 663, 664**).	

IMPERFECT

parā'**bar**, *I was being prepared, was prepared*   parābā'**mur**, *we were being pre-pared, etc.*

parābā'**ris**, *you were being pre-pared, etc.*   parābā'**minī**, *you were being prepared, etc.*

parābā'**tur**, *he was being pre-pared, etc.*   parāban'**tur**, *they were being prepared, etc.*

Similarly **habēbar, pōnēbar, capiēbar, mūniēbar** (see **661, 662, 663, 664**).

FUTURE

parā'**bor**, *I shall be prepared*   parā'**bimur**, *we shall be pre-pared*

parā'**beris**, *you will be pre-pared*   parābi'**minī**, *you will be pre-pared*

parā'**bitur**, *he will be pre-pared*   parābun'**tur**, *they will be pre-pared*

Similarly **habēbor, pōnar, capiar, mūniar** (see **661, 662, 663, 664**).

---

177. Drill. — Conjugate **pugnō, videō, dēfendō, accipiō,** and **inveniō** in the present system passive.

---

[1] For the vowel shortened before **-ntur**, see **20**, *a*.

178.   **Exercises**

Oral. 1. Reliquī nautae ad īnsulam mittentur. 2. Rōmānī proelium cum fīnitimīs committunt. 3. America terra līberōrum est. 4. Pauca signa proelī in fīnitimīs agrīs oppidīsque vidēbantur. 5. Multa praemia reliquīs puerīs puellīsque dōnābuntur. 6. Captīvī ad oppidum redūcentur et proelium committētur.

Written. 1. We shall be accused; he is being taught; it was not approved; they will be sent. 2. They will receive a few words of advice; a few words of advice will be received. 3. Where are the-rest-of the boys? Are they working in the fields? 4. The-rest-of the men will be sent to the island and will lead-back many prisoners.

Fig. 34. Forum Rōmānum

A view from the Capitoline Hill, facing east (cf. Figs. 32, 36). In the foreground, the **Basilica Iūlia** (a courthouse); to the left, the Forum proper; in the left background, the Colosseum (Fig. 41); on the right, the Palatine Hill, where the imperial palaces stood.

LESSON XXXII

ABLATIVE OF PERSONAL AGENT

179.   **Vocabulary**

appel'lō, –ā're, *call, call upon, name*   (appellate)
aut, conj., *or;* **aut . . . aut,** *either . . . or*
et . . . et, conj., *both . . . and*
ne'que (or **nec**), conj., *and not, nor;* **ne'que . . . ne'que,** *neither . . . nor*
praesi'dium, –ī, n., *garrison, guard, protection*

180.   **Latin Phrases in English**

magnum bonum, *great good.*

terra firma, *solid earth* (as opposed to water).

via media, *a middle way* or *course.*

cōnsiliō et armīs, *by counsel and by arms.*

nōn ministrārī, sed ministrāre, *not to be served, but to serve* (motto of Wellesley College).

In Deō spērāmus, *In God we trust* (motto of Brown University).

181.   **Ablative of Personal Agent**

1. **Amāmur ab amīcīs,** *We are loved by our friends.*
2. **Vir ā puerō vidētur,** *The man is seen by the boy.*

182. Rule. — *The ablative preceded by* **ā** *or* **ab** *is used with a passive verb to denote the person by whom anything is done.*

Caution. — The ablative of personal agent must be carefully distinguished from the ablative of means, both of which are frequently translated with *by*. Remember that *means refers to things*, while *agent always denotes a person*. Furthermore, the ablative of means *never takes a* preposition, while the ablative of personal agent is never used without the preposition **ā** (**ab**).

1. **Oppidum cōnsiliō capitur,** *The town is taken by strategy* (**means**).
2. **Oppidum ā nostrīs capitur,** *The town is taken by our men* (**agent**).

183. Agreement. — In both English and Latin, when two singular subjects are connected by *or* (**aut**), *either . . . or* (**aut . . . aut**), *neither . . . nor* (**neque . . . neque**), the verb is in the singular: *Neither the boy nor the girl **is** in the forest,* **Neque puer neque puella in silvā *est*.**

184.   **Exercises**

Oral. 1. Puer equōs dūcit; equī ā puerō dūcuntur. 2. Magister puerōs puellāsque docēbat; puerī puellaeque ā magistrō docēbantur. 3. Aut puerī aut virī equōs ad agrōs redūcent. 4. Neque servus neque equus in viīs vidēbitur. 5. Multa grāta praemia ā reliquīs puerīs puellīsque accipientur. 6. Neque praesidium neque auxilium ā nostrīs sociīs mittitur. 7. Et sociī et amīcī[1] ā multīs populīs appellābimur.

FIG. 35. A GAME OF KNUCKLEBONES

Bones an inch long were used to play the game now called jacks. They were also used in gambling, like dice.

Written. 1. The men see few signs of battle; few signs of battle are seen by the men. 2. The girls were frightened by the bad boys. 3. The grain is being carried by wagon to the town. 4. The troops were fleeing to the neighboring woods; there they were captured by our strong guard. 5. Neither water nor grain is being carried by the-rest-of the men.

---

[1] Observe that the predicate nominative (**13**, *b*) may be used with other verbs than **sum**.

LESSON XXXIII

PERFECT STEM. PERFECT ACTIVE INDICATIVE
OF THE FOUR CONJUGATIONS

185.   Vocabulary

āmit′tō, –ere, āmī′sī, *let go, lose*	[*mittō*]
an′nus, –ī, m., *year*	(annual)
lǐ′ber, lǐ′brī, m., *book*	(library)
nunc, adv., *now*	
perī′culum, –ī, n., *trial, danger*	(perilous)
prō, prep. with abl., *in front of, before, for*	
pro′perō, –ā′re, –ā′vī, *hasten*	

186.   Latin and English Word Formation

As a prefix **prō-** has its prepositional meanings, with
the additional one of *forward*. Define the following derivatives of words which you have already studied:

provoke, prospect, produce, proceed.

a.   **Latin Phrases in English**

prō patriā, *for (one's) country.*
prō bonō pūblicō, *for the public good.*
prō fōrmā, *for (as a matter of) form.*

187.   The Perfect Stem

In English, the **perfect** tense is formed by use of the auxiliary *have (has)* with the past participle: *I have prepared,
he has gone.*

In Latin, the **perfect stem** is used in forming the three
perfect tenses in the active — the **perfect, past perfect,** and
future perfect. The perfect stem is found by dropping the
personal ending **–ī** from the perfect active indicative: **āmīsī,
āmīs–.**

Note. — All verbs of the first conjugation thus far studied form the perfect
stem by adding –v to the present stem : **properā-**, **properāv-**.   No rules,
however, can be given for forming the perfect stem of verbs of the other conjugations.   Hereafter the first person singular of the perfect active indicative
will be given in the vocabularies as the third form.   This should be memorized.

188. **Perfect Active Indicative**

The following endings (used in no other tenses) are added
directly to the perfect stem in forming the **perfect indicative active** :

Perfect Endings		
–ī	parā′vī, *I have prepared, I prepared*	ha′buī, *I have had, I had*
–istī	parāvis′tī, *you have pre-pared*, etc.	habuis′tī, *you have had,* etc.
–it	parā′vit, *he has prepared,* etc.	ha′buit, *he has had,* etc.
–imus	parā′vimus, *we have pre-pared*, etc.	habu′imus, *we have had,* etc.
–istis	parāvis′tis, *you have pre-pared*, etc.	habuis′tis, *you have had,* etc.
–ērunt	parāvē′runt, *they have pre-pared*, etc.	habuē′runt, *they have had,* etc.

Similarly **posuī, cēpī, mūnīvī** (see **662, 663, 664**).

189. Drill. — Conjugate the following in the perfect indicative active :

convocō (convocāv–), agō (ēg–), excēdō (excess–), dēfendō (dē-
fend–), mittō (mīs–), trahō (trāx–), accipiō (accēp–), videō (vīd–), fugiō
(fūg–), veniō (vēn–).

190. **Exercises**

Oral. 1. Amīsimus; nūntiāvit; augēbis; occupāvistis; āmittitur; ēvocāminī. 2. Puer in viā librum āmīsit. 3. Ex oppidō excessimus et ad agrōs silvāsque properāvimus. 4. Multī vītam in bellō āmīsērunt sed magnam glōriam accēpērunt. 5. Multōs annōs in perīculō ēgimus; nunc ōtium habēmus. 6. Properāre dēbēmus, quod perīculum nunc est magnum. 7. Multī captīvī ā puerīs prō castrīs vidēbantur.

Written. 1. To lose; he has departed; we have intrusted; we shall be heard. 2. Were the girls being frightened by the horses? Where were the boys? 3. They have seen the danger and are fleeing to the camp. 4. I have intrusted the care of the camp to the guards.

FIG. 33. FORUM RŌMĀNUM

Thus it appeared during the Roman Empire (cf. Figs. 32, 34). In the left background, the temple of Jupiter on the Capitoline Hill.

LESSON XXXIV

PERFECT INDICATIVE OF *SUM*. THE USE OF THE IMPERFECT AND THE PERFECT

ELEMENTARY GRAMMAR: Review *Past and present perfect tenses*, **630**, *b, d.*

191. Vocabulary

agri′cola, –ae, m., *farmer*	[**ager**]
com′parō, –ā′re, –ā′vī, *get together, prepare*	[**parō**]
fī′lius, –ī, m., *son*	(filial)
nōs′cō, –ere, nō′vī, *learn;* in perf. tenses, " have learned " = *know*	
prōcē′dō, –ere, prōces′sī, *go forth, advance*	[**cēdō**]
sum, es′se, fu′ī, *be*	(essence)
ab′sum, abes′se, ā′fuī, *be away from, be absent*	

192. Perfect Indicative of *Sum*

The verb **sum** is conjugated regularly in the perfect:

fu′ī, *I have been, I was*	fu′imus, *we have been, we were*
fuis′tī, *you have been, you were*	fuis′tis, *you have been, you were*
fu′it, *he has been, he was*	fuē′runt, *they have been, they were*

193. How the Perfect and the Imperfect Differ in Latin

The perfect tense represents an act (*a*) as *now complete*, like the English present perfect, expressed by *has* and *have*: **vīdī**, *I have seen;* (*b*) as a *simple act* performed *once*, like the English past: **vīdī**, *I saw.* The latter use of the Latin perfect is to be carefully distinguished from the imperfect, which always denotes a state of being or an act as *repeated, customary,* or *continuous,* like the English progressive past:

    Perfect: **vīdī**, *I saw* (once).
    Imperfect: **vidēbam**, *I kept seeing* (all along), *I was seeing.*

The perfect tense is used more commonly in Latin than the imperfect.

194.   **Exercises**

Oral.   1. Multī puerī aberant. Nōnne valēbant? 2. Aquam portābam et reliquī puerī in magnō agrō castra pōnēbant. 3. Paucī (of us) labōrābāmus, sed reliquī puerī in castrīs semper manēbant.   4. Agricolārum fīliī multa dē agrīs et equīs nōvērunt.   5. Magistrī fīlius multa dē librīs nōvit, sed agrī fīlium agricolae docent.   6. Multī virī servī fuērunt; nunc līberī sunt. 7. Prō patriā ad pugnam prōcessērunt; prō patriā et arma et frūmentum comparāvērunt; prō patriā labōrāvērunt et pecūniam dōnāvērunt.

Written.   1. We are the sons of free (men) and love our native land.   2. We know much about many lands and peoples.   3. Much grain is being prepared by the farmers. 4. We hastened from the town into the fields and learned many (things).   5. The farmer has spent many years in the fields.

195.   **Latin and English Word Formation**

We have already studied the preposition **in** used as a prefix (**98**). There is another prefix **in-**, used chiefly with adjectives and nouns, which has an entirely different meaning and must be carefully distinguished from the former. It is a negative prefix (like " un- "), as in *injustice*. It is assimilated like the other prefix **in-**, *e.g. il-legal, im-moral, ir-regular.* Define the following derivatives of words which you have studied :

immemorial, immaterial, inglorious, ingratitude, illiberal, illiterate, infirm.

The prefix **dis-** in English and Latin means *apart;* but sometimes it is purely negative like **in-**. Distinguish carefully from **dē-**. It is either assimilated or left unchanged, as follows :

dis-inter, dis-locate, dis-arm, dif-fuse, di-vert, di-stant, dis-similar.

Define the first three of these words, derived from words in previous vocabularies.

PAST PERFECT AND FUTURE PERFECT INDICATIVE ACTIVE OF THE FOUR CONJUGATIONS

ELEMENTARY GRAMMAR: Review *Past perfect and future perfect,*
630, *e, f.*

196.   Vocabulary

dīmit′tō, –ere, dīmī′sī, *let go, send away*	[*mittō*]
inimī′cus, –a, –um, *unfriendly, hostile;* as a noun, *enemy*	[*amīcus*]
in′teger, –gra, –grum, *untouched, fresh*	(integer)
por′ta, –ae, f., *gate*	(portal)
prōdū′cō, –ere, prōdū′xī, *lead forth* or *out*	[*dūcō*]
reti′neō, –ē′re, reti′nuī, *hold back, restrain, keep*	[*teneō*]

197.   Past Perfect Indicative Active

In English, the **past perfect** tense is formed by use of the
auxiliary *had* with the past participle: *I had prepared,
they had prepared.*

In Latin, the **past perfect** (sometimes called pluperfect)
is formed by adding the tense sign **–erā–** to the perfect stem,
together with the personal endings used throughout the
present system. It is equivalent in form to the various
forms of the imperfect tense of **sum** added to the perfect
stem of the given verb:

---

parā′veram, *I had prepared*	parāverā′mus, *we had prepared*
parā′verās, *you had prepared*	parāverā′tis, *you had prepared*
parā′verat, *he, she, it had prepared*	parā′verant, *they had prepared*

Similarly **habueram, posueram, cēperam, mūnīveram.**
(For full conjugation see **661, 662, 663, 664**.)

198.   **Future Perfect Indicative Active**

In English, the **future perfect** tense is formed by use of the auxiliary *shall have* with the past participle: *I shall have prepared.*

In Latin, the **future perfect** is formed by adding the tense sign –**eri**– to the perfect stem, together with the personal endings of the present system. It is equivalent in form to the future tense of **sum** (with the exception of –**erint** in the third plural) added to the perfect stem of the given verb :

---

parā′verō,[1] *I shall have prepared*

parā′veris, *you will have prepared*

parā′verit, *he, she, it will have prepared*

parāve′rimus, *we shall have prepared*

parāve′ritis, *you will have prepared*

parā′verint, *they will have prepared*

Similarly **habuerō, posuerō, cēperō, mūnīverō.**

(For full conjugation see **661, 662, 663, 664.**)

Note. — The three tenses, perfect, past perfect, and future perfect, which are based upon the perfect stem, form the **perfect system.**

199. Drill. — Conjugate the following in the perfect system active : **videō, –ēre, vīdī ; cēdō, –ere, cessī ; efficiō, –ere, effēcī ; moveō, –ēre, mōvī ; incipiō, –ere, incēpī.**

200.   **Exercises**

Oral. 1. Inimīcōs nostrōs amāre dēbēmus.   2. Parvī puerī linguam retinēre dēbent.   3. Magister puerōs dīmīsit, quod fōrmās verbōrum nōn nōverant.   4. Nostrī castra movēre et proelium committere parāverint.   5. Integrae

---

[1] –i– disappears before final ō (**20,** *a*).

cōpiae nostrae bellum gerere incēpērunt et prō populīs līberīs pugnāvērunt.   6. Marius prō portīs castrōrum cōpiās prōdūxerat. 7. Virī ē castrīs vēnerant et ad oppidum prōcēdēbant.

FIG. 37. A PORTABLE HOT WATER HEATER

The heater has the form of a fortified camp. A charcoal fire was built in the interior. The water was poured into the towers and circulated around the fire. Note the modern-looking faucet at the right.

Written. 1. The slave deserved a large reward, because he had saved the life of our friend's son. 2. Marius had fought for his native land in Gaul. 3. We shall have seen strange lands, towns, and peoples. 4. We shall have sent away the messenger to the camp.

201.   Latin and English Word Formation

We have seen that prefixes are so called because they are attached to the beginnings of words (**87**). Particles which are attached to the ends of words are called **suffixes** (**sub**, *under, after;* **fīxus**, *attached*). Like the Latin prefixes, the Latin suffixes play a very important part in the formation of English words.

The suffix **–ia** usually has the form **–y** in English. Give the English forms of the following words found in the preceding vocabularies: **memoria, glōria, familia, iniūria.**

What must be the Latin words from which are derived *colony, luxury, perfidy?*

Some **–ia** nouns drop the **–ia** entirely in English (**126**): *concord, vigil, matter* (from **māteria**).

Fig. 38. Pompeii, a.d. 79

LESSON XXXVI

PAST PERFECT AND FUTURE PERFECT INDICATIVE OF *SUM*. INFINITIVE WITH SUBJECT ACCUSATIVE

ELEMENTARY GRAMMAR: Review *Infinitive*, **634.**

202.   Vocabulary

discē'dō, –ere, disces'sī, *go away, depart*	[*cēdō*]
e'tiam, adv., *also, even*	
iu'beō, –ē're, ius'sī, *order, command*	
lī'berī, –ō'rum, m., *children*	[*līber*]
red'igō, –ere, redē'gī, *drive* or *bring back, reduce*	[*agō*]
remo'veō, –ē're, remō'vī, *move back, remove, withdraw*	[*moveō*]

203.   Past Perfect and Future Perfect of *Sum*

PAST PERFECT	FUTURE PERFECT
fu'eram, *I had been*	fu'erō, *I shall have been*
fu'erās, *you had been*	fu'eris, *you will have been*
fu'erat, *he had been*	fu'erit, *he will have been*
fuerā'mus, *we had been*	fue'rimus, *we shall have been*
fuerā'tis, *you had been*	fue'ritis, *you will have been*
fu'erant, *they had been*	fu'erint, *they will have been*

204.   Infinitive Object as in English

1. **Virōs discēdere iussī,** *I ordered the men to go away.*
2. **Puerōs esse bonōs docēmus,** *We teach the boys to be good.*

Observe that (*a*) in English such verbs as *order, teach* (also *wish, forbid,* etc.) take an infinitive as *object*, often with a noun or pronoun in the accusative, which may be regarded as its *subject;* (*b*) in Latin certain verbs of similar meaning take the infinitive with subject accusative.

205. Rule. — *The subject of an infinitive is in the accusative.*

206. **Exercises**

Oral. 1. Līberōs nostrōs semper retinēre bonōs librōs docēmus. 2. Nōnne bonum est inimīcōs in amīcitiam et concordiam redigere? 3. Magister puerōs puellāsque etiam inimīcōs amāre docēbat. 4. Nostrī ex oppidō arma remōverant et ad fīnitima castra prōcesserant. 5. Fīnitimōs nostrōs dīmittere cōpiās et etiam discēdere ex īnsulā iussimus. 6. Cum Sociīs nostrīs fuerat et prō patriā nostrā in Galliā pugnāverat. 7. Novum erat vidēre magnum numerum captīvōrum in viīs oppidī.

Written. 1. I had been; we shall have been; they had been; you will have been. 2. It was good to see our forces near the gates of the town. 3. They had begun to remove the grain by wagon to the camp. 4. The children of the farmers are being taught to fight for (their) native land. 5. He has ordered the boy to lead out fresh horses to the gate. 6. We are preparing to carry the timber by wagon to the town.

207. **Latin and English Word Formation**

The Latin suffix –**tia** as a general rule has the form –**ce** in English. It is to be carefully distinguished from the Latin suffix –**ia**, which usually has the form –**y** in English (**201**).

Give the English forms of the following words found in the preceding vocabularies: **grātia, sententia.**

What must be the Latin words from which are derived *science, diligence, prudence?*

a. **Latin Verb Forms in English**

Present: *deficit.*
Perfect: *affidavit, vici.*

208. A CLEVER REPLY

Bellō [1] Pūnicō T.[2] Līvius Tarentum, oppidum Italiae, āmīsit et ad arcem [3] oppidī fūgit. Q.[4] Fabius Maximus magnā vigilantiā et magnō cōnsiliō oppidum recēpit. Tum ad arcem properāvit. Ibi Līvius superbus Fabiō dīxit [5]: " Meā operā Tarentum recēpistī." Fabius respondit: " Certē,[6] nam ego recēpī oppidum quod (*which*) tū āmīsistī."

FIG. 39. PORTA CASTRŌRUM

A fortified camp at Saalburg, Germany, part of the system of defense, consisting of camps and a wall, erected by the Romans.

---

[1] Abl.: *during.*   [2] T. = **Titus.**   [3] Acc. of **arx.**   [4] Q. = **Quīntus.**
[5] From **dīcō, dictus**; derivative?   [6] Adv.

LESSON XXXVII

PERFECT AND PAST PERFECT PASSIVE OF THE FOUR CONJUGATIONS

209.   Vocabulary

ēgre'gius, –a, –um, *distinguished, excellent*   (egregious)
exem'plum, –ī, n., *sample, example*   (exemplary)
per, prep. with acc., *through*
prōpō'nō, –ere, prōpo'suī, prōpo'situs, *set forth, present*   [*pōnō*]
rema'neō, –ē're, remān'sī, remānsū'rus,[1] *remain behind,*
  remain   [*maneō*]
sub, prep., *under, close to;* with acc. after verbs of motion ;
  with abl. after verbs of rest

210.   Latin and English Word Formation

The preposition **sub,** used as a prefix in Latin and English,
means *under, up from under:* **sus-tineō,** *to hold **up**;* **succēdō,** *to come **up**.* It is regularly assimilated before certain
consonants : *sup-port, suc-ceed, sug-gest, sus-ceptible, suf-fer,
sur-rogate, sus-tenance, sus-pend,* but *sub-mit, sub-trahend.*
We use it freely in English to form new words : *sub-let, sub-
lease.*

Per usually remains unchanged when used as a prefix.

211.   Perfect Participle

The **perfect participle** in Latin is passive and is declined
like **magnus, –a, –um.** It agrees with a noun or pronoun in
gender, number, and case like an ordinary adjective. The
perfect participle of each new verb will hereafter be given in
the vocabularies as the fourth part. In the first conjugation
it is regularly formed by adding **–tus** to the present stem :
parā–tus.

---

[1] A few verbs lack the perfect participle ; some of these have the future
active participle in **–ūrus,** which appears as the fourth principal part.

212.   **Perfect System Passive**

In English, all the passive tenses are compound, consisting of two or more parts.

In Latin, the tenses of the present and perfect systems thus far studied have been single or **simple** in form. The three perfect tenses in the passive, however, are **compound**, *i.e.* they are formed by combining the perfect participle of the given verb in turn with the present, imperfect, and future tenses of **sum** to form the perfect, past perfect, and future perfect tenses respectively.

213.   **Perfect Indicative Passive**

In English, the present perfect passive is formed by using the perfect tense of *to be* (i.e. *have been*) as an auxiliary with the past participle.

In Latin, the perfect passive is formed by using the *present* tense of **sum** as an auxiliary with the perfect participle.

parā′tus (–a, –um)	**sum**, *I was, have been prepared* **es**, *you were, have been prepared* **est**, *he was, has been prepared*	parā′tī (–ae, –a)	**su′mus**, *we were, have been prepared* **es′tis**, *you were, have been prepared* **sunt**, *they were, have been prepared*

Similarly **habitus sum, positus sum, captus sum, mūnītus sum.**
(For full conjugation see **661–664.**)

214.   **Past Perfect Indicative Passive**

In English, the past perfect passive is formed by using the past perfect tense of *to be* (i.e. *had been*) as an auxiliary with the past participle.

In Latin, the past perfect passive is formed by using the *imperfect* tense of **sum** (*i.e.* **eram**) as an auxiliary with the perfect participle (cf. the formation of the corresponding active tense by adding the imperfect tense of **sum** to the perfect stem: **parāv-eram**):

<table>
<tr><td rowspan="6">parā'tus
(-a, -um)</td><td>e'ram, I had been prepared</td><td rowspan="6">parā'tī
(-ae, -a)</td><td>erā'mus, we had been prepared</td></tr>
<tr><td>e'rās, you had been prepared</td><td>erā'tis, you had been prepared</td></tr>
<tr><td>e'rat, he had been prepared</td><td>e'rant, they had been prepared</td></tr>
</table>

Similarly **habitus eram, positus eram, captus eram, mūnītus eram.**
(For full conjugation see **661–664**.)

215. Drill. — Conjugate the following in the perfect and past perfect passive:

trahō, –ere, trāxī, trāctus   moveō, –ēre, mōvī, mōtus
videō, –ēre, vīdī, vīsus   agō, –ere, –ēgī, āctus

216. **Exercises**

Oral. 1. Ēgregium exemplum ā magistrō prōpositum est. 2. Arma carrīs ad castra portāta erant. 3. Equī ab agricolā per silvam ad aquam āctī erant. 4. Puellae magnīs undīs terrentur sed iniūriam nōn accipient. 5. Ēgregiumne exemplum amīcitiae memoriā tenētis? 6. Sub aquā remanēre nōn grātum est. 7. Vir ā puerō sub aquam trāctus erat sed et vir et puer servātī [1] sunt.

Written. 1. They have been seen; I had been dragged; you had been moved; he had been; they will have been. 2. The rest of the books had been removed by the boy's teacher. 3. The farmer's son had seen few towns but he knew much about horses and fields and woods. 4. In Gaul my son had fought for our country in many battles.

---

[1] Note that the participle is plural because it refers to both **vir** and **puer.**

LESSON XXXVIII

FUTURE PERFECT PASSIVE AND PRESENT INFINITIVE PASSIVE OF THE FOUR CONJUGATIONS

217. Vocabulary

ad'sum, ades'se, ad'fuī, adfutū'rus, *be near, be present* [**sum**]

de'us, –ī, m., *god* (deify)

ēdū'cō, –ere, ēdū'xī, ēduc'tus, *lead out* [**dūcō**]

permit'tō, –ere, permī'sī, permis'sus, *let go through, allow, in-trust* (with dat.) [**mittō**]

prī'mus, –a, –um, *first* (primary)

susci'piō, –ere, suscē'pī, suscep'tus, *take up, undertake* [**capiō**]

218. Latin Phrases in English

Deō grātiās, *thanks to God.*

Deī grātiā, *by the grace of God* (seen on Canadian coins).

per annum, *by (through) the year.*

sīc semper tyrannīs, *thus always to tyrants* (motto of the state of Virginia).

sub rosā, *under the rose, i.e.* in concealment.

FIG. 40. THE FORUM AT POMPEII

219. Future Perfect Indicative Passive

In English, the future perfect passive is formed by using the future perfect tense of *to be* (i.e. *shall have been*) as an auxiliary with the past participle.

In Latin, the future perfect passive is formed by using the *future* tense of **sum** (*i.e.* **erō**) as an auxiliary with the perfect participle (cf. the formation of the corresponding active tense by adding the future of **sum** to the perfect stem : **parāv-erō**) :

parā′tus (–a, –um)	e′rō, *I shall have been prepared* e′ris, *you will have been prepared* e′rit, *he will have been prepared*	parā′tī (–ae, –a)	e′rimus, *we shall have been prepared* e′ritis, *you will have been prepared* e′runt, *they will have been prepared*

Similarly **habitus erō, positus erō, captus erō, mūnītus erō.**
(For full conjugation see **661–664.**)

220. Drill. — Conjugate the following in the perfect system passive : **āmittō, –ere, āmīsī, āmissus ; ēdūcō, –ere, ēdūxī, ēductus ; suscipiō, –ere, suscēpī, susceptus.**

221. Present Infinitive Passive

In English, the present infinitive passive is formed by using the auxiliary *to be* with the past participle.

In Latin, the present infinitive passive is formed by changing the active infinitive ending **–re** to **–rī** :

Active : parā′**re**, *to prepare;* habē′**re**; mūnī′**re**
Passive : parā′**rī**, *to be prepared;* habē′**rī**; mūnī′**rī**

Note. — In the third conjugation, final **–ĕre** is changed to **–ī** :
Active : pō′nere, *to place;* ca′pere
Passive : pō′nī, *to be placed;* ca′pī

222. Drill. — Form the present passive infinitive of **videō, agō, trahō, suscipiō,** and **moveō.**

223.   Exercises

Oral. 1. Causam populī suscipere est officium bonōrum. 2. Vītam meam et fortūnās amīcīs permīsī. 3. Equī ex oppidō per agrōs ēductī erunt. 4. Pecūnia merērī et servārī ā puerīs puellīsque dēbet. 5. Deō grātiam habēre dēbeō, quod vītam meam regit. 6. Puerī adfuērunt prīmī, quod puellae tardae fuērunt. 7. Verbīs bonōrum virōrum semper incitārī et regī dēbēmus.

Written. 1. God teaches men to love (their) enemies. 2. The troops will have been ordered to advance and seize the town. 3. Where are the boys? They are absent, but the girls are present. 4. We have ordered the boys to be dismissed. 5. The boys ought to be called together by the teacher.

FIG. 41. THE COLOSSEUM

This amphitheater (cf. Fig. 7) was built in 80 A.D. and had room for at least 50,000 people. Much of its marble and limestone was carried away several centuries ago to build numerous palaces in Rome. To the right is the Arch of Constantine (cf. Fig. 47).

LESSON XXXIX

REVIEW

224. Rapid-fire Drills. — (*a*) *Give tense, person, and number, and translate:*

Appellantur, redūcēminī, āmīsērunt, nōvī, erant, āfuērunt, retinuit, dīmīserāmus, iusserō, prōcesserant, discessistī, prōdūxeram, redēgērunt, prōpositum est, remānsit, fuerō.

(*b*) *Give in Latin:*

1. It was committed; you have been away; we have hastened.   2. I have prepared; he had been; to remove.
3. To dismiss; to be presented; to be called.

225. Decline (*a*) **proelium integrum,** (*b*) **agricola bonus,** (*c*) **fīlius meus,** (*d*) **liber parvus,** (*e*) **perīculum magnum.**

226. Synopses [1]**:**   (Six tenses)

(*a*) 1. Give **iubeō** in the 1st sing., indic. act.
       2. Give **prōpōnō** in the 2nd sing., indic. pass.
       3. Give **prōdūcō** in the 3rd sing., indic. act.
       4. Give **appellō** in the 2nd plur., indic. pass.
(*b*) Give **sum** in the 1st sing.; **absum** in the 3rd sing.;
       adsum in the 2nd plur.

227.   A Color Scheme for Learning Verb Forms

It has been seen that a Latin verb need never be blindly memorized, for it is conjugated regularly throughout by combining certain stems with tense signs and personal endings in a logical way, as may be shown by the following color scheme:

Use white chalk for the present stem and yellow for the perfect stem; light red for all tense signs, light green for personal endings. For the compound tenses of the perfect system passive, use blue for the past participle, and white for the three tenses of **sum**.

---

[1] For definition of synopsis see **Elementary Grammar, 636**.

228. **English Word Study**

Find and use in sentences as many English derivatives as possible from **servō, moveō, dūcō, capiō.** For example: from **servō** is derived *conservation*, used as follows: *The* **conservation** *of our forests is a necessity.*

Enter the derivatives in your notebook, using a separate page for each Latin word.

229. **Hints for Developing "Word Sense"**

No word in any language, except a few prepositions, etc., has the same meaning at all times. While words, as a rule, have one general meaning, they may have several *shades of meaning*, which depend entirely upon their context or surroundings. You have doubtless seen the chameleon, a lizardlike creature which, for protection, changes its color to suit that of the leaf or limb upon which it rests. This we call "imitative coloring." Words, like chameleons, take on a local color. In translating a Latin word, therefore, it is necessary to derive its exact meaning (as opposed to its general or " vocabulary " meaning) from its context or setting; for example,

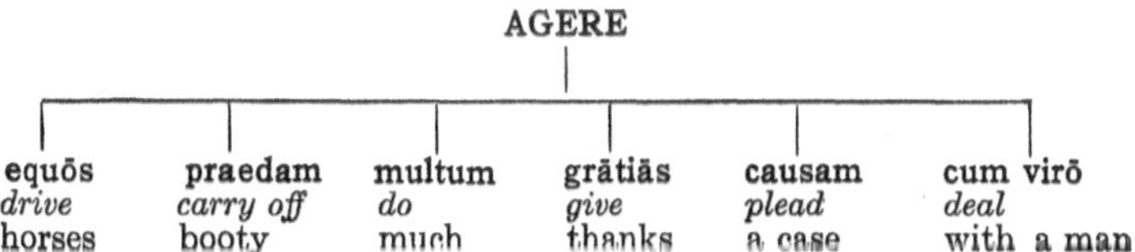

The above are only a few of the meanings of **agō.** From now on, do not confine yourself to the meanings given to words in the vocabulary, but select the one best suited to the context.

230. How to Study a Connected Passage

Do not turn to the vocabulary at the end of the book for a word you do not know. Read an entire paragraph before you look up a word. There are three ways to find the meaning of a word *without looking it up*:

1. *English derivatives* (nearly every Latin word has at least one English derivative).

2. *Related Latin words* (if you know the meaning of **re-** and **dūcō**, you know the meaning of **redūcō**).

3. *Sensible guessing.*

Use the vocabulary merely to verify results. In this way you will save time and gain a better command of Latin.

Fig. 42. Lūdus

A school scene from a stone relief found in Trier, Germany.

231. THE STORY OF LUCIUS (*Cont.*)

Lūdus

Lūciumne in memoriā habētis? Lūcius reliquīque puerī Rōmānī ā magistrō in Forum Rōmānum ductī erant. Nunc iterum dē Lūciō audiētis, quod bonī puerī puellaeque fuistis. Dē lūdō Lūcī nunc agēmus. Lūdus est locus ubi magister puerōs puellāsque docet. Prīmus lūdus vocābātur "lūdus litterārum." In Lūcī lūdō puellae nōn erant, et paucī puerī. Nōn erat pūblicus lūdus, sed tamen pretium disciplīnae erat

parvum. Puerī pecūniam et praemia ad magistrum portābant. Servī puerōs ad lūdum ante aurōram dūcēbant et
lanternam librōsque portābant. Nōnne dūrum erat puerum
Rōmānum esse? Servī in lūdō manēbant et puerōs ad
familiās redūcēbant.

WHAT ROMAN BOYS STUDIED

Etiam magister servus erat. Litterās et verba et numerōs
docēbat. Lingua lūdī erat Latīna, quod puerī Rōmānī erant.
Numerōs Lūcius nōn amābat. Magister puerīs fōrmās
litterārum mōnstrābat. Tum digitōs puerōrum tenēbat
et litterās faciēbant. Sententiae (*mottoes*) puerīs ā magistrō
mōnstrābantur. Exemplum sententiae est: "Ibi semper est
victōria ubi concordia est." Sententiās semper amābat
Lūcius et in memoriā tenēbat. Dīligentiā et studiō praemia
merēbat.

FIG. 43. LŪCIUS IN LŪDŌ POENĀ AFFICITUR

BAD LUCK

Tardī discipulī poenā afficiēbantur, sed Lūcius semper
prīmus veniēbat, quod ad lūdum properābat neque in viīs
remanēbat. Sed mala fortūna vēnit. Pecūnia ā Lūciō ad
magistrum portābātur et in viā āmissa est. Tardus fuit.
Magister puerōs appellāverat et reliquī puerī responderant,

"Adsum!" Tum magister Lūcium appellāvit. Puerī respondērunt, "Abest!" Tum vēnit Lūcius et magister puerīque dē pecūniā audīvērunt. Magister dūrus Lūcium ā puerīs sublevārī iussit et poenā eum (*him*) affēcit, quod pecūniam āmīserat et tardus fuerat.

FOUND!

· Magister discipulōs dīmīsit et singulī excessērunt. Lūcius cum servō discessit et pecūniam in viā invēnit. Ad lūdum properāvit et magistrō pecūniam dōnāvit. Magister bonō puerō grātiās ēgit et librum dōnāvit.

232.   **Conversation: School**

Magister. Discipulōs appellābō. Anna. **Anna**. Adsum.
M. Marīa. **Marīa.** Adsum.
M. Mārcus. **Discipulī.** Abest.
M. Ubi est Mārcus? **D.** Ad lūdum nōn vēnit. (Etc.)
M. Grātumne erat esse puerum Rōmānum? **D.** Nōn grātum erat esse puerum Rōmānum, quod puerī Rōmānī ante aurōram in lūdum dūcēbantur.
M. Ubi puerī Rōmānī labōrābant? **D.** In lūdō puerī Rōmānī labōrābant.
M. Multīne puerī in lūdō fuērunt? **D.** Paucī puerī in lūdō fuērunt.

Questions to Be Answered in Latin

1. Ubi nunc estis? 2. Estne grātum in lūdō esse? 3. Pecūniamne āmīsistī? 4. Ubi librum Latīnum āmīsistī? 5. Tardusne in lūdum vēnistī? 6. Semperne tardus in lūdum veniēs?

FIRST CONJUGATION : REVIEW OF PRINCIPAL PARTS

233.   Vocabulary

dīligen'tia, –ae, f., *carefulness, diligence*   (diligent)
dŏ,[1] dă're, de'dī, dă'tus, *give*   (dative)
in'ter, prep. with acc., *between, among*
ob, prep. with acc., *toward, on account of, for*
perti'neŏ, –ē're, –ti'nuī, –ten'tus, with **ad**, *extend to, pertain to*   [*teneō*]
submit'tō, –ere, –mī'sī, –mis'sus, (*send from under*), *dispatch*   [*mittō*]

234.   **Latin and English Word Formation**

As a prefix in Latin and English, **inter-** has its usual meanings. It is rarely assimilated. It is used rather freely in English to form new words: *inter-class, inter-state, inter-scholastic*, etc.

As a prefix **ob-** has the meaning *towards* or *against*. It is regularly assimilated before certain consonants: *oc-cur, of-ficial, o-mission, op-ponent;* but *ob-tain, ob-serve, ob-durate, ob-vious*.

235.   **Principal Parts**

(*a*) In English, every verb has three parts which, from their importance in forming the tenses, are called **principal parts**. Verbs that form the past tense by adding **–ed** to the present are said to be *regular*, while those which form the past tense in other ways — chiefly by changing the root vowel of the present — are said to be *irregular*. Note the following examples:

---

[1] **Dŏ** is irregular in three parts — perfect **dedī**, and **ă** in **dare** and **datus**. The **a** is short in all indicative forms except the present tense, second person singular.

	PRESENT	PAST	PAST PARTICIPLE
Regular:	call	called	called
Irregular:	be	was	been
	see	saw	seen
	do	did	done
	sing	sang	sung

Query. — Can you give the principal parts of *drink, write, go, come, run, give, sit, set, lie, lay?*

(*b*) In Latin, every verb regularly has four principal parts. They will hereafter be printed in the vocabularies and should be memorized. The principal parts of the model verbs of the four conjugations and of **sum** are as follows :

CONJUGATION	PRES. INDIC.	PRES. INFIN.	PERF. INDIC.	PERF. PART.
I	parō	parāre	parāvī	parātus
II	habeō	habēre	habuī	habitus
III	(*a*) pōnō	pōnere	posuī	positus
	(*b*) capiō	capere	cēpī	captus
IV	mūniō	mūnīre	mūnīvī	mūnītus
Irregular Verbs	sum	esse	fuī	futūrus [1]
	absum	abesse	āfuī	āfutūrus

236.　　　　　Tense Stems

Every Latin verb has approximately *one hundred and fifty forms*, all of which are built upon **three stems**, obtained from the principal parts as follows :

1. To find the **present stem**, drop –**re** from the present infinitive active : **parā–**, etc.

2. To find the **perfect stem**, drop –ī from the perfect indicative active : **parāv–**, etc.

---

[1] See **209**, footnote 1.

3. To find the **participial stem**, drop –us from the perfect participle : **parāt–**, etc.

Query. — What tenses are formed (*a*) upon the present stem, (*b*) upon the perfect stem, (*c*) with the perfect participle?

237. First Conjugation : Review of Principal Parts

Verbs of the first conjugation generally form the perfect stem by adding **–v** to the present stem (**187, Note**) and form the perfect participle by adding **–tus** to the present stem (**211**). Review the following and give their principal parts :

accūsō, amō, appellō, convocō, dōnō, ēvocō, exspectō, habitō, incitō, labōrō, mandō, mātūrō, migrō, mōnstrō, nāvigō, nūntiō, occupō, portō, probō, pugnō, servō, spectō, vāstō, vocō.

238.   Exercises

Oral. 1. Officium pūblicum est puerīs puellīsque disciplīnam dare. 2. Dīligentia puerōrum amīcīs nūntiāta erit. 3. Castra in altō locō erant inter oppidum et silvam. 4. Ob multās causās amīcitia et concordia inter līberōs esse dēbent. 5. America ob amīcitiam auxilium submīsit. 6. Ob magnum perīculum cōpiae nostrae colōnīs arma permīsērunt. 7. Agrī nostrī ad viam pertinent.

Written. 1. On-account-of the war we did not sail to Europe. 2. The fields had been laid waste and the town seized by the slaves. 3. He has been aroused by the messenger's harsh words. 4. We have dispatched a large number of reinforcements.

FIG. 44. ROMAN CUPS

LESSON XLI

DECLENSION OF THE RELATIVE PRONOUN *QUĪ*.
AGREEMENT OF THE RELATIVE

ELEMENTARY GRAMMAR: Review *Relative pronouns*, **615**, *c*.

239.   **Vocabulary**

cūr, interrog. adv., *why?*
nātū′ra, –ae, f., *nature*   (natural)
pul′cher, –chra, –chrum, *beautiful*   (pulchritude)
susti′neō, –ē′re, –ti′nuī, –ten′tus, *hold up, maintain, endure*   [**teneō**]

FIG. 45. A ROPE WALKER

240.   **Word Study: Intensive Prefixes**

Most of the Latin prepositions which are used as prefixes
in Latin and English may have intensive force, especially
con-, ex-, ob-, per-. They are then best translated either by
an English intensive, as *up* or *out*, or by an adverb, as *com-
pletely, thoroughly, deeply*. Thus **commoveō** means to *move
greatly*, **permagnus**, *very great*, **obtineō**, to *hold on to*, **concitō**,
to *rouse up*, **excipiō**, to *catch, receive*.

241.   **The Relative Pronoun *Quī***

The pronouns *who, which, what*, and *that* in English are
called **relative** pronouns because they *relate* or refer to some
foregoing word, called their **antecedent**.

There is only one relative pronoun in Latin, declined as
follows:

SINGULAR

Nom.	**quī** (*who*)	**quae** (*who*)	**quod** (*which*)
Gen.	**cu'ius** (*whose*)	**cu'ius** (*whose*)	**cu'ius** (*of which, whose*)
Dat.	**cui** (*to whom*)	**cui** (*to whom*)	**cui** (*to which*)
Acc.	**quem** (*whom*)[1]	**quam** (*whom*)[1]	**quod** (*which*)
Abl.	**quō** (*by whom*)	**quā** (*by whom*)	**quō** (*by which*)

PLURAL

Nom.	**quī** (*who*)	**quae** (*who*)	**quae** (*which*)
Gen.	**quō'rum**	**quā'rum**	**quō'rum**
Dat.	**qui'bus**	**qui'bus**	**qui'bus**
Acc.	**quōs**	**quās**	**quae**
Abl.	**qui'bus**	**qui'bus**	**qui'bus**

Note. — The plural is translated like the singular.

242. Relative Pronouns as Used in English

While *that* as a relative can be used to refer to both persons and things, *who* always refers to persons and *which* to things (in other words, *which* is the neuter of *who*). *Which* and *that* do not change form to indicate case, while *who* does:

Nom. *who* Gen. *whose* Dat. and Acc. *whom*

243. The Relative Pronoun as Used in Latin

In the following sentences the antecedent and relative are underscored. Give the number and gender of each:

1. (*a*) **Puella abest; puellam accūsō,** *The girl is absent; the girl I accuse.*

(*b*) **Puella quam accūsō abest,** *The girl whom I accuse is absent.*

2. **Oppidum quod vīdit erat parvum,** *The town which he saw was small.*

---

[1] Note that the genitive singular is alike in all genders, likewise the dative singular, and that the accusative singular, masculine and feminine, in both English and Latin ends in **-m.**

3. <u>Castra</u> ex <u>quibus</u> vēnimus erant magna, *The <u>camp from which</u> we came was large.*

4. <u>Virum</u> <u>cui</u> librum dedī vīdistī, *You saw the <u>man</u> to <u>whom</u> I gave the book.*

5. <u>Puer</u> <u>cuius</u> librum habeō est amīcus noster, *The <u>boy</u> <u>whose</u> book I have is our friend.*

Observe that the relative and the antecedent are always of the same number and gender but not necessarily in the same case.

244. Rule. — *The relative pronoun agrees with its antecedent in gender and number, but its case depends upon its use in its own clause.*

245. (*a*) While the relative may be omitted in English, it is never omitted in Latin: *The man (whom) I saw,* **Vir *quem* vīdī.**

(*b*) Fill in the blanks and write in Latin:

1. *I saw the horses —— were on the road.*
2. *The boy —— I saw was fighting.*

246.   **Exercises**

Oral. 1. Vir cui pecūniam permīsī erat amīcus meus. 2. Cūr nōn sustinētis fortūnam quam Nātūra dedit? 3. America bellum suscēpit ob iniūriās quās accēperat. 4. Virī quōrum fīliōs doceō ēgregiī agricolae sunt. 5. Cūr pecūniam puerō nōn dedistī quem in viā vīdistī? 6. Librōs quī ad fāmam et fortūnam pertinent puerī amant. 7. Via quā vēnimus erat pulchra.

Written. 1. The boy whom I saw in the woods is approaching. 2. He endured constant dangers on-account-of his enemies. 3. I saw the boy whose book I lost. 4. The war which was waged by our men in Europe had been approved by the people. 5. The men who did not fight maintained the country with money.

LESSON XLII

SECOND CONJUGATION: REVIEW OF PRINCIPAL PARTS. ABLATIVE OF MANNER

247.   **Vocabulary**

cōnser′vō, –ā′re, –ā′vī, –ā′tus, *save, preserve*	[***servō***]
intermit′tō, –ere, –mī′sī, –mis′sus, (lit., *let go between*), suspend, *stop, cease*	[***mittō***]
obti′neō, –ē′re, –ti′nuī, –ten′tus, *hold, obtain*	[***teneō***]
permo′veō, –ē′re, –mō′vī, –mō′tus, *move deeply, induce*	[***moveō***]
pe′tō, –ere, petī′vī, petī′tus, *seek, ask*	(petition)
tum, adv., *then*	

248.   **Interesting English Words**

Many English words that seem quite dull and ordinary have very interesting stories locked up within them. The key to these stories is Latin. Use this key and do not lose it. Let us try it now.

The "efficient" person is the one who *accomplishes* (**efficiō**) something

Fig. 46. A Roman Key

— remember this when you hear people talk about "efficiency." A "traction" company is engaged in *drawing* or *hauling* vehicles. What is a "tractor"? What sort of person is a "tractable" person? Politicians should remember that a public "office" is a *duty*. An "office" is also a place where one does his *duty* or *daily work.*

249. Second Conjugation: Review of Principal Parts

The following are verbs already studied, but whose principal parts have not been given in full. Memorize their principal parts and give the three stems of each:

dēbeō	dēbēre	dēbuī	dēbitus
mereō	merēre	meruī	meritus
terreō	terrēre	terruī	territus
valeō	valēre	valuī	valitūrus
teneō	tenēre	tenuī	tentus
contineō	continēre	continuī	contentus
retineō	retinēre	retinuī	retentus
doceō	docēre	docuī	doctus
augeō	augēre	auxī	auctus
maneō	manēre	mānsī	mānsus
iubeō	iubēre	iussī	iussus
moveō	movēre	mōvī	mōtus
removeō	removēre	remōvī	remōtus
videō	vidēre	vīdī	vīsus

Note. — It will be seen that no general rule can be given for forming the perfect and participial stems of verbs of the second conjugation. The most common type, however, is illustrated by **dēbeō**. Note the other types, which are arranged in groups.

250.   Ablative of Manner

In English, the manner of an action is expressed by an adverb or a phrase answering the question *How?* When a phrase is used, a preposition, such as *with*, introduces it.

In Latin, manner is similarly expressed. Examine the following:

1. **Cum studiō labōrat,** *He labors with eagerness (eagerly).*
2. **(Cum) magnō studiō labōrat,** *He labors with great eagerness (very eagerly).*

Note that when an adjective is used with the noun, **cum** may be omitted.

251. Rule. — *The ablative of manner with* **cum** *describes how something is done.* **Cum** *may be omitted if an adjective is used with the noun.*

252.   **Exercises**

Oral.   1. Magnā cūrā silvās nostrās cōnservābimus.
2. Servus pecūniam petet quae ab agricolā retenta est.
3. Magnā iniūriā tum populus regēbātur.   4. Puer quī
prīmum locum obtinuerat cum magnā cūrā et studiō labōrā-
verat. 5. Multī puerī studia ob bellum intermīsērunt.
6. Amīcus noster litterīs neque permōtus neque territus est
sed aequō animō ad castra prōcessit.   7. Frūmentō et
pecūniā et armīs causam Sociōrum nostrōrum sustinuimus.

Written.   1. He has been deeply moved by my words.
2. The teacher carefully taught the boys to save money.
3. The bad boy very carefully removed the teacher's books.
4. Why do you not seek the friendship of the girls who live
on High Street?   5. The slave was unjustly accused by the
prisoner.

FIG. 47. THE ARCH OF CONSTANTINE

Such arches were built in honor of generals and emperors. To the right
a corner of the Colosseum (cf. Fig. 41) is visible. Constantine died in
337 A.D.

LESSON XLIII

DECLENSION OF THE INTERROGATIVE PRONOUN *QUIS*

Elementary Grammar: Review *Interrogative pronouns,* **615**, *b.*

253.   Vocabulary

cō'gŏ, –ere, coē'gī, coāc'tus, (*drive together*), *collect, compel*   [**agō**]
Gallia, –ae, f., *Gaul* (modern France)
mo'dus, –ī, m., *measure, limit, manner*   (moderate)
mo'neō, –ē're, mo'nuī, mo'nitus, *remind, warn*   (monitor)
rĕg'num, –ī, n., *royal power, kingdom*   [**regō**]
tu'us, –a, –um, *your* (referring to one person)
ves'ter, –tra, –trum, *your* (referring to two or more)

254.   Latin Phrases in English

Cui bonō? (lit., *to whom for a good?*)   *What good is it?*
in absentiā, *in absence.*
in perpetuum, (*to perpetuity*), *forever.*
Īlium fuit, *Ilium has been* (i.e. *no longer exists*), said of Troy (Īlium)
after its destruction by the Greeks; now applied to anything that is
past.

255.   Interrogatives

I. **Pronoun.** — In English, the interrogative pronoun *who*
refers only to persons, *what* refers only to things.

In Latin, the interrogative pronoun corresponding to *who*
and *what* is **quis, quid,** declined as follows:

	M. AND F.	N.	M.	F.	N.
Nom.	**quis,** *who?*	**quid,** *what?*	quī	quae	quae
Gen.	**cu'ius,** *whose?*	**cu'ius,** *whose? of what?*	quō'rum	quā'rum	quō'rum
Dat.	**cui,** *to whom?*	**cui,** *to what?*	qui'bus	qui'bus	qui'bus
Acc.	**quem,** *whom?*	**quid,** *what?*	quōs	quās	quae
Abl.	**quō,** *by whom?*	**quō,** *by what?*	qui'bus	qui'bus	qui'bus

Note. — The plural is translated like the singular.

112

II. **Adjective.** — In English, the interrogative pronoun *who* can not be used as an adjective; we can not say, *Who man?* But *what* may be used as an adjective, referring to persons or things: *What man? What thing?*

In Latin, the interrogative adjective is **quī, quae, quod,** declined throughout like the relative pronoun (**241**). Compare the interrogative **quis** with the relative **quī** and note differences in the singular.

Note. — In English, *which* can be used as pronoun or adjective, referring to persons or things. It differs in meaning from *who* and *what* in that it implies a limited choice: *Which hat shall I wear? Which do you mean, Mr. Jones or Mr. Smith?* **Quis** and **quī** are used in this sense only when more than two are involved.

256. Drill. — Decline *what ally? what price? what nature?*

Lapsūs Linguae ("Slips of the Tongue"). — Have you ever said, *Who did you see?* Why is *who* incorrect? Give the correct form and translate the sentence into Latin.

257.   **Exercises**

Oral. 1. Quī puer verbīs bonī virī nōn permōtus est? 2. Quid amīcī tuī fēcērunt et quod praemium accipient? 3. Quō modō Sociī pecūniam coēgērunt? 4. Quod cōnsilium ā magistrō vestrō puerīs datum est? 5. Gallia tum multa rēgna continēbat quae ā populō Rōmānō occupāta erant. 6. Puerī magnā cūrā dē perīculīs monitī erant. 7. Quod fuit pretium librī quem ab amīcō tuō accēpistī? 8. Cui puerō, cui puellae, Nātūra nōn vītam grātam dedit?

Written. 1. To whom shall we give the money and present the rewards? 2. By what street did you come and whom did you seek? 3. In what manner did you obtain the money which you have? 4. Whose words were, " My kingdom for (**prō**) a horse!"? 5. How (in what manner) did you obtain your books? What did you give the man?

THIRD CONJUGATION: REVIEW OF PRINCIPAL PARTS

258.   **Vocabulary**

an′te, adv. and prep. with acc., *before* (of time or place)
cognōs′cō, –ere, **cognō′vī**, **cog′nitus**, *learn;* perf. tenses,
   " have learned " = *know*   [*nōscō*]
do′minus, –ī, m., *master, lord, ruler*   (dominate)
iam, adv., *already*
le′gō, –ere, **lē′gī**, **lēc′tus**, *gather, choose, read*   (legible)
pli′cō, –ā′re, –ā′vī, –ā′tus, *fold*   (implication)
scrī′bō, –ere, **scrīp′sī**, **scrīp′tus**, *write*   (Scripture)
trāns, prep. with acc., *across*

259.   **Latin and English Word Formation**

Ante- has its regular meaning and form when used as a
prefix. **Trāns-** means *through* or *across*, and sometimes has
the form **trā-**, as **trā-dūcō**.

Importance of the Verb. — The most important part of
speech in Latin for English derivation is the verb, and the
most important part of the verb is the *perfect participle*.
This form is also the most important for Latin word formation. Therefore *learn carefully* the principal parts of every
verb. Nothing is more important.

By associating Latin word and English derivative, you
can make the English help you in your Latin, and *vice
versa*. You can often tell the conjugation or the perfect
participle of a Latin verb by the help of an English derivative.
The English word *mandate* shows that **mandō** has **mandātus**
as its perfect participle and is therefore of the first conjugation. Similarly *migrate, donation, spectator*, etc. The
word *vision* helps one remember that the perfect participle of
videō is **vīsus**. Similarly *motion* from **mōtus**, *merit* from
meritus, *missive* from **missus**, *position* from **positus**, *active*
from **āctus**.

260. Third Conjugation : Review of Principal Parts

Memorize the principal parts of these verbs already studied and give the three stems of each. No rule can be given for the formation of the third and fourth parts, from which the perfect and participial stems are obtained, but the commonest type has a perfect ending in –sī. The participle ends in –tus or –sus :

I	cēdō	cēdere	cessī	cessus
	(Similarly accēdō, discēdō, excēdō, prōcēdō)			
	gerō	gerere	gessī	gestus
	mittō	mittere	mīsī	missus
	(Similarly āmittō, committō, dīmittō)			
	dūcō	dūcere	dūxī	ductus
	(Similarly prōdūcō, redūcō)			
	regō	regere	rēxī	rēctus
	trahō	trahere	trāxī	trāctus
	pōnō	pōnere	posuī	positus
	dēfendō	dēfendere	dēfendī	dēfēnsus
	agō	agere	ēgī	āctus
	nōscō	nōscere	nōvī	nōtus
II	capiō	capere	cēpī	captus
	accipiō	accipere	accēpī	acceptus
	incipiō	incipere	incēpī	inceptus
	faciō	facere	fēcī	factus
	afficiō	afficere	affēcī	affectus
	efficiō	efficere	effēcī	effectus
	fugiō	fugere	fūgī	fugitūrus

Note. — The change or lengthening of the vowel of the perfect and participial stems may be compared with the change of vowel in English *sing, sang, sung,* etc.

Query. — What is the sign of the future which is found in verbs of the third conjugation?

261.   **Exercises**

Oral.   1. Bellum trāns Ōceanum cum victōriā gessimus. 2. Signa ante cōpiās posita erant.   3. Litterās quās scrīpsī plicābō et ad amīcum meum mittam.   4. Bonus est dominus noster, quod populum cum cōnsiliō et concordiā regit. 5. Linguam Latīnam cum studiō legere et scrībere incipimus, quod multa nova verba iam cognōvimus.   6. Litterae quās ad meum amīcum mīsī cum cūrā plicātae erant.

FIG. 48. PORTA RŌMĀNA

This gate in the wall around Rome built by Aurelian (270–275 A.D.) leads to the road to Ostia (cf. Fig. 129).

Written.   1. The new words ought always to be learned. 2. I do not know the boy who lives across the street. 3. The prisoners had been dragged across the fields and placed in-front-of the camp.   4. Who wrote the letter which you are reading?

PERFECT PARTICIPLES USED AS ADJECTIVES AND NOUNS. CONJUGATION OF *POSSUM*

262. **Vocabulary**

cer'nō, –ere, crĕ'vī, crĕ'tus, (*separate*), *discern, see*   (*discretion*)
cer'tus, –a, –um, *fixed, sure*   [*cernō*]
commo'veō, –ē're, –mō'vī, –mō'tus, *move away, disturb*   [*moveō*]
fac'tum, –ī, n., *deed*   [*faciō*]
nam, conj., *for*
nō'tus, –a, –um, *known, familiar*   [*nōscō*]
parā'tus, –a, –um, *prepared, ready*   [*parō*]
possum, pos'se, po'tuī, ——, *can, be able* (with infinitive)   [*sum*]

263. Perfect Participles Used as Adjectives and Nouns

Perfect participles of many verbs came to be used as simple adjectives, just as in English : **parātus,** " prepared," *ready;* **nōtus,** " known," *familiar;* **certus,** " decided," *sure.* A participle, like any adjective, may be used substantively : **factum,** " having been done," *deed.*

264. Drill. — Decline **via nōta** and **signum certum.**

265.   Conjugation of *Possum*

Possum is a compound of **sum** and is therefore **irregular.** It has no passive voice. Review the conjugation of **sum.** **Possum** = pot(e) + **sum.** **Pot** becomes **pos** before all forms of **sum** which begin with **s.** The perfect tenses are regular.

PRESENT

pos'sum, *I can, am able*	**pos'sumus,** *we can, are able*
pot'es, *you can, are able*	**potes'tis,** *you can, are able*
pot'est, *he can, is able*	**pos'sunt,** *they can, are able*
Imperfect **pot'eram,** etc.,	Future **pot'erō,** etc.,
I could, was able	*I shall be able*

(For full conjugation see **667.**)

118　　ELEMENTARY LATIN

266.　　　　　　　**Exercises**

Oral.　1. " Semper parātus " est nōta sententia, quam bonī puerī memoriā tenēre dēbent.　2. Amīcus certus in malā fortūnā cernitur.　3. Perīcula vītae bonum virum commovēre nōn possunt.　4. Linguam Latīnam et legere et scrībere possum.　5. Facta virōrum clārōrum semper nōta erunt.　6. " Facta, nōn verba " nostra sententia esse dēbet.　7. Ante bellum patria nostra nōn parāta erat; nam magnās cōpiās nōn habēbāmus.

Written.　1. The great deeds of our troops will be remembered by a grateful people.　2. Few men can neither read nor write.　3. We came across the fields, because the road was not familiar.　4. They had not been able to come on-account-of the bad streets.　5. My motto is: " Always ready." Is it yours?

267.　　**Latin Words and Phrases in English**

errātum (plur., **errāta**), *error.*
ante bellum, *before the war.*
dē factō, *from* or *according to fact, actual;* as a **dē factō** government.

268.　　　　An Ancient Philanthropist

Plīnius, clārus Rōmānus, ad oppidum parvum in quō nātus[1] erat vēnit et ibi amīcum cum fīliō vīdit. Plīnius puerō dīxit[2]: " Discipulusne es? " Puer respondit: " Discipulus Mediōlānī (*at Milan*) sum." " Cūr nōn hīc (*here*) ? " " Quod magistrōs hīc nōn habēmus." Tum Plīnius amīcō dīxit: " Hīc lūdum habēre dēbētis. Nōn līberōs habeō sed tertiam partem[3] pecūniae quam dabitis parātus sum dare."

---

[1] From **nāscor.**　　[2] From **dīco.**　　[3] Acc.

LESSON XLVI

FOURTH CONJUGATION: REVIEW OF PRINCIPAL PARTS. NUMERALS

269.   Vocabulary

adhi′beō, –ē′re, –hi′buī, –hi′bitus, *apply, employ, summon*	[*habeō*]
antecĕ′dō, –ere, –ces′sī, –ces′sus, *go before, precede*	[*cēdō*]
crē′ber, –bra, –brum, *frequent, close together*	
Gallus, –ī, m., *a Gaul* (an inhabitant of **Gallia**)	
relin′quō, –ere, –lī′quī, –līc′tus, *leave behind, abandon*	(relinquish)
stō, –ā′re, ste′tī, sta′tus, *stand*	(station)
trādū′cō, –ere, –dū′xī, –duc′tus, *lead across*	[*dūcō*]
trānspor′tō, –ā′re, –ā′vī, –ā′tus, *carry over, transport*	[*portō*]

270.   **The Latin Influence upon English**

Latin words have kept coming into English continuously from the beginning of the language down to the present moment. Julius Caesar twice visited the island of Britain with his army and fought with the native Celts, as he relates in his book called the " Gallic War." But the Romans did not conquer the island until a century later. During the first four centuries of our era the Romans ruled Britain, and the towns at least became thoroughly Roman. Though they then abandoned it, they left a number of Latin words in the speech of the native population. Some of these words were afterwards adopted by the Angles and Saxons when they invaded the island nearly fifteen hundred years ago and gave their name (*Angle-land, Eng-land*) and language to the island. Their language was a form of German, for they came from northern Germany. Even there they had taken some Latin words into their language. So you see that one may say that Latin affected English even before English existed as a separate language.

As the Romans in Britain found it necessary to build many military camps, which developed into towns, the word **castra** is to be found in a number of town names, many of which have been used in our country also. So *Chester* (Pa.), *Ro-chester* (N. Y.), *Man-chester* (N. H.), *Wor-cester* (Mass.), *Glou-cester* (Mass.), *Lan-caster* (Pa.). What other names with these endings can you give?

FIG. 49. THE ROMAN WALL IN BRITAIN

The Romans left many traces of their occupation of Britain. The wall is one of the most important.

271. Fourth Conjugation: Review of Principal Parts

Memorize the principal parts of the following verbs, which have occurred in previous lessons:

audiō	audīre	audīvī	audītus
veniō	venīre	vēnī	ventus
conveniō	convenīre	convēnī	conventus
inveniō	invenīre	invēnī	inventus

272. Numerals: How Lucius Learned to Count

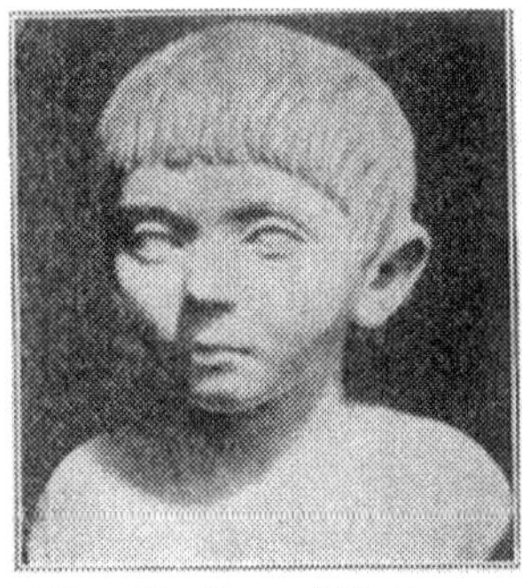

FIG. 50. PUER RŌMĀNUS

Ūnus [1] puer et ūnus puer sunt **duo** puerī; duo librī et ūnus liber sunt **trēs** librī; duo equī et duo equī sunt **quattuor** equī; trēs carrī et duo carrī sunt **quīnque** carrī; quattuor oppida et duo oppida sunt **sex** oppida; sex dominī et ūnus dominus sunt **septem** dominī; quīnque nautae et trēs nautae sunt **octō** nautae; septem agrī et duo agrī sunt **novem** agrī; sex puellae et quattuor puellae sunt **decem** puellae.

Summary: **ūnus, duo, trēs, quattuor, quīnque, sex, septem, octō, novem, decem.**

273. Exercises

Oral. 1. Multum frūmentum in Eurōpam trānsportāvimus. 2. Nūntium mīsimus ad Marium, quī cum auxiliīs antecesserat. 3. Ob equōs et carrōs crēbrōs in viā stāre nōn possumus. 4. Ubi pecūnia quam āmīserās inventa est? 5. Nōnne magnam dīligentiam in amīcōrum perīculīs adhibēre dēbēmus? 6. Gallī trāns agrōs in silvam cōpiās trādūxērunt. 7. Ob quās causās colōnī agrōs relīquērunt?

Written. 1. How did you hear about your friend's injury? 2. Marius ordered our forces to be led-across. 3. We ought to employ diligence and to labor with eagerness. 4. Why do you stand in the middle (of the) street?

---

[1] One.

LESSON XLVII

PARTICIPLES USED AS CLAUSES

274.   **Vocabulary**

addū′cō, –ere, –dū′xī, –duc′tus, *lead to, influence*	[*dūcō*]
cōn′sulō, –ere, –su′luī, –sul′tus, *consult* (with acc.)	(consultation)
fī′lia, –ae, f., *daughter*	[*fīlius*]
fu′ga, –ae, f., *flight;* **in fu′gam da′re**, *to put to flight*	[*fugiō*]
nōn iam, adv., *no longer*	
prōvi′deō, –ē′re, –vī′dī, –vī′sus, *foresee, provide*	[*videō*]
ti′midus, –a, –um, *fearful, afraid*	(timidity)

275.   **The Latin Influence upon English** (*Cont.*)

In the preceding lesson we saw that a number of Latin words came into English as a result of the Roman occupation of Britain. Other examples are *wall* (from **vāllum**), together with place names like *Walton* (*Wall-town*), *port* (from **portus**, *harbor*), together with place names like *Portsmouth*, *street* (from **strāta**), *Lin-coln* (from **colōnia**, *colony*); cf. *Cologne*, the name of a city in Germany, which was an ancient Roman colony.

A century and a half after the Angles and Saxons settled in England, Pope Gregory sent a number of missionaries, including the famous Augustine, to convert the island to Christianity. As the missionaries spoke Latin, they introduced a number of Latin words into English, especially words dealing with the Church, *e.g.* *temple* (**templum**), *disciple* (**discipulus**), *bishop* (**episcopus**).

276.   **Participles Used as Clauses**

The participle, although sparingly used in English, is exceedingly common in Latin. It often serves as a *one-word substitute* for a subordinate clause, introduced in English by *who*, etc., *when* or *after*, *since* or *because*, *although*, and *if*.

The meaning of the Latin sentence as a whole will always determine the precise meaning of the participle. Make it a rule to translate the participle *literally* before attempting to expand it into a clause. Note the various translations in the following:

Relative 1. **Oppida *capta* vīdī,** *I saw the towns* **which had been captured** (lit., *the captured towns*).

Temporal 2. ***Convocātī* ad proelium dūcentur,** *After they have been* ***called together***, *they will be led to battle* (lit., *having been called together*).

Causal 3. ***Territī* nōn prōcessērunt,** *Because they were terrified*, *they did not advance* (lit., *having been terrified*).

Adversative 4. ***Territī* nōn cessērunt,** *Though they were terrified*, *they did not yield.*

Conditional 5. ***Territī* cēdent,** *If terrified*, *they will yield.*

Observe that the *perfect* participle denotes time *before* that of the leading verb.

277. **Exercises**

Oral. 1. Malus puer, ab amīcīs monitus, verbīs addūcī nōn iam potest. 2. Fīlia mea est timida, quod multa perīcula semper prōvidet. 3. Monitī amīcōs dē perīculō cōnsulere nōn poterāmus. 4. Parātī ante bellum Germānī ā Sociīs in fugam datī sunt. 5. Germānī multa oppida occupāta relīquērunt. 6. Arma, ā Germānīs relicta in multīs oppidīs, ā nostrīs inventa sunt. 7. Perīculum prōvīsum nostrōs nōn terruit.

Written. 1. I saw many arms that had been captured [1] by our (men). 2. The boys read the book because they had been influenced by the teacher's words. 3. We have given help to the sailors abandoned on the island. 4. I have read the letter written by my son. 5. The Gauls captured the town although it was defended by the Germans.

---

[1] Express in two ways.

LESSON XLVIII

REVIEW

278.   General Review of Principal Parts

1. Give the four parts of the following verbs : **mittō, cēdō, dūcō.**

(*a*) Form three compounds from each of the above verbs and give their principal parts.

2. Give the four parts of the following : **agō, capiō, veniō, faciō, pōnō.**

(*a*) Form one compound from each of the above verbs and give its principal parts.

3. Give in Latin the principal parts of the following verbs : *defend, flee, have, be, see, remain, teach, increase, frighten, learn.*

279. 1. Give in English the principal parts and a synopsis of *be* and *have* in the 1st plural.

2. Give a synopsis of **audiō** in the act. 3rd plur.; **capiō** in the pass. 1st plur.; **moveō** in the act. 2nd sing.; **agō** in the pass. 3rd sing.

280. Decline **quae nātūra, modus vester, quod rēgnum, signum parātum, dominus monitus.**

281. Perception Device for Learning the Verb (*To the teacher*)

This device is intended to fix the general scheme of the Latin verb as represented in the first and second conjugations.

Select three pieces of white cardboard 10×6 in. and print upon each in large letters one of the three stems of some regular verb.   Next cut four pieces of cardboard 4×6 in., upon each of which place one of the four tense signs (**bā, bi,**[1] **erā, eri**).   Cut six cards of the same size for each of

---

[1] The future sign –ē– of the 3rd and 4th conjugations should be placed upon the reverse side.   In like manner, the subjunctive signs may be placed later on the back of the other tense-sign cards, in order to save duplication.

the active personal endings; the reverse side should be used for the corresponding passive endings. Similar cards should be prepared for the first three tenses of **sum**, used in forming the perfect system in the passive. After the four parts of the given verb have been written upon the blackboard and the three stems plainly underscored, proceed to build verb forms in the various tenses by holding up before the class a set of cards, as follows:

MOVĒ	BA	NTUR

Modifications in the present and imperfect tenses of the third and fourth conjugations (and elsewhere), due to the " connecting " vowel, must be explained by the teacher, for they can not be illustrated conveniently.

Drill on verb forms must be incessant.   Prompt recognition of tense, voice, and mood can be secured by having the student *translate* promiscuous verb forms selected from a large group written on the blackboard, representing both voices and every tense.

282.   Conversation: Counting

(The teacher assigns a number — " Ūnus," " Duo," " Trēs," etc. to each of ten pupils. The following questions and others like them should be answered by the pupil whose number furnishes the correct answer.)

M. Quot (*how many*) sunt duo et quattuor?   **D.** " **Sex.** " Duo et quattuor sunt sex.

M. Quot sunt quattuor et quīnque?   **D.** " **Novem.** " Quattuor et quīnque sunt novem.

Etc.   Etc.

Note.— A competitive game can be made by having two sets of ten (or less) and scoring one for the side whose representative answers first.

283.   English Word Study

Find and use in sentences as many English derivatives as possible from **vocō**, **videō**, **mittō**, and **faciō**.   Enter the derivatives in your notebook, using a separate page for each Latin word.

284.   THE STORY OF LUCIUS (*Cont.*)

Circus

Dē "lūdō" in quō magister docēbat lēgistis. Sed erat etiam "lūdus"[1] in quō ōtium agēbātur; nam puerī Rōmānī nōn semper labōrābant sed etiam lūdēbant. Dictum est: "Puerī puerī erunt."

"The Parade's Coming"

Fēriae erant. Lūcius, amīcus noster parvus, ad lūdōs pūblicōs in Circō factōs ā servō ductus est. Multī ad Circum conveniēbant; nam populus lūdōs amābat. Nōn paucī ante aurōram vēnerant. Lūcius et servus loca commoda invēnērunt et exspectāvērunt. Sed quid audiunt? "Pompa venit! Pompa venit!" Pompa per Forum et Sacram Viam ad Circum prōcesserat et nunc per portam in Circum prōcēdēbat. In pompā fuērunt deōrum fōrmae, virī, puerī, equī, quadrīgae,[2] aurīgae.[3]

Fig. 51. Equī

These magnificent bronze horses, made in Roman times, now stand over the entrance to the church of St. Mark's, Venice. During the World War they were taken down and carefully protected against airplane raids.

---

[1] See Vocabulary.

[2] Quattuor equī quī carrum trahunt "quadrīgae" appellantur.

[3] "Aurīgae" sunt virī quī quadrīgās agunt.

The Chariot Race: "They're Off!"

Pompa per Circum ducta est; Lūcius cum studiō exspectāvit. Tum sex quadrīgae, ad portam redāctae, signum exspectāvērunt. Signum datum est et equī ā portā missī sunt.

Inter aurīgās fuit Pūblius, quī magnam fāmam ob multās victōriās habuit. Erat amīcus familiae Lūcī nostrī, et Lūcius multa dē Circō ā Pūbliō cognōverat. Nunc Lūcius cum reliquīs Pūblium magnō studiō spectābat.

Publius Handicapped at the Start

Sed Fortūna nōn bona fuit. Pūblius habuit ūnum equum quī erat novus et tardus; reliquae quadrīgae antecessērunt. Lūcius magnā cūrā ob malam fortūnam amīcī affectus est. Sed victōria nōn āmissa erat; nam septem spatia erant.

Two Chariots Out of the Race

In mediō Circō erat longa spīna. Terminī spīnae "mētae" appellātī sunt. Magnum erat perīculum aurīgārum ad mētās. Itaque in prīmo spatiō nec prīmus nec secundus aurīga quadrīgās ā mētīs regere potuit. Ēiectī[1] per (*over*) terram equīs trāctī sunt et iniūriās accēpērunt. Servī virōs ad spīnam portāvērunt et auxilium dedērunt.

Publius Still Last

Nunc erant quattuor quadrīgae. Sex spatia restābant, sed Pūblius antecēdere nōn poterat. Quīnque, quattuor spatia restābant. Pūblius ultimus erat. Duo spatia restābant; populus cōnsilium multum Pūbliō dabat sed nōn

---

[1] From **ēiciō**.

Fig. 52. Magnum Erat Perīculum Aurīgārum ad Mētās

audiēbātur. Pūblius magnā cūrā equōs regēbat et etiam retinēbat, sed populus nōn cognōverat. Ūnum spatium restābat; Lūcius lacrimās retinēre nōn potuit. Fortūna inimīca erat.

"AND THE LAST SHALL BE FIRST!"

Sed quid vidēmus? Pūblius antecēdit! Nōn iam equōs retinet sed incitat. Ūnus equus, "Parātus" appellātus (nam semper parātus erat), integer fuit et properāre incipit. Nōn iam Pūblius erat ultimus; iam secundum locum tenet. Ūnus aurīga ante Pūblium restat. Aequī sunt — deī sunt bonī! — prīmus ad mētam ultimam Pūblius venit et praemia victōriae acci-

FIG. 53. PŪBLIUS ET PARĀTUS

From an ancient mosaic floor, made of bits of colored stone.

pit! Et Lūcius — quid faciēbat? "Iō! Iō! Pūblius! Parātus! Clāra victōria!" erant Lūcī verba.

Nōnne magnum erat puerum Rōmānum esse? Sed etiam nunc in circō quadrīgās vidēre potestis; nam circum pompamque ā Rōmānīs accēpimus.

LESSON XLIX

THIRD DECLENSION: MASCULINE AND FEMININE NOUNS

285. Vocabulary

dux, du′cis, m., *leader, general*	[*dūcō*]
ho′mŏ, ho′minis, m., *man, human being*	(homicide)
lēx, lē′gis, f., *law*	(legal)
mī′les, mī′litis, m., *soldier*	(military)
pāx, pā′cis, f., *peace*	(pacifist)
pre′mŏ, –ere, pres′sī, pres′sus, *press, press hard, oppress*	(pressure)
sa′lūs, salū′tis, f., *health, safety*	(salutary)

286. **Third Declension: Masculine and Feminine Nouns**

The genitive singular of nouns of the **third declension** ends
in –**is**; the base is obtained by dropping this ending. All
three genders are found among nouns of the third declension,
and no general rule can be given. The gender, as well as
the nominative and genitive singular, must therefore be
learned from the vocabulary.[1] Masculine and feminine
nouns are declined alike, as follows:

	Endings		*mīles, soldier* (base, **mīlit–**)		*lēx, law* (base, **lēg–**)	
	Sing.	Plur.	Sing.	Plur.	Sing.	Plur.
Nom.	— [1]	–**ēs**	mī′les	mī′lit**ēs**	lēx	lē′g**ēs**
Gen.	–**is**	–**um**	mī′litis	mī′lit**um**	lē′gis	lē′g**um**
Dat.	–**ī**	–**ibus**	mī′lit**ī**	mīli′t**ibus**	lē′g**ī**	lē′g**ibus**
Acc.	–**em**	–**ēs**	mī′lit**em**	mī′lit**ēs**	lē′g**em**	lē′g**ēs**
Abl.	–**e**	–**ibus**	mī′lit**e**	mīli′t**ibus**	lē′g**e**	lē′g**ibus**

a. **Observe** that the dative and ablative plural are alike; this is true
of all declensions.   The nominative and accusative plural also are alike
in the third declension.

---

[1] The ending of the nominative singular varies. When not omitted, it
is usually –**s** or –**x**.

287. Drill. — Decline **dux bonus, homō magnus, pāx aequa, salūs nostra.**

288. **Exercises**

Oral. 1. Hominem nunc exspectō cui quattuor librōs mandāvī. 2. Dux mīlitēs ēvocātōs ad pugnam per plāna loca prōdūxit. 3. Ob vigiliam praesidī, equī nōn removērī poterant. 4. Magna est glōria mīlitum quī bellō pressī nōn cessērunt sed firmō animō prō causā sacrā pugnāvērunt. 5. Salūs patriae nostrae in armīs mīlitum nostrōrum nōn iam pōnētur, quod pācem aequam effēcimus. 6. Bellō pācem et ōtium et salūtem obtinuimus. 7. Ibi potest valēre populus, ubi lēgēs valent.

Written. 1. Many books sent by boys and girls were received by the soldiers in the camps. 2. Why do you not approach (**ad**) the man? 3. " Safety first!" is a good motto. 4. The general ordered the soldiers to be called-together. 5. Why is he absent? He ought to set an example and be present.

289. **Latin Phrases in English**

pāx in bellō, *peace in (the midst of) war.*
Dux fēmina factī, *A woman (was) leader in (of) the deed.*
novus homō, *a new man* (in politics) ; hence, *an upstart.*
lēx scrīpta, *the written law.*

FIG. 54. CUPIDS IN A CHARIOT RACE

Deer are used instead of horses. The winner holds the prize, a palm branch. From a Pompeian wall painting (cf. Fig. 2).

LESSON L

ABLATIVE ABSOLUTE

290. Vocabulary

pēs, pe′dis, m., *foot;* pe′dibus, *on foot, afoot* (pedal)

  expe′diō, –ī′re, –pedī′vī, –pedī′tus, (lit., *make the foot free*),
   set free

  impedīmen′tum, –ī, n., *hindrance;* plur., *baggage*

  impe′diō, –ī′re, –pedī′vī, –pedī′tus, (lit., *entangle the feet*),
   hinder

rēx, rē′gis, m., *king* (regal)

ver′tō, –ere, ver′tī, ver′sus, *turn* (version)

291. Latin and English Word Studies

Latin words should not be memorized individually but
in groups — by *families,* so to speak. This is much easier,
much more useful, and much more interesting. For example,
there is the word **pēs,** the father of its family. From it are
derived many other words in Latin and in English. **Im-**

FIG. 55. ROMAN SCIS-
SORS

pediō means to *entangle the feet.* An
" impediment " is a *tangle,* something
in the way. Transportation is still a
big problem with an army; it is no
wonder that the Romans, without rail-
roads or motor trucks, called the bag-
gage train of the army **impedīmenta.** **Ex-pediō** means to
get the *foot out* of the tangle; therefore in English an " ex-
pedient " is a means of solving a difficulty. To " expedite "
matters is to hurry them along by removing obstacles in the
way.

You have already become acquainted with several other
" families " of words (**173**). Other words which should be
grouped together are **regō, rēgnum,** and **rēx**; **dō** and **dōnō**;
dūcō and **dux**; **ager** and **agricola**; **cōnsulō** and **cōnsilium.**

292. Ablative Absolute: The Participle Used Independently with a Noun

(*a*) In English, we occasionally say, *This meeting with your approval, I shall act accordingly.* Inasmuch as such phrases are used loosely and have no direct connection with either the subject or the predicate of the sentence, they are said to be in the **nominative absolute,** *i.e.* they are *absolutely free* in a grammatical sense from the rest of the sentence.

In Latin, this loose construction is very common, with this difference: the *ablative* is used instead of the nominative. This independent use of the participial phrase is known as the **ablative absolute.** The perfect participle is most frequently used in this construction.[1] Translate the participle *literally* before attempting to expand it into a subordinate clause of *time, cause, condition,* etc. (see **276**).

1. *Servō accūsātō* (lit., *the slave having been accused*) **dominus discessit,** *After accusing the slave, the master departed.*

2. *Litterīs nōn missīs* (lit., *a letter not having been sent*) **puer pecūniam nōn accēpit,** *Because he did not send a letter, the boy did not receive the money.*

3. *Oppidīs nostrīs captīs* (lit., *our towns captured*) **bellum gerēmus,** *If our towns are captured, we shall wage war.*

(*b*) In English, there is an active and a passive past participle: *having sent* (act.), *sent* or *having been sent* (pass.). *In Latin, there is only a passive perfect participle.* If, therefore, in English the active past participle is used with an object, the phrase must be recast so as to become passive in the same tense before it is translated into Latin:

English: *having given the signal* (active)
the signal having been given (passive)
Latin: **signō datō.**

---

[1] Occasionally a noun, adjective, or present participle (to be studied later) is used.

134 ELEMENTARY LATIN

Caution. — The ablative absolute can not be used when the noun or pronoun with which the participle agrees forms any part of the main sentence (subject or predicate). Compare the following sentence with those above (**292**, *a*) and note that the ablative absolute construction can not be used because the participle in this case must agree with the subject:

Servus accūsātus territus est, *The slave, having been accused, was terrified.*

293. Rule. — *A noun in the ablative case used with a participle, adjective, or other noun and having no grammatical connection with the subject or the predicate is called an ablative absolute.*

294. **Exercises**

Oral. 1. Dux Gallōrum, signō datō, cōpiās proelium committere iussit. 2. Captīvī, trāctī ad pedēs rēgis, pācem petēbant. 3. Duce captō, nostrī pācem nōn petēbant. 4. Impedīmentīs in oppidō relīctīs, mīlitēs salūtem fugā iam petīverant. 5. Hominēs, praedā armīsque impedītī, properāre nōn poterant. 6. Rōmānī, castrīs mūnītīs, Gallōs in fugam vertērunt. 7. Castrīs positīs, Gallī auxilia exspectāvērunt. 8. Expedītī ex perīculō Deō grātiam habēre dēbēmus.

Written. 1. Although called a friend, Marcus was my enemy. 2. By fortifying five towns the Gauls were able to hinder the king's soldiers. 3. Hindered by bad roads, we have not been able to come on foot. 4. After sending a messenger, the king came to the town with a few friends. 5. Though the signal had been given, the men did not advance. 6. If the town is captured, the Gauls will make peace or seek safety by flight.

LESSON LI

THIRD DECLENSION: NEUTER NOUNS

295.   **Vocabulary**

ca'put, ca'pitis, n., *head*	(capital)
cor'pus, cor'poris, n., *body*	(corporation)
flū'men, flū'minis, n., *river*	(fluid)
iūs, iū'ris, n., *right, justice*	(jury)
nō'men, nō'minis, n., *name*	(nominate)

296.   **Third Declension: Neuter Nouns**

ENDINGS			corpus, *body* (base, corpŏr-)		
	SINGULAR	PLURAL		SINGULAR	PLURAL
Nom.	—	-a		cor'pus	cor'pora
Gen.	-is	-um		cor'poris	cor'porum
Dat.	-ī	-ibus		cor'porī	corpo'ribus
Acc.	—	-a		cor'pus	cor'pora
Abl.	-e	-ibus		cor'pore	corpo'ribus

Observe that the nominative and accusative singular of neuter nouns are alike, and that the nominative and accusative plural both end in -a.

297. Drill. — Decline **nōmen clārum, homō bonus, flūmen longum.**

298   **Exercises**

Oral. 1. Dominō vīsō, servus malus fūgit. 2. Ob impedīmenta multōs mīlitēs ad flūmen relīquimus. 3. Corporibus nostrīs patriam dēfendēmus. 4. Litterae quās fīlia mea scrīpsit nec caput nec pedem habent. 5. Iūs et lēgēs bonōs hominēs nōn impediunt sed malōs terrent.

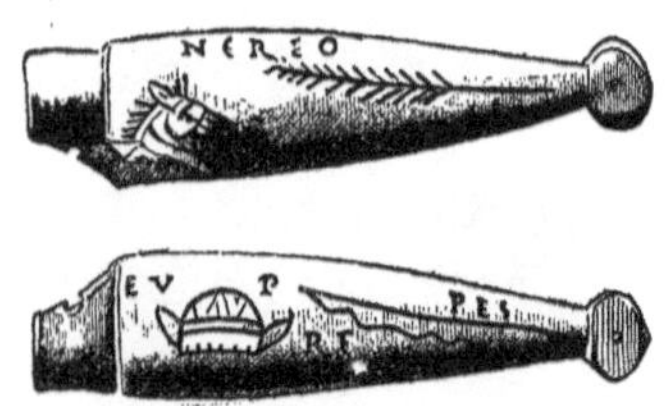

Fig. 56. Handle of a Pocket Knife

On one side is the name of a race horse; on the other, that of a driver.

6. Quae nōmina flūminum Galliae cognōvistis? 7. Iūra līberōrum populōrum America semper dēfendet. 8. Germānī, pressī ā multīs Gallīs, fugient.

Written. 1. The river which you see is deep. 2. The men were deeply-moved by the distinguished leader's words. 3. Horses have large bodies but small heads. 4. The body of a man was found in the river by soldiers.

299.　　English Word Studies

Many English words preserve the original Latin forms of the third declension, either in the singular or in the singular and plural. Examples of the masculine and feminine types are:

Singular	Plural	Singular	Plural
apex	apexes or apices	index	indexes or indices [1]
appendix	appendixes or appendices	vertex	vertexes or vertices
calyx	calyxes or calyces		

Nouns with their plurals in –s are consul, ratio, and a large number of nouns in –or: actor, doctor, factor, labor, victor, etc.

Examples of neuter nouns are:

Singular	Plural	Plural
genus	genera	viscera (singular rare)
stamen	stamina or stamens [1]	

Nouns with plurals in –s are: omen, specimen, etc.

The genitive case is preserved in *juris*diction, *juris*prudence, *legis*lator.

---

[1] With difference of meaning.

LESSON LII

SUMMARY OF ABLATIVE USES

300.   Vocabulary

auc′tor, auctō′ris, m., *maker, author*	(authorize)
clau′dō, –ere, clau′sī, clau′sus, *close*	(clause)
ōr′dō, ōr′dinis, m., *order, rank*	(ordinary)
tem′pus, tem′poris, n., *time*	(temporal)
vul′nus, vul′neris, n., *wound*	(vulnerable)

301.   Latin Phrases in English

Tempus fugit, *Time flies.*

per capita, *by heads* or *individuals.*

prō tem. (prō tempore), *for the time, temporarily.*

Fāta viam invenient, *The Fates will find a way.*

dē jūre, *according to right,* as a **dē jūre** government; cf. **dē factō** (**267**).

302.   Summary of Ablative Uses

The uses of the ablative may be grouped under three heads:

I. The **true** or "**from**" **ablative** (ab, *from,* and **lātus,** *carried*), used with the prepositions **ab, dē,** or **ex** — if any preposition is used. The ablative of agent (with **ab**) belongs here.

II. The **associative** or "**with**" **ablative,** used with the preposition **cum** — if any preposition is used. The ablatives of means, accompaniment, and manner belong here.

III. The **place** or "**in**" **ablative,** used with the prepositions **in** or **sub** — if any preposition is used.

Every ablative construction may be put into one of these groups. Sometimes the use is literal, as, *I am going **with** you.* Sometimes it is figurative, as, *I shall buy a book **with** the money.*

303.   **Exercises**

Oral.   1. Auctōris nōmen fāmam oppidī augēbit in quō
habitat.   2. Studiō et dīligentiā prīmum locum obtinēbis.
3. Nōn iam impedītī vulneribus properāre poterimus.
4. Pāce factā ōrdō in Eurōpā nōn reductus est.   5. Ob tempus
annī frūmentum trānsportāre nōn poterāmus.   6. Rēx,
victōriā Gallōrum territus, cōpiās trāns flūmen trādūxit.
7. Librō etiam clausō, auctōris verba memoriā tenēre possum.

Fig. 57. Porta Nigra in Trier, Germany
This magnificent " black gate " was built by the Romans.

Written.   1. I know the author whose books you have
read.   2. (There) were many wounds on the sailor's body.
3. The boys, having been warned by the teacher, will answer
one at a time in order.   4. Since the river is closed, grain can
no longer be transported.   5. The author had earned fame
by (his) many books.

LESSON LIII

THIRD DECLENSION: I-STEM NOUNS (Genitive Plural in –*ium*) OF ALL GENDERS

304.   Vocabulary

* cī'vis, cī'vis,[1] m., *citizen*	(civic)
* hos'tis, hos'tis, m., *enemy,*[2] usually plur.	(hostile)
* ma're, ma'ris, n., *sea*	(marine)
* mōns, mon'tis, m., *mountain*	(mount)
* nă'vis, nă'vis,[3] f., *ship*	(navy)

FIG. **58.** NĀVĒS IN MARĪ SUNT

(From " Julius Caesar.")

---

[1] Nouns marked with an asterisk (*) are i-stem nouns.

[2] *National enemy*, differing from **inimīcus**, *personal enemy.*

[3] The ablative singular ends in –ī.

305.   **Third Declension : I–stem Nouns**

The important group of nouns which have –ium instead of –um in the genitive plural are called **i–stem nouns**. In addition, neuters ending in –e, –al, and –ar have –ī instead of –e in the ablative singular, and –ia in the nominative and accusative plural. The classes of **i**–stem nouns are :

I. *Masculines and Feminines*
     1. Nouns ending in –is having no more syllables in the genitive than in the nominative : **cīvis**.
     2. Nouns of one syllable whose base ends in two consonants : **pars** (gen. **part–is**), **nox** (gen. **noct–is**).

II. *Neuters*
     3. Nouns ending in –e, –al, –ar : **mare, animal, calcar**.

cīvis, *citizen* (base, cīv–)		mare, *sea* (base, mar–)	
Nom. cī′vis	cī′vēs	ma′re	ma′ria
Gen. cī′vis	cī′vium	ma′ris	ma′rium
Dat. cī′vī	cī′vibus	ma′rī	ma′ribus
Acc. cī′vem	cī′vēs [1]	ma′re	ma′ria
Abl. cī′ve	cī′vibus	ma′rī	ma′ribus

306. Drill. — Decline **nāvis bona, mōns altus, mare pulchrum.**

307.   **Exercises**

Oral. 1. Parvā nāvī colōnī trāns mare ad Americam migrāvērunt. 2. Ob numerum hostium quī in montibus erant Gallī in castrīs remānsērunt. 3. Bonī cīvēs officia pūblica suscipere dēbent. 4. Altōs montēs et flūmina alta in Eurōpā vīdī. 5. Multōs librōs, scrīptōs ā clārīs auctōribus, līberī legunt. 6. Nāvibus hostium captīs, trāns mare frūmentum trānsportāre ad Sociōs nostrōs poterāmus. 7. Lūcius cīvēs frūmentum comparāre iussit.

---

[1] Occasionally –īs is preferred to –ēs in the accusative plural of nouns of this type.

Written.   1. I saw a large number of ships on the sea.
2. If [1] the sea is closed, the enemy's ships will not be able
to transport reinforcements.   3. I have ordered the citizens
to close the gates of the town.   4. The enemy were seen
on the mountain by our men.

308.   English Word Studies

Many Latin i–stem nouns ending in –is are preserved in
their original form in English. The original plural in –es
is pronounced like " ease " :

axis	**axes**
basis	**bases**
finis	————

Distinguish **axes** from *axes* (plural of ax), **bases** from *bases* (plural
of base). **Finis** has no plural in English.

Neuter i–stems in English (with plurals in –s) are **animal, exemplar,
tribunal.**

309.   Romulus and Remus

Silvius Proca, rēx Albānōrum, Numitōrem et Amūlium
fīliōs habuit. Numitōrī rēgnum relīquit, sed Amūlius,
pulsō [2] Numitōre, rēxit. Rhēa Silvia, fīlia Numitōris, geminōs (*twin*) fīliōs, Rōmulum et Remum, habuit. Amūlius
puerōs in Tiberī flūmine pōnī iussit. Sed aqua geminōs in
siccō (*on dry ground*) relīquit. Lupa accessit et puerōs
aluit. Posteā (*afterwards*) Faustulus, pāstor rēgis, puerōs
invēnit et ēducāvit. Post multōs annōs Rōmulō et Remō
dīxit: "Numitor est avus vester." Adductī pāstōris verbīs,
geminī Amūlium interfēcērunt et Numitōrī avō rēgnum
dedērunt. Posteā oppidum mūnīvērunt in locō in quō
ēducātī erant, quod dē nōmine Rōmulī Rōmam appellāvērunt.

---

[1] Use abl. abs.   [2] From **pellō.**

FIG. 59. ROME FROM AN AIRPLANE

The Colosseum (Fig. 41) in the foreground; beyond it the Forum (Figs. 32, 34, 36).

LESSON LIV

CHOICE OF WORDS

310. **Vocabulary**

* **fi′nis, fi′nis,** m., *end, limit;* plur., *borders, territory* (final)
i′ter, iti′neris, n., *journey, road, march* (itinerary)
post, prep. with acc., *behind* (of place); *after* (of time)
  post′eā, adv., *afterwards*
ten′dō, –ere, teten′dī, ten′tus, *stretch* (tendon)

311. **The Right Word in the Right Place**

We have observed from a study of **agō (229)** that a Latin
word may have many shades of meaning, which are suggested
by the context. In translating, therefore, do not confine
yourself to the " vocabulary " meaning of the word but
select the particular meaning demanded by English usage.
Observe the varying translation of **magnus, –a, –um** when
used with the following nouns:

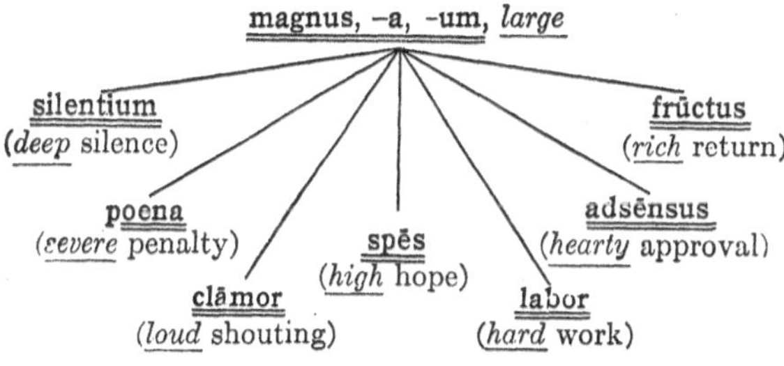

Exercise. — (*a*) Combine **magnus, –a, –um** with each of
the following nouns already studied and translate freely
and naturally : **perīculum, studium, cōpiae, pretium.**

(*b*) How does **altus, –a, –um** differ when applied to rivers
and mountains?

(*c*) Translate **puella pulchra** and **homō pulcher.**

143

312.   **Gender of Third Declension Nouns**

1. Nouns ending in –**or** are almost all masculine : **auctor, labor.**
2. Nouns ending in –**dŏ** and –**gŏ** are feminine : **magnitŭdŏ, imăgŏ.**
3. Nouns ending in –**tās** and –**tŭs** are feminine : **cīvitās, virtūs.**

313.   **Exercises**

Oral.   1. Flūmina Italiae ex montibus ad mare tendunt.
2. Aut viam inveniam aut faciam.   3. Post castra nostra
erat mōns altus, in quō paucī mīlitēs hostium vidēbantur.
4. Poteruntne hostēs, montibus occupātīs, posteā iter facere
per fīnēs nostrōs?   5. Nōnne grātum erat vidēre mīlitēs
nostrōs post fīnem bellī?   6. Dēbēmusne, pāce factā,
numerum nostrōrum mīlitum et nāvium augēre?

Written.   1. The enemy were afterwards put to flight
by the Romans.   2. After a long journey my friend is
approaching (**ad**) the end of life.   3. Our soldiers were
not frightened by the dangers of the journey.   4. The
road stretches through the mountains to the territory of the
Gauls.

314.   **English Word Studies**

a. The suffix –**tās** is usually found in nouns formed from
adjectives and indicates condition. Its English form is
–**ty**, which is to be carefully distinguished from –**y (201).**
What must be the Latin words from which are derived
commodity, integrity, liberty, publicity, timidity, variety?
Note that the letter preceding the ending is usually **i.**

b.   **Latin Phrases in English**

  ad fin. (**ad fīnem**), *near the end* (of the page).
  P.S. (**post scrīptum**), *written after* (at the end of a letter).

LESSON LV

THIRD DECLENSION : ADJECTIVES

315.   Vocabulary

cī'vitās, cīvitā'tis, f., *citizenship, state*   [*cīvis*]
fa'cilis, fa'cile, (lit., " do-able "), *easy*   [*faciō*]
for'tis, for'te, *strong, brave*   (fort)
līber'tās, lībertā'tis, f., *freedom*   [*līber*]
om'nis, om'ne, *all, every*   (omniscient)
păr, gen., pa'ris, *equal* (with dat.)   (parity)

316.   **Adjectives of the Third Declension**

The adjectives thus far studied, such as **magnus, –a, –um**
and **sacer, –cra, –crum**, have been declined like nouns of
the first and second declensions.   Many adjectives, however,
are declined like **i**–stem nouns and are therefore called
adjectives of the third declension.   With the exception of
one important class, which will be studied later, practically
all adjectives of the third declension are **i**–stems.   They are
divided into classes according to the number of forms which
are used in the nominative singular to denote gender, as
follows :

1. **Two endings** [1] — masculine and feminine in **–is**, neuter in **–e** :
fortis, forte.
2. **One ending** — one form for all genders : **păr.**

Adjectives of the third declension have **–ī** in the ablative
singular, **–ium** in the genitive plural, and **–ia** in the neuter
nominative and accusative plural.   Note particularly that
the ablative singular, unlike that of most **i**–stem *nouns,* ends
in **–ī.**

---

[1] A few adjectives in **–er** have *three endings* in the nominative singular,
one for each gender : **celer, celeris, celere.**

	M. AND F.	N.	M. AND F.	N.
Nom.	for'tis	for'te	pār	pār
Gen.	for'tis	for'tis	pa'ris	pa'ris
Dat.	for'tī	for'tī	pa'rī	pa'rī
Acc.	for'tem	for'te	pa'rem	pār
Abl.	for'tī	for'tī	pa'rī	pa'rī
Nom.	for'tēs	for'tia	pa'rēs	pa'ria
Gen.	for'tium	for'tium	pa'rium	pa'rium
Dat.	for'tibus	for'tibus	pa'ribus	pa'ribus
Acc.	for'tēs [1]	for'tia	pa'rēs [1]	pa'ria
Abl.	for'tibus	for'tibus	pa'ribus	pa'ribus

317. Drill. — Decline **cīvitās pār, puer fortis, iter facile, oppidum omne.**

318. **Exercises**

Oral. 1. Vir fortibus factīs cīvitātem obtinuit. 2. Post bellum lībertās omnibus captīvīs data est. 3. Nōvistīne nōmen hominis quem in nāvī vīdimus? 4. Terminus agrōrum nostrōrum est via longa et pulchra. 5. In nostrā patriā omnēs cīvēs sunt līberī et parēs. 6. Facilī itinere inventō, dux fortis omnēs cōpiās dē montibus dūcere mātūrāvit.

Written. 1. All free men love liberty and peace. 2. Nature has given men many beautiful (things). 3. We shall defend the freedom of our country on the sea. 4. We ought not to undertake a long journey now, because the time of the year is not suitable. 5. After pitching camp, the Romans led-forth fresh troops to battle.

---

[1] Occasionally **-īs** is preferred to **-ēs** (**305**, footnote 1).

319. English Word Studies

A number of English nouns and adjectives preserve the nominative singular and a few, the nominative plural of Latin adjectives of the third declension : **par, pauper, simplex, duplex,** etc. ; **September,** etc. ; **amanuensis.** Neuter forms occur in **simile, facsimile, insignia** (singular rare), **regalia**

FIG. 60. A ROMAN HOUSE

Note the chairs, table, boxes of manuscript rolls (librī), and statuary.
(From " Julius Caesar.")

(singular rare), **forte** (singular only). The dative plural is preserved in **omnibus** (a vehicle *for all*) and the ablative singular in **velocipede** (a vehicle *with swift foot*). Note that this word shows that in the third declension most *adjectives* have –ī in the ablative, while most *nouns* have **–e.**

LESSON LVI

ABLATIVE OF RESPECT

320.   Vocabulary

auctŏ′ritās, auctŏritā′tis, f., *authority, influence*   [*auctor*]
ce′ler, ce′leris, ce′lere, *swift*   (celerity)
  cele′ritās, celeritā′tis, f., *swiftness*
cŏnfir′mō, –ā′re, –ā′vī, –ā′tus, *make firm, encourage, establish*   [*firmus*]
pel′lō, –ere, pe′pulī, pul′sus, *drive, defeat*   (repulsive)
su′perō, –ā′re, –ā′vī, –ā′tus, *overcome, excel*   (insuperable)

321.   Latin Phrases in English

Dominus prŏvidēbit, *The Lord will provide.*
ex tempore, *without preparation* (lit., *according to the time*).
in omnia parātus, *prepared for all things.*
Fortēs Fortūna adiuvat, *Fortune aids the brave.*
Arma nŏn servant modum, *Arms (war) do not preserve restraint.*
Vānitās vānitātum et omnia vānitās, *Vanity of vanities, and all (is)
vanity* (from the Vulgate, or Latin translation of the Bible, *Ecclesi-
astes, i,* 2).

322.   Ablative of Respect

1. **Equī et hominēs nŏn sunt parēs celeritāte,** *Horses and men are
not equal in swiftness.*
2. **Puer erat vir factīs,** *The boy was a man in deeds.*
3. **Superāmur numerō, nŏn animō,** *We are surpassed in number, not
in courage.*

Observe the following points:
(*a*) The ablative limits the application respectively of an
adjective, a noun, and a verb.

(*b*) No preposition is used in Latin, though in English we
use the preposition *in.*

323. Rule. — *The ablative of respect (or specification) tells
in what respect something is true.*

148

324.   **Exercises**

Oral. 1. Puer erat celer pede sed studiīs ab omnibus superābātur.   2. Mīlitēs nostrī cum magnā celeritāte ad flūmen prōcessērunt.   3. Homō erat magnus auctōritāte. 4. Erāmus parēs hostibus neque mīlitibus neque nāvibus. 5. Omnēs hostēs ē nostrīs fīnibus pellēmus.   6. Pāx et amīcitia cum fīnitimīs cīvitātibus ā Rōmānīs cōnfirmātae sunt.   7. Colōnī ex patriā migrant et in variīs terrīs cīvitātem petunt.

Written. 1. We can not all be swift of foot.   2. He was king in name, but he had not the authority of a king. 3. Does a horse excel a boy in swiftness?   4. Inasmuch as we have been carefully taught, we ought to remember new words.   5. (Now that) peace has been established,[1] free citizens will maintain the freedom of the state.

Fig. 61. Forum of Trajan, Rome, as It Was

---

[1] See **292.**

REVIEW

325.   Review of the Third Declension

(1) Decline **dux fortis, lībertās nostra, omnis mīles, rēx magnus, nāvis pulchra.**

(2) Give the following in Latin:
   (a) *small authority* in the nom., sing. and plur.
   (b) *an easy journey* in the gen., sing. and plur.
   (c) *a good citizen* in the dat., sing. and plur.
   (d) *a brave enemy* in the acc., sing. and plur.
   (e) *the deep sea* in the abl., sing. and plur.

(3) Review the **classes of i–stem nouns**, with one example of each, giving (a) genitive singular, (b) ablative singular, (c) genitive plural, (d) accusative plural.

326.   Review of Verbs

Give the synopsis of **impediō**, 3rd plur., act. ; **premō**, 1st plur., pass.; **superō**, 3rd sing., act. ; **videō**, 2nd plur., pass. ; **fugiō**, 2nd sing., act.

327.   How to Learn Words

Repetition is the first law of memory, or, as the Romans said, **Repetītiō est māter studiōrum.** New words must be repeated often enough to fix them in your mind for future use. You will find the following device helpful:

After studying the new vocabulary, noting carefully the genitive singular and gender of every noun, the principal parts of each verb, etc., close the book and write on a narrow slip of paper the English meanings (not the Latin) of as many of the Latin words as you can recall. Then open your book and check up your list, filling in any blanks. Close the book again and, on the other side of the slip, write the full Latin form of each English word, and afterwards check mistakes by referring to the book. Close the book once more.

With the slip in your hand, give the English meanings from the Latin list. After mastering the Latin words so that you do not need to turn the slip for the meaning of a single word, take the English side and proceed in the same way until you can give the Latin for every English word, without turning the paper. Another way is to write a Latin word on one side of a slip of paper or a small card and the English meaning on the other side.

Association is the second law of memory. In order to make use of this important principle in mastering new words, try at once to give an English derivative for every new Latin word.[1] Wherever possible, recall the *primitive* or simple word from which the new word has been formed; *e.g.* **amīcus, inimīcus, amīcitia** — all from **amō**, *I love*.

328.   **Vocabulary Review**

(*a*) Give the nominative, genitive, gender, and meaning of the Latin noun suggested by each of the following: *civil, finish, submarine, navigate, author, corpulent, legislate, nominal, decapitate.*

(*b*) Give the principal parts and meaning of the Latin verb suggested by each of the following: *expedite, press, verse, attention, repellent.*

(*c*) Give the nominative forms and meaning of the Latin adjective suggested by each of the following: *omnipresent, celerity, facilitate, disparity, fortitude.*

329.   **English Word Studies**

Find and use in sentences as many English derivatives as possible from **parō, teneō, agō,** and **scrībō.**

Enter the derivatives in your notebook, using a separate page for each Latin word.

---

[1] Classes using the *vocabulary notebook* method will find nothing new in this suggestion.

330.   THE STORY OF LUCIUS *(Cont.)*

Deī

FIG. 62. IUPPITER

Rōmānī multōs deōs habuērunt. Deōs in omnibus locīs vīdērunt — in terrā, in agrīs, in frūmentō, in montibus, in silvīs, in undīs maris, in aquā flūminum, in omnī nātūrā. Erant magnī deī et parvī deī, deī deaeque. Inter magnōs deōs prīmus erat Iuppiter, rēx deōrum hominumque, quī in caelō habitābat et fulmine malōs terrēbat. Iūnō erat uxor Iovis[1] et rēgīna deōrum. Venus erat pulchra dea amōris. Mārs, deus bellī, arma pugnāsque amābat. Mercurius erat celer nūntius deōrum. Neptūnus erat deus maris, quī equōs in undīs regēbat. Reliquī magnī deī erant Cerēs, dea frūmentī, Minerva, dea sapientiae, Diāna, dea silvārum, Vulcānus, deus ignis, Apollō, deus ōrāculōrum, Bacchus, deus vīnī.

STRANGE GODS

Lūcius noster nōmina omnium magnōrum et multōrum parvōrum deōrum cognōverat — quod nōn facile erat; nam magnus erat numerus deōrum deārumque. Etiam "terminus agrōrum"

FIG. 63. VENUS

deus erat. Concordiam, Victōriam, Salūtem, Pācem, For-

---

[1] Gen. sing. of **Iuppiter**.

tūnam Rōmānī deās vocāvērunt, quod sacrae erant et ā
Rōmānīs amābantur. Etiam pecūnia ā Rōmānīs amābātur,
sed tamen (ut scrībit auctor Rōmānus, Iuvenālis) nōn dea
fuit neque in templō habitāvit.

Gods of the Home

Erant etiam deī fa-
miliae, prīmī quōs Lū-
cius cognōverat. Lār
erat deus quī familiam
cōnservābat. Penātēs
erant deī quī cibum
servābant. Vesta erat
dea focī, in quō cibus
parābātur. Ad focum
erant parvae fōrmae
deōrum. Ibi, omni-
bus līberīs convocātīs,
pater Lūcī deīs grā-
tiās agēbat et cibum
dōnābat. Quondam
nōn multus cibus erat,
sed tamen pater deīs
dōnābat. Lūcius ā
patre petit: "Cūr

FIG. 64. AN ALTAR

Relief depicts the sacrifice of an ox (cf. Fig. 66).

cibus deīs datur? Nōn multum habēmus." Pater respondit: "Cibō datō, deī hominibus magna praemia et
longam vītam dabunt."

LESSON LVIII

THE DEMONSTRATIVES *HIC* AND *ILLE*

ELEMENTARY GRAMMAR: Review *Demonstrative pronouns and adjectives*, **615**, *d.*

331.   Vocabulary

cur'rō, –ere, cucur'rī, cur'sus, *run*	(current)
mā'ter, mā'tris, f., *mother*	(maternal)
pa'ter, pa'tris, m., *father*	(paternal)
prae'ceps, praeci'pitis, *headlong, steep*	(precipice)

332. English Word Study: Importance of the Third Declension

The third declension is very important in Latin on account of the number of words which belong to it. Hence more English words are derived from nouns and adjectives of this declension than from any other declension. The English word is usually derived from the base, and not from the nominative. It is therefore doubly important to memorize the genitive, from which the base is obtained. It would be difficult to see that *itinerary* is derived from **iter** if one did not know that the genitive is **itineris.** Examine the words of the third declension studied thus far, and see how many have derivatives from the base. Note the help given for English spelling: *temporal, corporal, military, maritime, nominal,* etc.

On the other hand, the English derivative will help you determine the genitive. In the following list of words, a derivative is placed after each; give the genitive: **religiō** (*religion*), **sermō** (*sermon*), **latus** (*lateral*), **rādix** (*radical*), **orīgō** (*original*), **ēruptiō** (*eruption*), **cūstōs** (*custody*), **dēns** (*dental*), **mōs** (*moral*).

333.   **The Demonstratives *Hic* and *Ille***

In English, *this* and *that* are used to point out persons or objects and are therefore called **demonstratives**. They may be used as adjectives or pronouns; as, ***This*** *man did not write* ***that***.

In Latin, **hic** means *this* (*near* the speaker in place or thought), while **ille** means *that* (*more distant* from the speaker). From such expressions as *this man, that woman,* etc., the demonstrative adjectives **hic** and **ille** came to be used as substitutes for a third person pronoun *he, she, it.* The personal pronoun, however, is usually not required in Latin.

<table>
<tr><th colspan="7" align="center">hic, this</th></tr>
<tr><th colspan="3" align="center">SINGULAR</th><th colspan="4" align="center">PLURAL</th></tr>
<tr><td>Nom.</td><td>hic</td><td>haec</td><td>hoc</td><td>hī</td><td>hae</td><td>haec</td></tr>
<tr><td>Gen.</td><td>hu′ius</td><td>hu′ius</td><td>hu′ius</td><td>hō′rum</td><td>hā′rum</td><td>hō′rum</td></tr>
<tr><td>Dat.</td><td>huic</td><td>huic</td><td>huic</td><td>hīs</td><td>hīs</td><td>hīs</td></tr>
<tr><td>Acc.</td><td>hunc</td><td>hanc</td><td>hoc</td><td>hōs</td><td>hās</td><td>haec</td></tr>
<tr><td>Abl.</td><td>hōc</td><td>hāc</td><td>hōc</td><td>hīs</td><td>hīs</td><td>hīs</td></tr>
</table>

<table>
<tr><th colspan="7" align="center">ille, that</th></tr>
<tr><th colspan="3" align="center">SINGULAR</th><th colspan="4" align="center">PLURAL</th></tr>
<tr><td>Nom.</td><td>il′le</td><td>il′la</td><td>il′lud</td><td>il′lī</td><td>il′lae</td><td>il′la</td></tr>
<tr><td>Gen.</td><td>illī′us</td><td>illī′us</td><td>illī′us</td><td>illō′rum</td><td>illā′rum</td><td>illō′rum</td></tr>
<tr><td>Dat.</td><td>il′lī</td><td>il′lī</td><td>il′lī</td><td>il′līs</td><td>il′līs</td><td>il′līs</td></tr>
<tr><td>Acc.</td><td>il′lum</td><td>il′lam</td><td>il′lud</td><td>il′lōs</td><td>il′lās</td><td>il′la</td></tr>
<tr><td>Abl.</td><td>il′lō</td><td>il′lā</td><td>il′lō</td><td>il′līs</td><td>il′līs</td><td>il′līs</td></tr>
</table>

Observe that both **hic** and **ille** in the plural are declined regularly, like **bonus, −a, −um**, with the exception of the nominative and accusative plural neuter of **hic** (**haec**). Note that **hic** and **ille** resemble **quī** in the genitive singular.

334.   **Position of Demonstratives**

Demonstrative adjectives regularly precede their nouns in Latin and English: *this boy,* **hic puer**; *that girl,* **illa puella**. Therefore, when *that* precedes its noun, it is a demonstrative adjective (**ille**); when it follows, it is a relative pronoun (**quī**), equivalent to *who* or *which: The man that I saw was famous,* **Vir** *quem* (not **illum**) **vīdī clārus erat**.

335.   **Exercises**

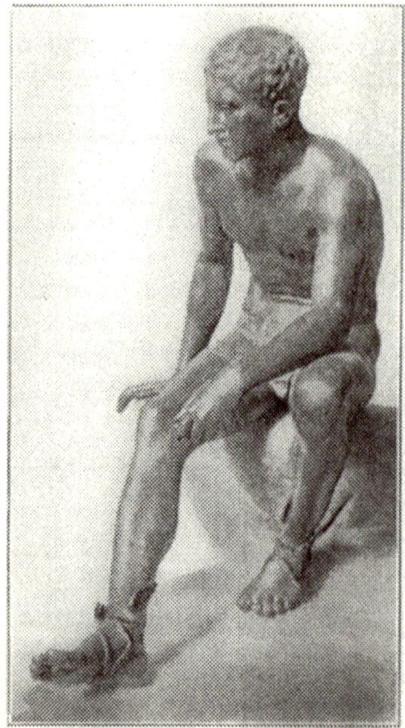

Fig. 65. Mercurius

As messenger of the gods Mercury sometimes became weary in spite of his winged feet.

Oral. 1. Haec est mea patria; nam cīvis Americānus sum. 2. Hī hominēs sunt patris meī amīcī; illī sunt inimīcī. 3. Hunc cognōvī sed illum ante hoc tempus nōn vīdī. 4. Ille erat dux ducum. 5. Praeceps in illum virum cucurrī, quod illum nōn vīdī. 6. Māter mea huic hominī magnam grātiam habet, quod hic patrem meum ex undīs servāvit.

Written. 1. I am expecting my father and my mother. 2. This is my money; that is yours. 3. This boy excels that (one) in (his) studies. 4. This road is steep; that is easy. 5. Our soldiers defeated the enemy's forces by capturing that town.

LESSON LIX

ABLATIVE OF TIME WHEN

336. Vocabulary

aes′tās, aestā′tis, f., *summer*
cor, cor′dis, n., *heart*   (cordial)
hi′ems, hi′emis, f., *winter*
ni′hil (indeclinable), *nothing*   (nihilist)
ti′meō, –ē′re, ti′muī, ——, *fear, be afraid*   (timid)

337. Latin Phrases in English

Alma Māter, *fostering mother*, applied to an educational institution.
A.D. (annō Dominī), *in the year of our Lord.*
aut Caesar aut nihil, *either Caesar or nothing.*
iūstitia omnibus, *justice for all* (motto of the District of Columbia).
Pater Noster, *Our Father*, *i.e.* the Lord's Prayer, which begins with these words.
prīmus inter parēs, *first among his equals.*
Stābat Māter, *The mother was standing* — a 13th century Latin hymn which begins with these words.

338. Ablative of Time When

In English, adverbial phrases with or without the prepositions *in, on*, etc. are used to express time: *last summer, in winter.*

In Latin, time when is expressed by the ablative *without a preposition.*

1. **Illō annō hostēs nōn timuimus,** *That year we did not fear the enemy.*

2. **Aestāte agrī sunt pulchrī,** *In summer the fields are beautiful.*

Note. — Compare with the ablative of place where (**75**, *a*). Observe that when *at, in*, or *on* denotes *time* instead of *place*, no preposition is used in Latin.

157

339.　　　　　　**Exercises**

Oral.　1. Prō Deō et patriā! Haec clāra verba corda virōrum semper incitāvērunt.　2. Hōc annō nihil timēmus, quod cōpiam frūmentī habēmus.　3. Cūr cīvitās huic cīvī pecūniam dedit? Quod patriam annō Bellī Magnī servāvit. 4. Oppidō occupātō, mīlitēs nostrī, paucī numerō sed corde fortēs, auxilia exspectābant.　5. Hic puer et aestāte et hieme labōrat, quod pater māterque pecūniam nōn habent. 6. Omnēs servī, lībertāte obtentā, ad flūmen cum magnā celeritāte fūgērunt.

Written.　1. Good citizens fear God and love (their) country.　2. If[1] Marcus is our leader, we shall not be de- feated by the enemy this winter.　3. In summer the fields are beautiful.　4. In a few years America will have many ships on every sea.

Fig. 66. Sacrificial Utensils

Torch, pitcher, knife, saucer, ladle, ax (cf. Fig. 64).

---

[1] Use abl. abs.

LESSON LX

THE DEMONSTRATIVE *IS*

340. Vocabulary

commū'nis, –e, *common* (communistic)
dum, conj., *while*
incer'tus, –a, –um, *uncertain* [*cernō*]
* **pars, par'tis,** f., *part* (partition)
remit'tō, –ere, remī'sī, remis'sus, (lit., *let back*), *relax,*
 send back [*mittō*]
spē'rō, –ā're, –ā'vī, –ā'tus, *hope (for)* (despair)
spī'rō, –ā're, –ā'vī, –ā'tus, *breathe* (inspiration)

341. The Demonstrative *Is*

is, *this, that; he, she, it*					
SINGULAR			**PLURAL**		
Nom.	is	e'a	id	e'ī (i'ī)	e'ae	e'a
Gen.	e'ius	e'ius	e'ius	eō'rum	eā'rum	eō'rum
Dat.	e'ī	e'ī	e'ī	e'īs (i'īs)	e'īs (i'īs)	e'īs (i'īs)
Acc.	e'um	e'am	id	e'ōs	e'ās	e'a
Abl.	e'ō	e'ā	e'ō	e'īs (i'īs)	e'īs (i'īs)	e'īs (i'īs)

342. How *Is* Is Used. — Instead of pointing, in a forceful
way, to a definite person or thing, as **hic** and **ille** do, **is**
usually refers to somebody or something just mentioned.
When used without a noun, it is commonly translated as a
personal pronoun, *he, she,* or *it;* accordingly, the genitive
eius may be translated *his, her, its,* while **eōrum** (m. and n.)
and **eārum** (f.) mean *their.* **Is** often serves as the antecedent
of a relative clause; as, **Is quī videt probat,** *He who sees
approves.*

343. **Exercises**

Oral. 1. Dum spīrō spērō. 2. Commūne perīculum concordiam facit. 3. Certa āmittimus dum incerta petimus. 4. Is cui librōs dedī eōs nōn remīsit. 5. Magna pars eius viae ā Rōmānīs mūnīta est. 6. Puellās et eārum mātrem in oppidō vīdī. 7. Hostibus pulsīs, vigiliam nostram nōn remittēmus. 8. Eī puerī quōs aestāte vīdimus erant eius discipulī.

Written. 1. This man is my teacher; that man is her father. 2. We saw him and his mother on the street. 3. To whom have you given a part of the money and booty? 4. We shall see her and her father this summer.

344. English Word Studies: The Names of the Months

In early Roman times the year began March 1, and February was the last month. We still use the ancient Roman names of the months. **March** was named after Mars. **April** was the *opening* month (**aperiō**), when the earth seems to open up. **May** is the month when things become *bigger* (**maior**). **June** is Juno's month. **July** was originally called **Quinctīlis**, the *fifth* month, but was renamed in honor of Julius Caesar when he had the calendar reformed. Similarly **August** was originally **Sextīlis**, the *sixth* month, but was renamed after the Emperor Augustus. **September** was originally the *seventh* month and kept its name even after it later became the ninth; similarly, **October, November, December**. **January** was named after **Janus**, the god of beginnings. **February** was the time of purification (**februa**), like the Christian Lent.

345.

A LATIN PLAY

VICTŌRIA MĀTRIS

Persōnae

Gāia, *Rōmāna*
Mārcus, *parvus fīlius Gāiae*

Pyrrhus, *rēx Graecōrum*
Mīlitēs Graecī

Locus: in castrīs relīctīs in Campāniā. Tempus: annō CCLXXV ante Christum.

Gāia. Iuppiter, tē (*thee*) vocāmus! Nōbīs (*to us*) et Rōmae auxilium dare potes!

Mārcus. Māter! Quid dīcis? Cūr pater nōn venit?

Gāia. Pater longē abest. Nōn veniet.

Mār. Sed cūr nōn cum patre sumus?

Gāia. Cum duce Dentātō pugnat — magnum est perīculum Rōmae nostrae! Graecī nunc per Campāniam veniunt!

Mār. Per Campāniam?

Gāia. Sed ad haec castra relīcta fūgimus. In hōc locō nōs (*us*) nōn invenient.

Mār. Nōn timeō. Cum Graecīs pugnābō!

Gāia. Mātrēs et puerī patriae auxilium dare nōn possunt; pugnāre est virōrum officium.

Mār. Vir sum! Possum pugnāre! Nōnne vidēs? (*Gladium relīctum capit.*)

Gāia. Āh, meus puer erit fortis mīles! — sed quid est? Pedēs equōrum audiō.

Vōx Mīlitis Graecī. Castra relīcta sunt; nēmō adest!

Mār. Cūr territa es, māter? Cūr mē tenēs?

Gāia. Graecī sunt! Iuppiter, tē vocāmus! (*Per portam veniunt Pyrrhus et mīlitēs Graecī.*)

Pyrrhus. Ho! Quis adest?

Mīles Graecus. Puer et eius māter!

Gāia. Cūr ad hunc locum vēnistis, Graecī? Haec terra, haec castra sunt Rōmāna!

Mīles. Sunt Rōmāna — sed erunt Graeca!

Mār. Nōn erunt Graeca! Virī Rōmānī sunt fortēs!

Pyr. O-ho! Etiam puer fortis esse vidētur. Fortem puerum petō. Potesne litterās ad castra Graecōrum portāre?

Gāia. Nōn portābit; Rōmānus est!

Pyr. Nōnne omnēs viās cognōvistī, puer? Vidēsne hanc pecūniam? Tua erit —

Gāia. Graecī pecūniam capiunt et patriam relinquunt; nōs sumus Rōmānī!

Pyr. Pyrrhus sum, rēx Graecōrum. Hunc puerum interficere possum. Properāre dēbēmus. Puer litterās portābit. (*Mīlitēs ad Gāiam et Mārcum accēdunt. Gāia gladium relīctum capit et tenet, sed Pyrrhus eum nōn videt.*)

Gāia. Meus fīlius servus Graecōrum nōn erit!

Mīles. Quid faciētis? Fugere nōn potestis, pugnāre nōn potestis!

Gāia. Sed hoc facere possum — prō patriā meā!

Mār. Māter! (*Gāia gladiō Mārcum interficit, tum sē (herself).*

Mīlitēs. Oh! (*Pyrrhus Gāiam et Mārcum spectat.*)

Pyr. Ita mātrēs Rōmānae pugnant! Quid virī facient?

(Exeunt tardē)

FIG. 67. A COIN OF CAESAR

On the left, the head of Venus; on the right, Aeneas carrying his father, Anchises, and the image of Athena (Minerva) from Troy.

LESSON LXI

THE DEMONSTRATIVE *ĪDEM*

346.   Vocabulary

expug'nō, –ā're, –ā'vī, –ā'tus, (lit., *fight it out*), *capture by assault* [*pugnō*]
ge'nus, ge'neris, n., *birth, race, kind*   (generation)
interci'piō, –ere, –cē'pī, –cep'tus, *intercept*   [*capiō*]
nō'bilis, –e, (lit., "know-able"), *distinguished, noble*   [*nōscō*]
suppli'cium, –ī, n., *punishment*   [*plicō*]

347.   Latin Phrases in English

i.e. (id est), *that is.*
id. (idem), *the same* (*i.e.* as mentioned above).
ibid. (ibīdem), *in the same place.*
semper īdem, *always the same.*

348.   The Demonstrative *Īdem*

The demonstrative **īdem** is a compound of **is** and **–dem**,
with slight changes for ease of pronunciation:

	īdem, *same*		
	SINGULAR		
Nom.	ī'dem	e'ădem	ĭ'dem
Gen.	eius'dem	eius'dem	eius'dem
Dat.	eī'dem	eī'dem	eī'dem
Acc.	eun'dem	ean'dem	ĭ'dem
Abl.	eō'dem	eā'dem	eō'dem
	PLURAL		
Nom.	eī'dem (ī'dem)	eae'dem	e'ădem
Gen.	eōrun'dem	eārun'dem	eōrun'dem
Dat.	eīs'dem (īs'dem)	eīs'dem (īs'dem)	eīs'dem (īs'dem)
Acc.	eōs'dem	eās'dem	e'ădem
Abl.	eīs'dem (īs'dem)	eīs'dem (īs'dem)	eīs'dem (īs'dem)

349.   **Exercises**

Oral.   1. Eōdem annō lībertās servīs data est.   2. Īdem dux eum ad supplicium trahī iussit.   3. Dum omnia timēmus, victōriam spērāre nōn possumus.   4. Is eōdem tempore bellum in fīnibus Germānōrum gerēbat.   5. Omnēs hominēs līberī parēsque esse dēbent, quod omnēs eundem Deum habent.   6. Hic homō nōbilī genere et auctōritāte sed nōn magnīs factīs antecēdit.   7. Oppidō expugnātō, Caesaris cōpiae impedīmenta hostium intercēpērunt. 8. Temporibus magnī perīculī quem aut quid timēbimus? Dominus prōvidēbit.

Written.   1. His punishment terrified the rest.   2. Their towns were taken-by-assault.   3. He will not send back the same book.   4. When I heard that, I was no longer afraid. 5. I shall not see the same boys this summer.

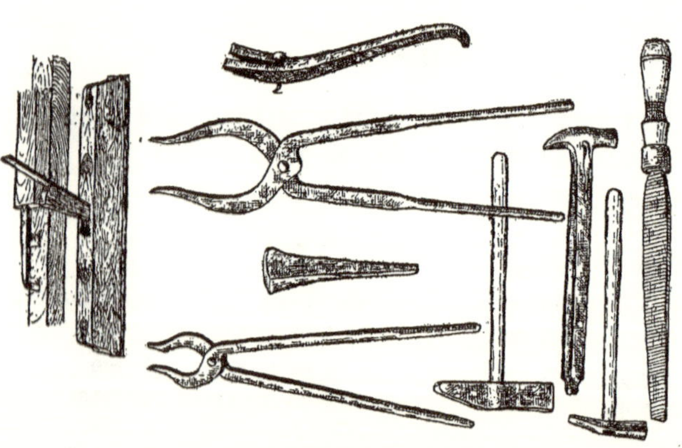

FIG. 68. ROMAN TOOLS

These tools, and many others exactly like ours, were found in a Roman fort in Germany.

LESSON LXII

THE INTENSIVE *IPSE*

350.   **Vocabulary**

co′lō, –ere, co′luī, cul′tus, *till, dwell in, worship*	(cultivate)
frā′ter, frā′tris, m., *brother*	(fraternal)
se′deō, –ē′re, sē′dī, ses′sus, *sit*	(session)
so′ror, sorō′ris, f., *sister*	(sorority)

351.   **English Word Studies: Spelling**

Latin words are often very helpful in fixing the spelling of English words. In this lesson we shall consider words in which a double consonant occurs.

If the Latin word has a double consonant, it is usually preserved in English, except at the end of a word: *terrestrial*, but *inter* (from **terra**); *carriage*, but *car* (**carrus**); *rebelled*, but *rebel* (**bellum**); *deterred*, but *deter* (**dēterreō**); *remitted*, but *remit* (**remittō**). *Letter* has two *t*'s and *literature* only one in the root of the word because the spelling of Latin **littera** varied.

352.   **The Intensive in English and Latin**

In English, compound pronouns are formed by joining *self* to *my, your, him, her, it,* and the plural *selves* to *our, your, them.* These compounds may be used in an intensive or emphatic sense; as, *I saw the man myself.*

In Latin, the pronoun **ipse** is a compound of **is** (**341**) and the intensive particle –**pse**, and therefore has purely intensive force: **Ipse hominem vīdī,** *I saw the man myself.* Note that **ipse** may be used alone in the nominative to emphasize an omitted subject. It is declined like **ille**, except in the neuter nominative and accusative singular.

165

ipse, *self*					
SINGULAR			**PLURAL**		
Nom. ip′se	ip′sa	ip′sum	ip′sī	ip′sae	ip′sa
Gen. ipsī′us	ipsī′us	ipsī′us	ipsō′rum	ipsā′rum	ipsō′rum
Dat. ip′sī	ip′sī	ip′sī	ip′sīs	ip′sīs	ip′sīs
Acc. ip′sum	ip′sam	ip′sum	ip′sōs	ip′sās	ip′sa
Abl. ip′sō	ip′sā	ip′sō	ip′sīs	ip′sīs	ip′sīs

353. Exercises

Oral. 1. Nōnne idem ipsī vīdistis? 2. Frātrēs et sorōrēs eiusdem familiae paria iūra habēre dēbent. 3. Quis est puer quī cum meā sorōre sedet? 4. Eō tempore ducem ipsum cum omnibus eius cōpiīs vīdī. 5. Quae officia soror tua ipsa suscipiet? 6. Colōnī agrōs in novā terrā colunt et ibi remanent. 7. Ille homō "agricola" appellātur quod agrōs colit. 8. Rōmānī deōs multōs habēbant quōs colēbant.

Written. 1. These (men) are standing; those are sitting. 2. The same winter they saw and heard him themselves. 3. These letters were written by the king himself. 4. We ourselves shall get much money together in a few years. 5. My brother was in that battle.

FIG. 69. CUPIDS PLAYING HIDE AND SEEK

From an ancient wall painting.

354.   HORATIUS AT THE BRIDGE [1]

Tarquiniī,[2] ā Rōmānīs pulsī, ā Porsenā, rēge Etrūscōrum, auxilium petīvērunt. Itaque Porsena cum magnīs cōpiīs (*to*) Rōmam vēnit. Rōmānī territī sunt, quod magna erat potestās Etrūscōrum magnumque Porsenae nōmen. Rōmānī ex agrīs in oppidum migrant; oppidum ipsum praesidiīs dēfendunt. Pars urbis mūrīs, pars Tiberī flūmine mūnīta est. Pōns sublicius (*made of piles*) iter hostibus dabat, sed ēgregius vir prohibuit, Horātius Coclēs, illō cognōmine appellātus quod in proeliō oculum āmīserat. Is, extrēmā pontis parte occupātā, cōpiās hostium sōlus sustinuit et Rōmānōs quī fugiēbant pontem rumpere iussit. Ipsa audācia hostēs terruit. Ponte ruptō,[3] armātus in Tiberim dēsiluit et per multa tēla incolumis (*unharmed*) ad Rōmānōs trānāvit. Grāta ob factum clārum eius cīvitās fuit. Multī agrī eī datī sunt et statua eius in Comitiō posita est.

FIG. 70. PŌNS MULVIUS

This bridge, built in 109 B.C., is just north of Rome, across the Tiber. The four central arches are ancient. A number of ancient bridges are in use throughout the lands of the old Roman Empire.

---

[1] Read Macaulay's *Lays of Ancient Rome*, "Horatius," 26–67.   [2] The Etruscan kings who ruled Rome in the sixth century, B.C.   [3] Cf. **rumpō**.

LESSON LXIII

DECLENSION OF IRREGULAR ADJECTIVES

355. A small but important group of adjectives of the first and second declensions resembles **ipse** in having –ĭus in the genitive and –ī in the dative singular of all genders. In other cases they are declined regularly, like **magnus, –a, –um:**

a'lius, a'lia, a'liud,[1] *other, another* (alias)
  (a'lius ... a'lius, *one ... another;* a'liī ... a'liī, *some ... others*)
al'ter, al'tera, al'terum,[2] *the other* (of two) (alternate)
  (al'ter ... al'ter, *the one ... the other*)
neu'ter, neu'tra, neu'trum, *neither* (of two) (neutral)
nūl'lus, nūl'la, nūl'lum, *no, none* (nullify)
sō'lus, sō'la, sō'lum, *alone, sole, only* (solitary)
tō'tus, tō'ta, tō'tum, *whole* (total)
ūl'lus, ūl'la, ūl'lum, *any*
ū'nus, ū'na, ū'num,[3] *one* (unit)

a. **Note.** — Like **hic, ille,** and **is,** these adjectives are emphatic and accordingly precede their nouns.

b. **Decline** each as follows:

	SINGULAR			PLURAL
Nom.	tō'tus	tō'ta	tō'tum	
Gen.	tōtī'us	tōtī'us	tōtī'us	
Dat.	tō'tī	tō'tī	tō'tī	(regular)
Acc.	tō'tum	tō'tam	tō'tum	
Abl.	tō'tō	tō'tā	tō'tō	

356. Drill. — Decline in the singular **alius frāter, neutra soror,** and **tōtum oppidum.**

---

[1] Note that the neuter nominative and accusative singular ends in –**d,** not –**m.**

[2] The genitive singular of **alter** ends in –ĭus.

[3] **Uter,** *which* (of two), and **uterque,** *each, both,* are likewise irregular and belong to this group but are comparatively unimportant.

Fig. 71. A Roman Lady in Her Garden

357.   **Exercises**

Oral. 1. Hostēs agrōs oppidaque tōtīus īnsulae vāstāvērunt. 2. Rēx neutrī fīliō rēgnum committet. 3. Is homō ipse ab aliīs accūsātus est sed ab aliīs dēfēnsus est. 4. Cōnsilia alterius ducis nōn erant grāta alterī. 5. Tōtum praesidium ex oppidō remōtum ad mare prōcēdere mātūrat. 6. Omnēs amīcī eius iam discessērunt et is sōlus nunc manet. 7. Accēpistīne ipse ūlla praemia prō meritīs tuīs? (*See* **168.**) Nūlla accēpī neque ūlla exspectō.

Written. 1. To one sister I shall give money, to the other this book. 2. My brother and father spent part of that same summer alone in the woods. 3. Have you seen my mother and sister? I have seen neither. 4. In the summer the farmer tills the fields, but what does he do in winter? 5. We have already dispatched reinforcements, but there is no danger now.

358.   **English Word Studies: Spelling**

Many prefixes bring about the doubling of consonants by assimilation. The most important are **ad-**, **con-**, **in-**, **ob-**, **ex-**, and **sub-**. If you will analyze the English word, you can often tell whether the consonant is to be doubled: **con-** and **modus** form **commodus**; prefix **ad-** and you get the English derivative *ac-com-modate* with two *c's* and two *m's*. Similarly *commend* has two *m's*; *re-com-mend* has two *m's* but only one *c* because **re-** is never assimilated. Other examples of doubling through assimilation are *im-material*, *ac-celerate*, *suf-ficient*, *ef-ficient* (but *de-ficient*, for **dē-** is not assimilated).

A Latin Pun

Equus in stabulō est sed nōn ēst, The horse *is* in the stable but does not *eat* (**est** means *is;* **ēst** means *eat*).

LESSON LXIV

THE PARTICIPLE: PRESENT AND FUTURE ACTIVE

ELEMENTARY GRAMMAR: Review *Participles*, **635**.

359. Vocabulary

aliē′nus, –a, –um, *another's, unfavorable*	[*alius*]
conten′dō, –ere, –ten′dī, –ten′tus, *struggle, hasten*	[*tendō*]
expel′lō, –ere, ex′pulī, –pul′sus, *drive out*	[*pellō*]
gra′vis, –e, *heavy, serious, severe*	(gravitation)
op′primō, –ere, –pres′sī, –pres′sus, *overwhelm, surprise*	[*premō*]
ro′gō, –ā′re, –ā′vī, –ā′tus, *ask*	(interrogative)
vŏx, vō′cis, f., *voice, remark*	[*vocō*]

360. Latin Phrases in English

Homō prōpōnit, sed Deus dispōnit, *Man proposes, but God disposes.*
ipsō factō, *by the fact itself, thereby.*
Vŏx populī vŏx Deī, *The voice of the people (is) the voice of God.*
ūnā vŏce, *with one voice, unanimously.*

361. Present Participle

In English, the **present participle** has both an active and a
passive form: (a) *I have a brother **fighting** in France;* (b) *The
battle now **being fought** will be decisive.* In both examples
the present participle *modifies a noun.* It is likewise used in
making the progressive verb form: *My brother **is fighting**.*
Here " fighting " does not modify the noun but is a part of
the verb and denotes progressive action (*see* **20, *b***).

In Latin, the **present participle** has only the active form.
It is used to modify nouns or pronouns and never combines
with the verb **sum** to form verb phrases. *My brother is fighting*
becomes in Latin simply **frāter meus pugnat.** The present
participle, like the present infinitive, represents an act *as
taking place at the time indicated by the main verb.*

170

362. Formation and Declension. — The present participle of the four conjugations is formed by adding **–ns** to the present stem. It is declined like a third declension adjective of one ending (**316**), with the base ending in **–nt–**, as follows:

	M. AND F.	N.	M. AND F.	N.
Nom.	pa'rāns	pa'rāns	paran'tēs	paran'tia
Gen.	paran'tis		paran'tium	
Dat.	paran'tī		paran'tibus	
Acc.	paran'tem	pa'rāns	paran'tēs(īs)	paran'tia
Abl.	paran'te(ī)		paran'tibus	

Note. — (*a*) The ablative singular ending is regularly **–e**, but **–ī** is used instead whenever the participle is used simply as an adjective. (*b*) In verbs of the fourth conjugation, and **–iō** verbs of the third, **–ie–** appears throughout, forming the base **–ient–**, as **audiēns, audientis**; **capiēns, capientis**. (*c*) **Sum** has no present participle; that of **possum** is **potēns**.

363. Future Active Participle

Latin, unlike English, has a **future active participle**. This is formed by dropping the **–us** of the perfect participle and adding **–ūrus, –a, –um**: **parātūrus, –a, –um**, *about to prepare, going to prepare*; **futūrus, –a, –um**, *going to be*. It is declined like **magnus, –a, –um**.

364. Drill. — Form and translate the participles of **rogō**, **opprimō**, and **expellō** in the present and future active.

365. Exercises

Oral. 1. Cūr in hōc locō mānsūrus es? 2. Vōcēs amīcōrum rogantium auxilium audītae sunt. 3. Paucīs annīs nūllōs mīlitēs per viās nostrās iter facientēs vidēbimus. 4. Rōmānīs prōcēdentibus, hostēs fūgērunt. 5. Multī mīlitēs pugnantēs captī sunt. 6. Vulneribus gravibus acceptīs, nostrī ē castrīs hostēs expulērunt. 7. Oppressī in aliēnō locō, hostēs cum equīs impedīmentīsque ad montēs contentūrī sunt.

(Instead of clauses, use participles wherever possible.)

Written. 1. The number of (those) approaching is not large. 2. The weapons given to the other soldier are heavy but not long. 3. He was accused (while) defending the public cause. 4. Hearing many voices, the children were frightened. 5. He folded the letter which he had written and sent (it) to (his) friend.

FIG. 72. A STREET CORNER IN POMPEII

Notice the fountain, the stepping stones for use in wet weather, and the ruts in the pavement.

LESSON LXV

THE PERFECT ACTIVE INFINITIVE

366.   Vocabulary

cōnscrī'bō, –ere, –scrīp'sī, –scrīp'tus, *enlist, enroll*	[*scrībō*]
cōnsis'tō, –ere, cōn'stitī, cōn'stitus, *stand still, stop*	[*sistō*]
dī'cō, –ere, dī'xī, dic'tus, *say, tell*	(diction)
ia'ciō, –ere, iē'cī, iac'tus, *throw, cast, hurl*	(projectile)
levis, –e, *light* (in weight)	(levity)
osten'dō, –ere, –ten'dī, –ten'tus, (*stretch out*), *show, display*	[*tendō*]
prohi'beō, –ē're, –hi'buī, –hi'bitus, *prevent, keep from*	[*habeō*]
vīs, —,[1] f., *force, violence;* plur., vī'res, vī'rium, *strength*	(vim)

367.   Latin and English Word Studies

The suffix **–or**, when added to the participial stem, indicates the doer of an action : **monitor** (*one who warns*), **scrīptor** (*one who writes*), **inventor** (*one who finds*). It is used in English in the same way.

When the suffix **–or** is added to the present base of a verb, it usually indicates a state of being or condition : **timor, amor, terror.** It is used in English.

Exercise. — Find five English words which are formed by adding the suffix **–or** to the stems of verbs that you have studied.

368.   Perfect Active Infinitive

The **perfect active infinitive** is formed by adding **–isse** to the perfect stem : **parāvisse**, *to have prepared;* **habuisse,** etc.

369. Review infinitive used as subject and object, see **106, 107;** infinitive with subject in the accusative as in English, see **204.**

---

[1] Genitive and dative singular rarely found (see **645**).

370. Exercises

Oral. 1. Prohibēre vim et pācem cōnservāre est nōbile. 2. Omnibus bonum exemplum ostendere dēbēmus. 3. Mīlitēs cōnsistentēs arma levia cum magnā vī iēcisse dīcuntur. 4. Caesar captīvōs coāctōs cōnscrībī iubēbit. 5. Rēgis fīlia librum scrīpsisse dīcitur. 6. Rōmānī paucās nāvēs ad Galliam mīsisse dīcuntur. 7. Dux iussit cōpiās cum magnā celeritāte ad oppidum prōcēdere et ibi cōnsistere.

Written. 1. The king is said to have fortified the town. 2. We can not breathe under water. 3. Are you preparing to come with your father and mother? 4. Those men are said to have sailed to a strange land. 5. For these reasons we ought to lead the men out of camp with great speed.

371. Cincinnatus, the Plowman-Dictator

Hostēs Minucium, ducem Rōmānum, et cōpiās eius premēbant. Ubi id Rōmānīs nūntiātum est, parāvērunt Cincinnātum dictātōrem facere, quod is sōlus cīvitātem ē perīculō servāre poterat. Ille trāns Tiberim eō tempore parvum agrum colēbat. Nūntiī missī eum in agrō labōrantem invēnērunt. Salūte (*greeting*) datā acceptāque, Cincinnātus togam parāre uxōrem iussit; nam nōn oportēbat (*it was fitting*) sine togā nūntiōs audīre.

Nūntiī eum dictātōrem appellant et dīcunt: "Cōpiae nostrae ab hostibus premuntur et cīvēs nostrī timent." Itaque Cincinnātus prōcessit et, Minuciō servātō, hostēs sub iugum (*under the yoke* [1]) mīsit. Triumphāns cōpiās redūxit. Ductī sunt ante eum ducēs hostium, capta arma ostenta sunt; post eum mīlitēs vēnērunt praedam portantēs. Et haec omnia Cincinnātus magnā celeritāte gessit: dictātūrā in (*for*) sex mēnsēs acceptā, sextō decimō diē (*day*) ad agrōs discessit, nōn iam dictātor sed triumphāns agricola.

---

[1] *I.e.* an arch of spears. This act signified unconditional surrender.

FIG. 73. THE FOUNTAIN NEAR THE COLOSSEUM, AS IT WAS

LESSON LXVI

PERFECT PASSIVE AND FUTURE ACTIVE INFINITIVE. INDIRECT STATEMENT

372.   Vocabulary

iūs'tus, –a, –um, *just*	[*iūs*]
la'bor, labō'ris, m., *work, trouble*	[*labōrō*]
mū'nus, mū'neris, n., *duty, service, gift*	(munificent)
pu'tō, –ā're, –ā'vī, –ā'tus, *think*	(reputation)
sci'ō, scī're, scī'vī, scī'tus, *know*	(science)
secun'dus, –a, –um, *second*	(secondary)
sol'vō, –ere, sol'vī, solū'tus, *loose, pay*	(solution)
spa'tium, –ī, n., *space, time, distance*	(spacious)

373.   English Word Study: Spelling

The base of the Latin present participle is –**ant**, –**ent**, or –**ient**, according to the conjugation (**362**). This is used as a suffix in English, with the same meaning as the participial ending –*ing*.

A common mistake in the spelling of English words is due to the confusion of –**ant** and –**ent**. Reference to the Latin partly solves the difficulty:

(*a*) All English words derived from the first conjugation follow the Latin spelling with an –**a**– : *expectant, emigrant.*

(*b*) All adjectives and most nouns derived from the other conjugations follow the Latin spelling with an –**e**– : *continent, regent, agent, efficient.*

(*c*) But some *nouns* have an –**a**– : *tenant, defendant.*

Exercise. — Give eight English words with suffix –**ant** or –**ent** derived from Latin words previously studied.

374. Perfect Passive and Future Active Infinitive

a. The **perfect passive infinitive** is a compound tense, formed by using the perfect participle with the present

infinitive **esse** : **parātus, –a, –um esse,** *to have been prepared;*
habitus, –a, –um esse, etc. (cf. perfect passive indicative :
parātus sum).

b. The **future active infinitive** is a compound tense, formed
by using the future active participle with the present infinitive **esse** : **parātūrus, –a, –um esse,** *to be going to prepare;*
habitūrus, –a, –um esse, etc.

There was no future passive infinitive in common use in Latin.

c. **Learn** the infinitives, active and passive, of the model
verbs (**660–664**) and **sum** (**666**).

375. Drill. — Form and translate the infinitives, active
and passive, of **iaciō, ostendō,** and **prohibeō**.

376.   Infinitive with Verbs of Saying, etc.

In English, we use a "that" clause after verbs of *saying,
thinking, knowing, hearing,* and the like : *He says (that* [1])
the boys are coming. But sometimes we use the infinitive :
*The boys are said to be coming; I know him to be a good man;
I heard him say this.*

In Latin, the infinitive is *always* used after such words :
Dīcit puerōs venīre. Note that **puerōs** is in the accusative
because it is the subject of an infinitive (**205**). The word
that is not translated.

377.   Direct and Indirect Statement

    1. **Dīcit, " Puerī veniunt,"** *He says, " The boys are coming."*
    2. **Dīcit puerōs venīre,** *He says that the boys are coming.*

In the first sentence the exact words of the speaker are
given, as shown by the use of quotation marks. Such a
sentence is called a **direct statement**. In the second sentence

----
[1] *That* is occasionally omitted.

the exact words are not given. Such a sentence is called an **indirect statement.**

378. Rule. — *Statements that convey indirectly the thoughts or words of another, used as the objects of verbs of* **saying**, **thinking**, **knowing**, **hearing**, **perceiving**, *or the like, require subjects in the accusative and verbs in the infinitive.*

379. Who or Whom? — Explain how a knowledge of indirect statement in Latin will enable one to use *who* and *whom* correctly, as follows : (a) *A man* **who**, *I believe*, **is** *honest;* (b) *A man* **whom** *I believe* **to be** *honest.*

380.   **Exercises**

Oral. 1. Dīcunt, " Cīvis iūstus lībertātem amat." 2. Cīvis iūstus lībertātem amāre dīcitur. 3. Dīcunt cīvem iūstum lībertātem amāre. 4. Putāmus nostra mūnera futūra esse levia. 5. Scīmus in spatiō vītae esse cūrās et labōrēs. 6. Ille homō erit prīmus aut secundus ōrdine. 7. Putāsne hunc hominem pecūniam dēbitam solvisse aut solūtūrum esse? 8. Putō pecūniam ab illō nōn solūtam esse.

Written. 1. Galba said, " My father is a soldier." 2. We all know that his father is brave. 3. I hear that Galba's brother was a sailor and was not terrified by the sea. 4. I think that Galba himself will be a soldier. 5. He himself said, " I am going to be a soldier, for my father is a soldier."

Fig. 74. Puerī Lūdunt

LESSON LXVII

INDIRECT STATEMENT (*Cont.*)

381. Vocabulary

ā′cer, ā′cris, ā′cre,[1] *sharp, keen* (acrid)
clā′mō, –ā′re, –ā′vī, –ā′tus, *cry out, shout* (clamor)
hae′reō, –ē′re, hae′sī, hae′sus, *stick* (adhesive)
īn′stō, –ā′re, īn′stitī, ——, *press on, threaten* [*stō*]
perve′niō, –ī′re, –vē′nī, –ven′tus, (*come through*), *arrive* [*veniō*]
sen′tiō, –ī′re, sēn′sī, sēn′sus, *feel, realize* (sense)
sī, conj., *if*
tan′gō, –ere, te′tigī, tāc′tus, *touch* (tangent)

382. English Word Studies

By addition of the suffix –ia (**201**) to the base of the present participle, a suffix –**antia** or –**entia** is formed which becomes –**ance**, –**ence**, –**ancy**, or –**ency** in English (cf. the change of –**tia** to –**ce**, **207**): **scientia**, *science.* The difficulty in spelling is again removed by reference to the Latin (cf. **373**).

Exercise. — Give eight English nouns with this suffix derived from Latin words previously studied.

383. How Indicative and Infinitive Differ in Tense

1. *It was thought that he was present.*
2. *He was thought to be present.*

In the first sentence, the verb in the subordinate clause is in the past indicative. In the second sentence, the infinitive *to be* refers to the same time but is in the present tense. The tenses of the **indicative** are determined by their *relation to present time*, but the tenses of the **infinitive** are determined *by their relation to the verbs on which they depend.* This is true in Latin as in English and should be remembered in translating a Latin infinitive into an English " that " clause.

---

[1] Cf. **316**, footnote 1.

384.   How the Tenses of the Infinitive Differ

1. The present infinitive represents time or action as *going on*, from the standpoint of the introductory verb:

Dīcit **Dīxit** } eōs pugnāre,   *He* { *says* / *said* } *(that) they* { *are* / *were* } *fighting.*

2. The future infinitive represents an act that will occur *later*, from the standpoint of the introductory verb:

Dīcit **Dīxit** } eōs pugnātūrōs esse,   *He* { *says* / *said* } *(that) they* { *will* / *would* } *fight.*

3. The perfect infinitive represents time or action as *completed before* that of the introductory verb:

Dīcit **Dīxit** } eōs pugnāvisse,   *He* { *says* / *said* } *(that) they* { *have* / *had* } *fought.*

385. *a.* **Note** that the participle in the compound forms of the infinitive must agree with its subject (see 2 above).

b. **A helpful hint:** In translating indirect statements into Latin, use the tense of the infinitive corresponding to that which would have been used in a direct statement.

386.   Exercises

Oral.   1. (*a*) Omnēs scīmus Americānōs mīlitēs esse ācrēs et fortēs. (*b*) Substitute *scīvimus* for *scīmus* in (*a*) and translate. 2. Rōmānī dīcēbant Caesarem esse fortem ducem nec superātum esse. 3. Sī meum frātrem tangēs, eum dēfendam. 4. Servī spērāvērunt labōrem futūrum esse facilem. 5. Omnēs sēnsimus perīculum īnstāre. 6. Omnēs puerī sciunt Columbum ab Eurōpā nāvēs solvisse [1] et ad Americam pervēnisse. 7. Puer, perīculō īnstantī territus, nōn clāmāre potuit, quod vōx haesit. 8. Quis dīxit amīcum meum pervēnisse?

---

[1] Use the English idiom.

Written.   1. Who said that America would not fight? 2. The boy thought that (his) father had been saved by a sailor. 3. My mother wrote that the islands were beautiful. 4. We can prove that our cause is just.   5. The general says that the soldiers were brave and keen.

FIG. 75. CAESAR AT THE RUBICON

The Rubicon river in northeastern Italy was the southern boundary of the province over which Caesar had been given military control. His decision to cross it with his army (49 B.C.) was in defiance of the Senate and meant civil war. (From "Julius Caesar.")

LESSON LXVIII

REVIEW

387. Review of Participles

We have seen that the Latin participle furnishes a convenient means for conveying various ideas expressed by dependent clauses in English.   Review **276**.

388. Noun and Adjective Review

(*a*) Decline **haec pars, idem supplicium, pater ipse, ea aestās, hoc
genus, nūlla vōx, sōlus frāter.**

(*b*) Give the genitive and dative singular of **nūllus pater, ūlla māter,
altera soror, sōlum flūmen, neutrum iter.**

389. Verb Review

(*a*) Give a synopsis of **timeō** in the 3rd plural active; of **remittō** in
the 3rd singular passive.

(*b*) Form the participles, active and passive, of **dīcō, iaciō, sciō,** and
rogō.

(*c*) Form the infinitives, active and passive, of **sentiō, intercipiō,
currō,** and **expugnō.**

(*d*) Conjugate **sum** and **possum.**

390. Vocabulary Review

(*a*) Give the nominative, genitive, gender, and meaning of the Latin
nouns suggested by the derivatives : *cordial, partial, generation, frater-
nity, sorority, vocal, maternal.*

(*b*) Give the principal parts of the Latin verbs suggested by the derivatives : *sedentary, cursive, remiss, inspiration, cult, expulsive, op-
pressive, diction, ostensible, prohibit.*

391. Vocabulary Matches (*To the teacher*)

Latin word contests, especially between two divisions of the same class,
excite keen rivalry and lead to a ready mastery of words. After every
member of the class has faithfully prepared all the vocabularies of a given

182

number of lessons, have two leaders choose sides, as in an old-fashioned spelling bee. The teacher dictates the English word, and the students in turn give the Latin word in full (*i.e.* principal parts, if a verb; genitive singular and gender, if a noun). When a student misses a word or one of its parts, he takes his seat. Much interest is added if a descriptive name is given to the contesting sides, such as " Altī *vs.* Brevēs," " Puerī *vs.* Puellās," etc.

392.   English Word Studies: A Review

Find and use in sentences as many English derivatives as possible from **dīcō**, **putō**, **iaciō**, **audiō**, and **sedeō**.

Enter the derivatives in your notebook, using a separate page for each Latin word.

393.   THE STORY OF LUCIUS (*Cont.*)

Virginēs Vestālēs

Etiam cīvitās focum Vestae habuit. Templum Vestae in Forō Rōmānō stābat. Ibi sex puellae, Virginēs Vestālēs appellātae, ignem sacram Vestae semper servābant. Magna erat glōria Vestālium et maximē ā populō Rōmānō amābantur. Eīs in viīs vīsīs, omnēs dē viā dēcessērunt. Facile erat eās cognōscere, quod omnēs semper candidās vestēs gessērunt neque ūlla alia fēmina vestēs eiusdem generis gessit. In Circō loca ēgregia eīs dabantur. Sed dūrum fuit supplicium Vestālis quae mala fuit: ea vīva sub terrā posita est.

Fig. 76. Vestālis

The costume suggests one reason why the Vestals have been called the first nuns.

FIG. 77. THE CHIEF VESTAL PASSES
Omnēs dē viā dēcessērunt.

EXACTING DUTIES

Iūlia, soror Lūcī, Vestālis erat et multa dē vītā Vestālium nārrābat.   Cum reliquīs Vestālibus in Ātriō Vestae ad templum habitāvit sed saepe patrem et mātrem et frātrēs vidēbat. Dīxit vītam Vestālium fēlīcem esse sed labōrem nōn facilem esse: eās omnia magnā cūrā dīligentiāque facere dēbēre. Dīxit Vestālēs ligna in focō eōdem modō semper pōnere et omnia certīs temporibus facere.   Itaque spatium disciplīnae longum erat.   Puellae sex annōrum, ā patribus mātribusque Vestae datae, prīmōs decem annōs discipulae ēgērunt, tum decem annōs in officiīs ēgērunt et posteā parvās puellās docuērunt.   Post trīgintā annōs lībertās eīs data est et eae ad amīcōs familiāsque redīre[1] potuērunt, sed multae in Ātriō Vestae permānsērunt.   Sex sōlae Vestālēs in Ātriō ūnō tempore habitāvērunt.

---

[1] Infinitive of **red-eō**, *go back*.

MISFORTUNE

Quondam Iūlia, aquam sacram dē fonte portāns, vīdit aliam Vestālem ante portam sedentem flentemque et ad eam cucurrit. Causā dolōris petītā, audīvit alteram sīvisse[1] ignem sacram exstinguī; vigiliā cōnfecta, somnō oppressa erat. Iūlia, malā fortūnā amīcae permōta, tamen illī nūllum cōnsilium dare potuit. Itaque illa pontificī omnia nārrāvit et hic eam verberāvit — nihil aliud facere potuit, quod ita lēgēs iussērunt.

Fig. 78. Vestālis Somnō Oppressa Est

RIGHT OR WRONG

Hōc audītō, Lūcius dīxit illam nōn merēre ob lassitūdinem poenā afficī et ōtium habēre dēbēre, sed eius soror, Iūlia, aliam sententiam habuit: " Etiam amīca mea ipsa quae verberāta est sentit supplicium aequum fuisse. Mūnera nostra gravia sunt. Sī dīligentiam nōn adhibēbimus, salūs cīvitātis in perīculō erit. Itaque poena neglegentiae gravis esse dēbet. Sī ignem exstinguī sinam (quod spērō numquam futūrum esse) gravī poenā afficī dēbēbō."

---

[1] From **sinō.**

THE IRREGULAR VERB *FERŌ*

394. **Vocabulary**

cōnfi'ciō, **–ere**, **–fē'cī**, **–fec'tus**, (*do thoroughly*), *complete,*
  exhaust (cf. "do up")   [*faciō*]
fe'rō, **fer're**, **tu'lī**, **lā'tus**, *bear, carry, bring* (with **ad** or **in** and acc.) (*ferry*)
  cōn'ferō, **cōnfer're**, **con'tulī**, **collā'tus**, *bring together, collect*
  dē'ferō, **dēfer're**, **dē'tulī**, **dēlā'tus**, *carry away, refer, offer*
  re'ferō, **refer're**, **ret'tulī**, **relā'tus**, *bring back, report, give back*
interfi'ciō, **–ere**, **–fē'cī**, **–fec'tus**, *kill* (cf. " done for ")   [*faciō*]
o'pus, **o'peris**, n., *work*   (*operate*)
prīn'ceps, **prīn'cipis**, m., *first man, chief, leader*   [*prīmus + capiō*]

395. **Conjugation of *Ferō***

The indicative of **ferō** is irregular in the present tense
only; in all other tenses it is conjugated like a verb of the
third conjugation. The present active infinitive **ferre** is contracted from **ferĕre**, while the passive (**ferrī**) is formed by
changing final **–e** to **–ī**, as in other verbs. Give all forms
of the indicative, together with the participles and infinitives
(see **668**).

PRESENT INDICATIVE			
ACTIVE		PASSIVE	
fe'rō	fe'rimus	fe'ror	fe'rimur
fers	fer'tis	fer'ris	feri'minī
fert	fe'runt	fer'tur	ferun'tur

396. **Exercises**

Oral. 1. Cūr frāter tuus librum nōn refert quem eī
dedī? 2. Puerī, opere cōnfectō, praemia quae meruerant
accēpērunt et dīmissī sunt. 3. Sociī nostrī in magnō perī-

culō erant, quod America eō tempore auxilium ferre nōn poterat. 4. Nostrī, hostibus expulsīs, in ūnum locum impedīmenta cōnferēbant. 5. Mīles dīxit verba nūntī ad prīncipem dēlāta esse. 6. Aliī ad oppidum prōcēdere mātūrāvērunt, aliī pugnantēs interfectī sunt. 7. Captīvī, vulneribus gravibus cōnfectī, arma ferre nōn potuērunt.

Written. 1. It was said that the enemy's plans were being reported to the Romans. 2. The rest were killed (while) bringing water to the men. 3. Do you know the names of any parts of the body? 4. The Romans thought that the mind was not in the head but in the heart. 5. We heard that the boys and girls had collected books and had sent them to the soldiers.

397.   Phrases and Quotations

inter alia, *among other things.*

magnum opus, *a great piece of work* (as a book or painting).

Iacta ālea est, *The die is cast,* i.e. *the decision is made* (Caesar at the Rubicon river; cf. Fig. 75).

Timeō Danaōs et dōna ferentēs, *I fear the Greeks even when they bring gifts* (Virgil).

in locō parentis, *in place of a parent.*

obiter dictum, *(something) said by the way* (ob iter).

FIG. 79. SCENE IN AN INN

This ancient picture shows, on the left, two men quarreling over a game; on the right, the innkeeper telling them to do their quarreling outdoors.

LESSON LXX

COMPARISON OF REGULAR ADJECTIVES.
DECLENSION OF COMPARATIVES

398.   Vocabulary

condi'ciō, condiciō'nis, f., *condition, terms*	(conditional)
li'gō, –ā're, –ā'vī, –ā'tus, *tie, bind*	(ligament)
quam, conj., *than*	
ra'piō, –ere, ra'puī, rap'tus, *seize, carry off*	(rapture)
respon'deō, –ē're, respon'dī, respōn'sus, *answer*	(response)
sta'tuō, –ere, sta'tuī, statū'tus, (*make stand*), *place, establish, determine*	[**stō**]
ū'tilis, –e, *useful*	(utility)
vin'cō, –ere, vī'cī, vic'tus, *conquer*	(invincible)

399.   Comparison of Adjectives

Adjectives are inflected to show degree. This is called **comparison.** There are three degrees: **positive, comparative, superlative.** The positive is the simple form of the adjective, the others indicate a greater degree.

In English, the comparative is formed by adding –**er** (–**r**) to the positive: *high-**er**, brave-**r**.* The superlative is formed by adding –**est** (–**st**) to the positive: *high-**est**, brave-**st**.* But adjectives of more than one syllable are often compared by the use of *more* and *most: more skillful, most skillful.*

In Latin, adjectives regularly add to the base of the positive the endings –**ior** (m. and f.), –**ius** (n.), to form the comparative, and –**issimus, –a, –um** to form the superlative:

POSITIVE	COMPARATIVE	SUPERLATIVE
altus, –a, –um, *high* (base **alt–**)	**altior, altius,** *higher*	**altissimus, –a, –um,** *highest*
fortis, –e, *brave* (base **fort–**)	**fortior, fortius,** *braver*	**fortissimus, –a, –um,** *bravest*

a. **Hints for translating.** — The comparative may often be translated *more, too, rather;* the superlative, *most, very, exceedingly.*

400.   Declension of the Comparative

Adjectives are declined as follows in the comparative:

	M. AND F.	N.	M. AND F.	N.
Nom.	al'tior	al'tius	altiō'rēs	altiō'ra
Gen.	altiō'ris	altiō'ris	altiō'rum	altiō'rum
Dat.	altiō'rī	altiō'rī	altiō'ribus	altiō'ribus
Acc.	altiō'rem	al'tius	altiō'rēs	altiō'ra
Abl.	altiō're	altiō're	altiō'ribus	altiō'ribus

Observe that, while comparatives are declined like adjectives of the
third declension, they do not have –ī in the abl. sing., –ium in the gen.
plur., or –ia in the nom. and acc. plur. neuter.

401. Drill. — (*a*) Compare **grātus, –a, –um ; nōbilis, –e ;
clārus, –a, –um ; levis, –e ; longus, –a, –um.** (*b*) Decline
novus, –a, –um in the comparative.

402. Remember that in Latin the same case is used after **quam** as before it, but in English the nominative is often used after *than:* **Forti-
ōrem virum quam illum nōn vīdī,** *A braver man than he I have not seen.*

403.   Exercises

Oral.   1. Captīvus, nōn ligātus, arma rapuit et fūgit.
2. Quid est ūtilius et nōbilius quam prō patriā pugnāre?
3. Novissimum librum, ab eōdem auctōre scrīptum, ad
frātrem meum mittere statuī.   4. Gallī vīribus corporis
Rōmānōs superābant sed nōn erant fortiōrēs virī.   5. Hominem dē viīs rogāvī ; respondit hanc esse plāniōrem quam
illam.   6. Ostendimus duo itinera per Galliam — alterum
facile, alterum longius et incertius.   7. Condiciōnēs pācis
durissimae et gravissimae ab hostibus victīs semper esse
habentur.   8. Quid fers? Nihil.

Written. 1. Why are not the rivers of Italy very long? 2. Even more severe peace-terms[1] will be determined (upon) than these. 3. I know that that river is swift and very deep. 4. Nothing is more useful than water. 5. Peace has nobler and truer victories than war.

404. **English Word Studies**

It is important to distinguish different words from the same stem. " Plain " and " plane " both come from **plānus**, *level*. A " plain " is a *level* field; a " plain " person is not above the average *level* in appearance, etc. A " plane " is a *level* surface (hence " plane " geometry); it is also a tool which makes surfaces *level*. " Plane " is therefore used in a more literal, "plain," in a less literal sense.

A " corpse " is a dead *body* (from **corpus**); a " corps " (pronounced "core") is a *body* of men forming part of an army. The former is literal, the latter, figurative. A " corporation " is a *body* of men united for commercial or other purposes. A " corpuscle " is a little *body* in the blood. " Corporal " punishment is punishment inflicted upon the *body*, *i.e.* a whipping. Anything " corporeal " has a *body*, *i.e.* it is not imaginary. Similarly, a "principal" is the *leading* person in a school; a " principle " is a *leading* rule.

A Punning Epitaph

It is said that on the tombstone of a certain Roman lady, Victoria, who outlived her " man," one may read this triumphant statement:

VICTŌRIA VIRUM VĪCIT

---

[1] Cf. Oral 7.

Fig. 80. The Peristyle of a Roman House. (From "Julius Caesar.")

LESSON LXXI

FORMATION AND COMPARISON OF REGULAR ADVERBS

405.   **Vocabulary**

ap′tus, –a, –um, *fit, suitable*	(adapt)
*****gēns, gen′tis,** f., *tribe, people, nation*	[***genus***]
īn′struō, –ere, –strū′xī, –strūc′tus, *arrange, provide*	[***struō***, arrange]
iū′dicō, –ā′re, –ā′vī, –ā′tus, *judge, decide*	(judicial)
nē′mō, dat. **nē′minī,** acc. **nē′minem** (no other forms), *no one*	[***homō***]
ōrā′tiō, ōrātiō′nis, f., *speech*	(orator)
re′giō, regiō′nis, f., *district, region*	[***regō***]
repel′lō, –ere, rep′pulī, repul′sus, *drive back, repulse*	[***pellō***]

406.   **English Word Study: The Suffix** *–iō*

In Latin, the suffix **–iō** is added to verb stems, usually to
the participial stem. As this generally ends in **–t** or **–s**, words
of this origin generally end in **–tiō** or **–siō**. The suffix
indicates an act or the state which results from an act:
ōrātiō is the act of speaking, or the result, *i.e.* a speech.
Nouns with this suffix have **–iōnis** in the genitive. Accordingly, the base ends in **–n**. Hence the English form of the
suffix, which is very common, is **–ion** (**–tion, –sion**): *region,
oration, session.* It often has the force of the suffix *–ing.*

Exercise. — Give and define ten English words with the suffix **–ion**
derived from Latin verbs which you have studied.

407.   **Formation of Adverbs**

In English, adverbs are commonly formed from adjectives
by adding the suffix *–ly;* as, adj., *high,* adv., *highly;* adj.,
brave, adv., *bravely.*

In Latin, adverbs are likewise formed from adjectives.
Like adverbs in English, they can be compared but not declined.

(*a*) Adverbs are formed from adjectives of the first and second declensions, as a rule, by adding –**ē** to the base : adj., **altus**, adv., **altē** ; adj., **līber**, adv., **līberē**.

(*b*) Adverbs are formed from adjectives of the third declension, as a rule, by adding –**iter** to the base; as, adj., **fortis**, adv., **fortiter** ; adj., **ācer**, adv., **ācriter**.

408. The **comparison of adverbs** is similar to that of adjectives :

Positive	Comparative	Superlative
al'tē	al'tius	altis'simē
for'titer	for'tius	fortis'simē

Note that the comparative adverb has the same form as the neuter accusative singular of the comparative adjective.

409. Drill. — Form and compare adverbs from the following adjectives already studied :

longus, ūtilis, clārus, levis, firmus, gravis, vērus

410. **Exercises**

Oral. 1. Sciō hoc flūmen esse longius quam illud. 2. Gentēs Galliae celerius vincī poterant, quod nātūrā locī continēbantur. 3. Nostrī fortissimē pugnāvērunt sed ab hostibus repulsī sunt. 4. Pater meus omnia iūstē et celeriter iūdicat; nam nēmō est iūstior quam ille. 5. Hī mīlitēs, ē castrīs ēductī, ad proelium ā duce īnstruuntur. 6. Cūr hae gentēs aliās regiōnēs partēsque Galliae perpetuē petunt? 7. Puerī magistrō librum dedērunt et ille ōrātiōne aptā respondit.

Written. 1. We certainly hope that peace has been established among all nations. 2. We shall drive the enemy back, because our men fight more bravely. 3. No one approves a very long speech. 4. The battle was sharply fought, but few men received severe wounds.

LESSON LXXII

COMPARISON OF ADJECTIVES ENDING IN *-ER* AND *-LIS*. DATIVE WITH ADJECTIVES

411.   Vocabulary

ca′dŏ, –ere, ce′cidī, cā′sus, *fall*   (casualty)
 ac′cidŏ, –ere, ac′cidī, ——, *fall to, befall, happen* (with dat.)
diffi′cilis, –e, *difficult*   [*facilis*]
ex′plicō, –ā′re, –ā′vī, –ā′tus, *unfold, spread out, explain*   [*plicō*]
hu′milis, –e, *low, humble*   (humility)
pro′prius, –a, –um, *one's own, fitting*   (propriety)
si′milis, –e, *like*   (similarity)
 dissi′milis, –e, *unlike*

412.   Comparison of *-er* Adjectives

All adjectives ending in **–er** form the superlative by adding **–rimus, –a, –um** to the nominative singular masculine of the positive:

POSITIVE	COMPARATIVE	SUPERLATIVE
crē′ber, crē′bra, crē′brum	crē′brior, crē′brius	crēber′rimus, –a, –um
lĭ′ber, lĭ′bera, lĭ′berum	lībe′rior, lībe′rius	līber′rimus, –a, –um
ā′cer, ā′cris, ā′cre	ā′crior, ā′crius	ācer′rimus, –a, –um

413. Drill. — Compare **sacer, celer, pulcher, firmus, altus.**

414. Five Adjectives with Superlative in *-limus*

The superlative degree of five adjectives ending in **–lis** is formed by adding **–limus, –a, –um** to the base of the positive:

fa'cilis, –e	faci'lior, faci'lius	facil'limus, –a, –um
diffi'cilis, –e	diffici'lior, diffici'lius	difficil'limus, –a, –um
si'milis, –e	simi'lior, simi'lius	simil'limus, –a, –um
dissi'milis, –e	dissimi'lior, dissimi'lius	dissimil'limus, –a, –um
hu'milis, –e	humi'lior, humi'lius	humil'limus, –a, –um

Note. — Other –lis adjectives, such as **nōbilis, –e, ūtilis, –e,** etc. form the superlative regularly — *i.e.* by adding –issimus, –a, –um to the base of the positive: **nōbil–is'simus, –a, –um.**

415. **Dative with Adjectives**

1. **Hic liber est similis illī,** *This book is similar to that.*
2. **Ille homō est frātrī meō inimīcus,** *That man is unfriendly to my brother.*

Observe that the dative is often used with Latin adjectives whose English equivalents are followed by *to* (for rule, see **593, 2**).

416. **Exercises**

Oral. 1. Nihil est ūtilius quam bonus liber; nam est nōbilissimus amīcōrum, semper firmus et vērus. 2. Humilis homō nec altē cadere nec graviter potest. 3. Rōmānōrum deī dissimillimī nostrō Deō erant. 4. Hic equus similior meō est quam ille. 5. Cūr capis id quod nōn tuum proprium est? 6. Mīlitēs iussī sunt explicāre ōrdinēs, sed id erat difficillimum ob parvum spatium. 7. Quid sorōrī tuae accidit? Cūr nōn vēnit cum reliquīs?

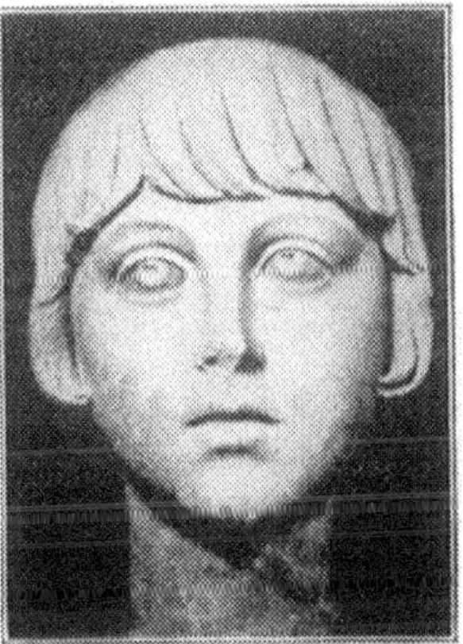

FIG. 81. PUELLA RŌMĀNA

Written. 1. Not all the neighboring nations were friendly to the Romans. 2. The teacher in a very beautiful speech unfolded the life of Caesar. 3. As our men approached, the enemy fought more bravely. 4. The places in which our soldiers fell are the most sacred in Gaul. 5. This region is fit for (to) some men, but not for others.

417. **Legal Phrases in English**

Lawyers use so many Latin phrases daily that they must be familiar with Latin. A few such phrases are:

subpoenā, a summons to court *under penalty* for failure to attend.

ex post factō, *resulting after the fact; e.g.* a law which makes punishable acts committed before its passage.

in fōrmā pauperis, *in the form* (or *manner*) *of a poor man;* to sue as a poor man and so avoid the costs of the suit.

in propriā persōnā, *in one's own person* (not through someone else).

Exercise. — Look through the court records and legal items in the newspapers for other Latin phrases.

FIG. 82. THEATER OF POMPEY, ROME

As some of the Romans had a prejudice against theaters, Pompey built a temple of Venus and a theater together, so arranged that the seats of the theater served as steps leading to the temple. Both have now disappeared.

LESSON LXXIII

COMPARISON OF IRREGULAR ADJECTIVES AND ADVERBS

418. **Vocabulary**

extrē'mus, –a, –um, *farthest, last, end of*	(extremist)
īnfe'rior, īnfe'rius, *lower*	(inferiority)
pro'ximus, –a, –um, *nearest, next* (with dat.)	(proximity)
sum'mus, –a, –um, *highest, top of*	(summit)
ulte'rior, ulte'rius, *farther;* ul'timus, –a, –um, *farthest*	(ultimate)

419. **Irregular Adjectives Compared**

In English, certain adjectives in common use are compared irregularly, such as *good, better, best; bad, worse, worst.*

In Latin, the following adjectives, among others, are compared irregularly and should be memorized:

POSITIVE	COMPARATIVE	SUPERLATIVE
bonus, –a, –um (*good*)	melior, melius (*better*)	optimus, –a, –um (*best*)
malus, –a, –um (*bad*)	peior, peius (*worse*)	pessimus, –a, –um (*worst*)
magnus, –a, –um (*large*)	maior, maius (*larger*)	maximus, –a, –um (*largest*)
parvus, –a, –um (*small*)	minor, minus (*smaller*)	minimus, –a, –um (*smallest*)
multus, –a, –um (*much*)	——; plūs [1] (*more*)	plūrimus, –a, –um (*most*)

Exercise. — Find English derivatives of the above words.

420. **Irregular Adverbs Compared**

Adverbs formed from the above adjectives are compared, in general, according to the rule (**407**); irregularities not explained by reference to the corresponding adjective forms are underscored and should be noted carefully:

---

[1] Gen. **plūris**; there is no masculine and feminine singular, and no dative in any gender; the plural is **plūrēs**, **plūra**, gen., **plūrium**, etc. See **651.**

Positive	Comparative	Superlative
bĕnĕ (*well*)	**melius** (*better*)	**optimē** (*best*)
malĕ (*badly*)	**peius** (*worse*)	**pessimē** (*worst*)
——	**magis** (*more*)	**maximē** (*most*)
——	**minus** (*less*)	**minimē** (*least*)
multum (*much*)	**plūs** (*more*)	**plūrimum** (*most*)

Note.—Certain other irregular adjectives and adverbs occur less frequently in the comparative and superlative forms and have accordingly been omitted from the list to be memorized. A few will be introduced as vocabulary words in the form in which they most frequently occur.

421. Extrēmus and Summus.—In English, it is necessary to employ nouns to translate adjectives like **extrēmus** and **summus**: **in extrēmā ōrātiōne**, *at the end of the speech;* **summus mōns**, *top of the mountain* (cf. **reliquī mīlitēs**, *rest of the soldiers;* **in mediō flūmine**, *in the middle of the river*). When thus used the adjective commonly precedes its noun.

422. **Exercises**

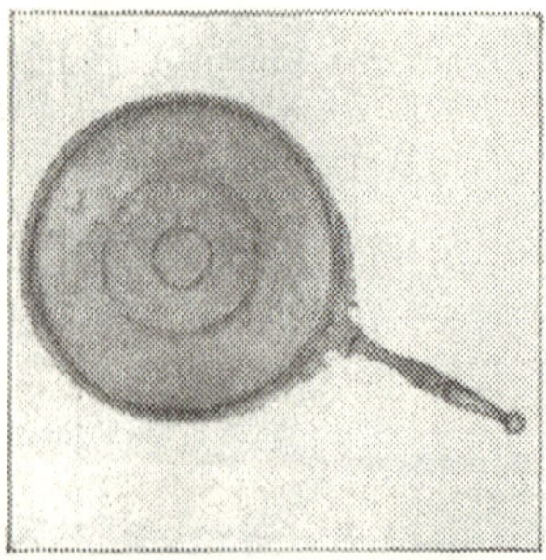

Fig. 83. A Roman Mirror

Mirrors were made of silver and other polished metals.

Oral. 1. Nōnne spērās proximam hiemem nōn futūram esse dūriōrem quam hanc? 2. Optimī cīvēs patriam semper fortissimē dēfendent. 3. Pessimī hominēs in ultimās regiōnēs mittī dēbent. 4. Rōmānī ad īnferiōrem partem flūminis ab extrēmīs Galliae fīnibus iter facient. 5. Summus mōns ā nostrīs facillimē occupātus est. 6. Hostēs magis territī sunt quod Rōmānōs cum maximā celeritāte ad castra prōcessūrōs esse putāvērunt. 7. Rōmānī cum maiōre salūte pugnābant quod plūrimī eōrum meliōra arma quam Gallī habēbant.

Written. 1. He said that boys and girls ought to read the best books. 2. Can a horse run more swiftly than a man? 3. We shall do this very quickly and well. 4. Our men fought more bravely than the enemy. 5. The smallest boy is not always the worst.

423. **English Word Studies**

A number of English words preserve the forms of the comparative and superlative of Latin irregular adjectives : *major* (cf. *mayor*), *maximum, minor, minus, minimum, plus, nonplus, inferior, superior, ulterior, prior, anterior, posterior, interior, exterior, junior, senior.*

424. A "Pyrrhic Victory"

Pyrrhus, rēx Epīrī, ā Tarentīnīs in Italiam vocātus est, quī eō tempore cum Rōmānīs pugnābant. Is ad Italiam vēnit et elephantōrum auxiliō vīcit, quod Rōmānī elephantōs nōn anteā vīsōs timuērunt. Sed multī Pyrrhī mīlitēs interfectī sunt. Pyrrhus, ubi omnia corpora Rōmānōrum interfectōrum vulnera in fronte habēre vīdit, haec verba fēcit: "Cum tālibus (*such*) mīlitibus tōtum orbem (*earth*) vincere possum!" Amīcīs dē victōriā agentibus dīxit :

Fig. 84. Pyrrhus

"Sī iterum eōdem modō vīcerō, nūllōs mīlitēs in Ēpīrum redūcam."

SUBJUNCTIVE MOOD: PRESENT TENSE OF THE SECOND, THIRD, AND FOURTH CONJUGATIONS

425.   Vocabulary

crūdē′lis, −e, *cruel*   (cruelty)
dam′nō, −ā′re, −ā′vī, −ā′tus, *condemn*   (condemnation)
exstin′guō, −ere, −stīn′xī, −stīnc′tus, *extinguish, destroy* [**stinguō**, *put out*]
fal′lō, −ere, fefel′lī, fal′sus, *deceive*   (fallacy)
lū′men, lū′minis, n., *light*   (luminous)
nē, conj., *not, that not, lest* (with subjunctive)
prehen′dō, −ere, −hen′dī, −hēn′sus, *grasp, take hold of*   (comprehension)
tri′buō, −ere, tri′buī, tribū′tus, *bestow, grant*   (contribute)

426.   Use of the Subjunctive

Thus far every sentence in this book has either stated a fact or asked a question, and the indicative mood has been used. We shall now study sentences which do not state facts but have **modal** force. In English, various auxiliaries, such as *let, may, might, should,* are used to express this force, just as other auxiliaries are used to indicate tense. Yet occasionally we use a separate verb form, called the **subjunctive**; *e.g.* we may say, *If this **be** true* (subjunctive), or *If this **should be** true* (auxiliary). At one time English had a complete set of subjunctive forms, but the subjunctive is now little used. We still prefer, however, to say, *If this **were*** (subjunctive) *true, my friend would not come here any more,* instead of *If this **was*** (indicative) *true, my friend would not come here any more.*

In Latin, the subjunctive is freely used to express modal ideas and even, under certain conditions, to state facts. It is differentiated from the indicative by its signs, which are added to the various stems.

427.   **Present Tense**

The mood sign of the **present subjunctive** in the second, third, and fourth conjugations is –ā–. This is added directly to the present stem, with the resultant loss of the short stem vowel (ĕ) of the third conjugation and the shortening of the long stem vowels of the second and fourth.[1] The subjunctive has the same personal endings as the indicative. Learn the present subjunctive of the following model verbs:

ACTIVE		PASSIVE	
ha'be**am** [2]	habeā'**mus**	ha'be**ar**	habeā'**mur**
ha'be**ās**	habeā'**tis**	habeā'**ris**	habeā'**minī**
ha'be**at**	ha'be**ant**	habeā'**tur**	habe**an'tur**

pōn–
capi– } {
mūni– }

ACTIVE
–**am**, –**ās**, –**at**; –ā'**mus**, –ā'**tis**, –**ant**

PASSIVE
–**ar**, –ā'**ris**, –ā'**tur**; –ā'**mur**, –ā'**minī**, –**an'tur**

Note. — The verb **ferō** (**395**) is regular in the subjunctive.

428. Drill. — Form the present subjunctive, active and passive, of **teneō**, **agō**, **ferō**, **efficiō**, and **sentiō**.

429.   **Volitive Subjunctive**

Patriam dēfendimus, *We are defending the country.*
Patriam dēfendāmus, *Let us defend the country.*
Patriam nōn dēfendit, *He is not defending the country.*
Patriam nē dēfendat, *Let him not defend the country.*

Observe (*a*) that we translate the subjunctive by *let;* (*b*) that the mood idea is that of *will,* hence called **volitive** (Latin **volō**, *I will*); (*c*) that the negative is **nē**.

---

[1] A vowel before another vowel is short (**608**).

[2] The translation of subjunctive forms varies with the use and must be determined by the context.

430.   **Exercises**

Oral.   1. Lūmen exstinguāmus et excēdāmus.   2. Audi-
ātur etiam altera pars.   3. Semper optimōs ūtilissimōsque
librōs retineāmus.   4. Ubi nunc crūdēlissimus rēx, ab
omnibus populīs damnātus, habitat?   5. Hic homō, ā
vigiliīs prehēnsus, ad supplicium quod meret rapiātur.
6. Mūnera pessimīs hominibus nē tribuāmus.   7. Sī pecūniam meam neutrī illōrum hominum mandābō, nōn fallar.

Written.   1. Let us not be deceived by the opinions of
others.   2. Why don't you go-away?   Why do you stick
in the same place?   3. Let the condemned men be sent
across the sea.   4. Let us realize that men of all kinds live
on this earth.   5. After spending nine years in leisure,
you ought to think more about your duties.

431.   **Phrases and Quotations**

nē plūs ultrā, *nothing more beyond* (i.e. *nothing finer*).
Stet, *Let it stand* (printers' term).
In hōc signō vincēs, *In this sign you will conquer* (motto of the first
Christian emperor, Constantine).
Labor omnia vincit, *Work overcomes everything* (Virgil).
ad maiōrem Deī glōriam, *to the greater glory of God.*
Spērō meliōra, *I hope for better things.*
ē plūribus ūnum, *one from many* (find this on a U. S. coin).

FIG. 85. A COIN OF THE EMPEROR AUGUSTUS (27 B.C.–14 A.D.)

LESSON LXXV

PURPOSE CLAUSES WITH *UT* AND *NĒ*

432.   Vocabulary

aes'timō, –ā're, –ā'vī, –ā'tus, *estimate, value* (in
  money)   [**aes**, *bronze, money*]
*ars, ar'tis, f., *skill, art*   (artistic)
cōnspi'ciō, –ere, –spe'xī, –spec'tus, *catch sight of, see*   [**speciō**, *look*]
e'mō, –ere, ē'mī, ēmp'tus, *get, buy*
  red'imō, –ere, redē'mī, redēmp'tus, *buy back, ransom*   (redemption)
flu'ō, –ere, flū'xī, flū'xus, *flow*   (fluency)
in'cidō, –ere, in'cidī, ——, *fall into* or *upon, happen*   [**cadō**]
pen'dō, –ere, pepen'dī, pēn'sus, *hang, weigh, pay*   (pendant)
ut, conj., *in order that, that, so that*

433.   Purpose Clauses

Venīmus ut videāmus, *We come that we may see,* or *We come to see.*
Fugit nē videātur, *He flees that he may not be seen.*

Observe that (*a*) the subordinate verbs **videāmus** and **videātur** express the purpose of the preceding acts;

(*b*) the conjunction **ut** introduces the positive clause and **nē** the negative;

(*c*) *in English* the more common way of expressing purpose is by use of the *infinitive*, which is *never so used in Latin prose writers.*

434. Rule. — *The subjunctive is used in a subordinate clause with **ut** (negative **nē**) to express the purpose of the act in the principal clause.*

435.   Exercises

Oral. 1. Hunc ūtilissimum librum emam ut semper teneam. 2. Magister docuit lībertātem esse mātrem artium omnium. 3. Crūdēlī dominō magnam pecūniam pendam ut hunc humilem servum redimam. 4. Reliquī mīlitēs ācrius pugnāvērunt quod nostrās cōpiās in summō monte cōnspexerant.   5. Hunc equum minōre pecūniā ēmī quam aestimāveram.   6. Hoc nunc facimus nē ab aliīs posteā impediāmur.   7. Per illam terram fluunt decem flūmina quae in mare incidunt.

(**Caution**. — *Think of the meaning of every infinitive before you translate.*)

Written.   1. He will send money to pay for (**prō**) the books.   2. Do you think it is better to be thrown into the river than to fall-in?   3. He labors swiftly and with much skill to complete the work.   4. We ought to come-together and consult that we may not be surprised by the enemy. 5. From the-top-of the mountain I caught-sight-of a very beautiful river, which flowed into the sea.

436.   Latin Abbreviations Used in English

etc., et cētera, *and the rest, and so forth.*
et al., et aliī, *and others;* or **et alibī,** *and elsewhere.*
s. v., sub vōce, *under the word* (*e.g.* "Look *s.v.* . . . in the dictionary").
ult., ultimō mēnse, *last month* (*e.g.* " the 26th ult.").
prox., proximō mēnse, *next month.*

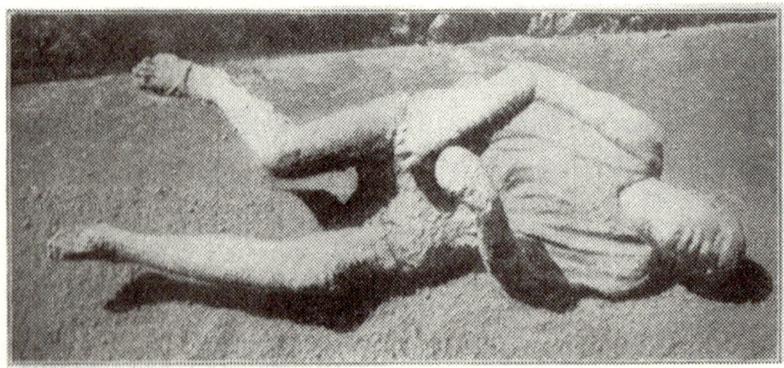

FIG. 86. CAST OF A SLAVE AT POMPEII

The slave was guarding his master's treasures when suffocated by the ashes (cf. Fig. 18). As the body decayed the ashes formed a perfect mold which the excavators filled with plaster.

LESSON LXXVI

SUBJUNCTIVE: PRESENT TENSE OF THE FIRST CONJUGATION AND OF *SUM*. TENSE SEQUENCE

437. **Vocabulary**

a'lō, –ere, a'luī, a'litus, *feed, nourish*	[*altus*]
ascen'dō, –ere, ascen'dī, ascēn'sus, *climb up, ascend*	[*scandō, climb*]
com'pleō, –ē're, –plē'vī, –plē'tus, *fill up*	[*pleō, fill*]
cōnsti'tuō, –ere, –sti'tuī, –stitū'tus, *set up, establish, determine*	[*statuō*]
intel'legō, –ere, –lē'xī, –lēc'tus, *understand*	(intellect)
potes'tās, potestā'tis, f., *power, authority, chance*	[*possum*]
* tes'tis, tes'tis, m., *witness*	(testify)
vol'vō, –ere, vol'vī, volū'tus, *roll*	(revolution)

438. **Present Subjunctive : First Conjugation**

The mood sign of the present subjunctive in the first conjugation is –ē–, not –ā– as in the other conjugations. It could not be –ā– because there would be no difference in form between indicative and subjunctive.

	ACTIVE		PASSIVE	
	pa'rem	parē'mus	pa'rer	parē'mur
	pa'rēs	parē'tis	parē'ris	parē'minī
	pa'ret	pa'rent	parē'tur	paren'tur

439. Drill. — Give the present subjunctive, active and passive, of **spectō, rogō, timeō, volvō, iūdicō, sciō, ferō.**

440. **Present Subjunctive of *Sum***

sim	sī'mus
sīs	sī'tis
sit	sint

a. **Drill.** — Give the present subjunctive of **possum.**

441.　　　　　**Tense Sequence (Harmony)**

We have learned that the tense of a participle or an infinitive in English and Latin is determined by its time relation to the leading verb (**361, 384**). How the infinitive and indicative differ in tense has been shown in **383**. In English and Latin, the subordinate verbs in the indicative and subjunctive shift their tenses to match those of the main verb. Study the following examples:

1. *He **is said** to **be** at home.*
2. *He **was said** to **be** at home.*

But　　1. *They **say** that he **is** at home.*
2. *They **said** that he **was** at home.*

1. *He* { *studies* / *will study* / *has studied* } *that he **may learn**.*
2. *He **studied** that he **might** learn.*

442.　　　　　　**Exercises**

Oral.　　1. Haec omnia explicābimus ut omnēs intellegātis et parātī sītis.　　2. (Is) multōs timēre dēbet quem multī timent.　　3. Convenīmus ut testēs adhibeāmus et dē factīs pessimī hominis iūdicēmus.　　4. Permōtī potestāte auctōritāteque testis, minimā poenā pessimum hominem affēcērunt.　　5. Maximās nāvēs frūmentō complent ut id in Eurōpam trānsportent, ubi multī populī eō alentur. 6. Mīles, vulnere acceptō, pedēs regere nōn potuit et praeceps in mare volūtus est.[1]　　7. Ducēs convocātī dē perīculō cōnsulunt et nāvēs ascendere [2] cōnstituunt nē ab hostibus intercipiantur.

Written.　　1. I am sending him to find my brother. 2. We fight bravely so-as-not-to be conquered by the enemy.

---

[1] *Tumbled.*　　　　[2] What is the English idiom?

3. We shall come to look-at your new wagon.   4. We shall fill the wagon with grain to feed the horses.   5. If you will stop in the middle (of the) street, I shall climb into the wagon.

FIG. 87. PUERĪ ET PUELLAE LŪDUNT

On the left is a game of marbles — with apples for marbles. More often nuts were used. On the right is a game of handball.

443.   English Word Studies

In two earlier lessons (**126**, **128**) we saw how many English words are simply the base of a Latin noun, adjective, or verb, or the base plus silent –**e**. A great many such words are derived from the Latin words in this book. A few are *par, facile, prime, just, cede, part*. In the case of verbs, the base of the present indicative, present participle, or perfect participle, or of all three, may furnish an English word : *convene, convenient, convent; remove, remote; refer, relate.*

As previously noted, there are sometimes changes in the base, *e.g.* the dropping of one of two final consonants, as in *remit, expel*, and particularly the addition of a vowel to the main vowel of the word, as in the following (the added vowel is underscored) : *peace, mount, reign, remain. Contain, retain,* etc. are from the compounds of **teneō**. The compounds of *cede* are spelled in the same way as the simple verb (*accede, precede, concede, recede, intercede, secede*), except *proceed, succeed,* and *exceed.*

Exercise. — Find fifteen more words illustrating the above principles.

LESSON LXXVII

SUBJUNCTIVE: IMPERFECT OF THE FOUR CONJUGATIONS, *SUM*, *POSSUM*, AND *FERŌ*. SEQUENCE IN PURPOSE CLAUSES

444. Vocabulary

af'ferō, affer're, at'tulī, allā'tus, *bring* (*to* or *against*), *report*   [*ferō*]
benefi'cium, –ī, n., *kindness*   [*bene* + *faciō*]
con'trahō, –ere, –trā'xī, –trāc'tus, *draw* or *bring together*,
   contract   [*trahō*]
crī'men, crī'minis, n., *charge*   [*cernō*]
dēpō'nō, –ere, –po'suī, –po'situs, *put* or *lay aside*   [*pōnō*]
fun'dō, –ere, fū'dī, fū'sus, *pour, rout, scatter*   (confusion)
īnsig'nis, –e, *remarkable, notable*   [*signum*]
vir'tūs, virtū'tis, f., *manliness, courage*   [*vir*]

445. Word Formation

Certain Latin suffixes had such broad or weakened meanings that their chief value consisted in furnishing means for forming new words. It is helpful to be familiar with them so as to be able to recognize the roots to which they are attached. They have no further value in English. Examples are:

-men: **lū-men, flū-men** (fluō), **nŏ-men** (nōscō), **volū-men** (volvō), **ag-men** (agō)
-ium: **iūdic-ium, cōnsil-ium** (cōnsulō), **benefic-ium**
-tūs: **vir-tūs**

446. Imperfect Subjunctive

The imperfect subjunctive of verbs of all conjugations, regular and irregular, may be readily obtained by adding the personal endings to the present active infinitive, as follows:

<table>
<tr><td colspan="2" align="center">ACTIVE</td><td colspan="2" align="center">PASSIVE</td></tr>
<tr><td>parā'rem</td><td>parārē'mus</td><td>parā'rer</td><td>parārē'mur</td></tr>
<tr><td>parā'rēs</td><td>parārē'tis</td><td>parārē'ris</td><td>parārē'minī</td></tr>
<tr><td>parā'ret</td><td>parā'rent</td><td>parārē'tur</td><td>parāren'tur</td></tr>
</table>

Similarly **habērem, habērer; pōnerem, pōnerer; caperem, caperer; mūnīrem, mūnīrer; essem; possem; ferrem, ferrer.**

447. Tense Sequence (Harmony) in Purpose Clauses

There are no future tenses in the subjunctive. To remedy this defect, the present and imperfect tenses, in addition to their regular uses, have a future force. In dependent purpose clauses the *present* subjunctive is used when the main verb is *present* or *future;* the *imperfect* subjunctive is used when the main verb is *past* (*i.e.* imperfect, perfect, or past perfect) ; *e.g.*

1. **Venīmus ut videāmus,** *We come that we may see.*
2. **Vēnimus ut vidērēmus,** *We came that we might see.*

448. Exercises

Oral. 1. Vēra potestās sōlā virtūte emitur. 2. Omnēs nāvēs ē fīnitimīs regiōnibus in ūnum locum coāctae contrāctaeque sunt ut parātae essent. 3. Quō modō poterimus dēpōnere memoriam illīus crūdēlis bellī? 4. Hoc crīmen in (*against*) amīcum vestrum allātum est ut poenam prō malīs factīs penderet. 5. Ubi nūntiātum est ēgregium auctōrem pervēnisse, labōrem intermīsimus ut ōrātiōnem eius audīrēmus. 6. Fundere aquam in flūmen nōn ūtilius est quam portāre māteriam in silvam. 7. Multa īnsignia beneficia ab eōdem amīcō accēpī, sed nūllum maius est quam hoc ultimum. 8. Frātrī meō pecūniam mīsī ut librōs novōs emere posset. 9. Ob maximam virtūtem et īnsignem artem hic vir plūrima praemia accēpit.

Written.   1. After the enemy had been routed, the general led his soldiers back to camp.   2. After a severe winter we can expect a similar summer.   3. We sent a messenger to intercept our friend and to show him the way.   4. What is more pleasing than to lay-aside cares?   5. The leaders of many nations assembled to prevent war and enforce (**cōnfirmō**) peace.

449.   PYRRHUS AND FABRICIUS

Lēgātī Rōmānī ad Pyrrhum missī sunt ut captīvōs redimerent et ab eō bene acceptī sunt.   Ūnus ex lēgātīs Rōmānōrum, Fabricius, Pyrrhō maximē grātus erat.   Eī Pyrrhus sēcrētō dīxit: " Cūr nōn in Ēpīrō manēs?   Quārtam rēgnī meī partem tibi (*to you*) dabō."   Sed contemptus[1] est ā Fabriciō.   Proximō annō Fabricius missus est ut cum Pyrrhō pugnāret.   Medicus rēgis nocte ad eum vēnit et prōmīsit sē (*he*) prō praemiō Pyrrhum interfectūrum esse.   Fabricius iussit hunc ligātum redūcī ad dominum et Pyrrhō omnia dīcī.   Tum rēx maximē mōtus dīxit: " Ille est Fabricius, quī nōn facilius ab honestāte quam sōl ā cursū suō āvertī potest! "

FIG. 88. A SHOP IN POMPEII AS IT IS

---

[1] Cf. **contemnō.**

LESSON LXXVIII

PERSONAL AND REFLEXIVE PRONOUNS.
POSSESSIVE ADJECTIVES

ELEMENTARY GRAMMAR: Review *Personal pronouns,* **615,** *a;* *Possessive adjectives,* **616,** *b,* 3.

450. Vocabulary

cae′dō, −ere, cecī′dī, cae′sus, *cut, kill*	(incision)
con′trā, adv. and prep. with acc., *against*	
crē′dō, −ere, crē′didī, crē′ditus, *believe, intrust* (with dat.)	(credit)
cre′ō, –ā′re, –ā′vī, –ā′tus, *create, elect*	(creative)
gubernā′tor, gubernātō′ris, m., *pilot, governor*	(government)
prae, prep. with abl., *before, in front of*	
sū′mō, −ere, sūmp′sī, sūmp′tus, *take, assume*	(assumption)
tem′perō, –ā′re, –ā′vī, –ā′tus, *regulate, refrain from* (with **ab**)	(temperance)

FIG. 89. A Shop in Pompeii as It Was

Like Fig. 88, this shows a place for the sale of food and drink.

451.   How Personal Pronouns Are Used

In English, personal pronouns are used to indicate the person of the verb: *I* am, *you* are. In Latin, as we have seen (**20**), personal endings perform this function. When, however, emphasis or sharp contrast in subjects is desired, the Latin employs the personal pronouns **ego** (*I*) and **tū** (*you*). We have already seen that **is, ea, id** serves as the personal pronoun of the third person (*he, she, it*). Review **is** (**341**) and memorize the declensions of **ego** and **tū**:

	SINGULAR	PLURAL
Nom.	**e′go**, *I*	**nōs**, *we*
Gen.	**me′ī**, *of me*	**nos′trum**, *of us*
Dat.	**mi′hi**, *to (for) me*	**nō′bīs**, *to (for) us*
Acc.	**mē**, *me*	**nōs**, *us*
Abl.	**mē**, *with (from, etc.) me*	**nō′bīs**, *with (from, etc.) us*

	SINGULAR	PLURAL
Nom.	**tū**, *you*	**vōs**, *you*
Gen.	**tu′ī**, *of you*	**ves′trum**, *of you*
Dat.	**ti′bi**, *to (for) you*	**vō′bīs**, *to (for) you*
Acc.	**tē**, *you*	**vōs**, *you*
Abl.	**tē**, *with (from, etc.) you*	**vō′bīs**, *with (from, etc.) you*

452.   Reflexive Pronouns

In English, the pronouns *myself*, *ourselves*, etc. may be used in apposition with a noun or pronoun for emphasis, like Latin **ipse** (**352**): **I saw him** *myself*, *Ipse* **eum vīdī**. They are also used alone as objects of verbs or of prepositions to refer to the subject of the verb; they are then called **re-flexive pronouns**: *I saw* **myself**.

In Latin, the personal pronouns of the first and second persons may be used reflexively, but in the third person

Latin has a special reflexive pronoun, **suī**, declined alike in the singular and plural:

Gen. **su'ī,**		*of himself, herself, itself, themselves*			
Dat. **si'bi,**	*to*	"	"	"	"
Acc. **sē (sē'sē),**		"	"	"	"
Abl. **sē (sē'sē),** *with (from, etc.)*	"	"	"	"

Query. — Why is **suī** without a nominative?

453.   How Reflexive Pronouns Are Used

(ego) mē rogō, *I ask myself*	**(nōs) nōs rogāmus,** *we ask ourselves*
(tū) tē rogās, *you ask yourself*	**(vōs) vōs rogātis,** *you ask yourselves*
(is) sē rogat, *he asks himself*	**(eī) sē rogant,** *they ask themselves*

454. Drill. — Give a synopsis with the reflexive of **damnō**, 1st sing.; **fallō**, 2nd plur.; **caedō**, 3rd sing.

455.   Possessive Adjectives

From the base of **ego (me–)**, **nōs (nostr–)**, **tū (tu–)**, and **vōs (vestr–)**, the possessive adjectives **meus, noster, tuus,** and **vester** are derived.

In place of a possessive adjective of the third person, the genitives of **is (eius** and **eōrum)** are used, as we have seen **(342).**

From **suī** we get the reflexive adjective **suus, –a, –um,** *his own,* etc., which *always refers to the subject of the verb.*

The possessive adjectives follow the noun except when emphatic.

Caution. — Never use the genitives **meī, tuī, nostrum, vestrum,** and **suī** to show possession; use the corresponding possessive adjectives **meus, tuus, noster, vester,** and **suus.**

Query. — What is the difference between **tuus** and **vester**?

456. Rapid-fire Drill. — *Translate:* my books, your books, his books; to our book, to your book, to their book; with his own book, with my book, with her book.

457. **Exercises**

Oral. 1. Captīvus sē suaque omnia mihi crēdidit. 2. Mīlitēs quī prae sē equōs agēbant, hostibus vīsīs, cōnstitērunt. 3. Gubernātor, sedēns in nāvī, eius celeritātem temperat et posteā eam ad terram vertet. 4. Crēditisne Deum mare terramque prō sē aut prō nōbīs creāvisse? 5. Videō tē eum cecīdisse; quō modō hoc fēcistī? 6. Arma sūmpsimus ut nōs dēfenderēmus contrā crūdēlissimōs hostēs. 7. Ego, quī sum puer, sum fortior quam tū, quae es puella; sed tū pulchrior es quam ego.

Written. 1. Do you believe that either he or I took your money? 2. If he kills (*future*) himself, I shall throw myself into the river. 3. I know that he has four brothers because I saw them myself. 4. If you will refrain from injury, we also shall abandon our hostile plans. 5. The general himself sent the prisoners before him one-by-one to prevent danger.

458. **Latin Phrases in English**

alter ego, " another I," *a second self*, a dear friend.
inter nōs, *between us.*
Et tū, Brūte, *You too, Brutus !* (said by Caesar on receiving the death-blow from his friend, Brutus).
Tē Deum, *Thee, God* (*we praise*); the name of a hymn.
Pāx vōbīscum, *Peace* (be) *with you !*
per sē, *by itself.*
suī generis, *of its own kind,* i.e. *unique.*

FIG. 90. "ET TŪ, BRŪTE"

Caesar's murder in the Senate, 44 B.C. (From "Julius Caesar.")

REVIEW

459. Indirect Statement: General Review

1. The following verbs, already studied, are used to introduce indirect statements. Review their meanings and quote the rule (see **378**):

cōnfirmō, iūdicō, nūntiō, putō, spērō; memoriā teneō, respondeō, videō; cognōscō, crēdō, dīcō, intellegō, scrībō; audiō, inveniō, referō, sciō, sentiō.

Summary

In Latin	In English
(a) No conjunction is used.	(a) "That" is regularly used.
(b) The subject is in the accusative.	(b) The subject is in the nominative.
(c) The verb is in the infinitive.	(c) The verb is in the indicative.

460. Noun and Adjective Review

1. Decline in the singular: **nūlla ars**; **tōta regiō**; **ūnum beneficium**; **alia potestās**; **sōlum opus**; **neuter socius**.

2. Decline in the plural: **ūtilior liber**; **certius lūmen**; **melior testis**; **aptissima ōrātiō**; **maxima gēns**; **crūdēlissimus prīnceps**.

Remember that all third declension adjectives are **i**–stems, *i.e.* they have **–ī** in the ablative singular, **–ia** in the neuter nominative and accusative plural, and **–ium** in the genitive plural. *The only exceptions are comparatives, none of which are i–stems.* Present participles are i–stems but have **–e** in the ablative singular when used as verbs, not adjectives.

461. Rapid-fire Drill. — *Give in Latin:*

(a) *more difficult* in the nom., sing. and plur.

(b) *most beautiful* in the gen., sing. and plur.

(c) *rather long* in the dat., sing. and plur.

(d) *very remarkable* in the acc., sing. and plur.

(e) *too cruel* in the abl., sing. and plur.

462. Verb Review

1. Conjugate **aestimō**, **respondeō**, **emō**, and **possum** in the present and imperfect subjunctive.

2. Give the principal parts of **cōnficiō**, **intellegō**, **dēferō**, **cōnstituō**, **contrahō**, **ascendō**, **fluō**, **repellō**, **pendō**, **dēfendō**, **exstinguō**.

463. Rapid-fire Drill

a. State **mood, tense**, and **voice** : cōnficiēmus, ferāmus, interficiunt, ligāns, respondēre, victus, raptūrus, iūdicārī, repellimur, cecidisse, plicābō, tribuēbant, volvunt, sūmpserat, creātus erit, dēpōnēminī, aestimāverō, flūxit, cōnspiceris, ascendentur.

b. **Give in Latin** : to cut, to have caught sight of, to be hung, to have been condemned, to be going to drive back, having been filled.

464. Vocabulary Review

Give the Latin words and their meanings, together with genitive and gender of nouns, principal parts of verbs, etc., suggested by the following English derivatives :

accident, appropriate, artistic, complete, conditional, conference, conspicuous, credible, damnation, deposit, extinct, fallacious, gubernatorial, implicate, incisor, instructive, ligature, opera, prehensile, profuse, proximity, rapture, regional, redemptive, repulsive, revolve, tribute, victor, virtuous.

465. English Word Studies

Find and use in sentences as many English derivatives as possible from **nāvigō**, **doceō**, **timeō**, **vincō**, **sūmō**.

Enter the derivatives in your notebook, using a separate page for each Latin word.

466.   THE STORY OF LUCIUS (*Cont.*)

Caesaris Triumphus

Quondam pater Lūcī ā Forō revertit et dīxit triumphum Caesaris futūrum esse et posteā magnōs lūdōs.   C.[1] Iūlius

FIG. 91. C. IŪLIUS CAESAR

Caesar tum erat maximus Rōmānōrum.   Galliam, Alexandrīam, Pontum, Āfricam vīcerat.   Decem annōs in Galliā ēgerat et, multīs gentibus pulsīs, illam terram in prōvinciam Rōmānam redēgerat.   Pompeius, cum Caesare prō summā potestāte contendēns, in fugam datus erat.   Tum Caesar in Aegyptum prōcesserat et, Alexandrīnīs fūsīs, Cleopātrae nōmen rēgīnae Aegyptiōrum dederat.   In Asiā rēgem Pontī celeriter vīcerat et dē eius rēgnō nōtās illās litterās mīserat in quibus erant sōla verba, "Vēnī, vīdī, vīcī."   Nunc futūrī erant quattuor triumphī, quod Caesar dē bellīs reverterat.

WAITING

Lūcius numquam triumphum vīderat et dē eō multa rogāvit.   Pater eī dīxit triumphum esse similem pompae in Circō habitae et Caesarem per Circum et Sacram Viam prōcessūrum esse et Capitōlium ascēnsūrum.   Lūcius permōtus vix exspectāre poterat.   Sed omnia ad eum quī exspectat veniunt; tempus triumphōrum aderat.   Prīmus et īnsignissimus triumphus quem Caesar ēgit erat Gallicus. Pater Lūcī cognātus Caesaris erat et optima loca obtinuit. Ubi Caesar in Campō Mārtiō mīlitēs īnstrūxit et ex praedā collātā eīs praemia tribuit, pompa tardē prōcēdere incipit.

---

[1] C. = Gāius.

"Here They Come!"

Post longum tempus (ut Lūciō vīsum est) pompa aderat. Prīmī fuērunt cōnsulēs et senātōrēs, post quōs vēnērunt cornicinēs, quī Lūciō grātissimī fuērunt. Tum cōnspexit titulōs[1] ducum oppidōrumque captōrum cum fōrmīs exemplīsque[2] oppidōrum. Dē nōminibus nōn nōtīs multa rogāvit:

Fig. 92. Triumphus Caesaris

Caesar sits on top of the float. Note the **titulī**. (From "Julius Caesar.")

"Quī sunt Aquītānī? Quī sunt Belgae?" Pater respondit: "Gallia est omnis dīvīsa[3] in partēs trēs; quārum ūnam incolunt Belgae, aliam Aquītānī, tertiam eī quī ipsōrum linguā Celtae, nostrā Gallī appellantur. Hōrum omnium fortissimī sunt Belgae." "Quī sunt Helvētiī?" "Helvētiī cōnstituērunt per prōvinciam nostram iter facere ut maiōrēs fīnēs habērent, sed ā Caesare prohibitī sunt." "Quis est Ariovistus?" "Ariovistus erat superbus crūdēlisque rēx Germānōrum, ā Caesare ex Galliā expulsus." "Quī sunt

---

[1] *Placards* (with names of towns, etc.).   [2] *Models* (of wood, etc.).
[3] From **dīvidō**. Use derivative.

Germānī?" "Maxima pars Germānōrum trāns Rhēnum flūmen incolunt. Etiam trāns Rhēnum Caesar mīlitēs suōs trādūxit ut cum eīs contenderet." "Quid est Britannia?" "Britannia est ultima īnsula, ā barbarīs culta, in quam Caesar cōpiās bis dūxit."

Hail! The Conquering Hero Comes!

Posteā Lūcius cōnspexit arma captōrum prīncipum et prīncipēs ipsōs ligātōs, inter quōs erat Vercingetorīx. Nunc populus maximē clāmat. "Quis est ille?" rogat Lūcius. Pater respondet: "Ille est extrēmus dux Gallōrum, quī victōs Gallōs ad bellum permōvit. Pompā ad Capitōlium accēdente, interficiētur." Nunc clāmōrēs audiuntur: "Caesar adest! Caesar adest!" Currus imperātōris, quattuor equīs trāctus, cernitur. Caesar ipse togam pictam[1] gerit et scēptrum tenet. In currū[2] stat servus corōnam super Caesaris caput tenēns. Sed subitō omnēs terrentur: axe frāctō, Caesar paene ē currū ēicitur. Hic sōlus nōn commōtus est. Dum novum currum exspectat, Lūcium cōnspicit et eum rogat: "Tū, quis es?" Lūcius respondet: "Ego sum Lūcius Iūlius, cognātus tuus. Mīles erō et multās gentēs vincam." Caesar rīdēns eius caput tetigit et dīxit: "Bene incipis. Putō tē imperātōrem futūrum esse." Pompa rūrsus prōcēdit et nunc lēgātī et mīlitēs Caesaris accēdunt, clāmantēs, "Iō triumphe,[3] Iō triumphe!" Etiam carmina canunt. Inter alia Lūcius intellegere potest haec:
"Ecce Caesar nunc triumphat quī subēgit Galliās." Itaque omnēs discēdunt, Lūciō clāmante, "Iō triumphe! Iō triumphe!"

---

[1] *Embroidered* (with gold).   [2] Abl.   [3] Exclamation: *Triumph!*

FIG. 93. CAESAR AND VERCINGETORIX. (From "Julius Caesar.")

LESSON LXXX

RESULT CLAUSES WITH *UT* AND *UT NŌN*

467.   **Vocabulary**

clā′mor, clāmō′ris, m., *shout*   [*clāmō*]
i′ta, adv., *so, in such a way, thus*
* mors, mor′tis, f., *death*   (mortal)
perter′reō, –ē′re, –ter′ruī, –ter′ritus, *frighten thoroughly, alarm*   [*terreō*]
praemit′tō, –ere, –mī′sī, –mis′sus, *send ahead*   [*mittō*]
tan′tus, –a, –um, *so great*   (tantamount)
ti′mor, timō′ris, m., *fear*   [*timeō*]
trā′dō, –ere, trā′didī, trā′ditus, *give* or *hand over, deliver*   [*dō*]

468.   **Word Studies**

Prae, when used as a prefix, has its literal meaning *before, in front of:* **praedīcō**. In English it takes the form *pre-*, as *pre-pare, pre-fix*. **Contrā** likewise has its literal meaning when used as a prefix. In English it is found in the forms *contra-* and *counter-*, as *contra-dict, counter-act*.

Exercise. — Give ten other examples of each of these prefixes in English words.

The adverbs **bene** and **male** are used as prefixes in Latin and English, as in *bene-diction, male-factor*.

469.   **Result Clauses**

Tantum est perīculum ut paucī veniant, *So great is the danger that few are coming.*
Ita bene erant castra mūnīta ut nōn capī possent, *So well had the camp been fortified that it could not be taken.*

Observe that (*a*) the verbs of the subordinate clauses are in the subjunctive, and that they express the *result* of the state or act described in the main clause;

(*b*) the tense sequence, or harmony, is the same as in purpose clauses.

470. Rule. — *The result of the action of the principal verb is expressed by a subordinate clause with* **ut** (*negative* **ut nōn**) *and the subjunctive.*

471.　How Purpose and Result Clauses Differ

(*a*) Result clauses are usually anticipated by such words as **ita** and **tantus**, while purpose clauses are not.

(*b*) Negative result clauses are introduced by **ut nōn**, negative purpose clauses by **nē**.

(*c*) In English, result clauses require the indicative; purpose clauses employ the auxiliaries *may* and *might*.

472. Verbal Signboards. — Such words as **ita**, **tantus**, etc., in main clauses, used to point to subordinate clauses of result, are like signboards, which seem to say, " Stop, Look, Think!　A Result Clause Is Coming!"

473.　　　　Exercises

Oral.　1. Ita agere dēbēmus ut ab omnibus amēmur. 2. Puer malus ita pedēs suōs tetendit ut puerum alterum tangeret.　3. Tantus erat timor populī ut putāret omnēs hominēs esse suōs hostēs.　4. Hae litterae ita male ā tē scrīptae erant ut eās legere nōn possēmus.　5. Plūrimī mīlitēs praemissī sunt ut clāmōribus hostēs perterrērent. 6. Timor mortis est peior quam mors ipsa. 7. Servus crūdēlis dominō sē trādidit nē ā reliquīs servīs caederētur.

Written.　1. Our soldiers are so brave that they can not be conquered.　2. I sent a friend ahead to warn you about the danger.　3. So loud (great) were the shouts of the boys that we could not hear the famous man's speech.　4. The enemy's soldiers were so close-together that it was easy to kill them.　5. Fortune is so changing that we ought not to intrust everything to her.

ORDINAL NUMERALS. DECLENSION OF *DUO*, *TRĒS*, AND *MĪLLE*

474.   **Vocabulary**

cen'tum, indecl. adj., *hundred*	(centennial)
fran'gŏ, –ere, frĕ'gī, frăc'tus, *break*	(fraction)
perfi'ciŏ, –ere, –fē'cī, –fec'tus, *finish*	[*faciō*]
reser'vŏ, –ā're, –ā'vī, –ā'tus, *save up, reserve*	[*servō*]

475.   **Ordinal Numerals**

We have already learned the **cardinal** numbers used in counting from 1–10 (**272**). To show order or succession other numbers, called **ordinals** (*first, second,* etc.), are used. The Latin ordinals are declined like **magnus, –a, –um.** Memorize the first ten ordinals as follows[1]:

prī'mus, –a, –um, *first*	sex'tus, –a, –um, *sixth*
secun'dus, –a, –um, *second*	sep'timus, –a, –um, *seventh*
ter'tius, –a, –um, *third*	octā'vus, –a, –um, *eighth*
quăr'tus, –a, –um, *fourth*	nŏ'nus, –a, –um, *ninth*
quĭn'tus, –a, –um, *fifth*	de'cimus, –a, –um, *tenth*

a. **Drill.** — Suggest and define one English derivative from as many ordinals as possible.

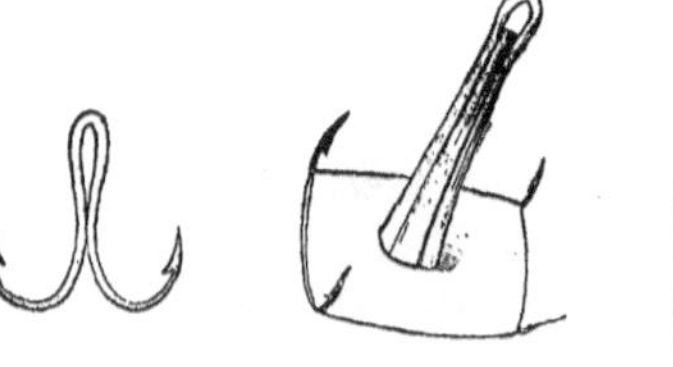

FIG. 94. ROMAN FISH HOOKS

---

[1] For complete list of cardinals and ordinals, see **653**.

476. Declension of *Duo* and *Trēs*

The cardinal numbers from 4 to 100 are indeclinable. We have seen, however, that **ūnus, –a, –um** is declined like **tōtus** (**355**, *b*). **Duo**, *two*, and **trēs**, *three*, are declined as follows:

	M.	F.	N.	M. AND F.	N.
Nom.	du′o	du′ae	du′o	trēs	tri′a
Gen.	duō′rum	duā′rum	duō′rum	tri′um	tri′um
Dat.	duō′bus	duā′bus	duō′bus	tri′bus	tri′bus
Acc.	du′ōs	du′ās	du′o	trēs	tri′a
Abl.	duō′bus	duā′bus	duō′bus	tri′bus	tri′bus

477. Declension and Use of *Mīlle*

Mīlle, when used to denote one thousand, is usually an indeclinable adjective (like **centum**): **mīlle hominēs**. When used of two or more thousands, it is a neuter plural **i**-stem noun (cf. **mare, 305**). The word used with the plural forms of **mīlle** must be in the genitive: **duo mīlia hominum** (lit., *two thousands **of** men*), *two thousand men*.

	SINGULAR	PLURAL
Nom.	mīl′le	mī′lia
Gen.	mīl′le	mī′lium
Dat.	mīl′le	mī′libus
Acc.	mīl′le	mī′lia
Abl.	mīl′le	mī′libus

478. Exercises

Ōral. 1. Nāvī frāctā, omnēs certē interficientur. 2. Duōs bonōs librōs reservābō ut eōs hāc aestāte legam. 3. Sī plūrimī puerī aut absunt aut tardī sunt, disciplīnam accipere nōn possunt; certō tempore adesse dēbent.

4. Dux mīlle nautās et trēs firmās nāvēs cum tribus gubernātōribus praemīsit ut hostēs interciperent.   5. Post septimam pugnam nōn iam vim hostium sustinēre poterāmus et eīs nōs trādidimus.   6. Properābāmus condiciōnēs pācis prōpōnere, sed hostēs centum mīlia mīlitum iam ēdūxerant.   7. Tertiō annō Bellī Magnī mīlitēs ad sociōs nostrōs ita celeriter mittere incēpimus, ut ante fīnem quīntī annī bellum perficerētur.

FIG. 95. PUELLA

Written.   1. All the sailors were saved, although two ships were lost.   2. Anna was fourth in rank but her brother was tenth.   3. Our men finished the march, although pressed-hard by the enemy.   4. The boundaries of two nations extend to the lower part of this river.   5. The price of these seven books is so great that I can not present them to you.

479.   English Word Studies

Much difficulty is caused in English spelling by silent or weakly sounded letters. This difficulty is often solved by referring to the Latin original: *laboratory, repetition, library, separate, auxiliary, comparative, debt, complement, reign, receipt.* The Latin original often helps in other difficulties: *consensus, annuity, deficit, accelerate.*

Exercise. — Define the above words and give their Latin originals.

Much confusion is caused in English by the combinations *ei* and *ie*. It will be helpful to remember that the derivatives of compounds of **capiō** have *ei*, as *receive.*

ACCUSATIVE OF EXTENT. WORDS OFTEN CONFUSED

480.   Vocabulary

ae′tās, aetā′tis, f., *age, time of life*	(eternal)
attin′gō, –ere, at′tigī, attāc′tus, *touch, reach*	[*tangō*]
distri′buō, –ere, –tri′buī, –tribū′tus, *distribute*	[*tribuō*]
exer′ceō, –ē′re, –er′cuī, –er′citus, *occupy, train*	(exercise)
exīs′timō, –ā′re, –ā′vī, –ā′tus, *think, consider*	[*aestimō*]
in′colō, –ere, –co′luī, –cul′tus, *dwell, inhabit*	[*colō*]
iun′gō, –ere, iūn′xī, iūnc′tus, *join to* (with dat. indir. obj.)	(junction)
strin′gō, –ere, strīn′xī, stric′tus, *draw tight, graze*	(strict)

481.   Accusative of Extent

Duōs annōs remānsit, *He remained two years.*
Flūmen decem pedēs altum est, *The river is ten feet deep.*

Observe that (*a*) **duōs annōs** answers the question, *How long?*
(*b*) **decem pedēs** answers the question, *How much?*
(*c*) both express *extent* by the accusative;
(*d*) the English and Latin constructions are identical and are not to be confused with the direct object.

482. Rule. — *Extent of time or space is expressed by the accusative.*

483.   Stop! Look! Think!

The following words, which have already been used, closely resemble one another in form or sound and must be carefully discriminated. For difference in meaning, see the Latin-English Vocabulary at the end of the book:

aetās, aestās	**gēns, genus**	**ob, ab**
accēdō, accidō	**ibi, ubi**	**pars, pār**
alius, alter, altus	**liber, līber, līberī**	**pōnō, possum**
caedō, cadō, cēdō	**nē, –ne**	**vīs, vir**
cīvis, cīvitās		

484. **Exercises**

Oral. 1. Exīstimō hunc montem esse mīlle pedēs altum, illud flūmen duōs pedēs altum. 2. Pater pecūniam ita distribuit ut omnēs suī līberī parēs partēs habērent. 3. Virī quibuscum[1] contendēbāmus sēsē ita bene dēfendēbant ut eōs commovēre nōn possēmus. 4. Illī hominēs multōs annōs ita in artibus bellī sē exercuērunt[2] ut nunc plūrimum valeant. 5. Ille vir tantam aetātem attigit[2] ut nōn iam vīrēs habeat nec bene vidēre possit. 6. Nāvis, undīs redācta, īnsulam strīnxit sed ā gubernātōre in altam aquam versa est. 7. Mīlia Germānōrum, quī trāns flūmen Rhēnum incoluerant, pāce factā, Rōmānīs sēsē iūnxērunt.

FIG. 96. CATAPULT

Roman artillery consisted in part of catapults which shot arrows. The power was derived from twisted strands of rawhide. (From a model made by a high school boy.)

Written. 1. My brother will arrive next year and remain with me the whole summer. 2. The letter had been folded with such great care that I did not unfold it. 3. The greater part of the winter we remain in town, but in summer we hasten to the fields. 4. Don't you think that the courage of these men is so great that they will not retreat? 5. Caesar waged war in Gaul for nine years in-such-a-way that all nations gave themselves up to him.

---

[1] **Cum** (*with*) becomes an enclitic (**120**) when used with relative, personal, and reflexive pronouns: **mēcum**, *with me;* **sēcum**, *with himself.*

[2] When the perfect tense has present perfect force (translated with *has* or *have*), it has the same sequence as the present.

485. . **Word Studies**

The name *Caesar* has given us several interesting words. As Julius Caesar was the founder of the Roman Empire, his successors kept the name *Caesar* and it soon became a mere title, like *emperor*. Modern imitators of the Caesars adopted it, and as a result we have the words *Kaiser* and *Czar*. Many places were named *Caesarea* in honor of the Caesars. One was an island between France and England, in whose name, *Jersey*, it is not easy to recognize the original form. From *Jersey* we get the name of the garment and that of the state, *New Jersey*.

Many other ancient names have furnished us with interesting words. An "atlas" is so called because it usually has on its cover a picture of *Atlas* supporting the world on his shoulders. "Volcanoes" are named after *Vulcan*, god of fire; "martial" is derived from *Mars*, god of war.

Exercise. — Find other examples of English· words derived from ancient names.

FIG. 97. ROMAN TEMPLE AT NÎMES, FRANCE

In its fine state of preservation it is a rival of the Greek temple at Paestum
(cf. Fig. 6).

LESSON LXXXIII

INDIRECT QUESTIONS

486.   Vocabulary

ex'igō, –ere, –ē'gī, –āc'tus, *drive out, demand*		[**agō**]
* **frōns**, **fron'tis**, f., *forehead, front*		(frontal)
ho'nor, **honō'ris**, m., *honor, office*		(honest)
interclū'dō, –ere, –clū'sī, –clū'sus, *shut off, cut off*		[**claudō**]
occī'dō, –ere, –cī'dī, –cī'sus, *kill*		[**caedō**]
quae'rō, –ere, **quaesī'vī**, **quaesī'tus**, *seek, inquire*		(inquisitive)
qui'a, conj., *because*		
vo'veō, –ē're, **vō'vī**, **vō'tus**, *vow, promise*		(devotion)

487.   **Latin and English Word Formation**

We have seen (**134**) that when a Latin word is compounded
with a prefix, a short **a** or **e** is usually changed to short **i**.
Similarly, **ae** is changed to long **ī**. From **aestimō** we have
exīstimō; from **aequus, inīquus**; from **caedō, occīdō** (English *incision, decisive, concise*, etc.). The compounds of
caedō, with long **ī**, must be carefully distinguished from the
compounds of **cadō**, with short **i**.

Au is often changed to **ū** in compounds: **accūsō** is from
causa; **interclūdō** and **exclūdō** are from **claudō** (English
recluse, etc.).

Exercise. — Illustrate these rules by further examples of English
derivatives of **caedō, quaerō, claudō**.

488.   **Indirect Questions**

An **indirect question** is a question *indirectly* quoted or
expressed after some introductory verb, such as *ask, doubt,
learn, know, tell, hear,* etc. Examine the following:

    1. **Quis est?** *Who is he?*
    2. **Rogat quis sit,** *He asks who he is.*

Observe that (*a*) sentence 1 is a simple, *direct* question, and that the Latin verb is in the indicative;

(*b*) sentence 2 is complex, containing the same question in *indirect* form, reduced to a subordinate clause, and that its verb in the Latin is in the *subjunctive*.

489. Rule. — *The verb in an indirect question is in the subjunctive.*

490. How Indirect Questions and Statements Differ

In English, indirect statements are introduced by *that* (expressed or understood); indirect questions, by an interrogative word, such as *who, where,* etc.

In Latin, indirect statements are expressed by the infinitive without an introductory word; indirect questions, by the subjunctive with an introductory interrogative.

491. Tenses. — The tenses in the following exercises are determined by the rules for sequence, or harmony, explained in **441, 447**.

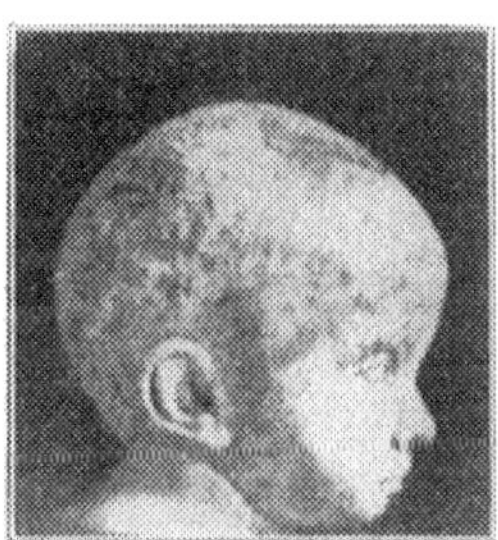

FIG. 98. A ROMAN BABY

492. Exercises

Oral. 1. Cūr nōn ā magistrō quaeris quis summum honōrem mereat? 2. Rogāsne cūr paucī multōs amīcōs et reliquī nūllōs habeant? 3. Hic puer tibi mōnstrābit ubi amīcus tuus habitet; nam videō viam tibi nōn nōtam esse.   4. Fāma est plūrimōs mīlitēs, ā viā interclūsōs, sē expedīre nōn potuisse et occīsōs esse.   5. Ā nōbīs quaesīvit quō modō sub rēgnō crūdēlis hominis multōs annōs vītam sustinēre possēmus.   6. Vōvistis nōbīs octāvam partem praedae dare, sed nōs fefellistis.   7. Ē castrīs exāctī, nostrī oppressī sunt quia in fronte flūmine fuga interclūsa est.

Written.   1. I do not know who is coming. 2. He doesn't seem [1] to know who's who or what's what.   3. I didn't inquire who lived across the street.   4. We did not understand why he was demanding such-great honors. 5. We realized that we were being led-forth to battle, but fear was not in our hearts.

493.   THE HERO REGULUS

Contrā Carthāginiēnsēs bellum [2] ā Rōmānīs susceptum est. Victī Carthāginiēnsēs pācem ā Rōmānīs petīvērunt. Quam [3] Rēgulus, dux Rōmānōrum, dīxit sē nōn datūrum esse nisi dūrissimīs condiciōnibus. Itaque Āfrī auxilium ā Lacedaemoniīs petīvērunt. Tum Rōmānīs victīs Rēgulus captus est. Sed Carthāginiēnsēs aliīs proeliīs superātī, Rēgulum Rōmam mīsērunt ut pācem ā Rōmānīs obtinēret et permūtātiōnem captīvōrum faceret. Ille ductus in senātum Rōmānum dīxit sē esse captīvum, nōn iam Rōmānum. Itaque etiam uxōrem ā sē remōvit. Dīxit Carthāginiēnsēs, frāctōs multīs proeliīs, spem (*hope*) nūllam nisi in pāce habēre ; nōn esse ūtile multa mīlia captīvōrum propter sē ūnum, aetāte cōnfectum, reddī. Senātus verbīs eius permōtus nōn pācem cum hostibus fēcit. Itaque Rēgulus ad Āfricam nāvigāvit ubi ā Carthāginiēnsibus omnibus suppliciīs occīsus est.

---

[1] The passive of **videō**, *see*, may have the meaning " seem."

[2] First Punic or Carthaginian War, 264–241 B.C. These wars were for the supremacy of the ancient world. Carthage was in northern Africa.

[3] In Latin, a relative is often used at the beginning of a sentence to connect with the preceding sentence. In English, a demonstrative is used instead.

Fig. 99. A Scene in the Roman Senate

Note the purple-edged togas of the senators. (From "Julius Caesar.")

LESSON LXXXIV

SUBJUNCTIVE MOOD: PERFECT AND PAST PERFECT TENSES OF ALL CONJUGATIONS. SEQUENCE

494.   Vocabulary

animadver'tō, –ere, –ver'tī, –ver'sus, *turn the mind to,*
  notice, punish (with **in** and acc.)   **[*vertō*]**
crēs'cō, –ere, crē'vī, crē'tus, *grow, increase*   (crescent)
dē'serō, –ere, –se'ruī, –ser'tus, *desert*   **[*serō, weave, join*]**
du'plex, du'plicis, *twofold, double*   **[*duo + plicō*]**
īnsti'tuō, –ere, –sti'tuī, –stitū'tus, *establish, commence, train*   **[*statuō*]**
mātū'rus, –a, –um, *ripe, early*   **[*mātūrō*]**
quan'tus, –a, –um, *how great, (as great) as*   (quantity)
red'dō, –ere, red'didī, red'ditus, *give back, deliver*   **[*dō*]**

495.   Subjunctive Perfect and Past Perfect

<table>
<tr><td colspan="2">Perfect Active (tense sign –erī–)</td><td colspan="2">Past Perfect Active (tense sign –issē–)</td></tr>
<tr><td>parā'verim</td><td>parāverī'mus</td><td>parāvis'sem</td><td>parāvissē'mus</td></tr>
<tr><td>parā'verīs</td><td>parāverī'tis</td><td>parāvis'sēs</td><td>parāvissē'tis</td></tr>
<tr><td>parā'verit</td><td>parā'verint</td><td>parāvis'set</td><td>parāvis'sent</td></tr>
<tr><td colspan="2">Similarly habuerim, posu-
erim, cēperim, mūnīverim</td><td colspan="2">Similarly habuissem, posuis-
sem, cēpissem, mūnīvissem</td></tr>
<tr><td colspan="2">Perfect Passive</td><td colspan="2">Past Perfect Passive</td></tr>
<tr><td colspan="2">parā'tus, –a, –um sim, etc.;
ha'bitus sim, etc.; po'situs
sim, etc.; cap'tus sim, etc.;
mūnī'tus sim, etc.</td><td colspan="2">parā'tus, –a, –um es'sem, etc.;
ha'bitus es'sem, etc.; po'situs
es'sem, etc.; cap'tus es'sem,
etc.; mūnī'tus es'sem, etc.</td></tr>
<tr><td colspan="4" align="center">(For full conjugation see 660–664.)</td></tr>
</table>

Observe that:

(*a*) The perfect active subjunctive is the same as the future perfect active indicative — with one exception. What is it? Note the difference, also, in the quantity of the **i** in the tense sign –erī–.

(*b*) The past perfect subjunctive active of any verb may be formed by adding the active personal endings to the perfect active infinitive, as **fuisse–m**, etc. (cf. the formation of the imperfect subjunctive by use of the present active infinitive, **446**).

(*c*) The tenses of the passive are formed like the corresponding tenses in the indicative — by use of the proper tenses and moods of **sum**.

496. Drill.—Give the perfect and past perfect subjunctive of **sum, possum,** and **ferō.**

497.   Distinction in Tense

The perfect subjunctive, like the perfect indicative, states an act as finished from the *present point of view;* while the past perfect subjunctive, like the past perfect indicative, represents an act as finished from the *past point of view.*

498.   Summary of Sequence (Harmony)

(*a*) **Primary tenses** (referring to the present or future)
Indicative: Present, " present " perfect, future, future perfect.
Subjunctive: Present, perfect.

(*b*) **Secondary tenses** (referring to the past)
Indicative: Imperfect, perfect,[1] past perfect.
Subjunctive: Imperfect, past perfect.

499. Rule. — *Primary tenses are followed by primary tenses, secondary by secondary.*

500.   Exercises

Oral.   1. Cūr nōn mē rogās cūr in eum nōn animadverterim?   2. Ab eō quaesīvī quantum esset pretium frūmentī in aliīs oppidīs.   3. Respondit pretium frūmentī in aliīs oppidīs esse minus quam in hōc oppidō.   4. Duplex ōrdō vigiliārum prō castrīs positus est nē mīlitēs timidī

---

[1] The perfect, when not translated with *has* or *have*, is regarded as secondary.

dēserere īnstituerent.   5. Puerī Rōmānī in librīs lēgērunt quō modō cīvitās sua glōriā crēvisset.   6. Nōnne amīcus tuus dīxit ob quam causam pecūniam nōn reddidisset?

7. Ita mātūrae erant aestātēs in hīs locīs ut Caesar omnēs suōs mīlitēs ēvocāre statueret.

Written.   1. I have not heard why he deserted us. 2. We did not notice who closed the gate.   3. It is difficult to realize now how-great the fear of the prisoners was. 4. He was asked why he had left his own country.   5. Don't you think that boys are trained best by hard work?

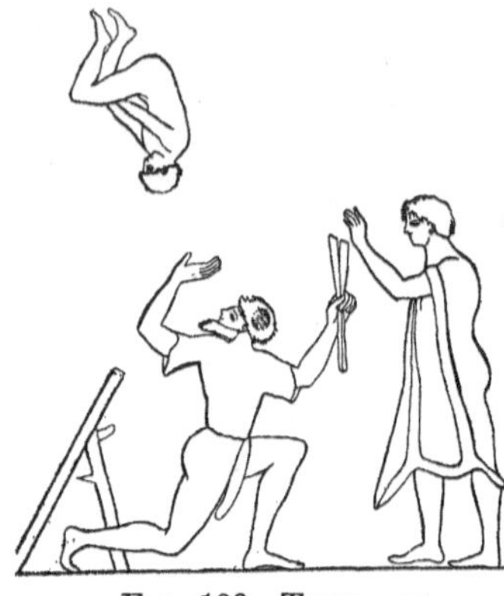

Fig. 100. Tumblers

501.   English Word Studies

A knowledge of the Latin root with its meaning will often help one use an English word correctly. You should not speak of an " endorsement " on the *front* of a document because **dorsum** means *back*. As **gravis** means *heavy, serious,* one may speak of an " aggravated " case of illness, but not of " aggravating " a person. To " *ef*fect " something is to *accomplish* it (**efficiō**, *do out* or *thoroughly, accomplish*). An " *ef*fect " is something *accomplished,* a *result.* To " *af*fect " is to *do* something *to* someone, to *influence* in some way. Other words whose meaning is made clear by the prefix are **ac***cess,* **ex***cess;* **ac***cept,* **ex***cept;* **e***migration,* **im***migration.*

Distinguish also the following according to etymology: *causal, casual; quantity, number; vocation, avocation.*

Fig. 101. A Pompeian Garden

LESSON LXXXV

DEPONENT VERBS

502.   **Vocabulary**

ar′bitror, arbitrā′rī, arbitrā′tus sum, *think, believe*	(arbitration)
expe′rior, experī′rī, exper′tus sum, *test, try, experience*	[*perīculum*]
familiā′ris, –e, (*belonging to the family*), *friendly;* as noun, *friend*	[*familia*]
fateor, fatē′rī, fas′sus sum, *confess*	(confession)
gra′dior, gra′dī, gres′sus sum, *step, walk*	(congress)
mī′ror, mīrā′rī, mīrā′tus sum, *wonder, admire*	(admirable)
quā′lis, –e, *what kind of,* (*such*) *as*	(quality)
se′quor, se′quī, secū′tus sum, *follow, pursue*	(sequence)

503.   Deponent Verbs of Four Conjugations

Some Latin verbs are *active in meaning* but *passive in form.* They are called **deponents** because they have *put away* (**dē-pōnō**) their active forms: **arbitror,** *I think.* Deponent verbs are conjugated throughout the indicative and subjunctive like regular verbs of the four conjugations in the passive (for complete synopses see **665**).

504.   Participles and Infinitives of Deponent Verbs

In deponent verbs the present and future participles and the future infinitive (formed from the future participle) are active in both form and meaning. The perfect participle, while passive in form, is active in meaning.

PARTICIPLES	INFINITIVES
Pres. **ar′bitrāns,** *thinking*	**arbitrā′rī,** *to think*
Perf. **arbitrā′tus,** *having thought*	**arbitrā′tus es′se,** *to have thought*
Fut. **arbitrātū′rus,** *going to think*	**arbitrātū′rus es′se,** *to be going to think*

238

505. Drill. — Give a synopsis of **miror** in the 3rd sing. and **sequor** in the 3rd plur., with meanings. Give the participles and infinitives of these words.

506. **Exercises**

Oral. 1. Mīror cūr ille mē secūtus sit. 2. Fateor mē nōn scīre quālis homō familiāris tuus sit. 3. Caesar arbitrātus est id bellum celeriter cōnficī posse. 4. Mīlitēs, perīcula bellī expertī, praemia et honōrēs exēgērunt. 5. Trēs tuās sorōrēs in Viā Altā gradientēs vīdī et ab eīs quaesīvī ubi tū essēs. 6. Arbitrārisne illōs quattuor hominēs nōs secūtūrōs esse? Illī nōn sequentur sī celerius gradiēmur. 7. Hōc opere effectō, mīrābāmur quid posteā facerēmus. 8. Mīrātus quid facerēs ā mātre tuā quaesīvī.

Written. 1. The slave, after killing his master, walked slowly to the next town. 2. The witness, after confessing that he had deceived us, was led-out to·punishment. 3. The mother wondered what boy had broken her daughter's new wagon. 4. He was so brave that five men could not hold him back. 5. Eight men were sent-ahead by the general to buy grain.

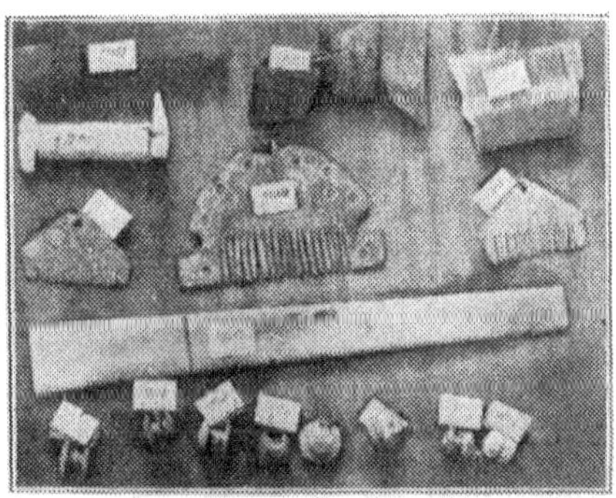

FIG. 102. ROMAN COMBS AND BUTTONS

507.   Latin and English Word Formation

The suffixes –ilis and –bilis are added to verb stems to form adjectives. They indicate what *can be done:* **facilis** is "do-able," *easy.* –ilis usually becomes –ile in English: *facile, fertile.* The more common suffix –**bilis** becomes –*ble*, –*able*, –*ible* in English: *noble, credible, terrible, amiable, visible, comparable.*

The suffixes –**āris** and –**ārius**, meaning *pertaining to*, are added to nouns and adjectives to form adjectives: **familiāris, mīlitāris, frūmentārius, ōrdinārius.** The former becomes –*ar* in English, the latter –*ary: familiar, singular; ordinary, secondary.*

Exercise. — Find ten other examples of suffix –*ble* (–*able*, –*ible*) and five of the suffixes –*ar* and –*ary* in English words derived from Latin words already studied.

FIG. 103. CAVĒ CANEM: "LOOK OUT FOR THE DOG"
From a mosaic at the entrance of a house in Pompeii.

LESSON LXXXVI

POST, *POSTEĀ*, AND *POSTQUAM* DISTINGUISHED

508. **Vocabulary**

cir'cum, prep. with acc., *around*	
circumve'niŏ, –ī're, –vē'nī, –ven'tus, *surround*	[*veniō*]
flec'tŏ, –ere, fle'xī, fle'xus, *bend, curve, turn*	(reflex)
nās'cor, nās'cī, nā'tus sum, *be born*	(native)
negō'tium, –ī, n., *business*	[*ōtium*]
post'quam, conj., *after*	[*post* + *quam*]
su'per, prep. with acc., *over, above*	[*superō*]
super'sum, –es'se, –fuī, –futū'rus, *be left over*	[*sum*]

509. **Latin and English Word Formation**

Ne- is sometimes used as a negative prefix in Latin: **nēmŏ** (ne–homŏ), **negōtium** (ne–ōtium), **neuter** (ne–ūter), **nūllus** (ne–ūllus).

Circum and **super** have their usual meanings when used as prefixes in Latin and English. **Super-** sometimes takes the form *sur-* in English, in which case it must be distinguished from assimilated **sub-**: *surplus, surmount.*

Exercise. — Find six English words with prefixes **circum-** or **super-** compounded with Latin words which you have studied.

510. **Post, Posteā, and Postquam**

The conjunction **postquam**, meaning *after*, must be distinguished carefully from the adverb **posteā**, meaning *afterwards*, and the preposition **post**,[1] meaning *after* (with acc.). Examine the following:

1. **Post illud bellum pāx cōnfirmāta est**, *After that war peace was established.*

2. **Cōnsidius posteā fuerat in Galliā**, *Considius had afterwards been in Gaul.*

---

[1] Sometimes used as an adverb like **posteā**.

3. **Caesar, postquam Gallōs fugere vīdit, cum omnibus cōpiīs secūtus est,** *After Caesar saw the Gauls fleeing, he followed with all his troops.*

Note that (*a*) the addition of **quam** to **post** makes **postquam** a conjunction;

(*b*) **posteā** means literally *after that*, hence *afterwards;*

(*c*) the real difficulty is in the English use of *after*, as both a conjunction and a preposition.

511. **Exercises**

Oral. 1. Quis cōnspexit nautās nāvigantēs " plānīs " (in locō nāvium) super caput? 2. Post labōrēs bellī omnēs perpetuam pācem spērant. 3. Ita praeceps erat frōns montis ut nōn eum ascendere possēmus et iter circum eum flectere cogerēmur. 4. Postquam duo līberī nātī sunt, tōta familia in Americam migrāvit. 5. Ubi hunc hominem ante portam vestram gradientem animadvertī, eum rogāvī quem peteret. 6. Mīror cui hoc difficile negōtium mandāre possim, sī ego ipse hoc nōn suscipiam. 7. Postquam hostēs ā fugā interclūsī et posteā circumventī sunt, plūrimī occīsī sunt et paucī superfuērunt.

Fig. 104. Posing for Their Picture

Written. 1. We cried-out (on) seeing the threatening danger. 2. We tied the prisoner but afterwards granted him freedom. 3. After the eighth year of ·the war, we enlisted 100,000 men and routed the enemy. 4. After they fought for ten years, so few were left that the nation was quickly destroyed. 5. Influenced

Fig. 105. A Roman Jug

by the speech of their leader, the men vowed they would take the town by assault.

512. Scipio

P. Cornēlius Scīpiō, puer duodēvīgintī annōrum, patrem, quī graviter vulnerātus erat, scrvāvit.[1] Post pugnam Cannēnsem, in quā Rōmānī gravissimē victī sunt, omnibus probantibus, ad Scīpiōnem, puerum vīgintī annōrum, summum imperium dēlātum est. Post sex annōs in Hispāniam prōcessit et Carthāginem Novam diē quō vēnit expugnāvit. Scīpiōnem clēmentissimē sē gerentem Hispānī rēgem appellāvērunt; sed Scīpiō, silentiō factō, dīxit: " Nōmen imperātōris quō mē meī mīlitēs appellāvērunt, mihi maximum est: rēgis nōmen, apud aliōs magnum, Rōmānī ōdērunt. Sī id quod rēgāle est amplissimum iūdicātis, vōbīs licet exīstimāre rēgālem in mē esse animum." Posteā, Hispāniā pācātā, Scīpiō in Āfricam prōcessit et ibi Carthāginiēnsēs victōriīs ita terruit ut Hannibalem ex Italiā ad patriam revocārent. Sed Scīpiō eum (*at*) Zamae[2] vīcit et ille, clārissimus et maximus omnium ducum quī contrā Rōmānōs pugnāvērunt, ex patriā in exsilium fūgit. Scīpiō ob hanc victōriam Āfricānus appellātus est.

---

[1] In the Second Punic War, the greatest of the three wars against Carthage, 218–201 B.C.
[2] 202 B.C.

SUBORDINATE CLAUSES REVIEWED. SUBSTANTIVE CLAUSES: VOLITIVE AND RESULT

ELEMENTARY GRAMMAR: Review *Clauses*, **638**.

513. Vocabulary

dis'cō, –ere, di'dicī, ——, *learn*	[*disciplīna*]
ēi'ciō, –ere, ēiē'cī, ēiec'tus, *throw* or *thrust out*	[*iaciō*]
fre'quēns, frequen'tis, *in great numbers, often*	(frequently)
imā'gō, imā'ginis, f., *a likeness* (*i.e.* statue or picture)	(imaginary)
impel'lō, –ere, im'pulī, impul'sus, *drive on, incite, persuade*	[*pellō*]
im'perō, –ā're, –ā'vī, –ā'tus, *command, order* (with dat. of person)	(imperial)
ō'rō, –ā're, –ā'vī, –ā'tus, *beg, ask*	[*ōrātiō*]
pi'us, –a, –um, *dutiful, loyal*	(piety)

514. Subordinate Clauses Reviewed

Subordinate clauses are substitutes for single parts of speech, either *nouns*, *adjectives*, or *adverbs*. In previous lessons we have studied the following:

(*a*) *Substantive* (or *noun*) *clause:* Indirect question, used as direct object.

(*b*) *Adjective clause:* Relative clause, modifying an antecedent like an adjective.

(*c*) *Adverbial clauses:* Clauses introduced by **sī** (condition), **quod** and **quia** (cause), **dum, ubi,** and **postquam** (time), **ut** and **nē** (purpose), **ut** and **ut nōn** (result).

515. Substantive Clauses: Volitive and Result

a. Volitive Substantive Clauses. Verbs of will or desire, like **addūcō** (*influence*), **cōgō** (*compel*), **impellō** (*persuade*), **imperō** [1] and **mandō** (*order*), **moneō** (*advise*), **ōrō** and **petō**

---

[1] **Iubeō** (*order*) always takes the infinitive.

(*beg*), **permittō** (*grant*), **rogō** (*ask*), take object clauses in the subjunctive with **ut** or **nē** :

1. **Rogō *ut veniās*,** *I ask you to come.*
2. **Impellit *nē remaneāmus*,** *He persuades us not to stay.*

b. Substantive Clauses of Result. Verbs meaning *to happen* (**accidō**) or *to cause* or *effect* (**efficiō**) require clauses of result in the subjunctive with **ut** or **ut nōn**, used as subject or object of the main verb:

(As subject) **Accidit *ut mē nōn vidēret*,** *It happened that he did not see me.*

(As object) **Efficiam *ut veniat*,** *I shall cause him to come.*

516. **Exercises**

Oral. 1. Tē ōrāmus nē discēdās dum pater noster abest. 2. Relātum est mīlitēs, nōn singulōs sed frequentēs, impellī ut dēsererent. 3. Fīlius pius imāginem patris magnā dīligentiā cōnservābat.
4. Imperāvimus Mārcō, gubernātōrī sextae nāvis, ut suam nāvem in mare flecteret et quīnque reliquās sequerētur.
5. Accidit ut in aquam inciderem sed, flūmine dēlātus, in terram ēiectus sum. 6. Familiārem dē hīs crīminibus cōnsuluī et ille effēcit ut nōn damnārer.
7. Tibi nōn permittam ut studia dēpōnās, quia dēbēs .discere, inter alia, quālem cīvitātem habeāmus.

FIG. 106. MĀRCUS AURĒLIUS
This good emperor (161–180 A.D.) was also a philosopher.

Written. 1. It happened that we could not see him, for the time was not convenient. 2. Dutiful children do not shout and thrust-out their tongues. 3. These men, though well-trained, were surrounded and compelled to give themselves up. 4. They thought it was better to enlist fresh troops than to ransom those not fit for battle. 5. I commenced to lead the soldiers over the mountain but was persuaded by their shouts to lead them around it.

517.   **Legal Phrases in English**

Caveat ēmptor, *Let the buyer beware* (for he buys at his own risk).

habeās corpus, (*I command that*) *you have the body* (*of a certain person brought into court*), a writ issued by a judge to see whether a person is justly imprisoned.

post mortem, *after death,* e.g. a *post mortem* examination of a body.

scīre faciās (*I demand that*) *you cause to know* (*why a certain court action should not be carried out*).

supersedeās, (*I command that*) *you suspend* (*proceedings*).

Fig. 107. The Small Theater at Pompeii as It Is

This theater was a covered one, which was unusual. Prominent men had chairs down in front, while the rest of the audience sat on the stone seats above. Over the entrances were private boxes.

LESSON LXXXVIII

CONJUGATION OF *EŌ*

518. Vocabulary

ē'dō, –ere, ē'didī, ē'ditus, *put forth, publish*   [*dō*]
e'ō, ī're, i'ī, i'tus, *go*   [*iter*]
   ex'eō, exī're, ex'iī, ex'itus, *go out* or *forth*
   red'eō, redī're, red'iī, red'itus, *go back*
me'mor, me'moris, *mindful of, remembering* (with gen.)   [*memoria*]
pa'tior, pa'tī, pas'sus sum, *suffer, endure*   (passion)
qui'ēs, quiē'tis, f., *rest, sleep*   (quietus)
tur'bō, –ā're, –ā'vī, –ā'tus, *disturb, agitate*   (turbulent)

519. **Conjugation of *Eō***

Eō is irregular in the present, future, and perfect tenses.
Note that the stem –ī– is changed to –e– before **a, o, u.**

PRESENT SYSTEM (present stem ī–)

	PRESENT		IMPERFECT	FUTURE	
Indic.	e′ō	ī′mus	ī′bam, *etc.*	ī′bō	ī′bimus
	īs	ī′tis		ī′bis	ī′bitis
	it	e′unt		ī′bit	ī′bunt
Subjunct.	e′am, *etc.*		ī′rem, *etc.*		

PERFECT SYSTEM (perfect stem i–)

	PERFECT		PAST PERF.
Indic.	i′ī	i′imus	i′eram, *etc.*
	īs′tī	īs′tis	FUT. PERF.
	i′it	iē′runt	i′erō, *etc.*
Subjunct.	i′erim, *etc.*		īs′sem, *etc.*

	INFINITIVES		PARTICIPLES
Pres.	ī′re	*Pres.*	i′ēns (*gen.*, eun′tis)
Perf.	īs′se	*Perf.*	i′tus, –a, –um
Fut.	itū′rus esse	*Fut.*	itū′rus, –a, –um

(Note. — As eō is intransitive, passive forms are rare.)

520. Drill. — Conjugate **exeō** and **redeō** in the present system.

521. **Exercises**

Oral. 1. Carrī quī sē movēre videntur celerius eunt quam eī quī equīs trahuntur. 2. Melius est līberōs beneficiō addūcere ut discant quam vī cōgere. 3. Ob mare turbātum quiētī nōs trādere nōn poterāmus. 4. Ex iīs quaesīvit cūr ex fīnibus suīs exīssent. 5. Postquam hic liber ēditus est, auctor maximōs honōrēs accēpit. 6. Nōnne memorēs estis graviōrum malōrum quae mēcum multōs annōs passī estis? 7. Frūmentō collātō et nāvibus contrāctīs, Caesar imperāvit timidīs ut ad castra redīrent.

Written.   1. The teacher asked who inhabited the farthest regions of Gaul.   2. The one sister was very beautiful, but the other was very unlike her.   3. After suffering many evils in this town, I shall go-back to the fields to till them.   4. My friend and I [1] were born in the same year, but he knows more than I.   5. We begged him not to go but we could not persuade him to remain.

522.   English Word Studies: The Norman-French Influence

We saw in earlier lessons (**270, 275**) how Latin words were introduced into English at its very beginning. A very important period of influence was after the Norman conquest of England (1066). The language of the Normans was an old form of French, itself descended from Latin. In the course of a few centuries, the English language underwent striking changes and adopted many French (Latin) words. These sometimes show considerable changes in the original spelling. Especially common is the addition of a vowel (cf. **443**).

Exercise. — Look up the Latin originals of *captain, vizor, sue, pursue, duke, peer, treason.*   See Scott's *Ivanhoe*, Chap. I, for *pork, beef,* etc.

FIG. 109. A ROMAN ARCH IN REIMS, FRANCE

---

[1] Latin order: *I and my friend were born* (first plural).

LESSON LXXXIX

DESCRIPTIVE *CUM* CLAUSES

523.   **Vocabulary**

cum, conj., *when*	
dēi'ciō, –ere, dēiē'cī, dēiec'tus, *throw from*	[*iaciō*]
dē'ligō, –ere, dēlē'gī, dēlēc'tus, *select*	[*legō*]
dig'nus, –a, –um, *worthy*	(dignity)
pin'gō, –ere, pīn'xī, pic'tus, *paint*	(picture)
ra'pidus, –a, –um, *swift*	[*rapiō*]
re'or, rē'rī, ra'tus sum, *think, calculate*	(rational)
sa'tis, adv. and indecl. adj., *enough*	(satisfaction)

524.   **Descriptive *Cum* Clauses**

In previous lessons **ubi** (*when*) and **postquam** (*after*) have been used with the indicative to introduce clauses purely temporal. A third conjunction, **cum**, meaning *when*, is used to introduce temporal clauses. In secondary sequence the Romans came to use **ubi** and **postquam** with the indicative and **cum** with the subjunctive. Such **cum** clauses are called **descriptive *cum* clauses.**

> *Examples:* **Postquam mīlitēs rediērunt, Caesar ōrātiōnem fēcit,**
> *After the soldiers returned, Caesar made a speech.*
>
> **Cum mīlitēs redīssent, Caesar ōrātiōnem fēcit,** *When the soldiers had returned, Caesar made a speech.*
>
> **Cum mīlitēs redīrent, Caesar ōrātiōnem faciēbat,** *When the soldiers returned, Caesar was making a speech.*

525. Rule. — *In secondary sequence, **ubi** and **postquam** are used with the perfect indicative, **cum** with the imperfect or the past perfect subjunctive.*

526.   **Exercises**

Oral.   1. Nōnne rēris mortem dignissimōs virōs rapere? 2. Semper plūs timet animus perīculum nōn nōtum.

3. Postquam imāginem suī patris pīnxit, ōrāvī ut meī patris imāginem pingeret. 4. Dīxit sē dē equō dēiectum esse sed ego exīstimō eum cecidisse. 5. Cum Caesar cerneret hostium frequentēs mīlitēs īnstrūctōs, dēlēgit decem nūntiōs ut hoc reliquīs ducibus referret. 6. Cum nostrī ob rapidum flūmen nōn satis commodē redīre possent, dux iussit auxilia submittī. 7. Cum allātum esset summa loca hostibus complērī neque ūlla auxilia cōnspicī, Caesar cōnstituit continēre cōpiās suās in castrīs.

Written. 1. When I had put-out the light and gone to rest, I thought I caught-sight-of a familiar shape. 2. When the enemy had been repulsed, the general permitted his men to take a rest. 3. I wonder why you do not select worthy friends. 4. So swiftly did the river flow that the boy could not grasp the boat. 5. When I noticed that my friend was struggling against nine men, I ran to him.

527.   **English Word Studies**

Most of the names of our states are Indian, but several of them are of Latin origin or form. Vermont means *green mountain* (**viridis mōns**), New Jersey is "New Caesarea" (cf. **485**), Pennsylvania is *Penn's woods* (**silva**), Virginia is the *maiden's* land (named after Queen Elizabeth, the virgin queen), Florida is the *flowery* land (**flōs, flōris**), Colorado is the land of the *colored* or *red* river, Montana is *mountainous* (**mōns**), Nevada is the land of *snow* (**nix, nivis**), and Rhode Island is named after the Greek island of Rhodes, meaning *rose*.

State names with Latin feminine forms are Carolina (Charles II), Georgia (George II), Louisiana (Louis XIV), and Indiana.

LESSON XC

REVIEW

528.   Noun and Adjective Review

1. Decline **tantus clāmor, mors mātūra, quantus timor, aetās pia, frōns alta, maximus honor, nūllum negōtium, imāgō familiāris**.

2. Review the Latin forms of the ordinal numerals 1st–10th. Decline the Latin forms of 1000, 2000, 3000.

529.   Verb Review

1. Give a synopsis of (*a*) **perterreō**, 1st sing., indic. act. ; (*b*) **trādō**, 2nd sing., subjunct. pass. ; (*c*) **perficiō**, 3rd sing., indic. act. ; (*d*) **reservō**, 1st plur., subjunct. pass. ; (*e*) **experior**, 2nd plur., indic. ; (*f*) **supersum**, 3rd plur., subjunct.

2. Conjugate **eō, exeō**, and **redeō** throughout.

3. **Rapid-fire drill on verb forms.** — *Locate the form:* praemīsit, frēgisset, attāctus est, distribuistis, exīstimem, incoluisse, iūnctūrus esse, exercērī, strictus esse, exāctus, interclūdēns, animadvertēmus, crēscēns, dēserunt, turbant, vovent, quaesītūrus, discēmus, nāta est, fatēberis, mīrābāminī, ēdunt.

530.   Syntax Review

Quote the rules for the following constructions and illustrate each in Latin with a short original sentence : *result clause; accusative of extent; indirect question; sequence (harmony) of tenses.*

531.   Synonyms

We rarely find a word in any language which has exactly the same meaning as another word. Words which have approximately the same meaning are called **synonyms**. The diagram may help you to remember the margin of difference between the synonyms **homō** and **vir**, which are often confused.

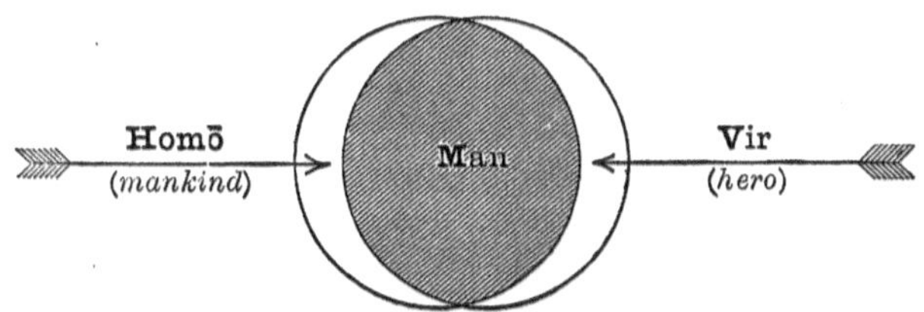

The following synonyms have occurred in previous vocabularies. Note differences and discriminate in their use:

1. **terra**, *land* (as opposed to water), then some particular *land* or *country*.

    fīnēs, *borders*, hence a *land* or *country* with reference to its boundaries.

    patria, *fatherland*, the *land* of one's birth.

2. **dux** [**dūcō**], *a leader* in a military sense, then in any field.

    prīnceps, [**prīmus + capiō**], the *first* or *chief* man in a group — usually non-military.

3. **putō**, " reckon," *be inclined to think*.

    reor, *think carefully and deliberately, come to a conclusion.*

    iūdicō, *judge*.

    aestimō, *value, estimate*, in a literal sense.

    exīstimō and **arbitror** are less carefully distinguished.

4. **videō**, *see*, the most general word.

    cernō, *see clearly*.

    cōnspiciō, *catch sight of*.

5. **labor**, *hard work, toil, suffering*.

    opus, usually *a piece of work*.

    negōtium, *lack of leisure* [**ōtium**], *business*.

6. **potestās**, *power* in general, *opportunity*.

    auctōritās, *influence*.

    rēgnum, *royal power*.

    imperium, *military power, command*.

532. A Derivative Match (*To the teacher*). The desirability of holding frequent word contests was discussed in **391**. The same method may be applied to derivative work. After choosing sides dictate Latin words and have each student in turn give one English derivative, or, *vice versa*, dictate English words and have him give the Latin form of each.

533. THE STORY OF LUCIUS (*Concluded*)

Cīvis Novus Iter Facit

Cum Lūcius aetātem quīndecim annōrum attigisset, pater eius dīxit eum ita crēvisse ut dēbēret togam praetextam dēpōnere et virīlem togam sūmere. (Puerī Rōmānī togās praetextās gerēbant sed virī tōtās albās. Brācae, quae ā virīs nunc geruntur, ā barbarīs, nōn ā Rōmānīs, illīs temporibus gerēbantur.) Itaque pater Lūcī cōnstituit ut Lūcius togam virīlem sūmeret proximīs Līberālibus,[1] quō tempore plūrimī puerī Rōmānī togās praetextās dēpōnēbant.

The New Citizen

Līberālia aderant. Multī cognātī et amīcī convēnērunt. Lūcius, postquam mōrem antīquum servāns togam praetextam ante Larēs posuit, novam virīlem togam sūmpsit. Omnēs familiārēs cum eō ad Forum pedibus iērunt, et posteā ad Capitōlium, ubi nōmen eius ad numerum cīvium ascrīptum est. Nunc potest dīcere, "Cīvis Rōmānus sum!" Omnēs Lūcium domum [2] redeuntem secūtī sunt, ubi optima cēna parāta erat. Multī cibī dē ultimīs terrīs portātī erant, aliī dē Graeciā, aliī dē Asiā, aliī dē Āfricā. Hospitēs cēnam variō sermōne prōdūxērunt et cum Lūciō dē officiīs cīvium, dē bellō et pāce, dē negōtiīs ēgērunt. Cum Lūcius quiētī sē daret, sēnsit quid esset cīvem Rōmānum esse.

The Journey

Paulō (*shortly*) post pater Lūciō, nunc virō, permīsit ut sēcum iter faceret. Itaque per portam Capēnam ex urbe exiērunt. Raedā ibi inventā, in Appiā Viā prōcessērunt. Sepulchrīs ad viam vīsīs, Lūcius dīxit sē semper mīrātum esse cūr sepulchra ad viās pōnerentur. Pater respondit:

---

[1] The Liberalia, a festival held March 17.
[2] *Place to which* with **redeuntem**: "*home.*"

"Ut omnēs ea videant." Lūcius fassus est sē nōn satis fortem esse ut nocte inter sepulchra iter facere audēret.

Good Roads and Great Men

Ita facile et commodum erat iter ut Lūcius dīceret: "Nōnne arbitrāris Appiam Viam optimam omnium esse?" Pater respondit: "Omnēs nostrae viae optimae sunt. Ob eam causam hostēs vīcimus, potestātem nostram auximus, et nunc gentēs regimus.

Aliī imāginēs pulchriōrēs pingunt, aliī ōrant (*plead*) causās melius, sed nōs regimus populōs." " Etiam causās optimē ōrāmus," respondit Lūcius. " Quis melior ōrātor fuit aut est aut erit quam Cicerō? Hic ōrātor etiam cōnsul fuit et populum Rōmānum rēxit. Ego eum ōrātiōnem habentem in Forō audīvī et eius ōrātiōnēs in lūdō lēgī." " Lēgistīne ōrātiōnēs in Catilīnam, illum quī cīvitātem ēvertere statuit?"

Fig. 110. M. Tullius Cicerō

" Illās et aliās lēgī. In prīmā dīxit dē Catilīnā: 'Ō tempora! Ō mōrēs! Senātus haec intellegit, cōnsul videt; hic tamen vīvit.'" "Optimē!" dīxit pater, " In secundā, sī rēctē memoriā teneō, dīxit, postquam Catilīna ex urbe exiit: 'Abiit, excessit, ēvāsit,[1] ērūpit[2]!' Ex Cicerōnis linguā fluēbat ōrātiō dulcior quam mel."

Scenes by the Way

Tum altōs et pulchrōs arcūs[3] aquaeductūs[4] cernunt, quī

---

[1] Ēvādō, ēvāsus — derivative?   [3] Acc. plur.
[2] Ērumpō, ēruptus — derivative?   [4] Gen. sing.

optimam aquam dē montibus ad urbem affert. Pater Lūciō dīxit prīmum aquaeductum ab Appiō factum esse. Appius fuit ille quī Appiam Viam mūnīvit. Ita prōcēdunt, nunc agrōs et vīllās, montēs silvāsque spectantēs, nunc hominēs frequentēs in viā ipsā, quōrum aliī gradiēbantur, aliī aut equō aut raedā aut lectīcā ferēbantur.

Epilogue

Nōn iam vīvit Lūcius et eius amīcī, nōn iam vīvunt Caesar et Cicerō, virī clārissimī, sed lingua eōrum vīvit, vīvunt eōrum dicta et facta, lēgēs et mōrēs, glōria et fāma. Haec omnia in eōrum librīs inveniuntur. Eīs quī itinera parva per illōs librōs faciunt Rōmānī ipsī vīvere videntur.

Fig. 111. Aquaeductus

Named after its builder, the emperor Claudius (41–54 A.D.), this aqueduct was one of many which brought pure water to Rome from a distance.

LESSON XCI

IDIOMS. THE DATIVE AND ACCUSATIVE WITH *TO* REVIEWED

534. **Vocabulary**

cōn′sequor, –sequī, –secū′tus sum, *follow, overtake, attain*	[*sequor*]
dē′sum, dees′se, dē′fuī, dēfutū′rus, *be lacking*	[*sum*]
ex′struō, –ere, –strū′xī, –strūc′tus, *pile up, build up*	[*struō*]
hūmā′nus, –a, –um, *human*	[*homō*]
impe′rium, –ī, n., *command, power*	[*imperō*]
necessā′rius, –a, –um, *necessary*	(necessity)
reci′piō, –ere, –cē′pī, –cep′tus, *take back, receive*	[*capiō*]
va′cō, –ā′re, –ā′vī, –ā′tus, *be free, uninhabited*	(vacation)

535. **Idioms**

Review the idioms **committere proelium, alius . . . alius, aliī . . . aliī, alter . . . alter, summus mōns, extrēma via.** Memorize the following new idioms:

1. **sē recipere,** with **ad,** *to retreat.*
2. **certiōrem eum facere dē,** *to inform him about;* as, **Fēcī eōs certiōrēs dē itinere,** *I informed them about the road* (what literally?).
3. **quam,** when used with the superlative of an adjective or adverb, means *as . . . possible.* Cf. **quam plūrimī,** *as many as possible;* **quam celerrimē,** *as quickly as possible.*

536. *To* **with Verbs of Motion**

The dative is essentially the " to " or "for" case. We have noticed, however, that, when *to* implies literally *motion toward* a place or person, the accusative is used. The following are " motion verbs," previously studied, that take the accusative with **ad** or **in** :

accēdō, cēdō, cōnferō, contendō, dēferō, dūcō, eō, ferō, fugiō, mātūrō, mittō, moveō, nāvigō, portō, prōcēdō, prōdūcō, properō, redigō, redūcō, trānsportō, sequor, veniō.

537. Dative of Indirect Object: A Summary

When *to* or *toward* does not imply literal motion but indicates the person *to whom* something is given or *toward whom* a benefit, injury, feeling, or quality is directed, the dative must be used. The following verbs, already familiar, are transitive and admit an accusative of the *direct object* and a dative of the *indirect object*:

committō, dīcō, dō, dōnō, iungō, mandō, mōnstrō, nūntiō, ostendō, permittō, prōpōnō, reddō, relinquō, respondeō, submittō, trādō, tribuō, voveō.

538. Exercises

Oral. 1. Homō sum; nihil hūmānī ā mē aliēnum[1] putō. 2. Necessārium vīsum est patrem meum dē hīs factīs certiōrem facere et omnia eī dīcere. 3. Tōtam aestātem māteriae magnam cōpiam exstruēbāmus nē hieme deesset. 4. Reliquam partem hiemis sē alēbant cōpiīs[2] ā cīvitāte distribūtīs. 5. Cum nostrī cōnspexissent hostēs ad castra sē recipere, eōs cum omnibus cōpiīs quam celerrimē cōnsecūtī sunt. 6. Hostēs crūdēlēs haec loca vāstāvērunt quia ratī sunt quam maximam esse glōriam loca fīnitima vacāre. 7. Postquam Rōmānōs ex hīs regiōnibus expulērunt, ipsī sub imperium Rōmānum redāctī sunt.

Written. 1. The just man refrains from wrong and guards the rights of others. 2. After the slave delivered the letter to me, I sent him back to my mother. 3. He told me that the highest power had been offered to my brother, but I did not believe him (*dat.*). 4. We informed our allies that the enemy would not begin battle, and they retreated to their ships. 5. It is not enough to select worthy friends: you ought to promise them constant friendship.

---

[1] *Foreign, of no concern to* (lit., *from*). [2] *Supplies.*

539. Latin and English Word Formation

We have seen (**507**) that the suffixes –**āris** and –**ārius** mean *pertaining to.* Other adjective suffixes with this meaning are –**ānus** (English *–an, –ane, –ain*), –**ālis** (English *–al*), –**icus** (English *–ic*), –**īvus** (English *–ive*). They are added to noun and adjective stems. Examples in English are *Roman, humane, captain; liberal; public; native.*

The suffix –**ōsus** (English *–ous* or *–ose*) is added to noun stems and means *full of:* **cōpiōsus,** *copious;* **ōtiōsus,** *otiose.*

Exercise. — Find ten examples of these suffixes in English words derived from Latin words which you have studied.

FIG. 112. TRIUMPHAL PROCESSION, ARCH OF TITUS, ROME
Note the famous seven-branched candlestick from the temple at Jerusalem, captured in 70 A.D.

LESSON XCII

SPECIAL VERBS THAT TAKE THE DATIVE

540.   **Vocabulary**

cŏnfī'dŏ, –ere, cŏnfī'sus sum,[1] *have confidence* (*in*)	[*fīdŏ, trust*]
fa'veŏ, –ē're, fā'vī, fau'tus, *be favorable to*	(favor)
invi'deŏ, –ē're, invī'dī, invī'sus, *be envious toward, envy*	[*videŏ*]
no'ceŏ, –ē're, no'cuī, no'citus, *do harm to*	(noxious)
pā'reŏ, –ē're, pā'ruī, pā'ritus, (*appear*), *be obedient to, obey*	(apparent)
pla'ceŏ, –ē're, pla'cuī, pla'citus, *be pleasing to*	(implacable)
prae'stŏ, –ā're, prae'stitī, prae'stitus, *stand before, excel*	[*stŏ*]
resis'tŏ, –ere, re'stitī, ——, *stand against, resist*	[*sistŏ*]

541.   **The Dative with Special Verbs**

a. **Dative and infinitive.** — The verbs in **537** are transitive
and take a direct object in addition to an indirect object.
Some of these verbs, however, have as the direct object
either a neuter pronoun or an infinitive: **dīcŏ, respondeŏ,
nūntiŏ, voveŏ.**

b. **Dative and *ut* clause.** — Similarly, other verbs require
a subordinate **ut** clause as direct object, as we have seen
(**515**): **imperŏ, permittŏ, mandŏ.**

Verbs of both these classes take an indirect object of the
person; as, *Eī* **imperŏ ut,** etc., *I order **him** to,* etc.

Note. — With some of these verbs, either the direct or the indirect
object is often omitted:

	this to him	eī hoc	
I (*in*)*trust*	*that this is true*	hoc vērum esse	crēdŏ
	him	eī	

So also **cōnfīdŏ.**

c. **Dative only — no direct object.** — Certain other verbs
rarely take any case but the dative. Memorize carefully:
dēsum, faveŏ, invideŏ, noceŏ, pāreŏ, placeŏ, praestŏ, resistŏ.

---

[1] Semi-deponent, *i.e.* deponent in perfect system only.

542. **Exercises**

Oral. 1. Imperāre sibi maximum imperium est. 2. Quod cōnfīdēbāmus eōs nōn nōbīs resistere posse, eōs cum omnibus cōpiīs cōnsecūtī sumus. 3. Mihi placet audīre familiārem meum, optimum puerum, reliquīs puerīs praestāre. 4. Sī hostēs sē recipient, agricolīs quī illās regiōnēs incolunt nocēbunt. 5. Nēmō potest dīcere quantam aetātem ille vir attigerit. 6. Cum cōnspiceret pecūniam mihi nōn deesse, nōn iam mihi favēbat sed invidēbat. 7. Hic aliīs imperāre poterit, quia imperiīs pārēre didicit. 8. Pārēbitisne patribus vestrīs aut eīs resistētis?

Written. 1. I confess that an early death is not pleasing to me. 2. He brought back much booty, which he displayed to his admiring friends. 3. A twofold danger was threatening: behind them one part of the enemy was pressing (on), in-front-of them the other part was being led against them. 4. The general commanded his soldiers not to do-harm to fields, but they were not obedient-to him. 5. It is necessary that men have-confidence-in themselves in order to obtain power.

543. **English Word Studies : Abbreviations of Latin Titles**

A.B.   **Artium Baccalaureus,** *Bachelor of Arts.*
S.B.   **Scientiae Baccalaureus,** *Bachelor of Science.*
A.M.   **Artium Magister,** *Master of Arts.*
Ph.D.   **Philosophiae Doctor,** *Doctor of Philosophy.*
LL.D.   **Lēgum Doctor,** *Doctor of Laws* (double **L** is a sign of the plural).

Exercise. — Find and explain other abbreviations of titles and degrees.

LESSON XCIII

THE IRREGULAR VERBS *VOLŌ* AND *NŌLŌ*

544.   Vocabulary

dī′vidō, –ere, dīvī′sī, dīvī′sus, *divide*   (division)
explō′rō, –ā′re, –ā′vī, –ā′tus, *investigate, explore*   [*plōrō, call out*]
magnitū′dō, magnitū′dinis, f., *greatness, size*   [*magnus*]
multitū′dō, multitū′dinis, f., *multitude, great number*   [*multus*]
pe′cus, pe′coris, n., *cattle*   [*pecūnia*]
proficīs′cor, –ficīs′cī, –fec′tus sum, *start, set out*   [*faciō*]
prōgre′dior, prō′gredī, prōgres′sus sum, (*step forward*),
   advance   [*gradior*]
ra′tiō, ratiō′nis, f., *account, plan, manner, reason*   [*reor*]
vo′lō, vel′le, vo′luī, ——, *want, be willing, wish*   (volition)
nō′lō, nōl′le, nō′luī, ——, *be unwilling, not wish*   [*ne + volō*]

545.   Conjugation of *Volō* and *Nōlō*

The present indicative of both verbs is irregular. The
present subjunctive employs the tense sign –ī–, as in **sim**.
The other tenses are regularly formed. There is no passive.

	INDICATIVE		SUBJUNCTIVE	
Pres.	**vo′lō**	**nō′lō**	**ve′lim**	**nō′lim**
	vīs	**nōn vīs**	**ve′līs**	**nō′līs**
	vult	**nōn vult**	**ve′lit**	**nō′lit**
	vo′lumus	**nō′lumus**	**velī′mus**	**nōlī′mus**
	vul′tis	**nōn vul′tis**	**velī′tis**	**nōlī′tis**
	vo′lunt	**nō′lunt**	**ve′lint**	**nō′lint**

Impf. **volē′bam**, etc. **nōlē′bam**, etc. **vel′lem**, etc. **nōl′lem**, etc.

PRESENT PARTICIPLE		INFINITIVES	
vo′lēns	**nō′lēns**	*Pres.* **vel′le**	**nōl′le**
		Perf. **voluis′se**	**nōluis′se**

(For full conjugation see **670**)

Observe that (*a*) the present stem is **vel-** in the subjunctive but **vol-** in the indicative; (*b*) the imperfect subjunctive of both **volō** and **nōlō** is formed regularly upon the present infinitive (**velle, nōlle**) — this explains why the l is doubled.

546. Caution. — Volō and nōlō, like **iubeō**, usually demand the infinitive construction (instead of **ut** and the subjunctive).

547.   Exercises

Oral.   1. Ille volēbat nōscere nōmen meum et quō modō ego cecidissem, sed ego nōlēbam eī dīcere.   2. Incertī animī multitūdinis ōrātiōne rēgis permōtī sunt et omnēs lēgibus pārēre cōnstituērunt.   3. Explōrāvistīne quae genera pecorum agrīs minimō noceant?   4. Ob magnitūdinem perīculī cum maximā cūrā prōgressī sunt nē ab hostibus pellerentur.   5. Iussī eum proficīscī ad hostium castra ut eōrum ratiōnem proclī cognōsceret et referret.   6. Cum cīvēs extrēmae cīvitātis pācem cōnfirmāvissent, Caesar dīxit sē velle cōpiās suās dīmittere.   7. Rōmānī Galliae gentēs dīvidere voluērunt ut eīs facilius imperārent.

Written.   1. What will you do if he shall be unwilling to go-back with[1] you?   2. Reason is the greatest gift which God has given to the human race.   3. I asked him why he wanted to reserve this witness for (**ad**) the last, but I could not persuade him to answer.   4. He ran so swiftly and lightly that he seemed to graze, not touch, the earth.   5. The size of the cattle was such that the boys were thoroughly-frightened.

548.   English Word Studies

The suffix **-tūdō** (English *-tude*) is added to adjective stems to form nouns and means *state of being:* **magnitūdō,** *magnitude.*

---

[1] See **484**, footnote 1.

The suffix –**mentum** (English –*ment*) is added to verb stems to form nouns and indicates the *means:* **impedīmentum,** *impediment.*

The suffix –**tūra** (English –*ture*) is added to verb stems to form nouns but has no very definite meaning: **nātūra** (from **nā–scor**), *nature.*

The verb suffix –*fy* in English is derived from **faciō** (–**ficiō**) and means *to make: satisfy* (**satisfaciō**). It is usually added to adjectives.

Exercise. — Find five examples of each of these suffixes in English words derived from Latin words which you have studied.

Fig. 113. Rome and the Tiber

LESSON XCIV

THE FOURTH DECLENSION

549.   Vocabulary

că′sus, –ŭs, m., *fall, chance, accident*	[*cadō*]
cruciă′tus, –ŭs, m., *torture*	[*crux*, *cross*]
dēsi′liŏ, –ĭ′re, –si′luĭ, –sul′tus, *jump down*	[*saliō, jump*]
dēspí′ciŏ, –ere, –spe′xĭ, –spec′tus, *look down on, despise*	[*speciō*]
do′mus, –ŭs,[1] f., *house, home*	(domestic)
ēvā′dŏ, –ere, –vā′sĭ, –vā′sus, *go out, escape*	[*vādō, go*]
exer′citus, –ŭs, m., *(trained) army*	[*exerceō*]
im′petus, –ŭs, m., *attack*	[*petō*]
iū′rŏ, –ā′re, –ā′vĭ, –ā′tus, *swear*	[*iūs*]
ma′nus, –ŭs, f., *hand, group, force*	(manual)

550.   Fourth Declension

We have seen that nouns of the first three declensions are distinguished by the ending in the genitive singular — first declension –**ae**, second declension –**ī**, third declension –**is**. The majority of Latin nouns belong to these three declensions. A few nouns, however, have –**ūs** in the genitive singular and belong to the **fourth declension**. Many of these are derived from verbs.

	Case Endings		casus, *chance* (base, căs–)	
Nom.	–us	–ūs	că′sus	că′sūs
Gen.	–ūs	–uum	că′sūs	că′suum
Dat.	–uĭ	–ibus	că′suĭ	că′sibus
Acc.	–um	–ūs	că′sum	că′sūs
Abl.	–ū	–ibus	că′sū	că′sibus

551. Gender. — Nouns of the fourth declension in –us are mostly masculine; the only exceptions in this book are **manus** and **domus**, both of which are feminine.

---

[1] Usually has abl. sing. **domō** and acc. plur. **domōs (645)**.

552. Drill. — Decline **exercitus noster, impetus fortis.**

553. **Exercises**

Oral. 1. Iūrāvit per (*by*) deōs sē nōn dēsertūrum esse suōs amīcōs, sed hī eī crēdere nōluērunt. 2. Omnēs ōrāvērunt nē in suīs propriīs domibus cruciātū interficerentur. 3. Lībertās iūraque nūllīus[1] dēspicientur; nam nōs omnēs parēs sumus. 4. Nautae singulī dē nāvī dēsiluērunt ut ē morte īnstantī ēvāderent. 5. Postquam cāsus ducī nūntiātus est, novem nāvibus contrāctīs, ad īnsulam rediit. 6. Exercitus noster impetum in (*on*) ōrdinēs Gallōrum ita ācriter fēcit ut hī perterritī sē quam celerrimē reciperent. 7. Cum nostrīs resistere nōn iam vellent, manūs tendere incēpērunt petentēs pācem salūtemque.

Written. 1. By chance I caught-sight-of the army (as it was) setting-out to begin battle. 2. Who has said that a house divided against itself can not stand? 3. On-account-of the many wagons (which were) rolling (along) on the street, we could not take a rest. 4. As our house was not finished, we did not know where we should live. 5. These regions are uninhabited; for I have seen no one.

554. **English Word Studies**

In the fourteenth century there began a great revival of interest in the ancient Latin and Greek authors. This revival is known as the **Renaissance**, or **Renascence (re-nāscor).** Beginning in Italy, it spread over western Europe and reached England in the sixteenth century. Ever since that time new words have been added to English from Latin and Greek in great numbers. As a result, over ninety per cent of the words in Caesar and Cicero have English derivatives. Words of this last period are easily distinguished by their similarity to the Latin originals.

---

[1] Used in place of the gen. sing. of **nēmō.**

One result of the introduction of new words directly from the Latin was the formation of a number of **doublets**, words derived at different periods from the same Latin word and having different meanings. Note the following (the earlier form precedes): *conceit, conception* (**concipiō**); *sample, example* (**exemplum**); *feat, fact* (**factum**); *Mr., master* (**magister**); *loyal, legal* (**lēx**); *mayor, major* (**maior**); *treason, tradition* (**trādō**); *chance, cadence* (**cadō**); *pursue, persecute* (**persequor**).

Exercise. — Show how the above doublets got their meanings from the original Latin meaning.

FIG. 114. A TEMPLE AT TIVOLI

Tivoli (ancient Tibur) has always been a favorite summer resort for the people of Rome. It is eighteen miles east of Rome in the Sabine Hills.

LESSON XCV

INDEFINITE PRONOUNS

555.   Vocabulary

a′liquis, a′liquid, *someone, some, any*   [*alius* + *quis*]
am′plius, compar. adv., *more, further*   (amplify)
au′tem (never first word), *moreover, on the other hand*
cōnsū′mō, –ere, –sūmp′sī, –sūmp′tus, (*take wholly*), *use up,*
   waste   [*sūmō*]
lo′quor, lo′quī, locū′tus sum, *talk, speak*   (loquacious)
mercā′tor, mercātō′ris, m., *trader, merchant*   [*merx, merchandise*]
quī′dam, quae′dam, quid′dam, *a certain one*   [*quī*]
tempes′tās, tempestā′tis, f., *season, storm*   [*tempus*]
tri′plex, tri′plicis, *threefold*   [*trēs* + *plicō*]
ve′hō, –ere, ve′xī, vec′tus, *convey, carry*   (vehicle)

556.   Indefinite Pronouns

Review the declension of the interrogative **quis** (**255**) and
the relative **quī** (**241**).

(*a*) The most indefinite of all Latin pronouns is **quis** (declined like the interrogative pronoun), *some, any,* used only
after certain words (**sī** and **nē** in this book) : **sī quis**, *if anyone;* **nē quid**, *lest anything*, etc.

(*b*) **Aliquis**, a compound of **quis**, often means "*someone
— I don't know who."*   It is declined exactly like **quis**, except
that it has **aliqua** in the nominative and accusative plural
neuter.

(*c*) **Quīdam**, *a certain one*, is less indefinite than **quis** and
aliquis.   It often means " someone whose name I can men-
tion but won't."   It is declined like **quī** [1] — the suffix –**dam**
being indeclinable.

---

[1] Except in accusative singular **quendam, quandam, quiddam**, genitive
plural **quōrundam, quārundam, quōrundam**.   See **659** for full declension of
aliquis and **quīdam**.

557.   Exercises

Oral.   1. Loquar tēcum amplius posteā dē quibusdam condiciōnibus quās nunc explicāre nōlō.   2. Sī vīs esse aliquis, dēbēs et labōrāre cum maximā dīligentiā et discere ea quae magister iubet.   3. Imperāvit nostrō exercituī ut prōgrederētur et triplicem impetum in manūs hostium faceret. 4. Crūdēlis est, nōn fortis, quī puerōs occīdit.   5. Nāvis quā vehēbāmur tempestāte ita rapidē agēbātur ut gubernātor eam regere nōn posset.   6. Iussī quendam mercātōrem īre cum manū mīlitum ut frūmentum emeret.   7. Imperāvī autem eī nē ūllum tempus cōnsūmeret, nē quid hostibus nūntiārētur.   8. Audīvī aliquem dē quibusdam cāsibus loquentem sed nōn bene intellēxī.

FIG. 115. CAESAR AND THE SOOTHSAYER

Caesar is being warned to beware the Ides of March (March 15), on which day he was assassinated (cf. Fig. 90).   (From "Julius Caesar.")

FIG. 116. A CENTAUR

Written. 1. I wish to speak with you further about heroes,[1] wars, and battles. 2. Some say that a certain merchant bought the horse but did not pay for (**prō**) it. 3. It pleased me to see that the children had been well taught. 4. After having been conveyed to the-top-of the mountain by horses, we jumped-down from them and explored those regions on foot. 5. A certain man swore that he saw the body of a horse joined to a human head and body.

558. **Latin Phrases in English**

prŏ et con(trā), *for and against.*

quid prŏ quŏ, *something for something,* " tit for tat."

Deŏ volente, *God willing* (often abbreviated **D.V.**).

Possunt quia posse videntur, *They can because they think they can* (lit., *seem to be able*). — Virgil.

Dulce (*sweet*) **et decōrum** (*glorious*) **est prŏ patriā morī** (from **morior,** *die*).

cāsus bellī, *an occasion for war.*

mē iūdice, *in my judgment.*

in statū quō, *in the situation in which* (*it was before*) ; **status quō,** *the situation in which* (*it was before*).

559. THE GRACCHI

Ti. et C. Gracchī Scīpiōnis Āfricānī nepōtēs erant. Dīligentiā Cornēliae mātris puerī doctī sunt. Cum quaedam hospita (*guest*) ōrnāmenta sua pulcherrima eī ostenderet,

---

[1] Vir or homŏ — which?

Cornēlia līberōs suōs hospitae ostendēns, dīxit: "Haec sunt mea ōrnāmenta!" (*See Fig. 1.*)

Tiberius, cum adultus[1] esset, plēbī fāvit. Tribūnus plēbis creātus,[2] agrōs populō dīvidēbat. Cum dīxisset omnia per plēbem agī dēbēre, senātōrēs convocātī cōnsuluērunt quid facerent. Tiberiō accēdente Scīpiō Nāsīca, senātor, clāmāvit: "Quī rem[3] pūblicam salvam esse volunt, mē sequantur!" Tum omnēs ad Tiberium currunt et eum occīdunt.

Gāius voluit frātris mortem vindicāre et eius cōnsilia efficere. Tribūnus creātus, frūmentum plēbī dīvidēbat et cīvitātem omnibus quī in Italiā habitābant dabat. Sed fugere coāctus interfectus est.

Itaque senātōrēs mortem Gracchōrum effēcērunt sed cōnsilia eōrum exstinguere nōn potuērunt; nam Rōmānī eōrum vītam[4] multōs annōs in memoriā tenuērunt.

FIG. 117. THE HOUSE WITH THE BALCONY, POMPEII

---

[1] From **adolēscō**. [2] 133 **B.C.** [3] Acc. of **rēs**. [4] With plural meaning.

LESSON XCVI

CONJUGATION OF *FĪŌ*. PREDICATE NOUNS AND ADJECTIVES

560.   **Vocabulary**

adminis'trō, –ā're, –ā'vī, –ā'tus, *manage*   (administration)

dēmōns'trō, –ā're, –ā'vī, –ā'tus, *point out, show*   [*mōnstrō*]

fī'ō, fī'erī, fac'tus sum, *become, be made, happen*   (satisfy)

praefi'ciō, –ere, –fē'cī, –fec'tus, *put in charge of* (with acc.
    and dat.)   [*faciō*]

prae'sum, –es'se, –fuī, –futū'rus, *be in charge of* (with dat.)   [*sum*]

se'nex, se'nis, m., *old man*   (senior)

    senā'tus, –ūs, m., *senate*

sup'plex, sup'plicis, (*kneeling*), *suppliant, beseeching*   [*sub + plicō*]

temp'tō, –ā're, –ā'vī, –ā'tus, *test, try, attempt*   (temptation)

vi'olō, –ā're, –ā'vī, –ā'tus, *treat with violence, profane*   [*vīs*]

FIG. 118. MĀTER ET PATER

561. Conjugation of *Fīō*

Faciō does not have the present system in the passive. When the Romans, therefore, desired to express *be made, be done, become* in the present, imperfect, or future tenses, they used the verb **fīō**, which has these meanings, although active in form:

	INDICATIVE		SUBJUNCTIVE	INFINITIVE
Pres.	**fī'ō** ——	*Pres.*	**fī'am, fī'ās**, etc.	*Pres.* **fi'erī**
	fit fī'unt			
Impf.	**fīē'bam**, etc.	*Impf.*	**fi'erem**, etc.	
Fut.	**fī'am, fī'ēs**, etc.			

(The perfect system is regularly formed with the perfect participle **factus, –a, –um** and **sum, eram, erō**, etc. See **671**.)

a. **Observe** that the stem vowel **i** is lengthened throughout, except before **ĕ** and final –t.

b. **Caution.** — Compounds of **faciō**, such as **cōnficiō** and **efficiō**, form the passive regularly: **cōnficior, efficior**, etc.

562. Predicate Nouns and Adjectives

Fīō, like the passive forms of **appellō** (*call*), **dēligō** (*choose*), **creō** (*elect*), may take a predicate noun or adjective:

Caesar *dux* fīet, *Caesar will be made* **leader.**
Cicerō *Pater* Patriae appellātus est, *Cicero was called* **the Father** *of his Country.*

563. Exercises

Oral. 1. Nōnne arbitrāris sorōrem meam crēvisse? Ea fit altior pulchriorque. 2. Vōbīs supplex manūs tendit patria commūnis, vōbīs vītam, lībertātem salūtemque omnium cīvium committit. 3. Virum quī praesidiō praefuit huic negōtiō praeficiam ut omnia administret. 4. Senex, cum Prīmus Cīvis Cīvitātis creātus esset, ēmit humilem domum in quā nātus erat. 5. Certior factus sum hostēs loca sacra violāvisse, domōs agrōsque vāstāvisse, omnia pecora remōvisse, et iter per fīnēs aliēnōs per vim temptāvisse. 6. Caesar dēmōnstrāvit hunc dignum senem prō beneficiīs crēbrīs amīcum sociumque populī Rōmānī ā senātū appellātum esse. 7. Nihil melius emī potest quam amīcus firmus.

Fig. 119. Puer Rōmānus

Written. 1. Someone is speaking, but I do not understand what he is saying on-account-of the shouts of the boys. 2. Who will become king after the old man's death? 3. After a certain boy told me that he could breathe under water, I wanted him to try, but he was unwilling. 4. If anyone wishes to excel others, let him always command himself. 5. While I am-in-charge-of this force of soldiers, those (things) will be done which I judge are best.

564.   **Musical Terms in English**

Most of our musical terms come from the Italian and thus ultimately from the Latin. Explain the following, all derived from Latin words used in this book: *alto, forte, fortissimo, piano* (**plānus**), *accelerando* (**celer**), *ritardo* (**tardus**), *con amore, soprano* (**super**), *mezzo-forte* (**medius**), *da capo* (**dē capite**), *crescendo, opus, finale, libretto, trio, solo, tempo.*

Poēta nāscitur, nōn fit, *A poet is born, not made.*

LESSON XCVII

FIFTH DECLENSION

565.   Vocabulary

congre'dior, con'gredī, congres'sus sum, *come together with, fight with*	[*gradior*]
coniun'gō, –ere, –iūn'xī, –iūnc'tus, *join with, unite*	[*iungō*]
di'ēs, diē'ī, m., *day*	(diary)
diur'nus, –a, –um, *daily, by day*	
fin'gō, –ere, fīn'xī, fic'tus, *shape, form, invent*	(fiction)
rēs, re'ī, f., *thing, matter, affair*	(real)
spe'ciēs, speciē'ī, f., *appearance, pretense, kind*	[*speciō*]
spēs, spe'ī, f., *hope*	[*spērō*]
sur'gō, –ere, surrē'xī, surrēc'tus, *rise*	(resurrection)
tol'lō, –ere, sus'tulī, sublā'tus, *raise, remove*	[*ferō*]

566.   Fifth Declension

The last of the noun declensions embraces comparatively few words. **Rēs** and **diēs**, however, occur constantly and should be memorized. Other nouns of the **fifth declension**, as a rule, have no plural; all are feminine except **diēs**, which is commonly masculine.

Case Endings			diēs, *day* (base, di–) rēs, *thing* (base, r–)			
	Sing.	Plur.				
Nom.	–ēs	–ēs	di'ēs	di'ēs	rēs	rēs
Gen.	–ĕī	–ērum	diē'ī	diē'rum	re'ī	rē'rum
Dat.	–ĕī	–ēbus	diē'ī	diē'bus	re'ī	rē'bus
Acc.	–em	–ēs	di'em	di'ēs	rem	rēs
Abl.	–ē	–ēbus	di'ē	diē'bus	rē	rē'bus

Observe that e appears in every ending and that in **diēs** it is long in the genitive and dative singular, though preceding a vowel (**608**).

567. Drill. — Decline **rēs similis, alia spēs, diēs longus.**

568. **Exercises**

Fig. 120. A Roman Pitcher

Oral. 1. Memoria est satis magnum praemium prō beneficiō. 2. Puerī tantum clāmōrem sustulērunt ut ā patre suō audīrentur. 3. Alpēs montēs ab aliquō deō fictī esse videntur; nam multa mīlia pedum surgunt. 4. Gallī diurnīs proeliīs cum Germānīs congressī sunt. 5. Exercitus eius maiōrem partem nōnī diēī in castrīs remānsit, quia nūllam spem victōriae habuit. 6. Hīs rēbus cognitīs, Gallī, trāns flūmen trāductī, manūs suās coniūnxērunt ut Rōmānōs impedīrent et interclūderent. 7. Nova speciēs hominum nōn nōtōrum mē puerum perterrēbat et multōs annōs in memoriā haerēbat.

Written. 1. If anyone asks in which house I live, I hope that you will point it out to him. 2. On the seventh day after the grain was distributed by the merchants, it was used-up. 3. When it became necessary to put this old man in charge of affairs, we all promised to obey him. 4. By chance I heard the distinguished man say that there was no hope of peace before the fifth year of the war. 5. Under the pretense of friendship he offered terms of peace, but we knew that he was trying to deceive us.

569. **English Word Studies**

English words which preserve the forms of the Latin fourth declension are: **census, consensus, impetus, prospectus, status, apparatus** (plural **apparatuses** or **apparatus**; the latter preserves the Latin plural). Note that **consensus** (from **sentiō**) is spelled with an **s** but **census** (from **cēnseō**) with a **c**. An ablative form is seen in **impromptu**.

The fifth declension is represented by **rabies, series, species**. The last two are used in the plural with no change of form (as in Latin). The accusative singular is represented by **requiem**, the ablative by **specie**, and the ablative plural by **rebus**.

A. M., **ante merīdiem**, *before midday;* **P.M.**, **post merīdiem**, *after midday;* **M.**, **merīdiēs**, *midday.*

Latin verb forms preserved in English are **interest, fiat, exit, exeunt, exeat, posse**.

Exercise. — Define the words listed above.

Fig. 121. Roman Aqueduct at Segovia, Spain

LESSON XCVIII

DATIVES OF REFERENCE AND PURPOSE. ABLATIVE OF MEASURE OF DIFFERENCE

570.   Vocabulary

appā′reō, –ē′re, –pā′ruī, –pāritū′rus, *appear, become visible*	[*pāreō*]
coni′ciō, –ere, –iē′cī, –iec′tus, *throw (forcibly), throw together*	[*iaciō*]
du′bitō, –ā′re, –ā′vī, –ā′tus, *doubt, hesitate*	(dubious)
e′ques, e′quitis, m., *horseman*	[*equus*]
ignō′rō, –ā′re, –ā′vī, –ā′tus, *be ignorant of, not know*	[*nōscō*]
lūx, lū′cis, f., *light*	[*lūmen*]
occur′rō, –ere, occur′rī, –cur′sus, *run against, meet* (with dat.), occur	[*currō*]
rēs pū′blica, re′ī pū′blicae, f., *(public affairs), government*	(republic)
ser′viō, –ī′re, –ī′vī, –ī′tus, *serve* (with dat.)	[*servus*]
vī′vus, –a, –um, *alive, living*	(vivid)

571.   Dative of Reference

1. **Iussī eōs sibi frūmentum ferre,** *I ordered them to carry grain for themselves.*

2. **Sī mihi dignī esse vultis,** *If you wish to be worthy in my sight (for me).*

Observe that (*a*) in both examples *the dative denotes the person concerned or referred to;* (*b*) the literal translation of this dative is often " for " rather than " to." Sometimes it is best translated by a possessive in English.

572.   Dative of Purpose

1. **Locum castrīs dēlēgit,** *He chose a place for a camp.*
2. **Haec castra erunt praesidiō oppidō,** *This camp will be (for) a protection to the town.*

Observe that (*a*) *the dative may be used to express purpose;* (*b*) a second dative (of reference) is often used with it, especially when the verb is some form of **sum.**

573.   Ablative of Measure of Difference

1. **Tribus annīs ante eum vīdī,** *I saw him three years ago* (lit., *before by three years*).

2. **Pater est capite altior quam fīlius,** *The father is a head taller than his son* (lit., *taller by a head*).

Observe that *the ablative expresses the measure of difference.*

574.   Exercises

Oral. 1. Mē ignōrās, sī exīstimās mē amīcīs meīs dignē et humiliter nōn semper servīre.   2. Puer perīculīs occurrere nōn dubitat, quia nihil timet; senex autem multō tardius agit, quia prōvidet quid accidat. 3. Multī vīvī mortem timent quod nōn sciunt quid post mortem accidat. 4. Quī auctor clārus linguā nostrā dīxit "sūmere arma contrā mare cūrārum"? 5. Ita bene rēs pūblica ab hōc homine administrāta erat ut omnēs eī favērent. 6. Cum lūx appārēret, dux tria mīlia equitum praesidiō impedīmentīs antecēdere iussit.   7. Septem diēbus post sex mīlia sociōrum auxiliō nostrīs pervēnērunt et hostēs in fugam coniēcērunt.

FIG. 122. HADRIAN'S VILLA NEAR TIVOLI

The emperor Hadrian (117–138 A.D.) built a magnificent summer home, or rather a fair-sized town, near Rome. The wall here shown was intended to furnish a shady walk morning and afternoon, on the one side or the other.

Written.   1. To select a home for others is a most diffi-cult thing.   2. Our house is much larger than yours. 3. Thrown-out by the force of the storm, he grasped the boat with his hands and escaped death.   4. Let us not envy those who with great skill form or paint the likenesses of our notable men.   5. It was (for) a great honor to the humble soldier to be consulted by the general.

575.   **Latin in Medicine**

FIG. 123. SURGICAL INSTRUMENTS

Many Roman surgical instruments were like those used to-day. Modern surgeons have expressed their admiration of them.

Physicians daily make use of many Latin words and phrases. The science of anatomy, with which all physicians must be familiar, uses a large number of Latin terms. In writing prescriptions, physicians use Latin constantly, and drug-gists must be able to understand it. The letter ℞ at the top of a prescription stands for **recipe**, *take.* Other examples are: **aq(ua) pūr(a)**, *pure water;* **aq(ua) dēst(īl-lāta)**, *distilled water;* **t(er) i(n) d(iē)**, *three times a day;* **cap(iat)**, *let him take;* **gtt.** (abbreviation of **gut-tae**), *drops;* **sig(nā)**, *write.*

LESSON XCIX

FUTURE PASSIVE PARTICIPLE (GERUNDIVE)
AND ITS USE WITH *SUM*

576. **Vocabulary**

admo′neō, –ē′re, –mo′nuī, –mo′nitus, *remind*	[*moneō*]
concur′rō, –ere, –cur′rī, –cur′sus, *run together, rush*	[*currō*]
grex, gre′gis, m., *herd*	[*ēgregius*]
incen′dō, –ere, –cen′dī, –cēn′sus, *set on fire, burn*	(incense)
lā′bor, lā′bī, lāp′sus sum, *slip, glide by*	(lapse)
lēgā′tus, –ī, m., *envoy, lieutenant general*	[*lēgō, appoint*]
lī′berō, –ā′re, –ā′vī, –ā′tus, *set free*	[*līber*]
prae′dicō, –ā′re, –ā′vī, –ā′tus, *declare, proclaim*	[*dĭcō, proclaim*]
rum′pō, –ere, rū′pī, rup′tus, *break*	(rupture)
ū′tor, ū′tī, ū′sus sum, *use, make use of* (with abl.)	(usury)

577. Idiom. — $\left\{ \begin{matrix} \text{causā} \\ \text{grātiā} \end{matrix} \right\}$ *by reason of, for the sake of* (preceded by genitive).

Note. — *E.g.*, used in English in the sense of "for example," stands for **exemplī grātiā**, lit., *for the sake of example.*

578. **Future Passive Participle**

The **future passive participle** (commonly called the **gerundive**) is formed by adding –ndus, –a, –um to the present stem of any verb: **para–ndus, –a, –um,** *to be prepared.*[1]

a. **Drill.** — Form the future passive participle of **līberō, pāreō, cōnsūmō, serviō.**

579. **Uses of the Future Passive Participle**

1. **Ad eās rēs cōnficiendās Mārcus dēligitur,** *Marcus is chosen to accomplish these things* (lit., *for these things to be accomplished*).

2. **Caesaris videndī grātiā vēnit,** *He came for the sake of seeing Caesar* (lit., *for the sake of Caesar to be seen*).

---

[1] Add –**endus, –a, –um** in the case of –**iō** verbs: **mūni–endus, capi–endus.** The stem vowel is shortened before –**nd–**.

3. **Hoc opus vōbīs faciendum est,** *This work is to be done by you,* i.e. *This work* **must be done** *by you.*

Observe that (*a*) when used with **ad, causā,** or **grātiā,** the future passive participle expresses *purpose;* (*b*) when used with forms of **sum** as a predicate adjective, it naturally expresses *obligation* or *necessity;* (*c*) the person upon whom the obligation rests is expressed by the dative (**dative of agent**).[1]

580.   Exercises

Oral.   1. Agricola prae sē gregem pecorum agēns ad oppidum tardē graditur.   2. Admonēmur annīs lābentibus nōn esse tempus ad omnia agenda.   3. Cīvēs frequentēs, puerī et etiam senēs, nōn dubitāvērunt sed ad rem pūblicam servandam concurrērunt.   4. Lēgātus nōbīs imperāvit ut, equīs ūsī, quam celerrimē proficīscerēmur et omnia explōrārēmus.   5. Ita rapidē iter nōbīs faciendum erat ut paucīs diēbus magnum spatium cōnficerēmus.   6. Lēgātus praedicāvit sē iūstās condiciōnēs pācis rūpisse captīvōrum līberandōrum grātiā.   7. Cum Gallī animadvertissent hostēs ad sē contendere, omnēs suās domōs incendendās esse arbitrātī sunt quia scīvērunt eōs ab iniūriā nōn temperātūrōs esse.

Written.   1. In the summer we shall set-out to explore the woods.[2]   2. If a boy meets an old man, what ought[2] he to do?   3. I am confident that he does not wish to do-harm-to us.   4. The war was carried-on for-the-sake-of freeing the slaves.   5. What ought[2] to be done by the Senate if the envoys hesitate to accept the harsh peace terms?

---

[1] To be distinguished from the **ablative of agent** with **ā** or **ab**, regularly used with the passive voice of verbs.

[2] Express in two ways.

581.   **Latin Forms of English Names**

Many English names of boys and girls are derived from Latin words (*a*) without or (*b*) with change :

(*a*) Alma, *fostering;* Clara, *clear, bright;* Leo, *lion;* Stella, *star;* Sylvester, *pertaining to the woods.*

(*b*) Mabel, from **amābilis**, *lovable;* Belle, from **bella**, *beautiful;* Florence, from **flōrentia**, *flourishing;* Grace, from **grātia**, *grace, favor;* Margaret, from **margarīta**, *pearl.*

The following names were in common use among the Romans :

August, Augustus, *venerable;* Rufus, *red-haired;* Victor, *conqueror;* Vincent (**vincēns**), *conquering.*

Other Roman names still used in English are :

Emil and Emily (**Aemilius, Aemilia**); Cecilia (**Caecilia**); Claudia ; Cornelius, Cornelia ; Horace (**Horātius**); Julius, Julia ; Mark (**Mārcus**); Paul (**Paulus**).

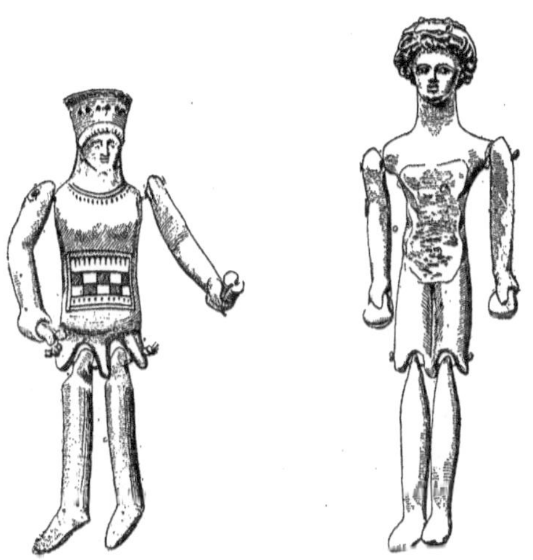

FIG. 124. ANCIENT DOLLS

Roman girls played with dolls to the time of marriage.

LESSON C

THE GERUND AND ITS USES. GENITIVE AND ABLATIVE OF DESCRIPTION

582.   Vocabulary

do'lor, dolō'ris, m., *pain, grief*   (doleful)
dor'miō, –ī're, –ī'vī, –ī'tus, *sleep*   (dormitory)
fa'ciĕs, faciē'ī, f., *face, appearance*   (surface)
frŭc'tus, frŭc'tūs, m., *enjoyment, fruit*   [*frūmentum*]
*mĕns, men'tis, f., *mind*   (mental)
mē'tior, mētī'rī, mĕn'sus sum, *measure, deal out*   (mensuration)
o'rior, orī'rī, or'tus sum, *arise, rise*   (orient)
te'gō, –ere, tē'xī, tēc'tus, *cover, conceal*   (detective)
te'xō, –ere, te'xuī, tex'tus, *weave*   (textile)
tor'queō, –ē're, tor'sī, tor'tus, *twist, torture*   (distorted)

583.   The Gerund

The gerund corresponds to the English verbal noun in –ing, as in *We learn to do by* **doing**. It is formed by adding –ndī, –ndō, –ndum, –ndō to the present stem of any verb.[1] It is accordingly declined in the singular only, in all cases except the nominative.

a. **Drill.** — Learn the gerunds of the model verbs (**660–4**).
Form and decline the gerunds of **admoneō, lābor, dormiō, mētior.**

584.   Uses of the Gerund

1. **Ad discendum vēnimus,** *We have come for learning* (i.e. *to learn*).
2. **Discendī causā** (or **grātiā**) **vēnimus,** *We have come for the sake of learning.*

Observe that the gerund, when used with **ad**, **causā**, or **grātiā**, expresses *purpose*.

---

[1] Add –endī, etc., in the case of –iō verbs.

585. Caution. — Do not confuse the gerund and the future passive participle (gerundive). The former has only *four* case forms, the latter has *thirty*. The gerund is a verbal *noun*, and as such has the constructions of a noun (object of a preposition, ablative of means, etc.), while the future passive participle is a verbal *adjective*, and as such must modify a noun and agree with it in gender, number, and case. Forms ending in –ī, –ō, or –**um** *may* be either gerund or future passive participle, according to the context; other forms *must* be the future passive participle. When either construction is possible, the Latin prefers the future passive participle.

586.   Genitive and Ablative of Description

1. **virī magnae virtūtis**, *men of great courage.*
2. **spatium decem pedum**, *a space of ten feet.*
3. **hominēs inimīcā faciē**, *men with* (or *of*) *an unfriendly appearance.*

Observe that in English we may say *men **of*** or ***with*** *an unfriendly appearance.* Both are descriptive. Note also that description is similarly expressed in Latin, *i.e.* either by the genitive or the ablative, but only when modified by an adjective.

While the **genitive** and the **ablative of description** are translated alike, the Latin confines the genitive largely to expressions of *measure and number* (see 2) and the ablative to *physical qualities* (see 3).

587.   Exercises

Oral. 1. Puella pulchrā faciē nōn semper mentem mīrandam habet.   2. Arbitrārisne tē dormiendī causā ad hunc locum vēnisse?   3. Scīsne quibus rēbus Rōmānī ad texendum ūsī sint?   4. Plūrima flūmina ex altīs montibus oriuntur.   5. Gallī circumventī mīlitibus frūmentum mētīrī nōn potuērunt et eōs frūctibus aluērunt.   6. Equitēs nūllam spem redeundī [1] habuērunt.   7. Captīvus magnae virtūtis quī torquōbātur faciem ob dolōrem tegēbat.

---

[1] Gerund of **redeō.**

Written. 1. Do you know that Roman girls painted their faces? 2. Marcus was a boy with a famous father. 3. Did he come to this place for-the-sake-of learning? 4. Some boys invent reasons of all kinds in-order-to escape work. 5. At the end of this journey we ought to give thanks to our leader.

588.   English Word Studies

The future passive participle is preserved in a number of English words: **propaganda, Amanda, memorandum, corrigendum, addendum, referendum.** It may also be seen in the following abbreviations, used in geometry: **Q. E. D. (Quod erat dēmōnstrandum), Q. E. F. (Quod erat faciendum).**

Latin Phrases in English

sine diē, *without a day (being set)* ; used of adjournment by a parliamentary body.
prīmā faciē, *on the first face (of it)* ; e.g. *prima facie* evidence.
in rē, *in the matter (of).*
bonā fidē, *in good faith.*
mēns sāna *(sound)* **in corpore sānō.**

LATIN INSCRIPTION ON LONGFELLOW'S GRAVE

589. Marius and Sulla

C. Marius, humilī locō nātus, ob singulārem virtūtem et cupiditātem ad perīcula suscipienda cōnsul ā Rōmānīs creātus est. Postquam Iugurtham, rēgem Numidiae, vīcit, bellum contrā Cimbrōs et Teutonēs suscēpit. Hī recentēs hostēs, ab extrēmīs Germāniae fīnibus fugientēs, novās sēdēs quaerēbant, et ā Rōmānīs petīvērunt ut sibi terram darent. Repulsī armīs petere cōnstituērunt. Trēs ducēs Rōmānī impetūs barbarōrum nōn sustinuērunt sed Marius imperium Rōmānōrum servāvit, nam Teutonēs sub Alpibus proeliō superāvit.

Victīs Teutonibus, Marius Cimbrīs occurrit. Hī lēgātōs mīsērunt ut agrōs urbēsque sibi et Teutonibus peterent — nihil enim dē cāsū Teutonum audīverant. Marius rīdēns, "Illī quidem tenent," inquit, "semperque tenēbunt terram ā nōbīs acceptam." Posteā pugnāre coepērunt, nec minor cum uxōribus Cimbrōrum est pugna quam cum virīs. Victae sē īnfantēsque suōs occīdērunt. Ad urbem reversus,[1] Marius triumphum ēgit.

Cum Sulla cōnsul contrā Mithridātem, rēgem Pontī, missus esset, Marius voluit imperātor fierī. Sulla cum exercitū ad urbem vēnit et eam armīs occupāvit. Interim Marius in Āfricam fūgit. Profectō ad bellum Sullā, Marius in Italiam rediit et Rōmam vāstāvit. Omnēs nōbilēs variīs suppliciōrum generibus affēcit. Post bellum Mithridāticum Sulla rediit et, Mariō ipsō mortuō (*dead*), omnēs quī Mariō fāverant superāvit. Dictātor creātus, tam multa mīlia cīvium interficī iussit ut quīdam dīceret vīvere aliquōs dēbēre ut essent quibus imperāret (*that there might be some left to govern*).

---

[1] Used here as a deponent verb.

A LATIN PLAY

SĀTURNĀLIA

Persōnae

Geta, *callidissimus servōrum*   **Hector**, *maximus servōrum*
Bellus, *pulcherrimus servōrum*   **Boadīx**, *coquus*
L. Calpurnius, *dominus*   **Aliī servī**

TEMPUS: Decembrī. LOCUS: in aedibus L. Calpurnī. (*Servī accēdunt.*)

Servī. Iō Sāturnālia! Iō Sāturnālia! Iō Sāturnālia!
　　　　(*Boadīx ā sinistrā parte accēdit, currēns*)

Boadīx. Quid est? Quem clāmōrem audiō? Quid accidit? Quis interfectus est?

Servī. Ho, ho, ho! Coquus est!

Bellus. Nōnne pulcher est? Tam gravis est, ut, eō currente, audīre videāmur —— montem cadentem!

Servī. Ha, ha!

Boadīx. Quid? Montem cadentem? Ubi?

Hector. Mōns nōn cadit; stupidus es!

Geta. Sāturnālia adsunt! Nōnne Sāturnālia in Galliā, tuā patriā, erant?

Boadīx. Quae sunt? Nūlla coxī!

Servī. Ha, ha! " Coxī! "

Geta. Sāturnālia! —— Sunt septem diēs quibus deō Sāturnō honōrēs dōnantur ——

Boadīx. Septem diēs! Deī Superī! Cūr rīdētis? Abīte[1] aut vōs omnēs interficiam!

Hector. Quid? Properāre nōn dēbēs!

Boadīx. Diēbus quibus deīs honōrēs dōnantur, tum labor coquī maximus est! Cūr tantum clāmōrem fēcistis? Cūr nōn permīsistis ut dominus noster ex memoriā hōs diēs dēpōneret? Cūr ——

Geta. Sed hīs diēbus servī līberī sunt! Rēgem habent, ē numerō servōrum dēlēctum! Rēx domum regit! Nūllus labor est!

Boadīx. Coquīs labor semper est! Abīte[1]!

---

[1] *Be off!*

Hector. Nunc nōn est tempus labōris. Tē teneō! Sī nōbīscum Sāturnālia nōn clāmābis, —— in viam tē ēiciēmus!

Bellus. Eat stupidus ad labōrem!

Geta. Eat!

Boadīx. Poenam dabitis, —— pessimī! (*Exit*)

Geta (*Hectorī*). Eat, —— nam dē graviōribus rēbus loquī dēbēmus!

Hector. Dē graviōribus quam dē Boadīce loquī nōn possumus! Ha, ha!

Geta (*Hectorī*). Nōnne tū cōnfīdis tē rēgem futūrum esse?

Servī. Iō Sāturnālia!

Hector. Rēgem?

Geta. Rēgem familiae, —— servum quī reliquōs servōs Sāturnālibus regit.

Hector. Mē?

Geta. Tē! Maximus servōrum es. Dominus tē amat. —— Mihi dīxit tē sibi cārissimum servōrum esse!

Hector. Dīxitne?

Geta. Dīxit. Sed Bellus putat sē rēgem futūrum esse!

Hector. Bellus! Puer est! Rēx nōn erit!

Geta. Tū rēx eris! Iō Sāturnālia!

Hector et reliquī Servī. Iō Sāturnālia!

Geta (*Bellō*). Nōnne tū cōnfīdis tē rēgem familiae futūrum esse?

Bellus. Mē?

Geta. Tē! Pulcherrimus servōrum es. Dominus tē amat. —— Mihi dīxit tē sibi cārissimum servōrum esse! Sed Hector putat sē rēgem futūrum esse!

Bellus. Hector? Nōn pulcher est!

Hector. Servī! Nōnne mē audītis?

Servī. Audīmus.

Hector. Rēx familiae erō!

Bellus. Quid? Ego rēx erō!

Hector. Puer es!

Bellus. Tē nōn timeō! Tē interficiam!

Hector. Tē in viam ēiciam!

Bellus. Em!

Hector. Em tibi! (*Pugnant*)

Servī. Bellus vincit! Bene, Hector! Bellus eum interficiet! Iō!

(*Calpurnius ā dextrā parte, Boadīx ā sinistrā parte accēdunt*)

Calpurnius et Boadīx. Quid hoc?

Servī. Dominus adest! Illī tamen pugnant!

Calpurnius. Quid hoc! Librum meum legere nōn possum!

Geta (*Calpurniō*). Diū pugnāvērunt! Ego eōs dēsinere pugnāre iussī, sed mihi nōn pāruērunt. Sī mē rēgem familiae faciēs, mihi pārēbunt! Rēx bonus erō. ——

Calpurnius. O-ho! Rēx familiae!

Hector et Bellus. Mēne vocās? Ōh! Dominus est!

Calpurnius. Ha, ha! Rēgem familiae dēligere dēbeō! In memoriā nōn habēbam! Dēligō ——

Hector et Bellus et Geta. Mē!

Calpurnius. Dēligō servum mihi cārissimum et optimum, —— coquum!

Servī. Coquum!

Calpurnius. Boadīx, rēx es! Em, vidēsne? Haec pecūnia tua est! Sī servī tibi pārēbunt, eīs partem dā[1]! Sed in memoriā tenē[2] tē rēgem esse! Bene rege[3]! Iō Sāturnālia! (*Exit*)

Boadīx. Rēx nunc sum! Vōs omnēs nunc mihi auxilium dabitis! Meus labor vester est! Iō Sāturnālia! —— Cūr nōn iam Sāturnālia clāmātis?

Servī. Ōh! Ōh! Sāturnālia dūra!

(*Exeunt*)

Fig. 125. An Unknown Roman

---

[1] *Give!*　[2] *Remember!*　[3] *Rule!*

FIG. 126.   A ROMAN FESTIVAL

SYNTAX OUTLINES FOR FINAL REVIEW

NOUN SYNTAX

(References are to sections)

591.　　　　　　NOMINATIVE

1. Subject of Verb (**13**).
2. Predicate Noun or Adjective (**13**).
   (*a*) Predicate nominative with passive of such verbs as *call, choose*, etc. (**562**).
   　(1. In the active these verbs take two accusatives.)

592.　　　　　　GENITIVE

1. Possession (**38**).
2. Description (**586**).

593.　　　　　　DATIVE

1. Indirect Object (**48**).
   (*a*) With transitive verbs (*give*, etc.) and Acc. of Dir. Obj. (**537**).
   (*b*) With certain intransitive verbs (*favor*, etc.) (**541**).
2. With adjectives meaning *like, fit, near*, etc. (**415**).
3. Reference (person concerned) (**571**).
4. Purpose (often with dat. of reference and **sum**) (**572**).
5. Agent (with future passive participle) (**579**).

594.　　　　　　ACCUSATIVE

1. Direct Object (**25**).
2. Place to Which with **ad** or **in** (**96**).
3. Subject of an Infinitive (**204**).
4. Extent of Time or Space (**481**).
5. Prepositions with acc.: **ad, ante, circum, contrā, ob, per, trāns, post, inter, super**; also **in** and **sub** after verbs of motion.
6. Two Accusatives: see Nominative, **2** (*a*) 1.

595.　　　　　　ABLATIVE

(a) With Preposition

1. Agent (person) with **ab** (**ā**) (**182**).
2. Place Where with **in, sub** (**75**, *a*).
3. Place from Which with **ab, dē, ex** (**84**).

4. Separation [1] with **ab, dē, ex** (**84**).
5. Accompaniment with **cum** (**150**).
6. Manner with **cum** [2] (**250**).
7. Prepositions with the abl.: **ab, cum, dē, ex, prae, prō**; also **in** and **sub** after verbs of rest or position.
    (b) *Without Preposition*
8. Means (thing) (**56**).
9. Time When (**338**).
10. Respect (**322**).
11. Ablative Absolute (**292**).
12. Measure of Difference (**573**).
13. Description (**586**).
14. Special Verbs (**576**).
15. Cause (**97**, footnote).

596.   VOCATIVE

A separate case of address, called the **vocative**, is used in the singular of –**us** and –**ius** nouns and adjectives of the second declension. The ending is –**e** in –**us** nouns and –**ī** in –**ius** nouns.

597.   LOCATIVE

In the singular of **domus** and of names of towns of the first and second declensions, a special case, known as the **locative**, identical in form with the genitive singular, is used to express Place Where.

FIG. 127. CUPIDS GATHERING GRAPES

---

[1] When the separation is not meant literally, the preposition is usually omitted: **Līberor timōre**, *I am freed from fear.*
[2] When an adjective is used with the noun, **cum** may be omitted.

VERB SYNTAX

598.   **SUBORDINATE CLAUSES**

1. Used as Adverbs

Name	*Introduced by*	*Translated by*	*Verb in*
Purpose (**434**)	**ut** (neg. **nē**)	*to, in order to, so that*	Subjunctive
Result (**470**)	**ut** (neg. **ut nōn**)	*that, so that*	Subjunctive
Cause (**133, 486**)	**quod, quia**	*because*	Indicative
Temporal (**340**)	**dum**	*while*	Pres. Indic.
Conditional (**381**)	**sī**	*if*	Indicative [1]
Past Temporal (**524**)	**cum**	*when, after*	Imperf. and Past Perf. Subjunct.
Past Temporal (**524**)	**ubi, postquam**	*when, after*	Perf. Indic.

2. Used as Adjectives

Simple Relative (**241**)	**qui**	*who, which*	Indicative

3. Used as Nouns (subject, object)

a. Finite

Name	*Introduced by*	*Translated by*	*Verb in*
Indirect Question (**488**)	**quis, ubi, cūr,** etc.		Subjunctive
Volitive (**515**)	**ut** (neg. **nē**)	*to, that*	Subjunctive
Result (**515**)	**ut** (neg. **ut nōn**)	*that, so that*	Subjunctive
Cause (**133**)	**quod**	*because, that*	Indicative

b. Infinitive

Use	*After Verbs*	*Translated by*
Subject or Object	as in English, without subject	Infinitive (**106, 107**)
Object	*order, teach,* etc., as in English, with subj. acc.	Infinitive (**204**)
Object (indir. statement)	*saying, thinking, knowing,* etc., with subj. acc.	"That" clause (**376**)

---

[1] Subjunctive uses have not been discussed.

599.   TENSE

a. Imperfect Indicative — state of being; repeated, customary, or continuous action (**193**)

Perfect Indicative — act performed once (**193**)

b.   Sequence (**441, 447, 498**)

Primary (present, future) followed by primary tenses
Secondary (past) followed by secondary tenses

Primary Tenses of the Subjunctive: present, perfect
Secondary Tenses of the Subjunctive: imperfect, past perfect

c.   **Summary of Subjunctive Uses by Tenses**

 I. Present Tense Only
  Independent Volitive. Negative **nē** (**429**)

 II. Present and Imperfect Tenses
   (*a*) Purpose, introduced by **ut**, negative **nē** (**434**)
   (*b*) Subordinate Volitive introduced by **ut**, negative **nē** (**515**, *a*)
   (*c*) Result, introduced by **ut**, negative **ut nōn** (**470, 515**, *b*)

 III. Imperfect and Past Perfect Tenses
  Cum Descriptive (**524**)

 IV. Any Tense Required
  Indirect Question (**488**)

600. **EXPRESSIONS OF PURPOSE SUMMARIZED**

    a. **For Short Statements**

Dative (confined to nouns) (**572**)
Future passive participle or gerund with **ad** [1] (**579, 584**)
Future passive participle or gerund with **causā** or **grātiā** (**577, 579, 584**)

    b. **For Longer Statements**

ut (negative **nē**) and the subjunctive (**434**)

---

[1] When there is a noun that can be modified, the future passive participle is preferred to the gerund.

601. **TENSES OF INFINITIVES AND PARTICIPLES**

(Determined by main verb)

Present : *same time as* main verb (**361**)
Perfect : *before* main verb (**384**)
Future : *after* main verb

602. **AGREEMENT**

Adjectives agree in number, gender, and case with the nouns which they modify (**15**).

Verbs agree in person and number with their subjects (**29**).

When two singular subjects are connected by **aut, aut . . . aut, neque . . . neque**, the verb is singular (**183**).

The **relative pronoun** agrees in gender and number with its antecedent but its case depends upon its use in its own clause (**244**).

Appositives agree in case (**130**).

FIG. 128. BATHS OF CARACALLA, ROME

The baths were really magnificent clubhouses which served as community centers for the Romans. Besides the baths and swimming pools there were gymnasiums, lecture rooms, reading rooms, etc.

© *International*

FIG. 129. OSTIA FROM AN AIRPLANE

This town at the mouth (**ostia**) of the Tiber was the busy seaport of ancient Rome.   It is now several miles inland because of the river deposits.

SUPPLEMENTARY READING

Cicero's Jests

Cum Cicerō Lentulum generum suum, parvae statūrae hominem, vīdisset longō gladiō accīnctum, "Quis," inquit, " generum meum ad gladium alligāvit?". . . Mātrōna quaedam, iūniōrem sē quam erat simulāns, dīcēbat sē trīgintā annōs habēre; cui Cicerō "Vērum est," inquit, " nam illam hoc dīcere iam vīgintī annōs audiō." . . . Dē Canīniō, quī quīnque hōrās cōnsul erat, Cicerō scrīpsit: " Maximā fuit vigilantiā Canīnius; nam tōtō suō cōnsulātū somnum nōn vīdit." . . . Hominī quī multa falsa dē annīs aetātis suae dīcēbat Cicerō respondit: "Itaque ubi ego et tū puerī in lūdō erāmus, nōn erās nātus."

Roman Wit [1]

No Friend of Mine

1. Nōn amo tē, Sabidī,[2] nec possum dīcere quārē;
   Hoc tantum possum dīcere, nōn amo tē.

No Change of Occupation

2. Nūper erat medicus, nunc est vispillo Diaulus,
   Quod vispillo facit, fēcerat et [3] medicus.

Nothing at All

3. Esse nihil dīcis quidquid petis, improbe [2] Cinna:
   Sī nīl,[4] Cinna, petis, nīl tibi, Cinna, negō.

A Deadly Friend

4. Omnēs quās habuit, Fabiāne,[2] Lycōris amīcās
   Extulit [5]: uxōrī fīat amīca meae.

Teeth

5. Thāis habet nigrōs, niveōs Laecānia dentēs.
   Quae ratiō est? Ēmptōs haec habet, illa suōs.

---

[1] These are epigrams of Martial, a Roman poet of the end of the first century, A.D. [2] See **596**. [3] = **etiam**. [4] = **nihil**. [5] *Buried* (lit., *carried out* — for burial).

Proverbs of Publilius Syrus

1. Bonus vir nēmō est nisi quī bonus est omnibus.
2. Fraus [1] est accipere quod nōn possīs reddere.
3. Gravissimum est imperium cōnsuētūdinis.
4. Iniūriārum remedium est oblīviō.
5. Īrācundiam quī vincit, hostem superat maximum.
6. Malum est cōnsilium quod mūtārī nōn potest.
7. Necessitās dat lēgem, nōn ipsa accipit.
8. Nūlla hominum maior poena est quam infēlīcitās.
9. Nōn nōvit [2] virtūs calamitātī cēdere.
10. Nēmō timendō ad summum pervenit locum.
11. Sēditiō cīvium hostium est occāsiō.
12. Ubi lībertās cecidit, audet lībere nēmō loquī.

Isaiah ii, 3–4. A Prophecy of World Peace [3]

Et ībunt populī multī et dīcent : Venīte,[4] ascendāmus ad montem Dominī et ad domum Deī Iacob [5] et docēbit nōs viās suās, et ambulābimus in sēmitīs eius ; quia dē Sīon exībit lēx, et verbum Dominī dē Ierūsalem, et iūdicābit gentēs, et docēbit populōs multōs ; et cōnflābunt gladiōs suōs in vōmerēs, et lanceās suās in falcēs ; nōn levābit gēns contrā gentem gladium, nec exercēbuntur ultrā ad proelium.

Julius Caesar

C. Iūlius Caesar nōbilissimā Iūliōrum familiā [6] nātus est. Dum adulēscēns ad Asiam nāvigat, ā pīrātīs captus est. Eīs pecūniam flāgitantibus plūs quam flāgitābant dedit. Sed līberātus ad proximam urbem properāvit ibique contrāctīs nāvibus impetum in pīrātās fēcit et eōs vīcit. Posteā quaestor in Hispāniam profectus est. Cum montēs trānsīret et, paupere quōdam vīcō cōnspectō, comitēs dīcerent ibi nūllum locum ambitiōnī esse, Caesar dīxit mālle sē ibi prīmum esse quam Rōmae [7] secundum. Cōnsul creātus

---

[1] Gen. **fraudis**; deriv.? [2] *Know how.* [3] From the Vulgate edition of the Bible. [4] *Come.* [5] Many Hebrew names are indeclinable in Latin. [6] Origin (*from, of*). [7] See **597**.

cum Pompeiō et Crassō sē iūnxit ut ipsī sōlī in rē pūblicā potestātem habērent. Post cōnsulātum Caesar Galliam prōvinciam accēpit. Gessit autem novem annīs haec: Galliam in prōvinciae fōrmam redēgit; Germānōs quī trāns Rhēnum incolunt prīmus Rōmānōrum ponte factō aggressus superāvit. Aggressus est Britannōs, ante nōn nōtōs.

Posteā inter Pompeium et Caesarem aemulātiō ērūpit. Caesar in Italiam rediit et ad Rubicōnem flūmen, quī prōvinciae eius fīnis erat, vēnit. Ibi cōnstitit et dīxit: " Etiam nunc regredī possumus; quod[1] sī ponticulum[2] trānsierimus, omnia armīs agenda erunt." Tum "Iacta ālea est," inquit, et exercitum trādūcī iussit.

Pompeiō victō, Caesar ipse omnem potestātem tenēbat. Sed post paucōs annōs in senātū occīsus est. Cum M. Brūtum, quem in locō fīlī habēbat, sē gladiō petentem vīdisset, ultima verba fuērunt: "Et tū, Brūte."

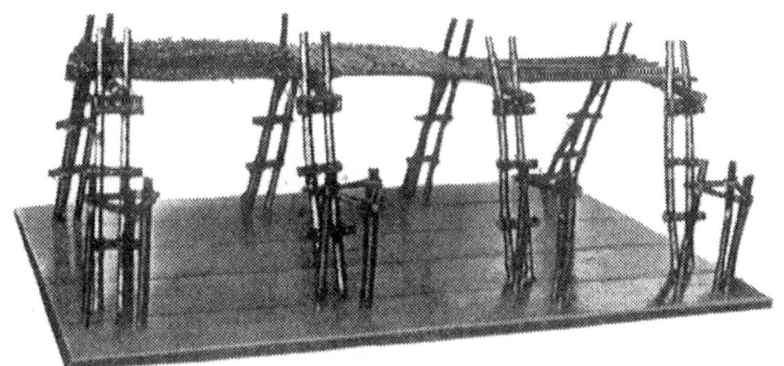

FIG. 130. CAESARIS PŌNS

Military bridges of considerable strength and permanence were used by Caesar in crossing important rivers. In his campaign against the Germans, he twice spanned the Rhine with a well-constructed bridge, 40 feet wide. (From a model made by a high school boy.)

---

[1] *But.*   [2] Diminutive of **pōns.**

Caesar

Selections from *The Gallic War*

1.　　　*Gaul, Its Divisions and Inhabitants*

Gallia est omnis dīvīsa in partēs trēs; quārum ūnam incolunt
Belgae,[1] aliam Aquītānī, tertiam quī ipsōrum linguā Celtae, nostrā
Gallī appellantur.　Hōrum omnium fortissimī sunt Belgae, quod
nōn ad eōs saepe mercātōrēs commeant atque ea quae ad effēmi-
nandōs animōs pertinent important; proximīque sunt Germānīs
quī trāns Rhēnum incolunt, quibuscum continenter bellum gerunt.
Quā dē causā Helvētiī[2] quoque reliquōs Gallōs virtūte praecēdunt,
quod ferē cotīdiānīs proeliīs cum Germānīs contendunt.

2. *The Helvetians Threaten to Invade the Roman Province and
Caesar Prepares to Check Them*

Caesarī cum id nūntiātum esset Helvētiōs per prōvinciam Rōmānam iter facere cōnārī, mātūrat ab urbe proficīscī, et, quam maxi-
mīs potest itineribus, in Galliam ulteriōrem contendit et ad Ge-
navam pervenit.　Ubi dē eius adventū Helvētiī certiōrēs factī sunt,
lēgātōs ad eum mittunt, nōbilissimōs cīvitātis, quī dīcerent[3] sibi
esse in animō sine ūllō maleficiō iter per prōvinciam facere, quod
aliud iter habērent nūllum.

3.　　*After Desperate Fighting the Helvetians Are Defeated*

Diūtius cum Helvētiī sustinēre nostrōrum impetūs nōn possent,
alterī sē, ut coeperant, in montem recēpērunt, alterī ad impedīmenta et carrōs suōs sē contulērunt.　Nam hōc tōtō proeliō, cum[4]
ab hōrā septimā ad vesperum pugnātum sit, āversum hostem vidēre
nēmō potuit.　Tandem impedīmentīs castrīsque nostrī potītī sunt.
Ibi Orgetorīgis fīlia atque ūnus ē fīliīs captus est.

---

[1] Ancestors of the modern Belgians.

[2] The name of the early Swiss.　"Helvetia" is used on Swiss stamps
and coins to-day.

[3] Relative clause of purpose.　　　　　[4] *Although.*

4. *Caesar Crosses the Aisne and Fortifies a Camp*

Postquam omnēs Belgārum cōpiās in ūnum locum coāctās ad sē venīre neque iam longē abesse ab Rēmīs [1] cognōvit, flūmen Axonam,[2] quod est in extrēmīs Rēmōrum fīnibus, exercitum trādūcere mātūrāvit atque ibi castra posuit. In eō flūmine pōns erat. Ibi praesidium pōnit et in alterā parte flūminis Q. Titūrium Sabīnum lēgātum cum sex cohortibus relinquit; castra in altitūdinem pedum duodecim vāllō fossāque duodēvīgintī pedum mūnīrī iubet.

FIG. 131. FIGHTING TOWER ON ROLLERS

Equipped with a battering-ram to attack walls. (From a model made by a high school boy.)

5. *An Ancient Remedy for Food Hoarding*

Vercingetorīx, ratiōne initā, dīxit sē exiguē diērum XXX habēre frūmentum, sed paulō etiam longius tolerārī posse parcendō. Frūmentum omne ad sē referrī iubet, capitis poenam eīs quī nōn pāruerint cōnstituit; pecus, cuius magna erat cōpia ā Mandubiīs compulsa, virītim distribuit, frūmentum parcē et paulātim mētīrī īnstituit.

6. *Caesar Invades Britain and Lands without Resistance*

Accessit Caesar ad Britanniam cum omnibus nāvibus merīdiānō ferē tempore; neque in eō locō hostis est vīsus, sed, ut posteā Caesar ex captīvīs cognōvit, cum magnae manūs eō convēnissent, multitūdine nāvium perterritae, ā lītore discesserant ac sē in superiōra loca abdiderant.

---

[1] The Remi gave their name to Reims, the city whose cathedral was ruined in the World War.

[2] The modern form of Axona is " Aisne," the river which saw so much fighting in the recent war.

Books for Supplementary Reading or Reference

The Children's Plutarch; Tales of the Romans.　(Harper)

Stories from the Classics.　Vol. 3.　By Eva March Tappan (Houghton Mifflin)

Pictures of Roman Life and Story.　By A. J. Church (Appleton)

The Story of Rome.　By Mary MacGregor (Stokes)

Lays of Ancient Rome.　By T. B. Macaulay (Macmillan Pocket Classics)

Last Days of Pompeii.　By Bulwer-Lytton (Macmillan Pocket Classics)

The Story of the Romans.　By H. A. Guerber　(American Book Co.)

Buried Cities.　By Jennie Hall (Macmillan)

The Private Life of the Romans.　By H. W. Johnston (Scott, Foresman)

The Development of Language.　By H. F. Scott and W. L. Carr (Scott, Foresman)

Word Study for High Schools.　By Norma L. Swan (Macmillan)

Fig. 132.　Roman Water Boiler

APPENDIX

PRONUNCIATION [1]

603. **Alphabet**

The English alphabet is one of the many things which we have borrowed from the Romans, but we have added two letters, *j* and *w*. The former is a variation of *i*, the latter, as its name and form show, is a " double *u* (or *v*)."

604. **Vowels**

At one time the English vowels were pronounced like the Latin, but the pronunciation of English has changed greatly. In French, Spanish, Italian, German, etc., which also have adopted the Latin alphabet, the vowels are still pronounced substantially as in Latin.

Each of the Latin vowels may be pronounced long or short, the difference being one of *time*. This is called **quantity**. In addition, all the long vowels except **a** have a different *sound* from the short vowels. This is called **quality**. The pronunciation is as follows :

(a) *Long*	*Short*	*Long and Short* as in
ā as in *father*	a as first *a* in *aha*	*Martha* (ā, ă)
ē as in *they*	e as in *let*	*lateness* (ē, ĕ)
ī as in *police*	i as in *bit*	*seasick* (ī, ĭ)
ō as in *rope*	o as in *obey, for*	*phonograph* (ō, ŏ)
ū as in *rude*	u as in *full*	*two-footed* (ū, ŭ)

In this book long vowels are regularly marked ¯; short vowels are usually unmarked, but ˘ is sometimes used.

(b) **Caution.** — It is very important to distinguish the *sounds* of the long and short vowels. For a person to say, *I heard the din in the hall*, when he meant the " dean," or *I forgot the debt*, when he meant the " date," is no worse than to confuse ī and ĭ, ē and ĕ in Latin.

The English equivalents of **e** and **o** are only approximate. Avoid pronouncing ŏ like *o* in *not* or in *note*.

---

[1] The best way to learn correct pronunciation is by careful imitation of the teacher; the rules are given for reference.

605. **Diphthongs**

The first three of the following diphthongs (two vowels making one sound) are the ones most commonly used :

    ae like *ai* in *aisle*

    au like *ou* in *out*

    oe like *oi* in *oil*

    ei like *ei* in *freight*

    eu like *eh–oo* (pronounced quickly)

    ui like *oo–ee* (pronounced quickly) ; only in **cui** and **huic**

606. **Consonants**

The Latin consonants have, generally speaking, the same sounds as in English.   The following exceptions, however, should be noted :

b before **s** or **t** has the sound of **p**.

c is always hard as in *cat*, never soft as in *city*.

g is always hard as in *go*, never soft as in *gem*.

i (consonant) has the sound of *y* in *year*.

(**i** is a consonant between vowels and before a vowel at the beginning
   of a word)

s always has the sound of *s* in *sin;* never of *s* in *these*.

t always has the sound of *t* in *ten;* never of *t* in *motion*.

v has the sound of *w* in *will*.

x has the sound of *x* in *extra*.

  (**ch** = **k**; **ph** = **f**; **th** = **t**)

Doubled consonants are pronounced separately : **an′–nus**.

607. **English Pronunciation of Latin.** — The above method of pronunciation is the ancient Roman method.   It should be remembered, however, that Latin words which have become thoroughly English should be pronounced as English words; *e.g.* in *terra firma,* the *i* is pronounced as in *firm,* not as in *miracle;* in *alumni,* the *i* is pronounced as in *mile*.

608. **Quantity of Vowels**

The quantity (and quality) of vowels must be learned as part of the word.   There are, however, a few general rules :

1. A vowel is short before another vowel or **h** (because **h** is weakly sounded).

2. A vowel is short before **nt**, **nd**, and final **m** and **t**.

609.   Syllables

Every Latin word has as many syllables as it has vowels or diphthongs: **vir-tū'-te, proe'-li-um.**

A single consonant between two vowels or diphthongs is pronounced with the second: **fī'-li-us, a'-git.** Compound words are divided into their component parts and are exceptions to this rule: **ad'-es.**

When two or more consonants occur between vowels or diphthongs, the division is made before the last consonant: **por'-tus, vīnc'-tī, an'-nus.** An exception to this rule occurs whenever a mute (**p, b, t, d, c, g**) is followed by a liquid (**l, r**), in which case the mute combines with the liquid and both are pronounced with the second vowel: **pū'-bli-cus, cas'-tra.**

The next to the last syllable of a word is called the **penult**; the one before the penult (or the third from the end) is called the **antepenult.**

610.   Quantity of Syllables

Some syllables of course take longer to pronounce than others, just as some vowels are longer than others.

1. A syllable is *naturally* long if it contains a long vowel or a diphthong.

2. A syllable is long (*by position*) if it contains a short vowel followed by two or more consonants or the double consonant **x** (= **cs**).

Note. — Exception is made in the case of a mute followed by a liquid (see above). **H** is so weakly sounded that it does not help make a syllable long.

Caution. — Distinguish carefully between long syllable and long vowel; in **ĕxĕm'plum** the first two syllables are long, though the vowels are short.

611.   Accent

The accented syllable of a word is the one that is pronounced with more stress or emphasis than the others; so in the word *an'swer*, the accent is on the first syllable. In Latin the accent is easily learned according to fixed rules:

1. Words of two syllables are accented on the first: **frā'ter.**

2. Words of three or more syllables are accented on the penult if it is long, otherwise on the antepenult: **lēgā'tus, exem'plum, dī'cĕre, si'mĭlis.**

ELEMENTARY GRAMMAR

The material here given may be reviewed in connection with the
Lessons, where cross references to it will be found.   For the use of those
who prefer to review Elementary Grammar before taking up the Lessons,
a number of explanations are given here which will also be found in the
body of the book.   Teachers can easily devise English exercises for drill
with classes which need it.   The sentences on these pages may be used
for that purpose.

612.   The Sentence.   Subject and Predicate

A **sentence** is a group of words which make complete *sense*.   Every
sentence consists of two parts — the **subject** about which something is
said and the **predicate** which says something about the subject: *The
sailor* (subject) *saved the girl* (predicate), **Nauta puellam servāvit.**

A subject or predicate is said to be **modified** by those words which
are closely associated with it.

613.   Parts of Speech

The words of a language are divided, according to their use, into
eight classes called **parts of speech.**   These are:

Nouns	Verbs	Prepositions
Pronouns	Adverbs	Conjunctions
Adjectives		Interjections

614.   Nouns

A **noun** (from Latin **nōmen,** *name*) is a word that names a person,
place, or thing: *Anna,* **Anna;** *island,* **īnsula;** *letter,* **littera.**

Nouns may be classified as:

a. **Common** (applied to any one of a class): *city,* **urbs;** *girl,* **puella.**

b. **Proper** (applied to a particular one of a class): *Rome,* **Rōma;**
Julia, **Iūlia.**

Note. — Proper nouns always begin with a capital letter.

615.   Pronouns

A **pronoun** (Latin **prō,** *for;* **nōmen,** *name*) is a word used instead of a
noun.   The noun whose place is taken by a pronoun is called an **antecedent** (Latin **ante,** *before;* **cēdere,** *go*).   There are five classes of pronouns:

a. **Personal** pronouns distinguish the three persons: the person speaking (*I*, **ego**; *we,* **nōs** — first person), the person spoken to (*you,* **tū, vōs** — second person), the person or thing spoken of (*he,* **is**; *she,* **ea**; *it,* **id**; *they,* **eī** — third person).

b. **Interrogative** pronouns are used to ask questions: *who,* **quis**; *which, what,* **quid.**

c. **Relative** pronouns relate to a preceding (antecedent) word and join to it a dependent clause: *who,* **quī**; *which, what, that,* **quod.**

d. **Demonstrative** pronouns point out persons or objects definitely — often accompanied with a gesture: *this,* **hic**; *that,* **ille**; *these,* **hī**; *those,* **illī.**

e. **Indefinite** pronouns refer to persons or objects in an indefinite way: *someone, some, any, anyone,* **aliquis**; *no one,* **nēmō**; *each, everyone,* **quisque.**

616.   Adjectives

An **adjective** is a word used to describe or limit the meaning of a noun or pronoun:

a. **Descriptive** adjectives are either **common** or **proper**: *good,* **bonus**; *Roman,* **Rōmānus** (see **614** *a, b,* and **Note**).

b. **Limiting**:

    1. **Article** — definite (*the*), indefinite (*a, an*). There is no word in Latin for " the " or " a."

    2. **Numerals** — **cardinals** (*one, two, three,* etc., **ūnus, duo, trēs,** etc.), **ordinals** (*first, second, third,* etc., **prīmus, secundus, tertius,** etc.)

    3. **Possessive** adjectives (formed from personal pronouns): *my, mine,* **meus**; *our, ours,* **noster**; *your, yours,* **tuus, vester**; *his, her, its,* **eius**; *their, theirs,* **eōrum.**

When interrogative, relative, demonstrative, and indefinite pronouns (**615**) are used as adjectives, they are called respectively:

    4. **Interrogative** adjectives: ***what** street?* **quae** via?

    5. **Relative** adjectives: *He spent a year in Italy, in **which** country he saw many beautiful things,* **Annum in Italiā ēgit, in *quā* terrā multa pulchra vīdit.**

    6. **Demonstrative** adjectives: ***that** road,* **illa via.**

    7. **Indefinite** adjectives: ***some** boy,* **aliquis** puer.

In English the demonstrative adjectives are the only ones that have different forms in the singular and plural: *this, these; that, those.*

617. **Verbs**

A **verb** is a word used to tell something about a subject and expresses action or situation: *He fought, Pugnābat; He is good, Bonus est.*

a. According to use verbs are either **transitive** or **intransitive**.

    1. A **transitive** verb (Latin **trāns**, *over;* **īre,** *go, pass*) is one in which the action expressed by the verb passes over to a receiver: *Anna is carrying water,* **Anna aquam** *portat.*

    2. An **intransitive** verb is one whose action does not pass over to a receiver: *Anna is working,* **Anna** *labōrat.*

Contrast "set" (transitive) with "sit" (intransitive), and "lay" (transitive) with "lie" (intransitive).

b. Intransitive verbs are either **complete** or **linking** (copulative).

    1. A **complete** verb is one which is complete in meaning without an object or other word: *He sails, Nāvigat.*

    2. A **linking** verb is one which links a noun or adjective to the subject: *They are good,* **Bonī** *sunt.*

The chief linking verbs in English are *be, appear, seem, become, feel, look, taste, smell.*

c. An **auxiliary** verb (Latin **auxilium,** *help*) is one used in the conjugation of other verbs: *I am learning;* ***Did*** *you see?* *They* ***have*** *given.*

618. **Adverbs**

An **adverb** is a word used to modify the meaning of a verb, adjective, or other adverb: *He is working* ***now,*** ***Nunc*** labōrat.

619. **Prepositions**

A **preposition** is a word used to show the relation of a noun or pronoun, called its **object,** to some word in the sentence: *He sails* ***to*** *the island,* ***Ad*** **insulam nāvigat.** The preposition is said to **govern** its object.

620. **Conjunctions**

A **conjunction** is a word used to join words, groups of words, and sentences. Conjunctions according to their use may be:

a. **Coördinate,** connecting words or sentences of equal rank (*and,* **et;** *but,* **sed;** *or,* **aut;** *nor,* **neque**).

b. **Subordinate,** connecting a subordinate part of a sentence with a principal part (*if,* **sī;** *while,* **dum;** *because,* **quod,** etc.).

c. **Correlative,** used in pairs (*both . . . and,* **et . . . et;** *neither . . . nor,* **neque . . . neque,** etc.).

621. Interjections

An **interjection** is a word used to show emotion. It has no direct relation to any other word in the sentence: *O! Alas! Ah! Oh!*

622. Inflection

The change of form which words undergo to indicate differences in use is called **inflection**: *boy — boys*, **puer** — **puerī**; *see, saw, seen*, **videō, vīdī, vīsus**. The inflection of nouns is called **declension**. Nouns and pronouns are declined to indicate change in number and case, and sometimes gender. Some pronouns indicate person (**615**, *a*).

623. Number

A noun or pronoun is **singular** when it refers to one person or thing: *girl*, **puella**; *house*, **aedificium**; *mouse*, **mūs**; *tooth*, **dēns**. It is **plural** when it refers to more than one: *girls*, **puellae**; *houses*, **aedificia**; *mice*, **mūrēs**; *teeth*, **dentēs**.

624. Gender

Gender is a distinction in the form of words corresponding to a distinction of sex. It is shown by change of word, by change of endings, or by use of a prefix: *father*, **pater** — *mother*, **māter**; *master*, **dominus** — *mistress*, **domina**; *he-goat* — *she-goat*. The first words given are **masculine**, the second are **feminine**. Most nouns in English have no gender and are therefore **neuter** ("neither" masculine nor feminine).

625. Case

Case is a change in the form of a noun or pronoun to show its use in the sentence: **She** (subject) *is here*, **Ea** adest; *I saw **her*** (object), **Eam** vīdī.

626. Subject and Object

a. The **subject** of a verb is that about which something is said (**612**).

b. The **direct object** is that which is directly affected by the action indicated in the verb: *Anna carries **water***, **Anna aquam** portat. The term object is also applied to a word dependent upon a preposition (**619**).

627.   **Names and Uses of the Cases**

a. **Nominative.** — A noun or pronoun used as the subject of a verb is in the **nominative** case: *The farmer is calling,* **Agricola vocat.**

b. **Accusative** (Objective). — A noun or pronoun used as the object of a verb or preposition is in the **accusative** case: *I sent a book to him,* **Ad eum librum mīsī.**

c. **Dative.** — The noun or pronoun that shows for whom or what the direct object is intended is called the **indirect object** and is put in the **dative** case: *I gave him a book,* **Eī librum dedī.**

d. **Genitive** (Possessive). — Possession is expressed by the genitive case: *the boy's book,* **puerī liber**; *the troops' victory,* **cōpiārum victōria.**

628.   **Conjugation**

The inflection of verbs is called **conjugation.** Verbs are conjugated to indicate *person, number, tense, voice,* and *mood.*

629.   **Person and Number**

A verb must agree with its subject in person and number: *The girl is good,* **Puella est bona**; *The girls are good,* **Puellae sunt bonae.**

630.   **Tense**

Tense is time. There are six tenses:

a. The **present** represents an act as taking place now: *He goes.*

b. The **past** represents an act as having already taken place: *He went yesterday.*

c. The **future** represents an act that will occur at some future date: *He will go to-morrow.*

d. The **present perfect** represents an act as completed but connected in thought with the present: *He has gone* (just left).

e. The **past perfect** represents an act as completed at some definite time in the past: *He had gone* (before something else occurred).

f. The **future perfect** represents an act as completed at or before some definite time in the future: *He will have gone* (before something else will occur).

631. **Progressive and Emphatic Verb Forms**

a. **Progressive** (time or action continuous; used with the auxiliary " be "): *They are studying, they were studying, they will be studying,* *they* **have been studying,** *they* **had been studying,** *they* **will have been studying.**

b. **Emphatic** (with the auxiliary " do," used only in the present and past) :

    1. Used in questions : **Do** (**did**) *you* **know** *this?*
    2. Negative : *I* **do** (**did**) *not* **know** *it.*
    3. Emphatic : *I* **do** (**did**) **believe** *it.*

632.   Voice

A transitive verb is in the **active voice** when it represents the subject as the doer or agent : *Anna* **accuses** *the sailor,* **Anna nautam accūsat.**

A transitive verb is in the **passive voice** when it represents the subject as the receiver of the action : *The sailor* **is accused,** **Nauta accūsātur.**

Note. — Intransitive verbs are used only in the active voice in English.

633.   Mood

The **indicative mood** is used to assert a fact or to ask a question : *Rome* **is a great city,** **Rōma est magna urbs;** *Where is Anna?* **Ubi est Anna?**

634.   Infinitive

The **infinitive** is a form of the verb to which *to* is usually prefixed in English : *to go,* **to** *sing.* It has tense and voice, but not person, number, or mood.

635.   Participle

The **participle** is a verbal adjective. As an adjective it modifies a noun or pronoun : *a* **losing** *fight.* As a verb it may have an object or adverbial modifiers : **losing** *his balance, he fell off.* The participles which are used in English are :

	ACTIVE	PASSIVE
Present	*seeing*	*being seen*
Past	*having seen*	*seen, having been seen*

636.   Synopsis

A synopsis is an outline, showing the given verb in a certain person and number in all moods and tenses (and in both voices if the verb is transitive).

637.   Phrases

A **phrase** is a group of words without subject and predicate.

One important kind of phrase is the **prepositional phrase**, that is, a preposition together with the word or words which it governs : *in great danger*, in **magnō perīculō**.

638.   Clauses

A **clause**, like a phrase, is a part of a sentence but differs from it in having a subject and a predicate.

Clauses are classified as :

a. **Principal**, when used as the leading or independent statement in a sentence : ***The girl** whom you saw on the street **is my sister**, **Puella** quam in viā vīdistī **est mea soror.**

b. **Subordinate**, when used as a dependent statement to modify the principal clause : *The girl **whom you saw on the street** is my sister,* **Puella *quam in viā vīdistī* est mea soror.**

Subordinate clauses are used as single parts of speech :

1. **Substantive clause**: *I saw **what you wrote*** (your writing), **Vīdī *quid scrīberēs*.**

2. **Adjective clause** : *This boy, **who is always good**, will receive a reward* (this good boy), **Hic puer, *quī semper bonus est*, praemium accipiet.**

3. **Adverbial clause** : *I gave him the money **because he earned it**,* **Eī pecūniam dedī *quod eam meruit*.**

639.   Sentences

a. **A simple sentence** contains one principal clause : *My friend, the farmer, has many horses,* **Amīcus meus, agricola, multōs equōs habet.**

b. **A compound sentence** contains two or more principal clauses connected by the coördinate conjunctions " and," " but," etc. : *My friend, the farmer, has many horses, but I have not seen them,* **Amīcus meus, agricola, multōs equōs habet, sed eōs nōn vīdī.**

c. **A complex sentence** contains one principal clause to which one or more subordinate clauses are joined by subordinate conjunctions or by relative or interrogative pronouns : *My friend, the farmer, has many horses which I have not seen,* **Amīcus meus, agricola, multōs equōs habet quōs nōn vīdī.**

SUMMARY OF INFLECTIONS

NOUNS

640. **FIRST DECLENSION (63)   SECOND DECLENSION (79)**

	Singular	Plural	Singular	Plural
Nom.	via	viae	servus	servī
Gen.	viae	viārum	servī	servŏrum
Dat.	viae	viīs	servŏ	servīs
Acc.	viam	viās	servum	servŏs
Abl.	viă	viīs	servŏ	servīs
(Voc.)			(serve)	

641.   **SECOND DECLENSION (90, 100)**

	Singular	Plural	Singular	Plural	Singular	Plural
Nom.	ager	agrī	puer	puerī	signum	signa
Gen.	agrī	agrŏrum	puerī	puerŏrum	signī	signŏrum
Dat.	agrŏ	agrīs	puorŏ	puerīs	signŏ	signīs
Acc.	agrum	agrŏs	puerum	puerŏs	signum	signa
Abl.	agrŏ	agrīs	puerŏ	puerīs	signŏ	signīs

642.   **THIRD DECLENSION (286, 296)**

	Singular	Plural	Singular	Plural	Singular	Plural
Nom.	mīles	mīlitēs	lēx	lēgēs	corpus	corpora
Gen.	mīlitis	mīlitum	lēgis	lēgum	corporis	corporum
Dat.	mīlitī	mīlitibus	lēgī	lēgibus	corporī	corporibus
Acc.	mīlitem	mīlitēs	lēgem	lēgēs	corpus	corpora
Abl.	mīlite	mīlitibus	lēge	lēgibus	corpore	corporibus

I-Stems (305)

	Singular	Plural	Singular	Plural
Nom.	cīvis	cīvēs	mare	maria
Gen.	cīvis	cīvium	maris	marium
Dat.	cīvī	cīvibus	marī	maribus
Acc.	cīvem	cīvēs (īs)	mare	maria
Abl.	cīve	cīvibus	marī	maribus

643.　　　**FOURTH DECLENSION (550)**

	SINGULAR	PLURAL	SINGULAR	PLURAL
Nom.	cāsus	cāsūs	cornū	cornua
Gen.	cāsūs	cāsuum	cornūs	cornuum
Dat.	cāsuī	cāsibus	cornū	cornibus
Acc.	cāsum	cāsūs	cornū	cornua
Abl.	cāsū	cāsibus	cornū	cornibus

644.　　　**FIFTH DECLENSION (566)**

	SINGULAR	PLURAL	SINGULAR	PLURAL
Nom.	diēs	diēs	rēs	rēs
Gen.	diēī	diērum	reī	rērum
Dat.	diēī	diēbus	reī	rēbus
Acc.	diem	diēs	rem	rēs
Abl.	diē	diēbus	rē	rēbus

645.　　**NOUNS OF IRREGULAR OR DEFECTIVE
DECLENSION**

	(366)		**(405)**	**(549)**	
	SING.	PLUR.	SING.	SING.	PLUR.
Nom.	vīs	vīrēs	nēmō	domus	domūs
Gen.	——	vīrium	(nūllīus)	domūs (–ī)	domuum (–ōrum)
Dat.	——	vīribus	nēminī	domuī (–ō)	domibus
Acc.	vim	vīrēs (–īs)	nēminem	domum	domōs (–ūs)
Abl.	vī	vīribus	(nūllō)	domō (–ū)	domibus
(Loc.)				(domī)	

ADJECTIVES

646. FIRST AND SECOND DECLENSIONS (79, 90, 100, 112)

	SINGULAR		
Nom.	magnus, *m.*	magna, *f.*	magnum, *n.*
Gen.	magnī	magnae	magnī
Dat.	magnō	magnae	magnō
Acc.	magnum	magnam	magnum
Abl.	magnō	magnā	magnō
(Voc.	magne)		

PLURAL

Nom.	magnī	magnae	magna
Gen.	magnōrum	magnārum	magnōrum
Dat.	magnīs	magnīs	magnīs
Acc.	magnōs	magnās	magna
Abl.	magnīs	magnīs	magnīs

SINGULAR

Nom.	līber, *m.*	lībera, *f.*	līberum, *n.*
Gen.	līberī	līberae	līberī
Dat.	līberō	līberae	līberō
Acc.	līberum	līberam	līberum
Abl.	līberō	līberā	līberō

PLURAL

Nom.	līberī	līberae	lībera
Gen.	līberōrum	līberārum	līberōrum
Dat.	līberīs	līberīs	līberīs
Acc.	līberōs	līberās	lībera
Abl.	līberīs	līberīs	līberīs

SINGULAR

Nom.	noster, *m.*	nostra, *f.*	nostrum, *n.*
Gen.	nostrī	nostrae	nostrī
Dat.	nostrō	nostrae	nostrō
Acc.	nostrum	nostram	nostrum
Abl.	nostrō	nostrā	nostrō

Plural, **nostrī, nostrae, nostra,** etc.

647.   THIRD DECLENSION (316)

a. THREE ENDINGS

	SINGULAR			PLURAL		
Nom.	ācer, *m.*	ācris, *f.*	ācre, *n.*	ācrēs	ācrēs	ācria
Gen.	ācris	ācris	ācris	ācrium	ācrium	ācrium
Dat.	ācrī	ācrī	ācrī	ācribus	ācribus	ācribus
Acc.	ācrem	ācrem	ācre	ācrēs (īs)	ācrēs (–īs)	ācria
Abl.	ācrī	ācrī	ācrī	ācribus	ācribus	ācribus

b. Two Endings

	SINGULAR		PLURAL	
Nom.	fortis, *m., f.*	forte, *n.*	fortēs	fortia
Gen.	fortis	fortis	fortium	fortium
Dat.	fortī	fortī	fortibus	fortibus
Acc.	fortem	forte	fortēs (–īs)	fortia
Abl.	fortī	fortī	fortibus	fortibus

c. One Ending

	SINGULAR		PLURAL	
Nom.	pār, *m., f.*	pār, *n.*	parēs	paria
Gen.	paris	paris	parium	parium
Dat.	parī	parī	paribus	paribus
Acc.	parem	pār	parēs (–īs)	paria
Abl.	parī	parī	paribus	paribus

648. PRESENT PARTICIPLE (362)

	SINGULAR		PLURAL	
Nom.	parāns, *m., f.*	parāns, *n.*	parantēs	parantia
Gen.	parantis	parantis	parantium	parantium
Dat.	parantī	parantī	parantibus	parantibus
Acc.	parantem	parāns	parantēs (–īs)	parantia
Abl.	parante (–ī)	parante (–ī)	parantibus	parantibus

649.

Nom.	ūnus, *m.*	ūna, *f.*	ūnum,[1] *n.*	trēs, *m., f.*	tria, *n.*
Gen.	ūnīus	ūnīus	ūnīus	trium	trium
Dat.	ūnī	ūnī	ūnī	tribus	tribus
Acc.	ūnum	ūnam	ūnum	trēs	tria
Abl.	ūnō	ūnā	ūnō	tribus	tribus

	(476)			(477)	
Nom.	duo, *m.*	duae, *f.*	duo, *n.*	mīlle	mīlia
Gen.	duōrum	duārum	duōrum	mīlle	mīlium
Dat.	duōbus	duābus	duōbus	mīlle	mīlibus
Acc.	duōs	duās	duo	mīlle	mīlia
Abl.	duōbus	duābus	duōbus	mīlle	mīlibus

---

[1] **Alius** has **aliud** in the nom. and acc. sing. neuter. The plural is regular.

650. COMPARISON OF ADJECTIVES

a. REGULAR (**399, 412, 414**)

POSITIVE	COMPARATIVE	SUPERLATIVE
altus, –a, –um	altior, altius	altissimus, –a, –um
fortis, forte	fortior, –ius	fortissimus, –a, –um
līber, –era, –um	līberior, –ius	līberrimus, –a, –um
ācer, ācris, ācre	ācrior, –ius	ācerrimus, –a, –um
facilis, facile	facilior, –ius	facillimus, –a, –um

b. IRREGULAR (**419**)

POSITIVE	COMPARATIVE	SUPERLATIVE
bonus, –a, –um	melior, –ius	optimus, –a, –um
malus, –a, –um	peior, –ius	pessimus, –a, –um
magnus, –a, –um	maior, –ius	maximus, –a, –um
parvus, –a, –um	minor, –us	minimus, –a, –um
multus, –a, –um	——, plūs	plūrimus, –a, –um
īnferus, –a, –um	īnferior, –ius	īnfimus *or* īmus, –a, –um
superus, –a, –um	superior, –ius	suprēmus *or* summus, –a, –um
——	prior, –ius	prīmus, –a, –um
——	propior, –ius	proximus, –a, –um
——	ulterior, –ius	ultimus, –a, –um

651. DECLENSION OF COMPARATIVES (400, 419)

	SINGULAR		PLURAL	
Nom.	altior, *m., f.*	altius, *n.*	altiōrēs	altiōra
Gen.	altiōris	altiōris	altiōrum	altiōrum
Dat.	altiōrī	altiōrī	altiōribus	altiōribus
Acc.	altiōrem	altius	altiōrēs	altiōra
Abl.	altiōre	altiōre	altiōribus	altiōribus

	SINGULAR	PLURAL	
Nom.	plūs,[1] *n.*	plūrēs, *m., f.*	plūra, *n.*
Gen.	plūris	plūrium	plūrium
Dat.	——	plūribus	plūribus
Acc.	plūs	plūrēs	plūra
Abl.	plūre	plūribus	plūribus

[1] Masculine and feminine lacking in the singular.

652.   COMPARISON OF ADVERBS (408, 420)

POSITIVE	COMPARATIVE	SUPERLATIVE
altē	altius	altissimē
līberē	līberius	līberrimē
fortiter	fortius	fortissimē
facile	facilius	facillimē
bene	melius	optimē
male	peius	pessimē
multum	plūs	plūrimum
———	minus	minimē
———	magis	maximē

653.   NUMERALS (272, 475)

	ROMAN NUMERALS	CARDINALS	ORDINALS
1.	I.	ūnus, –a, –um	prīmus, –a, –um
2.	II.	duo, duae, duo	secundus (alter)
3.	III.	trēs, tria	tertius
4.	IV.	quattuor	quārtus
5.	V.	quīnque	quīntus
6.	VI.	sex	sextus
7.	VII.	septem	septimus
8.	VIII.	octō	octāvus
9.	IX.	novem	nōnus
10.	X.	decem	decimus
11.	XI.	ūndecim	ūndecimus
12.	XII.	duodecim	duodecimus
13.	XIII.	tredecim	tertius decimus
14.	XIV.	quattuordecim	quārtus decimus
15.	XV.	quīndecim	quīntus decimus
16.	XVI.	sēdecim	sextus decimus
17.	XVII.	septendecim	septimus decimus
18.	XVIII.	duodēvīgintī	duodēvīcēsimus
19.	XIX.	ūndēvīgintī	ūndēvīcēsimus
20.	XX.	vīgintī	vīcēsimus
21.	XXI.	vīgintī ūnus *or* ūnus et vīgintī	vīcēsimus prīmus *or* ūnus et vīcēsimus
30.	XXX.	trīgintā	trīcēsimus
40.	XL.	quadrāgintā	quadrāgēsimus
50.	L.	quīnquāgintā	quīnquāgēsimus

60.	LX.	sexāgintā	sexāgēsimus
70.	LXX.	septuāgintā	septuāgēsimus
80.	LXXX.	octōgintā	octōgēsimus
90.	XC.	nōnāgintā	nōnāgēsimus
100.	C.	centum	centēsimus
101.	CI.	centum (et) ūnus	centēsimus (et) prīmus
200.	CC.	ducentī, –ae, –a	ducentēsimus
300.	CCC.	trecentī, –ae, –a	trecentēsimus
400.	CCCC.	quadringentī, –ae, –a	quadringentēsimus
500.	D.	quīngentī, –ae, –a	quīngentēsimus
600.	DC.	sescentī, –ae, –a	sescentēsimus
700.	DCC.	septingentī, –ae, –a	septingentēsimus
800.	DCCC.	octingentī, –ae, –a	octingentēsimus
900.	DCCCC.	nōngentī, –ae, –a	nōngentēsimus
1000.	M.	mīlle	mīllēsimus
2000.	MM.	duo mīlia	bis mīllēsimus

PRONOUNS

654. PERSONAL (451)

	Sing.	Plur.	Sing.	Plur.	M. F. N.
Nom.	ego	nōs	tū	vōs	is ea id
Gen.	meī	nostrum (nostrī)	tuī	vestrum (–trī)	(For declen-
Dat.	mihi	nōbīs	tibi	vōbīs	sion see **656**
Acc.	mē	nōs	tē	vōs	— demon-
Abl.	mē	nōbīs	tē	vōbīs	strative is)

655. REFLEXIVE (452)

FIRST PERSON   SECOND PERSON

Gen. **meī** (declined like **ego**)   **tuī** (declined like **tū**)

Note. — Reflexive pronouns are not used in the nominative.

THIRD PERSON

	Singular	Plural
Gen.	suī	suī
Dat.	sibi	sibi
Acc.	sē (sēsē)	sē (sēsē)
Abl.	sē (sēsē)	sē (sēsē)

656.　　　DEMONSTRATIVE (**333, 341, 348**)

	SINGULAR			PLURAL		
Nom.	hic, *m.*	haec, *f.*	hoc, *n.*	hĭ	hae	haec
Gen.	huius	huius	huius	hŏrum	hārum	hŏrum
Dat.	huic	huic	huic	hĭs	hĭs	hĭs
Acc.	hunc	hanc	hoc	hŏs	hās	haec
Abl.	hōc	hāc	hōc	hĭs	hĭs	hĭs
Nom.	is, *m.*	ea, *f.*	id, *n.*	eĭ (iĭ)	eae	ea
Gen.	eius	eius	eius	eŏrum	eārum	eŏrum
Dat.	eī	eī	eī	eĭs (iĭs)	eĭs (iĭs)	eĭs (iĭs)
Acc.	eum	eam	id	eŏs	eās	ea
Abl.	eō	eā	eō	eĭs (iĭs)	eĭs (iĭs)	(eĭs) iĭs

	SINGULAR			PLURAL		
Nom.	īdem, *m.*	eadem, *f.*	idem, *n.*	eīdem (īdem)	eaedem	eadem
Gen.	eiusdem	eiusdem	eiusdem	eŏrundem	eārundem	eŏrundem
Dat.	eīdem	eīdem	eīdem	eīsdem (īsdem)	eīsdem (īsdem)	eīsdem (īsdem)
Acc.	eundem	eandem	idem	eŏsdem	eāsdem	eadem
Abl.	eōdem	eādem	eōdem	eīsdem (īsdem)	eīsdem (īsdem)	eīsdem (īsdem)

DEMONSTRATIVE (333)

	SINGULAR		
Nom.	ille, *m.*	illa, *f.*	illud, *n.*
Gen.	illīus	illīus	illīus
Dat.	illī	illī	illī
Acc.	illum	illam	illud
Abl.	illō	illā	illō

(Plur. regular like **magnus**)

INTENSIVE (352)

	SINGULAR		
Nom.	ipse, *m.*	ipsa, *f.*	ipsum, *n.*
Gen.	ipsīus	ipsīus	ipsīus
Dat.	ipsī	ipsī	ipsī
Acc.	ipsum	ipsam	ipsum
Abl.	ipsō	ipsā	ipsō

(Plur. regular)

657.　　　RELATIVE (**241**)

	SINGULAR			PLURAL		
Nom.	quĭ, *m.*	quae, *f.*	quod, *n.*	quĭ	quae	quae
Gen.	cuius	cuius	cuius	quŏrum	quārum	quŏrum
Dat.	cui	cui	cui	quibus	quibus	quibus
Acc.	quem	quam	quod	quŏs	quās	quae
Abl.	quō	quā	quō	quibus	quibus	quibus

658.   INTERROGATIVE (255) [1]

SINGULAR

Nom.	quis,[2] *m., f.*	quid, *n.*
Gen.	cuius	cuius
Dat.	cui	cui
Acc.	quem	quid
Abl.	quō	quō

659.   INDEFINITE (556)

	SINGULAR		PLURAL		
Nom.	aliquis, *m., f.*	aliquid, *n.*	aliquī	aliquae	aliqua
Gen.	alicuius	alicuius	aliquōrum	aliquārum	aliquōrum
Dat.	alicui	alicui	aliquibus	aliquibus	aliquibus
Acc.	aliquem	aliquid	aliquōs	aliquās	aliqua
Abl.	aliquō	aliquō	aliquibus	aliquibus	aliquibus

(The adjective form is aliquī, –qua, –quod, etc.)

SINGULAR

Nom.	quīdam, *m.*	quaedam, *f.*	quiddam, *n.*
Gen.	cuiusdam	cuiusdam	cuiusdam
Dat.	cuidam	cuidam	cuidam
Acc.	quendam	quandam	quiddam
Abl.	quōdam	quādam	quōdam

PLURAL

Nom.	quīdam	quaedam	quaedam
Gen.	quōrundam	quārundam	quōrundam
Dat.	quibusdam	quibusdam	quibusdam
Acc.	quōsdam	quāsdam	quaedam
Abl.	quibusdam	quibusdam	quibusdam

(The adjective has quoddam for quiddam)

---

[1] Plural like that of quī.   [2] Interrogative adjective quī declined throughout like relative quī.

REGULAR VERBS

660.　　　FIRST CONJUGATION

Principal Parts: **parō, parāre, parāvī, parātus**
(Stems: **parā-, parāv-, parāt-**)

ACTIVE VOICE　　　　　　　PASSIVE VOICE

INDICATIVE

PRESENT (**20**)　　　　　　　PRESENT (**176**)

parō	parāmus	paror	parāmur
parās	parātis	parāris (–re)	parāminī
parat	parant	parātur	parantur

IMPERFECT (**33**)　　　　　　IMPERFECT (**176**)

parābam	parābāmus	parābar	parābāmur
parābās	parābātis	parābāris (–re)	parābāminī
parābat	parābant	parābātur	parābantur

FUTURE (**43**)　　　　　　　FUTURE (**176**)

parābō	parābimus	parābor	parābimur
parābis	parābitis	parāberis (–re)	parābiminī
parābit	parābunt	parābitur	parābuntur

PERFECT (**188**)　　　　　　PERFECT (**213**)

parāvī	parāvimus
parāvistī	parāvistis
parāvit	parāvērunt (–ēre)

parātus (–a, –um) { sum / es / est }　parātī (–ae, –a) { sumus / estis / sunt }

PAST PERFECT (**197**)　　　　PAST PERFECT (**214**)

parāveram	parāverāmus
parāverās	parāverātis
parāverat	parāverant

parātus (–a, –um) { eram / erās / erat }　parātī (–ae, –a) { erāmus / erātis / erant }

FUTURE PERFECT (**198**)　　　FUTURE PERFECT (**219**)

parāverō	parāverimus
parāveris	parāveritis
parāverit	parāverint

parātus (–a, –um) { erō / eris / erit }　parātī (–ae, –a) { erimus / eritis / erunt }

ACTIVE VOICE	PASSIVE VOICE

SUBJUNCTIVE

PRESENT (438) — PRESENT (438)

parem	parēmus	parer	parēmur
parēs	parētis	parēris (–re)	parēminī
paret	parent	parētur	parentur

IMPERFECT (446) — IMPERFECT (446)

pararem	parārēmus	parārer	parārēmur
parārēs	parārētis	parārēris (–re)	parārēminī
parāret	parārent	parārētur	parārentur

PERFECT (495) — PERFECT (495)

parāverim	parāverīmus	parātus (–a, –um) { sim / sīs / sit }	parātī (–ae, –a) { sīmus / sītis / sint }
parāverīs	parāverītis		
parāverit	parāverint		

PAST PERFECT (495) — PAST PERFECT (495)

parāvissem	parāvissēmus	parātus (–a, –um) { essem / essēs / esset }	parātī (–ae, –a) { essēmus / essētis / essent }
parāvissēs	parāvissētis		
parāvisset	parāvissent		

PRESENT IMPERATIVE

2nd sing. parā, *prepare (thou)*   parāre, *be (thou) prepared*
2nd plur. parāte, *prepare (ye)*   parāminī, *be (ye) prepared*

INFINITIVE (20, 221, 368, 374)

Present	parāre	parārī
Perfect	parāvisse	parātus esse
Future	parātūrus esse	

PARTICIPLES (211, 362–3, 578)

Present	parāns, *Gen.* –antis	
Perfect		parātus, –a, –um
Future	parātūrus, –a, –um	parandus, –a, um

GERUND (583)

Gen. parandī, *Dat.* parandō, *Acc.* parandum, *Abl.* parandō

661. SECOND CONJUGATION

Principal Parts: **habeō, habēre, habuī, habitus**
(Stems: **habē-, habu-, habit-**)

ACTIVE VOICE · PASSIVE VOICE

INDICATIVE

PRESENT (**69**) · PRESENT (**176**)

habeō	habēmus	habeor	habēmur
habēs	habētis	habēris (–re)	habēminī
habet	habent	habētur	habentur

IMPERFECT (**69**) · IMPERFECT (**176**)

habēbam	habēbāmus	habēbar	habēbāmur
habēbās	habēbātis	habēbāris (–re)	habēbāminī
habēbat	habēbant	habēbātur	habēbantur

FUTURE (**69**) · FUTURE (**176**)

habēbō	habēbimus	habēbor	habēbimur
habēbis	habēbitis	habēberis (–re)	habēbiminī
habēbit	habēbunt	habēbitur	habēbuntur

PERFECT (**188**) · PERFECT (**213**)

habuī	habuimus	habitus (–a, –um) { sum / es / est	habitī (–ae, –a) { sumus / estis / sunt
habuistī	habuistis		
habuit	habuērunt (–ēre)		

PAST PERFECT (**197**) · PAST PERFECT (**214**)

habueram	habuerāmus	habitus (–a, –um) { eram / erās / erat	habitī (–ae, –a) { erāmus / erātis / erant
habuerās	habuerātis		
habuerat	habuerant		

FUTURE PERFECT (**198**) · FUTURE PERFECT (**219**)

habuerō	habuerimus	habitus (–a, –um) { erō / eris / erit	habitī (–ae, –a) { erimus / eritis / erunt
habueris	habueritis		
habuerit	habuerint		

<table>
<tr><td>ACTIVE VOICE</td><td>PASSIVE VOICE</td></tr>
</table>

SUBJUNCTIVE

PRESENT (427)

		PRESENT (427)	
habeam	habeāmus	habear	habeāmur
habeās	habeātis	habeāris (–re)	habeāminī
habeat	habeant	habeātur	habeantur

IMPERFECT (446)

		IMPERFECT (446)	
habērem	habērēmus	habērer	habērēmur
habērēs	habērētis	habērēris (–r)	habērēminī
habēret	habērent	habērētur	habērentur

PERFECT (495)

		PERFECT (495)	
habuerim	habuerīmus		
habuerīs	habuerītis		
habuerit	habuerint		

habitus (–a, –um) { sim, sīs, sit }   habitī (–ae, –a) { sīmus, sītis, sint }

PAST PERFECT (495)

		PAST PERFECT (495)	
habuissem	habuissēmus		
habuissēs	habuissētis		
habuisset	habuissent		

habitus (–a, –um) { essem, essēs, esset }   habitī (–ae, –a) { essēmus, essētis, essent }

PRESENT IMPERATIVE

2nd sing. habē, *have (thou)*		habēre
2nd plur. habēte, *have (ye)*		habēminī

INFINITIVE (20, 221, 368, 374)

Present	habēre	habērī
Perfect	habuisse	habitus esse
Future	habitūrus esse	

PARTICIPLES (211, 362–3, 578)

Present	habēns, *Gen.* –entis	
Perfect		habitus, –a, –um
Future	habitūrus, –a, –um	habendus, –a, –um

GERUND (583)

Gen. habendī, *Dat.* habendō, *Acc.* habendum, *Abl.* habendō

662.   THIRD CONJUGATION

Principal Parts: **pōnō, pōnĕre, posuī, positus**
(Stems: **pŏnĕ-, posu-, posit-**)

ACTIVE VOICE	PASSIVE VOICE

INDICATIVE

PRESENT (**123**)		PRESENT (**176**)	
pōnō	pōnimus	pōnor	pōnimur
pōnis	pōnitis	pōneris (–re)	pōniminī
pōnit	pōnunt	pōnitur	pōnuntur

IMPERFECT (**123**)		IMPERFECT (**176**)	
pōnēbam	pōnēbāmus	pōnēbar	pōnēbāmur
pōnēbās	pōnēbātis	pōnēbāris (–re)	pōnēbāminī
pōnēbat	pōnēbant	pōnēbātur	pōnēbantur

FUTURE (**145**)		FUTURE (**176**)	
pōnam	pōnēmus	pōnar	pōnēmur
pōnēs	pōnētis	pōnēris (–re)	pōnēminī
pōnet	pōnent	pōnētur	pōnentur

PERFECT (**188**)		PERFECT (**213**)	
posuī	posuimus	positus (–a, –um) { sum, es, est }	positī (–ae, –a) { sumus, estis, sunt }
posuistī	posuistis		
posuit	posuērunt (–ēre)		

PAST PERFECT (**197**)		PAST PERFECT (**214**)	
posueram	posuerāmus	positus (–a, –um) { eram, erās, erat }	positī (–ae, –a) { erāmus, erātis, erant }
posuerās	posuerātis		
posuerat	posuerant		

FUTURE PERFECT (**198**)		FUTURE PERFECT (**219**)	
posuerō	posuerimus	positus (–a, –um) { erō, eris, erit }	positī (–ae, –a) { erimus, eritis, erunt }
posueris	posueritis		
posuerit	posuerint		

ACTIVE VOICE	PASSIVE VOICE

SUBJUNCTIVE

PRESENT (**427**)		PRESENT (**427**)	
pōnam	pōnāmus	pōnar	pōnāmur
pōnās	pōnātis	pōnāris (–re)	pōnāminī
pōnat	pōnant	pōnātur	pōnantur

IMPERFECT (**446**)		IMPERFECT (**446**)	
pōnerem	pōnerēmus	pōnerer	pōnerēmur
pōnerēs	pōnerētis	pōnerēris (–re)	pōnerēminī
pōneret	pōnerent	pōnerētur	pōnerentur

PERFECT (**495**)   PERFECT (**495**)

posuerim	posuerīmus
posuerīs	posuerītis
posuerit	posuerint

positus (–a, –um) { sim / sīs / sit }   positī (–ae, –a) { sīmus / sītis / sint }

PAST PERFECT (**495**)   PAST PERFECT (**495**)

posuissem	posuissēmus
posuissēs	posuissētis
posuisset	posuissent

positus (–a, –um) { essem / essēs / esset }   positī (–ae, –a) { essēmus / essētis / essent }

PRESENT IMPERATIVE

2nd sing.	pōne, *place (thou)*	pōnere, *be (thou) placed*
2nd plur.	pōnite, *place (ye)*	pōniminī, *be (ye) placed*

INFINITIVE (**20, 221, 368, 374**)

Present	pōnere	pōnī
Perfect	posuisse	positus esse
Future	positūrus esse	

PARTICIPLES (**211, 362–3, 578**)

Present	pōnēns, *Gen.* –entis	
Perfect		positus, –a, –um
Future	positūrus, –a, –um	pōnendus, a, –um

GERUND (**583**)

Gen. pōnendī, *Dat.* pōnendō, *Acc.* pōnendum, *Abl.* pōnendō

663. FOURTH CONJUGATION

Principal Parts: mūniō, mūnīre, mūnīvī, mūnītus
(Stems: mūnī-, mūnīv-, mūnīt-)

ACTIVE VOICE PASSIVE VOICE

INDICATIVE

PRESENT (136)		PRESENT (176)	
mūniō	mūnīmus	mūnior	mūnīmur
mūnīs	mūnītis	mūnīris (–re)	mūnīminī
mūnit	mūniunt	mūnītur	mūniuntur

IMPERFECT (136)		IMPERFECT (176)	
mūniēbam	mūniēbāmus	mūniēbar	mūniēbāmur
mūniēbās	mūniēbātis	mūniēbāris (–re)	mūniēbāminī
mūniēbat	mūniēbant	mūniēbātur	mūniēbantur

FUTURE (155)		FUTURE (176)	
mūniam	mūniēmus	mūniar	mūniēmur
mūniēs	mūniētis	mūniēris (–re)	mūniēminī
mūniet	mūnient	mūniētur	mūnientur

PERFECT (188)		PERFECT (213)	
mūnīvī	mūnīvimus		
mūnīvistī	mūnīvistis	mūnītus (–a, –um) { sum, es, est }	mūnītī (–ae, –a) { sumus, estis, sunt }
mūnīvit	mūnīvērunt (–ēre)		

PAST PERFECT (197)		PAST PERFECT (214)	
mūnīveram	mūnīverāmus		
mūnīverās	mūnīverātis	mūnītus (–a, –um) { eram, erās, erat }	mūnītī (–ae, –a) { erāmus, erātis, erant }
mūnīverat	mūnīverant		

FUTURE PERFECT (198)		FUTURE PERFECT (219)	
mūnīverō	mūnīverimus		
mūnīveris	mūnīveritis	mūnītus (–a, –um) { erō, eris, erit }	mūnītī (–ae, –a) { erimus, eritis, erunt }
mūnīverit	mūnīverint		

ACTIVE VOICE		PASSIVE VOICE	

SUBJUNCTIVE

PRESENT (427)   PRESENT (427)

mūniam	mūniāmus	mūniar	mūniāmur
mūniās	mūniātis	mūniāris (–re)	mūniāminī
mūniat	mūniant	mūniātur	mūniantur

IMPERFECT (446)   IMPERFECT (446)

mūnīrem	mūnīrēmus	mūnīrer	mūnīrēmur
mūnīrēs	mūnīrētis	mūnīrēris (–re)	mūnīrēminī
mūnīret	mūnīrent	mūnīrētur	mūnīrentur

PERFECT (495)   PERFECT (495)

mūnīverim	mūnīverīmus		
mūnīverīs	mūnīverītis	mūnītus (–a, –um) { sim / sīs / sit }	mūnītī (–ae, –a) { sīmus / sītis / sint }
mūnīverit	mūnīverint		

PAST PERFECT (495)   PAST PERFECT (495)

mūnīvissem	mūnīvissēmus		
mūnīvissēs	mūnīvissētis	mūnītus (–a, –um) { essem / essēs / esset }	mūnītī (–ae, –a) { essēmus / essētis / essent }
mūnīvisset	mūnīvissent		

PRESENT IMPERATIVE

2nd sing.	mūnī, *fortify (thou)*	mūnīre, *be (thou) fortified*
2nd plur.	mūnīte, *fortify (ye)*	mūnīminī, *be (ye) fortified*

INFINITIVE (20, 221, 368, 374)

Present	mūnīre	mūnīrī
Perfect	mūnīvisse	mūnītus esse
Future	mūnītūrus esse	

PARTICIPLES (211, 362–3, 578)

Present	mūniēns, *Gen.* mūnientis	
Perfect		mūnītus, –a, –um
Future	mūnītūrus, –a, –um	mūniendus, –a, –um

GERUND (583)

Gen. mūniendī, *Dat.* mūniendō, *Acc.* mūniendum, *Abl.* mūniendō

664.   THIRD CONJUGATION –*IŌ* VERBS

Principal Parts: **capiō, capĕre, cēpī, captus**
(Stems: **cape-, cēp-, capt-**)

<table>
<tr><th colspan="2">ACTIVE VOICE</th><th colspan="2">PASSIVE VOICE</th></tr>
</table>

INDICATIVE

PRESENT (**135**)		PRESENT (**176**)	
capiō	capimus	capior	capimur
capis	capitis	caperis (–re)	capiminī
capit	capiunt	capitur	capiuntur

IMPERFECT (**135**)	IMPERFECT (**176**)
capiēbam, etc.	capiēbar, etc.

FUTURE (**155**)		FUTURE (**176**)	
capiam	capiēmus	capiar	capiēmur
capiēs	capiētis	capiēris (–re)	capiēminī
capiet	capient	capiētur	capientur

PERFECT (**188**)	PERFECT (**213**)
cēpī, etc.	captus sum, etc.

PAST PERFECT (**197**)	PAST PERFECT (**214**)
cēperam, etc.	captus eram, etc.

FUTURE PERFECT (**198**)	FUTURE PERFECT (**219**)
cēperō, etc.	captus erō, etc.

SUBJUNCTIVE

PRESENT (**427**)		PRESENT (**427**)	
capiam	capiāmus	capiar	capiāmur
capiās	capiātis	capiāris (–re)	capiāminī
capiat	capiant	capiātur	capiantur

IMPERFECT (**446**)	IMPERFECT (**446**)
caperem, etc.	caperer, etc.

ACTIVE VOICE

PERFECT (495)

cēperim, etc.

PAST PERFECT (495)

cēpissem, etc.

PASSIVE VOICE

PERFECT (495)

captus sim, etc.

PAST PERFECT (495)

captus essem, etc.

PRESENT IMPERATIVE

2nd sing.	cape, *take (thou)*	capere, *be (thou) taken*
2nd plur.	capite, *take (ye)*	capiminī, *be (ye) taken*

INFINITIVE (20, 221, 368, 374)

Present	capere	capī
Perfect	cēpisse	captus esse
Future	captūrus esse	

PARTICIPLES (211, 362-3, 578)

Present	capiēns, *Gen.* capientis	
Perfect		captus, –a, –um
Future	captūrus, –a, –um	capiendus, –a, –um

GERUND (583)

Gen. capiendī, *Dat.* capiendō, *Acc.* capiendum, *Abl.* capiendō

665. DEPONENT VERBS (503)

arbitror, arbitrārī, arbitrātus sum	(1st Conj.)
fateor, fatērī, fassus sum	(2nd Conj.)
sequor, sequī, secūtus sum	(3rd Conj.)
gradior, gradī, gressus sum	(3rd Conj. –iō)
experior, experīrī, expertus sum	(4th Conj.)

INDICATIVE

Pres.	arbitror	fateor	sequor
Impf.	arbitrābar	fatēbar	sequēbar
Fut.	arbitrābor	fatēbor	sequar
Perf.	arbitrātus sum	fassus sum	secūtus sum
Past P.	arbitrātus eram	fassus eram	secūtus eram
Fut. P.	arbitrātus erō	fassus erō	secūtus erō

Pres.	gradior	experior
Impf.	gradiēbar	experiēbar
Fut.	gradiar	experiar
Perf.	gressus sum	expertus sum
Past. P.	gressus eram	expertus eram
Fut. P.	gressus erō	expertus erō

Subjunctive

Pres.	arbitrer	fatear	sequar
Impf.	arbitrārer	fatērer	sequerer
Perf.	arbitrātus sim	fassus sim	secūtus sim
Past P.	arbitrātus essem	fassus essem	secūtus essem

Pres.	gradiar	experiar
Impf.	graderer	experīrer
Perf.	gressus sim	expertus sim
Past. P.	gressus essem	expertus essem

Present Imperative

2d sing.	arbitrāre	fatēre	sequere
2d plur.	arbitrāminī	fatēminī	sequiminī

2d sing.	gradere	experīre
2d plur.	gradiminī	experīminī

Infinitive

Pres.	arbitrārī	fatērī	sequī
Perf.	arbitrātus esse	fassus esse	secūtus esse
Fut.	arbitrātūrus esse	fassūrus esse	secūtūrus esse

Pres.	gradī	experīrī
Perf.	gressus esse	expertus esse
Fut.	gressūrus esse	expertūrus esse

Participles

Pres.	arbitrāns	fatēns	sequēns
Perf.	arbitrātus	fassus	secūtus
Fut. Act.	arbitrātūrus	fassūrus	secūtūrus
Fut. Pass.	arbitrandus	fatendus	sequendus

Pres.	gradiēns	experiēns
Perf.	gressus	expertus
Fut. Act.	gressūrus	expertūrus
Fut. Pass.	gradiendus	experiendus

IRREGULAR VERBS

666.   Principal Parts: **sum, esse, fuī, futūrus**

INDICATIVE   SUBJUNCTIVE

(95)   PRESENT   (440)

sum	sumus		sim	sīmus
es	estis		sīs	sītis
est	sunt		sit	sint

(105)   IMPERFECT   (446)

eram	erāmus		essem	essēmus
erās	erātis		essēs	essētis
erat	erant		esset	essent

(105)   FUTURE

erō	erimus
eris	eritis
erit	erunt

(192)   PERFECT   (495)

fuī	fuimus		fuerim	fuerīmus
fuistī	fuistis		fuerīs	fuerītis
fuit	fuērunt (–ēre)		fuerit	fuerint

(203)   PAST PERFECT   (495)

fueram	fuerāmus		fuissem	fuissēmus
fuerās	fuerātis		fuissēs	fuissētis
fuerat	fuerant		fuisset	fuissent

(203)   FUTURE PERFECT

fuerō	fuerimus
fueris	fueritis
fuerit	fuerint

PRESENT IMPERATIVE

2nd sing. es   *2nd plur.* **este**

INFINITIVE (368, 374)	PARTICIPLE (363)
Pres. esse	———
Perf. fuisse	———
Fut. futūrus esse	futūrus, –a, –um

667. Principal Parts: possum, posse, potuī, ——

INDICATIVE (265)		SUBJUNCTIVE (440, 446, 495)	
Pres. possum	possumus	possim	possīmus
potes	potestis	possīs	possītis
potest	possunt	possit	possint
Impf. poteram, *etc.*		possem, *etc.*	
Fut. poterō, *etc.*			
Perf. potuī, *etc.*		potuerim, *etc.*	
Past P. potueram, *etc.*		potuissem, *etc.*	
Fut. P. potuerō, *etc.*			

INFINITIVE (262, 368)

Present posse   *Perfect* potuisse

PARTICIPLE (362)

Present potēns, *Gen.* –entis (adj.), *powerful*

668. Principal Parts: ferō, ferre, tulī, lātus

INDICATIVE (395)

ACTIVE		PASSIVE	
Pres. ferō	ferimus	feror	ferimur
fers	fertis	ferris (–re)	feriminī
fert	ferunt	fertur	feruntur
Impf. ferēbam, *etc.*		ferēbar, *etc.*	
Fut. feram, ferēs, *etc.*		ferar, ferēris, *etc.*	
Perf. tulī, *etc.*		lātus sum, *etc.*	
Past P. tuleram, *etc.*		lātus eram, *etc.*	
Fut. P. tulerō, *etc.*		lātus erō, *etc.*	

Subjunctive (**427, 446, 495**)

	ACTIVE	PASSIVE
Pres.	feram, ferās, *etc.*	ferar, ferāris, *etc.*
Impf.	ferrem, *etc.*	ferrer, *etc.*
Perf.	tulerim, *etc.*	lātus sim, *etc.*
Past P.	tulissem, *etc.*	lātus essem, *etc.*

Present Imperative

2nd Pers.	fer	ferte	ferre	feriminī

Infinitive (**395**)

Pres.	ferre	ferrī
Perf.	tulisse	lātus esse
Fut.	lātūrus esse	

Participles (**395, 578**)

Pres.	ferēns, –entis	
Perf.		lātus, –a, –um
Fut.	lātūrus, –a, –um	ferendus, –a, –um

Gerund (**583**)

Gen. ferendī, *Dat.* ferendō, *Acc.* ferendum, *Abl.* ferendō

669.   Principal Parts : eō, īre, iī, itus (**519**)

Indicative

PRESENT		IMPERFECT	FUTURE		PERFECT	
eō	īmus	ībam, *etc.*	ībō	ībimus	iī	iimus
īs	ītis		ībis	ībitis	īstī	īstis
it	eunt		ībit	ībunt	iit	iērunt (–ēre)

Past Perf. ieram, *etc.*   *Fut. Perf.* ierō, *etc.*

Subjunctive

PRESENT	IMPERFECT	PERFECT	PAST PERFECT
eam, *etc.*	īrem, *etc.*	ierim, *etc.*	īssem, *etc.*

IMPERATIVE		INFINITIVE	PARTICIPLES
Pres. ī	īte	īre	iēns, *Gen.* euntis
Perf.		īsse	itus, –a, –um
Fut.		itūrus esse	itūrus, –a, –um
			(*Passive*, eundus)

GERUND

Gen. eundī, *Dat.* eundō, *Acc.* eundum, *Abl.* eundō

670. Principal Parts: volō, velle, voluī (**545**); nōlō, nōlle, nōluī (**545**); mālō, mālle, māluī

INDICATIVE

PRESENT

volō	volumus	nōlō	nōlumus	mālō	mālumus
vīs	vultis	nōn vīs	nōn vultis	māvīs	māvultis
vult	volunt	nōn vult	nōlunt	māvult	mālunt

Impf.	volēbam, *etc.*	nōlēbam, *etc.*	mālēbam, *etc.*
Fut.	volam, *etc.*	nōlam, *etc.*	mālam, *etc.*
Perf.	voluī, *etc.*	nōluī, *etc.*	māluī, *etc.*
Past P.	volueram, *etc.*	nōlueram, *etc.*	mālueram, *etc.*
Fut. P.	voluerō, *etc.*	nōluerō, *etc.*	māluerō, *etc.*

SUBJUNCTIVE

PRESENT

velim	velīmus	nōlim	nōlīmus	mālim	mālīmus
velīs	velītis	nōlīs	nōlītis	mālīs	mālītis
velit	velint	nōlit	nōlint	mālit	mālint

Impf.	vellem, *etc.*	nōllem, *etc.*	māllem, *etc.*
Perf.	voluerim, *etc.*	nōluerim, *etc.*	māluerim, *etc.*
Past P.	voluissem, *etc.*	nōluissem, *etc.*	māluissem, *etc.*

PRESENT IMPERATIVE

nōlī   nōlīte

Infinitive

Pres.	velle	nōlle	mālle
Perf.	voluisse	nōluisse	māluisse

Participles

Pres.	volēns	nōlēns

671. Principal Parts : fīō, fierī, factus sum (561)

Indicative

PRESENT	IMPERFECT	FUTURE	PERFECT
fīō ——	fīēbam, *etc.*	fīam, *etc.*	factus sum, *etc.*
fit fīunt			

Past Perf. factus eram, *etc.*   *Fut. Perf.* factus erō, *etc.*

Subjunctive

PRESENT	IMPERFECT	PERFECT	PAST PERFECT
fīam, *etc.*	fierem, *etc.*	factus sim, *etc.*	factus essem, *etc.*

	IMPERATIVE	INFINITIVE	PARTICIPLES
Pres.	fī fīte	fierī	
Perf.		factus esse	factus, –a, –um
Fut.			faciendus, –a, –um

FRENCH AND SPANISH THROUGH LATIN

Nōtitia linguārum est prīma porta sapientiae, *A knowledge of languages is the first door to wisdom.* — BACON

672.   The Romance Languages

The Romance (**Rōmānus**, *Roman*) languages — French, Spanish, Italian, Portuguese, and Rumanian — are modern forms of Latin. Fully ninety per cent of the words in French and Spanish are derived from Latin. The Latin student, therefore, who is familiar with the principles that govern vowel and consonant changes, as well as other peculiarities of word transfer, can recognize at a glance a large proportion of words in French and Spanish derived from classical (as opposed to late) Latin.

The following pages are intended primarily for older students who have elected Latin after having begun the study of French or Spanish. These rules will, moreover, be found invaluable for reference by the Latin student who may later elect French or Spanish (see **1**).

673.   Pronunciation

The distinctions in sound between long and short **e** and **o** (**604**, *a*) are preserved in French and Spanish, though not in all derived words.

Spanish has no silent letters, except **h**, thus resembling Latin (**h** was weakly sounded in Latin).

674.   Syllable Division

Syllable division in French and Spanish is according to the Latin rule (**609**).

675.   Gender

Nouns which are masculine or feminine in Latin retain their gender in French and Spanish:

Lat.	**poëta**, *m.*	**liber**, *m.*	**mōns**, *m.*	**lībertās**, *f.*	**manus**, *f.*
Fr.	**poète**	**livre**	**mont**	**liberté**	**main**
Sp.	**poeta**	**libro**	**monte**	**libertad**	**mano**

Exception: Most Latin masculines in **–or** become feminine in French: **error**, *erreur*.

Nouns which are neuter in Latin become masculine in French and Spanish :

Lat.	*n.*	verbum	tempus
Fr.	*m.*	verbe	temps
Sp.	*m.*	verbo	tiempo

Exception: Many Latin neuters, especially those which were commonly used in the plural (which ends in –**a**, like the feminine singular) become feminine singular in French and Spanish :

Lat.	*n. plur.*	**arma**	**data**	**pecora**
Fr.	*f. sing.*	**arme**	**date**	**pécore**
Sp.	*f. sing.*	**arma**	**data**	**pécora**

FRENCH THROUGH LATIN

676. Accent

The French stress often preserves the Latin accent. The syllables after the accented syllable in Latin were dropped or became silent in French, which fact explains why the French stress is usually on the last syllable.

677. Vocabulary

Many Latin words remain unchanged in French, as in English: *agenda, alibi, errata, humus, omnibus, ultimatum,* etc.

678. Loss of Letters

1. The final syllable or letters of many Latin words are lost in French or changed to silent **e** : *ami* (**amīcum** [1]), *mont* (**montem**), *terre* (**terram**).

2. An unaccented short vowel within a word is often lost : *homme* (**homĭnem**), *livrer* (**līberāre**), *peuple* (**popŭlus**).

3. A consonant between two vowels is often lost : *cruel* (**crūdēlem**), *dire* (**dīcere**).

4. The first of two consonants is often lost : *frère* (**frātrem**).

---

[1] The accusative of all Latin nouns and adjectives is given because the French and Spanish forms are derived from it, not from the nominative.

679.   Vowels

The Latin vowels often remain unchanged in French, but the following changes are to be noted:

(A) *Change to a single vowel*

1. **a** sometimes becomes **e**: *père* (**patrem**), *aimer* (**amāre**), *gré* (**grātum**), *mer* (**mare**).
2. **e** sometimes becomes **i**: *six* (**sex**), *lire* (**legere**).
3. **i** sometimes becomes **e**: *ferme* (**firmum**), *lettre* (**litteram**).
4. **u** sometimes becomes **o**: *nombre* (**numerum**), *onde* (**undam**), *rompre* (**rumpere**).
5. **au** sometimes becomes **o**: *chose* (**causam**).
6. **ae** and **oe** are treated as **e**.

(B) *Change to two vowels*

This was very common in accented syllables (cf. **443, 522**).

1. **ai** is from **a**: *aimer* (**amāre**), *main* (**manum**).
2. **ei** is from **e** or **i**: *plein* (**plēnus**), *seing* (**signum**).
3. **oi** is from **e, i, o,** or **u**: *roi* (**rēgem**), *voie* (**viam**), *gloire* (**glōriam**), *croix* (**crux**).
4. **ui** is from **o** or **u**: *puis* (**post**), *suis* (**sum**).
5. **au** is from **al**, and **eau** from **el**: *haut* (**altum**), *vaut* (**valet**), *beau* (**bellum**).
6. **eu, oeu,** is from **o**: *seul* (**sōlum**), *coeur* (**cor**).
7. **ou** is from **o** or **u**: *nous* (**nōs**), *prouver* (**probāre**), *jour* (**diurnum**).
8. **ie** is from **e**: *bien* (**bene**), *pied* (**pedem**).

680.   Consonants

1. **b** and **p** sometimes become **v**: *livre* (**librum**), *avril* (**aprīlem**).

2. **p** and **v** sometimes become **b** or **f**: *double* (**duplicem**), *chef* (**caput**), *neuf* (**novum**).

3. **ct** sometimes becomes **it**: *fait* (**factum**), *fruit* (**frūctum**).

4. **t** followed by **i** and a vowel in certain cases becomes **s**: *raison* (**ratiōnem**).

5. **s** before a consonant is dropped and the preceding vowel receives a circumflex accent: *maître* (**magistrum**), *tempête* (**tempestātem**).

6. **c** before **a**, especially at the beginning of words, becomes **ch**: *char* (**carrum**), *chef* (**caput**), *chose* (**causam**).

7. Initial **sc, sp,** and **st** become **esc, esp,** and **est**: *espace* (**spatium**), *espèce* (**speciem**).

In some words the s is dropped and the e has an acute accent : *étude*
*s*tudium).

681. Word Formation

The Latin prefixes used in French have undergone the same changes
that have been noted for English in this book (cf. especially **com-, con-,
en-, em-, sur-, tra-**).   In addition, attention is called to the change
from **dis-** to **de-, dés-** (déshonneur), **inter-** to **entre-** (entrevoir), **per-** to
par- (parfait), **pro-** to **pour-** (poursuivre), **sub-** to **sou-, sous-** (souvenir),
ultra- to **outre-** (outremer).

Latin suffixes in French show much the same form as in English.
Note, however, the change of –ātum to é (am*ātum*, *aimé*), –ōrem to
–eur (auct*ōrem*, *auteur*), –ōsum to –eux (ōti*ōsum*, *oiseux*), –tātem to
-té (līber*tātem*, *liberté*).

682. Inflection

1. Nouns of the first Latin declension in –a end in silent –e in French.

2. The French definite article *le, la*, is derived from the last syllable
of ille, illa.

3. The comparative forms of Latin irregular adjectives are to some
extent preserved in French : *meilleur* (**melior**), *moins* (**minus**), *pire*
(**peior**).

4. The same forms constitute the principal parts of verbs in French
as in Latin, with the addition of the present participle.

5. Most French verbs belong to the first conjugation, with infinitive
in –er.   This corresponds to the Latin first conjugation, with infinitive
in –āre, but includes a number of verbs of the Latin second and third
conjugations.

6. The French second conjugation, with infinitive in –ir, corresponds
to the Latin fourth conjugation (–īre).

7. The French third conjugation, with infinitive in –re, corresponds to
the Latin third conjugation (–ĕre).

8. The Latin personal endings have undergone considerable changes
in French.   The endings of the French past definite can easily be traced
to those of the Latin perfect.   Many of the numerous irregular verbs
in French preserve forms derived from the Latin :

suis	(**sum**)	*sommes*	(**sumus**)
es	(**es**)	*êtes*	(**estis**)
est	(**est**)	*sont*	(**sunt**)

SPANISH THROUGH LATIN

683. Accent

Accent is greatly simplified in Spanish if the student understands Latin accent. The so-called irregular accent of nouns and adjectives in Spanish preserves the Latin accent of the accusative case:

Lat.	a'mant	a'nimum	ima'ginem	prōpo'situm	dormī're
Sp.	aman	a'nimo	imagen	propósito	dormir

684. Vocabulary

Hundreds of words in Spanish are either identical with the original Latin form or resemble it so closely that one who knows Latin can understand their meaning at a glance, without knowing the principles that govern word transfer:

Lat.	aqua	arma	causa	hōra	patria	trēs	victōria	dare	ūtilis
Sp.	agua	arma	causa	hora	patria	tres	victoria	dar	útil

685. Loss of Letters

1. Final letters and syllables are often lost in Spanish, but not to the same extent as in French: *amigo* (**amīcum**), *monte* (**montem**), *útil* (**ūtilem**).

2. An unaccented short vowel within a word is sometimes lost: *hombre* (**hominem**), *librar* (**līberāre**), *pueblo* (**popu**lum**).

3. A consonant (especially **b, d, g, h**) between vowels is sometimes lost: *leer* (**leg**ere**), *creer* (**crēd**ere**), *traer* (**tra**here**).

4. The first of two consonants is sometimes lost, especially **n** before **s**: *escrito* (**scrī**p**tum**), *autor* (**auctōrem**), *isla* (**ī**n**sulam**).

5. Double consonants become single: *oficio* (**of**f**icium**), *nulo* (**nū**ll**um**), *permitir* (**permi**tt**ere**). Double **n** becomes **ñ**: *año* (**an**n**um**); **ñ** is also for **ni**, etc.: *señor* (**sen**i**or**).

686. Vowels

The Latin vowels often remain unchanged in Spanish, but the following changes are to be noted:

(*A*) *Change to a single vowel*

    1. Short **i** sometimes becomes **e**: *lengua* (**linguam**), *letra* (**lit**teram**), *menos* (**minus**).

2. Short **u** sometimes becomes **o** : *onda* (**undam**), *romper* (**rum-pere**).

3. **au** sometimes becomes **o** : *oído* (**au**d**ī**tum), *cosa* (**causam**).

4. **ae** and **oe** are treated as **e**.

(B) *Change to two vowels*

1. Accented short **e** becomes **ie** : *bien* (**bene**), *cielo* (**caelum**), *cierto* (**certum**).

2. Accented short **o** becomes **ue** : *bueno* (**bonum**), *cuerpo* (**corpus**), *nuevo* (**novem**).

687.   Consonants

1. **c** sometimes becomes **g** : *amigo* (**amīcum**).

2. **p** sometimes becomes **b** : *pueblo* (**po**p**ulum**).

3. **t** sometimes becomes **d** : *maduro* (**mātūrum**), *padre* (**pa**t**rem**).

4. **ct** becomes **ch** : *dicho* (**dic**t**um**), *hecho* (**fac**t**um**), *ocho* (**oc**t**ō**).

5. **li** becomes **j** : *consejo* (**cōnsi**l**ium**), *hijo* (**fī**l**ium**), *mejor* (**me**l**ior**).

6. Initial **f** sometimes becomes **h** : *hacer* (**f**acere), *hijo* (**f**īlium).

7. Initial **cl** and **pl** sometimes become **ll** : *llamar* (**cl**āmāre), *llano* (**pl**ānum).

8. Initial **sc**, **sp**, and **st** become **esc**, **esp**, **est** : *escribir* (**sc**ribere), *esperar* (**sp**ērāre), *estar* (**st**āre).

688.   Word Formation

The Latin prefixes used in Spanish are easily recognizable. Note the following changes which sometimes occur : **ex-** to **ej-** (*ejercer*), **dis-** to **des-** (*descrédito*), **super-** to **sobre-** (*sobrehumano*).

The Latin suffixes are also used in Spanish. Note the following changes : **–ātum** to **–ado** (*amado*), **–tātem**, **–tūtem**, to **–tad, –tud** (*libertad, virtud*), **–tiōnem** to **–cion** (*oración*), **–tiam** to **–cia** (*gracia*).

689.   Inflection

1. Nouns of the first Latin declension ending in **–a** retain the **–a** in Spanish : *gracia* (**grāti**a), *tierra* (**terr**a).

2. Nouns of the second Latin declension in **–us** and **–um** end in **–o** in Spanish : *carro* (**carr**us), *reino* (**rēgn**um).

3. The comparative and superlative forms of Latin irregular adjectives are to some extent preserved in Spanish : *poor* (**peior**), *mayor* (**maior**), *óptimo* (**optimus**), *libérrimo* (**līberrimus**).

4. The Spanish first conjugation, with infinitive in **–ar**, corresponds to the Latin first conjugation (**–āre**).

5. The Spanish second conjugation, with infinitive in –er, corresponds to the Latin second and third conjugations (–ēre, –ĕre).

6. The Spanish third conjugation, with infinitive in –ir, corresponds to the Latin fourth conjugation (–īre) but also includes many verbs of the third conjugation.

7. Many of the tenses of the Spanish verb are very much like the Latin. Cf. the imperfect:

Lat. **amābam** **amābās** **amābat** **amābāmus** **amābātis** **amābant**
Sp. **amaba** **amabas** **amaba** **amábamos** **amabais** **amaban**

Observe that final –m and –t of the personal endings of Latin verbs disappear in Spanish.

The Spanish past definite is very similar to the Latin perfect.

8. The Latin perfect participle will suggest at once the past participle of the Spanish verb, no matter how irregular: **impressus**, Sp. *impreso;* **scrīptus**, Sp. *escrito.*

FIG. 133. A BRONZE STAND

HELPS FOR CLASSROOM CONVERSATION

690.   Vocabulary

I The Classroom

blackboard, **tabula (nigra)**
desk, **scrīnium**
door, **iānua**
open, close the door, **aperī, claude iānuam**
seat, **sella**
window, **fenestra**

chalk, **crēta**
pencil, **stilus**
pen, **calamus**
ink, **ātrāmentum**
paper, **charta**

    sit down, **cōnsīde, –ite**   *stand up*, **surge, –ite**

II The Lesson

page, **pāgina**
lesson, **pēnsum**
to speak, know Latin, **loquī, scīre Latīnē**
translate into English, **Anglicē redde**

III Grammar

parts of speech, **partēs ōrātiōnis :**
    nōmen, adiectīvum, prōnōmen (**persōnāle, relātīvum**,[1] etc.),
    verbum, adverbium, praepositiō, coniūnctiō, interiectiō
case, **cāsus : nōminātīvus, genitīvus, datīvus, accūsātīvus, ablā-**
    tīvus[1]
gender, **genus : masculīnum, fēminīnum, neutrum**
number, **numerus : singulāris, plūrālis**
person, **persōna : prīma, secunda, tertia**
declension, **dēclīnātiō** ; *to decline*, **dēclīnāre**
tense, **tempus : praesēns, imperfectum, futūrum, perfectum,**
    praeteritum perfectum, futūrum perfectum
mood, **modus : indicātīvus**,[1] etc.
voice, **vōx : actīva, passīva**
conjugation, **coniugātiō** ; *to conjugate*, **coniugāre**
participle, **participium**
deponent, **dēpōnēns**

IV Miscellaneous

good morning, **salvē, –ēte**
good bye, **valē, –ēte**
how are you? **quid agis ?**
good ! **bene !**

to-day, **hodiē**
yesterday, **heri**
to-morrow, **crās**
that's enough, **satis est**

---

[1] Similarly other words whose English forms end in *–ive*.

GAUDEAMUS IGITUR

Student Song

INTEGER VITAE

HORACE, Odes I. 22
(ca. 25 B.C.)

Dr. F. F. FLEMMING, ca. 1811

AMERICA

Tr. George D. Kellogg

Te cano, Patria,
Candida, libera;
Te referet
Portus et exulum
Et tumulus senum;
Libera montium
Vox resonet.

Tutor es unicus,
Unus avum Deus!
Laudo libens.
Patria luceat,
Libera fulgeat,
Vis tua muniat,
Omnipotens!

THE STAR–SPANGLED BANNER

Tr. F. A. Geyser

Oh, potestne cerni, profulgente die,
Salutatum signum circa noctis adventum?
Lati clav(i) et stellae, decertant(e) acie,
Gloriose cingunt oppidi munimentum!
Iaculumque rubens, globus sursum rumpens
Per noctem monstrant vexillum fulgens.
Stellatumne vexillum volans tegit nos,
Patriam liberam fortiumque domos?

Oh, sic esto semper, manus si libera
Arcet a patria belli vastationem!
Triumphante pace patria prospera
Deum laudet qui nos statuit nationem!
Victoria me(a) est, quando causa iust(a) est;
Haec nostra sit vox: " Deus salus nostr(a) est."
Stellatum vexillum triumphans teget nos,
Patriam liberam fortiumque domos!

LATIN-ENGLISH VOCABULARY

A

ā, ab, *prep. w. abl.*, from, away from, by.

abdō, –ere, –didī, –ditus, put away, hide.

abdūcō, –ere, –dūxī, –ductus, lead away.

abeō, –īre, –iī, –itus, go away.

absum, abesse, āfuī, āfutūrus, be away, be absent.

ac, *see* atque.

accēdō, –ere, –cessī, –cessus, approach.

accidō, –ere, accidī, —-, fall to, befall, happen (*w. dat.*).

accingō, –ere, –cīnxī, –cīnctus, gird.

accipiō, –ere, –cēpī, –ceptus, receive.

accūsō, –āre, –āvī, –ātus, blame, accuse.

ācer, ācris, ācre, sharp, keen.

aciēs, aciēī, *f.*, battle line.

ācriter, *comp.*, ācrius, *superl.*, ācerrimē, *adv.*, sharply.

ad, *prep. w. acc.*, to, toward, for, near.

addō, –ere, –didī, –ditus, add.

addūcō, –ere, –dūxī, –ductus, lead to, influence.

adhibeō, –ēre, –hibuī, –hibitus, apply, employ, summon.

adiciō, –ere, –iēcī, –iectus, throw to, add.

administrō, –āre, –āvī, –ātus, manage.

admoneō, –ēre, –monuī, –monitus, remind.

adolēscō, –ere, –olēvī, –ultus, grow up.

adsum, –esse, –fuī, –futūrus, be near, be present.

adulēscēns, –centis, *m.*, a youth.

adventus, –ūs, *m.*, a coming to, arrival.

aedēs, –ium, *f. pl.*, a house.

Aegyptiī, –ōrum, *m.*, the Egyptians.

Aegyptus, –ī, *f.*, Egypt.

aemulātiō, –iōnis, *f.*, rivalry.

aequus, –a, –um, even, equal, fair, just, calm.

aestās, aestātis, *f.*, summer.

aestimō, –āre, –āvī, –ātus, estimate, value (*in money*).

aetās, aetātis, *f.*, age, time of life.

Aetna, –ae, *f.*, (Mt.) Etna.

afferō, afferre, attulī, allātus, bring (to *or* against), report.

afficiō, –ere, –fēcī, –fectus, affect, afflict with, visit with.

Āfrī, –ōrum, *m.*, the Africans.

Āfrica, –ae, *f.*, Africa.

Āfricānus, –ī, *m.*, Africanus.

ager, agrī, *m.*, field, country.

aggredior, aggredī, aggressus sum, attack.

agō, –ere, ēgī, āctus, drive, live *or* spend (*of time*), do, treat, discuss; grātiās agere, thank;

triumphum agere, celebrate a triumph.

agricola, –ae, *m.*, farmer.

āh! *interj.*, ah !

Albānī, –ōrum, the Albans (*people of Alba Longa*).

albus, –a, –um, white.

ālea, –ae, *f.*, die (*pl.*, dice).

Alexandrĭa, –ae, *f.*, *a city in Egypt.*

Alexandrīnī, –ōrum, *the people of Alexandria.*

aliēnus, –a, –um, another's, unfavorable, foreign, of no concern.

aliquis, **aliquid**, some one, some, any.

alius, **alia**, **aliud**, other, another ; **alius ... alius**, one ... another ; **aliī ... aliī**, some ... others.

alligō, –āre, –āvī, –ātus, tie to.

alō, –ere, aluī, alitus, feed, nourish.

Alpēs, –ium, *f.*, the Alps.

altē, on high, highly, deeply, far.

alter, **altera**, **alterum**, the other (*of two*) ; **alter ... alter**, the one ... the other.

altitūdō, –tūdinis, *f.*, height, depth.

altus, –a, –um, high, deep, tall.

ambitiō, –iōnis, *f.*, ambition.

ambulō, –āre, –āvī, –ātus, walk.

America, –ae, *f.*, America.

Americānus, –a, –um, American.

amīcitia, –ae, *f.*, friendship.

amīcus, –a, –um, friendly ; **amīcus**, –ī, *m.*, **amīca**, –ae, *f.*, friend.

āmittō, –ere, āmīsī, āmissus, let go, lose.

amō, –āre, –āvī, –ātus, love, like.

amor, –ōris, *m.*, love.

amplē, fully ; *comp.*, **amplius**, more, further.

amplus, –a, –um, great, large, magnificent.

Amūlius, –ī, *m.*, Amulius.

animadvertō, –ere, –vertī, –versus, (turn the mind to), notice, punish (*w.* **in** *and acc.*).

animus, –ī, *m.*, mind, spirit, courage.

Anna, –ae, *f.*, Anna.

annus, –ī, *m.*, year.

ante, *adv. and prep. w. acc.*, before (*of time or space*).

anteā, *adv.*, before.

antecēdō, –ere, –cessī, –cessus, go before, precede, take the lead.

antīquus, –a, –um, ancient, of old.

Apollō, –inis, *m.*, Apollo.

appāreō, –ēre, –pāruī, –pāritūrus, appear, become visible.

appellō, –āre, –āvī, –ātus, call, call upon, name.

Appius, –ī, *m.*, Appius.

Appius, –a, –um, *adj.*, of Appius, Appian.

appropinquō, –āre, –āvī, –ātus, draw near to, approach.

aptus, –a, –um, fit, suitable (*w. dat.*).

apud, *prep. w. acc.*, among, at the home of.

aqua, –ae, *f.*, water.

aquaeductus, –ūs, *m.*, aqueduct.

Aquītānī, –ōrum, *m.*, *a people in Gaul.*

arbitror, **arbitrārī**, **arbitrātus sum**, think, believe.

arcus, –ūs, *m.*, arch.

arēna, –ae, *f.*, arena.

Ariovistus, –ī, *m.*, *a German chieftain.*

arma, –ōrum, *n.*, weapons, arms.

armō, –āre, –āvī, –ātus, arm.
ars, artis, *f.*, skill, art.
arx, arcis, *f.*, citadel.
ascendō, –ere, ascendī, ascēnsus, climb (up), ascend.
ascrībō, –ere, ascrīpsī, ascrīptus, add to (*in writing*).
Asia, –ae, *f.*, Asia.
Atlanticus, –a, –um, Atlantic.
atque (ac), *conj.*, and.
ātrium, –ī, *n.*, atrium, hall, house.
attingō, –ere, –tigī, –tāctus, touch, reach.
auctor, –ōris, *m.*, maker, author.
auctōritās, –tātis, *f.*, authority, influence.
audācia, –ae, *f.*, boldness.
audeō, –ēre, ausus sum, dare, venture.
audiō, –īre, –īvī, –ītus, hear.
augeō, –ēre, auxī, auctus, increase.
aurīga, –ae, *m.*, charioteer.
aurōra, –ae, *f.*, dawn.
aut, or; aut . . . aut, either . . . or.
autem, *conj.* (*never first word*), moreover, on the other hand.
auxilium, –ī, *n.*, help, aid, assistance; *pl.*, reinforcements.
āvertō, –ere, āvertī, āversus, turn away from.
avus, –ī, *m.*, grandfather.
axis, –is, *m.*, axletree.

B

Bacchus, –ī, *m.*, *god of wine.*
barbarus, –a, –um, foreign, barbarous; barbarus, –ī, *m.*, a barbarian.
Belgae, –ārum, *m.*, the Belgians.
bellum, –ī, *n.*, war; bellum gerere, wage *or* carry on war.

bene, *adv.*, well, well done; *comp.,* melius, better; *superl.*, optimē, best.
beneficium, –ī, *n.*, kindness.
bis, *adv.*, twice.
bonus, –a, –um, good; *comp.,* melior, melius, better; *superl.*, optimus, –a, –um, best.
brācae, –ārum, *f.*, trousers.
Britannī, –ōrum, *m.*, the Britons.
Britannia, –ae, *f.*, Britain.
Brūtus, –ī, *m.*, Brutus.

C

C., *abbreviation for* Gāius.
cadō, –ere, cecidī, cāsus, fall.
caedō, –ere, cecīdī, caesus, cut, kill.
caelum, –ī, *n.*, sky.
Caesar, –aris, *m.*, Caesar.
calamitās, –tātis, *f.*, misfortune.
callidus, –a, –um, *adj.*, crafty, clever.
Campānia, –ae, *f.*, *a district of Italy.*
Campus Mārtius, Campī Mārtī, *m.,* *a place of assembly in Rome.*
candidus, –a, –um, white.
Canīnius, –ī, *m.*, Caninius.
Cannēnsis, –e, *adj.*, of Cannae.
canō, –ere, cecinī, cantus, sing.
Capēna, *see* porta.
capiō, –ere, cēpī, captus, take, seize, capture.
Capitōlium, –ī, *n.*, the Capitol (*temple of Jupiter, at Rome*); the Capitoline Hill.
captīvus, –ī, *m.*, prisoner.
caput, capitis, *n.*, head.
carmen, –minis, *n.*, song.
carrus, –ī, *m.*, cart, wagon.
Carthāginiēnsēs, –ium, *m.*, the Carthaginians.

Carthāgō, –inis, *f.,* Carthage (*a city in Africa*).

cārus, –a, –um, dear.

castra, –ōrum, *n.,* camp; **castra pōnere,** pitch camp; **castra movēre,** break camp.

cāsus, –ūs, *m.,* fall, chance, accident.

Catilīna, –ae, *m.,* Catiline.

causa, –ae, *f.,* cause, reason; **causās ōrāre,** plead cases; **causā,** by reason of, for the sake of.

cēdō, –ere, cessī, cessus, move, retreat.

celer, celeris, celere, swift.

celeritās, –tātis, *f.,* swiftness, speed.

celeriter, *comp.,* **celerius,** quickly.

Celtae, –ārum, *m.,* Celts (*a people of Gaul*).

cēna, –ae, *f.,* dinner.

centum, hundred.

Cerēs, –eris, *f.,* *goddess of agriculture.*

cernō, –ere, crēvī, crētus, separate, discern, see.

certē, certainly, at least.

certus, –a, –um, fixed, certain, sure; **certiōrem eum facere dē,** inform him about.

cēterī, –ae, –a, the other, the rest.

Christus, –ī, *m.,* Christ.

cibus, –ī, *m.,* food.

Cicerō, –ōnis, *m.,* Cicero.

Cimbrī, –ōrum, *m.,* *a people of Germany.*

Cincinnātus, –ī, *m.,* Cincinnatus.

Cinna, –ae, *m.,* Cinna.

circum, *prep. w. acc.,* around.

circumdō, –dare, –dedī, –datus, put around, surround.

circumveniō, –īre, –vēnī, –ventus, surround.

circus, –ī, *m.,* circle, circus (*esp. the Circus Maximus at Rome*).

cīvis, cīvis, *m.,* citizen.

cīvitās, –tātis, *f.,* citizenship, state.

clāmō, –āre, –āvī, –ātus, cry out, shout.

clāmor, –ōris, *m.,* shout.

clārus, –a, –um, clear, brilliant, famous.

claudō, –ere, clausī, clausus, close.

clēmenter, mildly, with forbearance.

Cleopātra, –ae, *f.,* *queen of Egypt.*

Coclēs, *see* **Horātius.**

coepī, coepisse, coeptus (*used only in perf. tenses*), began.

cognātus, –ī, *m.,* relative.

cognōmen, –inis, *n.,* cognomen, surname.

cognōscō, –ere, –nōvī, –nitus, learn, recognize; *perf. tenses,* have learned, know, understand.

cōgō, –ere, coēgī, coāctus, drive together, collect, compel.

cohors, cohortis, *f.,* cohort (*a division of the Roman army*).

colō, –ere, coluī, cultus, till, dwell in, worship.

colōnus, –ī, *m.,* settler.

Columbus, –ī, *m.,* Columbus.

comes, comitis, *m.,* comrade.

Comitium, –ī, *n.,* *the assembly place of the Romans.*

commeō, –āre, –āvī, –ātus, visit.

committō, –ere, –mīsī, –missus, join together, commit, intrust; **proelium committere,** begin battle.

commodē, suitably, conveniently.

commodus, -a, -um, suitable, convenient.

commoveō, -ēre, -mōvī, -mōtus, move away, disturb.

commūnis, -e, common.

comparō, -āre, -āvī, -ātus, get ready, get together, prepare.

compellō, -ere, -pulī, -pulsus, drive together, collect.

compleō, -ēre, -plēvī, -plētus, fill up.

concitō, -āre, -āvī, -ātus, arouse, excite.

concordia, -ae, f., harmony.

concurrō, -ere, -currī, -cursus, run together, rush.

condiciō, -ōnis, f., condition, terms.

cōnferō, cōnferre, contulī, collātus, bring together, collect.

cōnficiō, -ere, -fēcī, -fectus, (do thoroughly), complete, exhaust.

cōnfīdō, -ere, cōnfīsus sum, have confidence (in), be confident.

cōnfirmō, -āre, -āvī, -ātus, make firm, encourage, establish.

cōnflō, -āre, -āvī, -ātus, melt.

congredior, congredī, congressus sum, come together with, fight with.

coniciō, -ere, -iēcī, -iectus, throw (forcibly), throw together.

coniungō, -ere, -iūnxī, -iūnctus, join with, unite.

cōnor, cōnārī, cōnātus sum, try.

cōnscrībō, -ere, -scrīpsī, -scrīptus, enlist, enroll.

cōnsequor, cōnsequī, cōnsecūtus sum, follow, overtake, attain.

cōnservō, -āre, -āvī, -ātus, save, preserve.

cōnsilium, -ī, n., plan, prudence, advice.

cōnsistō, -ere, cōnstitī, cōnstitus, stand still, stop.

cōnspiciō, -ere, -spexī, -spectus, catch sight of, see.

cōnstituō, -ere, -stituī, -stitūtus, set up, establish, determine.

cōnsuētūdō, -tūdinis, f., custom, habit.

cōnsul, -ulis, m., consul (the highest Roman official).

cōnsulātus, -ūs, m., consulship.

cōnsulō, -ere, -suluī, -sultus, consult.

cōnsūmō, -ere, -sūmpsī, -sūmptus, (take wholly), use up, waste.

contemnō, -ere, -tempsī, -temptus, scorn, despise.

contendō, -ere, -tendī, -tentus, struggle, hasten.

continenter, continually.

contineō, -ēre, -uī, -tentus, hold together, detain, contain, hem in.

contrā, adv. and prep. w. acc., against.

contrahō, -ere, -trāxī, -trāctus, draw or bring together, contract.

conveniō, -īre, -vēnī, -ventus, come together, assemble.

convocō, -āre, -āvī, -ātus, call together, summon.

cōpia, -ae, f., supply, abundance; pl., forces, troops.

coquō, -ere, coxī, coctus, cook.

coquus, -ī, m., cook.

cor, cordis, n., heart.

Cornēlia, -ae, f., Cornelia.

Cornēlius, -ī, m., Cornelius.

cornicen, -cinis, m., hornblower.

cornū, cornūs, *n.*, horn, wing (*of an army*).

corōna, -ae, *f.*, crown, wreath.

corpus, -poris, *n.*, body.

Corsica, -ae, *f.*, Corsica.

cotīdiānus, -a, -um, daily.

Crassus, -ī, *m.*, Crassus.

crēber, -bra, -brum, frequent, close together.

crēdō, -ere, -didī, -ditus, believe, intrust (*w. dat.*).

creō, -āre, -āvī, -ātus, create, elect.

crēscō, -ere, crēvī, crētus, grow, increase.

crīmen, -minis, *n.*, charge.

cruciātus, -ūs, *m.*, torture.

crūdēlis, -e, cruel.

cum, *prep. w. abl.*, with.

cum, *conj.*, when.

cupiditās, -tātis, *f.*, desire, greed.

cupidus, -a, -um, desirous, eager.

cupiō, cupere, cupīvī, cupītus, desire.

cūr, *adv.*, why.

cūra, -ae, *f.*, care, concern; (cum) magnā cūrā, very carefully.

currō, -ere, cucurrī, cursus, run.

currus, -ūs, *m.*, chariot.

cursus, -ūs, *m.*, course.

D

damnō, -āre, -āvī, -ātus, condemn.

dē, *prep. w. abl.*, from, down from, concerning.

dea, -ae, *f.*, goddess.

dēbeō, -ēre, dēbuī, dēbitus, ought, owe, be obliged to.

dēcēdō, -ere, -cessī, -cessus, depart, go away.

decem, ten.

December, -bris, *m.*, December.

decimus, -a, -um, tenth.

dēfendō, -ere, -fendī, -fēnsus, defend.

dēferō, -ferre, -tulī, -lātus, carry away, refer, offer.

dēficiō, -ere, -fēcī, -fectus, fail, revolt, rebel.

dēiciō, -ere, -iēcī, -iectus, throw from.

dēligō, -ere, -lēgī, -lēctus, select.

dēmōnstrō, -āre, -āvī, -ātus, point out, show.

dēns, dentis, *m.*, tooth.

Dentātus, -ī, *m.*, Dentatus.

dēpōnō, -ere, -posuī, -positus, put *or* lay aside.

dēscendō, -ere, -scendī, -scēnsus, descend.

dēserō, -ere, -seruī, -sertus, desert.

dēsiliō, -īre, -siluī, -sultus, jump down.

dēsinō, -ere, -siī, -situs, stop, cease.

dēsistō, -ere, -stitī, -stitus, desist from, cease.

dēspērō, -āre, -āvī, -ātus, lose hope, despair.

dēspiciō, -ere, -spexī, -spectus, look down on, despise.

dēsum, deesse, dēfuī, dēfutūrus, lacking.

deus, -ī, *m.*, god.

dexter, -tra, -trum, right (*hand*).

Diāna, -ae, *f.*, *goddess of hunting*.

Diaulus, -ī, *m.*, Diaulus.

dīcō, -ere, dīxī, dictus, say, tell.

dictātor, -ōris, *m.*, dictator.

dictātūra, -ae, *f.*, dictatorship.

dictum, -ī, *n.*, word, saying.

diēs, diēī, *m.*, day.

difficilis, –e, difficult.
difficultās, –tātis, *f.*, difficulty.
digitus, –ī, *m.*, finger.
dignē, worthily.
dignitās, –tātis, *f.*, worth, position.
dignus, –a, –um, worthy.
dīligenter, with care, diligently.
dīligentia, –ae, *f.*, carefulness, diligence.
dīmittō, –ere, –mīsī, –missus, let go, send away.
discēdō, –ere, –cessī, –cessus, go away, depart.
disciplīna, –ae, *f.*, training, instruction, learning.
discipulus, –ī, *m.*, **discipula, –ae**, *f.*, learner, pupil.
discō, –ere, didicī, —, learn.
dissimilis, –e, unlike.
distribuō, –ere, –tribuī, –tribūtus, distribute.
diū, *comp.*, **diūtius**, *superl.*, **diūtissimē**, *adv.*, for a long time.
diurnus, –a, –um, daily, by day.
dīvidō, –ere, –vīsī, –vīsus, divide.
dō, dare, dedī, datus, give; **poenam dare**, pay the penalty.
doceō, –ēre, docuī, doctus, teach.
dolor, –ōris, *m.*, grief, pain.
dominus, –ī, *m.*, master, lord, ruler.
domus, –ūs, *f.*, house, home.
dōnō, –āre, –āvī, –ātus, give, present.
dormiō, –īre, –īvī, –ītus, sleep.
dubitō, –āre, –āvī, –ātus, doubt, hesitate.
ducentī, –ae, –a, two hundred.
dūcō, –ere, dūxī, ductus, lead.
dulcis, –e, sweet.
dum, *conj.*, while.
duo, –ae, –o, two.

duodecim, twelve.
duodēvīgintī, eighteen.
duplex, *gen.* **duplicis**, *adj.*, twofold, double.
dūrus, –a, –um, hard, harsh.
dux, ducis, *m.*, leader, general.

E

ē, ex, *prep. w. abl.*, from, out from, out of.
ecce, *interj.*, behold!
ēdō, –ere, ēdidī, ēditus, put forth, publish.
ēducō, –āre, –āvī, –ātus, bring up, educate.
ēdūcō, –ere, ēdūxī, ēductus, lead out.
effēminō, –āre, –āvī, –ātus, weaken.
efficiō, –ere, –fēcī, –fectus, make out, bring about, complete.
ego, meī, I.
ēgregius, –a, –um, distinguished, excellent.
ēiciō, –ere, ēiēcī, ēiectus, throw *or* thrust out.
elephantus, –ī, *m.*, elephant.
em! *interj.*, here! there! take that!
emō, –ere, ēmī, ēmptus, get, buy.
enim, *conj.* (*never first word*), for.
eō, īre, iī, itus, go.
eō, *adv.*, there.
Ēpīrus, –ī, *f.*, *a province in Greece.*
eques, equitis, *m.*, horseman.
equester, –tris, –tre, *adj.*, cavalry.
equitātus, –ūs, *m.*, cavalry.
equus, –ī, *m.*, horse.
ēripiō, –ere, ēripuī, ēreptus, snatch away.
ērumpō, –ere, ērūpī, ēruptus, burst forth.

et, *conj.*, and, even; et ... et, both ... and.

etiam, *adv.*, also, even, too.

Etrūscī, –ōrum, *m.*, the Etruscans.

Eurōpa, –ae, *f.*, Europe.

ēvādō, –ere, ēvāsī, ēvāsus, go out, escape.

ēvertō, –ere, ēvertī, ēversus, overturn.

ēvocō, –āre, –āvī, –ātus, summon.

excēdō, –ere, –cessī, –cessus, go away, depart.

excipiō, –ere, –cēpī, –ceptus, take, accept.

exclūdō, –ere, –clūsī, –clūsus, shut out.

exemplum, –ī, *n.*, sample, example, model.

exeō, –īre, –iī, –itus, go out *or* forth.

exerceō, –ēre, –ercuī, –ercitus, occupy, train.

exercitus, –ūs, *m.*, (trained) army.

exigō, –ere, –ēgī, –āctus, drive out, demand.

exiguē, hardly.

exīstimō, –āre, –āvī, –ātus, think, consider.

exitus, –ūs, *m.*, a going forth, outcome, departure.

expediō, –īre, –īvī, –ītus, set free.

expellō, –ere, –pulī, –pulsus, drive out.

experior, experīrī, expertus sum, test, try, experience.

explicō, –āre, –āvī, –ātus, unfold, spread out, explain.

explōrō, –āre, –āvī, –ātus, investigate, explore.

expōnō, –ere, –posuī, –positus, set forth, explain.

expugnō, –āre, –āvī, –ātus, capture by assault.

exsilium, –ī, *n.*, exile.

exspectō, –āre, –āvī, –ātus, look out for, await, wait.

exstinguō, –ere, –stīnxī, –stīnctus, extinguish, destroy.

exstruō, –ere, –strūxī, –strūctus, pile up, build up.

extrēmus, –a, –um, farthest, last, end of.

F

Fabiānus, –ī, *m.*, Fabianus.

Fabius, –ī, *m.*, Fabius.

Fabricius, –ī, *m.*, Fabricius.

faciēs, –iēī, *f.*, face, appearance.

facile, *adv.*, easily.

facilis, –e, easy.

faciō, –ere, fēcī, factus, do, make, hold; verba facere, speak, make a speech; certiōrem eum facere dē, inform him about.

factum, –ī, *n.*, deed.

fallō, –ere, fefellī, falsus, deceive.

falsus, –a, –um, false.

falx, falcis, *f.*, sickle, pruning hook.

fāma, –ae, *f.*, report, fame, reputation.

familia, –ae, *f.*, household, family.

familiāris, –e, (belonging to the family), friendly; *as noun*, friend.

fateor, fatērī, fassus sum, confess.

Faustulus, –ī, *m.*, Faustulus.

faveō, –ēre, fāvī, fautus, be favorable to.

fēlīx, –īcis, happy.

fēmina, –ae, *f.*, woman.

ferē, *adv.*, almost, about.

fēriae, -ārum, holidays.
ferō, ferre, tulī, lātus, bear, carry, bring.
fidēs, -eī, _f._, good faith, protection.
fīlia, -ae, _f._, daughter.
fīlius, -ī, _m._, son.
fingō, -ere, fīnxī, fictus, shape, form, invent.
fīnis, fīnis, _m._, end, limit; _pl._, borders, territory.
fīnitimus, -a, -um, neighboring; fīnitimus, -ī, _m._, a neighbor.
fīō, fierī, factus sum, become, be made, happen.
firmus, -a, -um, strong, steadfast, firm, solid.
flāgitō, -āre, -āvī, -ātus, demand.
flectō, -ere, flexī, flexus, bend, curve, turn.
fleō, flēre, flēvī, flētus, cry, weep.
flūmen, flūminis, _n._, river.
fluō, -ere, flūxī, flūxus, flow.
focus, -ī, _m._, hearth.
fōns, fontis, _m._, spring.
fōrma, -ae, _f._, shape, image, form.
fortis, -e, strong, brave.
fortiter, bravely.
fortūna, -ae, _f._, fortune.
forum, -ī, _n._, market place; Forum (_at Rome_).
fossa, -ae, _f._, trench.
frangō, -ere, frēgī, frāctus, break, wreck.
frāter, frātris, _m._, brother.
fraus, fraudis, _f._, fraud.
frequēns, _gen._ frequentis, _adj._, in great numbers, often.
frōns, frontis, _f._, forehead, front.
frūctus, -ūs, _m._, enjoyment, fruit.
frūmentārius, _see_ rēs.
frūmentum, -ī, _n._, grain.

fuga, -ae, _f._, flight; **in fugam dare**, put to flight.
fugiō, -ere, fūgī, fugitūrus, flee.
fulmen, -minis, _n._, lightning.
fundō, -ere, fūdī, fūsus, pour, rout, scatter.
futūrus, _see_ sum.

G

Gāius, -ī, _m._, Gaius.
Galba, -ae, _m._, Galba.
Gallia, -ae, _f._, Gaul (_ancient France_).
Gallicus, -a, -um, Gallic.
Gallus, -ī, _m._, a Gaul.
Genava, -ae, _f._, Geneva.
gener, -erī, _m._, son-in-law.
gēns, gentis, _f._, tribe, people, nation.
genus, generis, _n._, birth, race, kind.
Germānia, -ae, _f._, Germany.
Germānus, -ī, _m._, a German.
gerō, -ere, gessī, gestus, carry on, manage, wear; **bellum gerere**, wage war; **sē gerere**, act.
gladius, -ī, _m._, sword.
glōria, -ae, _f._, glory, fame.
Gracchus, -ī, _m._, Gracchus.
gradior, gradī, gressus sum, step, walk.
Graecia, -ae, _f._, Greece.
Graecus, -a, -um, Greek; **Graecus**, -ī, _m._, a Greek.
grātia, -ae, _f._, gratitude, favor, influence, grace; **grātiam habēre**, feel grateful; **grātiās agere**, thank; **grātiā**, by reason of, for the sake of.
grātus, -a, -um, pleasing, grateful.
gravis, -e, heavy, serious, severe.
graviter, seriously.

grex, gregis, *m.,* herd.

gubernātor, –ōris, *m.,* pilot, governor.

H

ha! *interj.,* ha!

habeō, –ēre, habuī, habitus, have, hold, consider; **grātiam habēre,** feel grateful (*w. dat.*); **ōrātiōnem habēre,** deliver an oration.

habitō, –āre, –āvī, –ātus, live.

haereō, –ēre, haesī, haesus, stick.

Hannibal, –alis, *m., a Carthaginian general.*

Helvētiī, –ōrum, *m.,* the Helvetians (*lived in ancient Switzerland*).

Hibernia, –ae, *f.,* Ireland.

hic, haec, hoc, this; *as pron.,* he, she, it.

hiems, hiemis, *f.,* winter.

Hispānia, –ae, *f.,* Spain.

Hispānus, –a, –um, Spanish; **Hispānus, –ī,** *m.,* a Spaniard.

ho! *interj.,* ho!

homō, hominis, *m.,* man, human being.

honestās, –tātis, *f.,* honor, honesty.

honor, –ōris, *m.,* honor, office.

hōra, –ae, *f.,* hour.

Horātius, –ī, *m.,* Horatius; **Horātius Coclēs** (" One-eye "), *a famous Roman.*

hospes, –pitis, *m.,* guest.

hostis, hostis, *m.,* enemy (*usually pl.*).

hūmānus, –a, –um, human.

humilis, –e, low, humble.

humiliter, humbly.

I

iaciō, –ere, iēcī, iactus, throw, cast, hurl.

iam, *adv.,* already; **nōn iam,** no longer.

ibi, *adv.,* there.

īdem, eadem, idem, same.

idōneus, –a, –um, suitable.

ignis, –is, *m.,* fire.

ignōrō, –āre, –āvī, –ātus, be ignorant of, not know.

ille, illa, illud, *demonst. adj.,* that; *as pron.,* he, she, it.

imāgō, imāginis, *f.,* likeness (*i.e. a statue or picture*).

immortālis, –e, undying, immortal.

impedīmentum, –ī, *n.,* hindrance; *pl.,* baggage.

impediō, –īre, –īvī, –ītus, hinder.

impellō, –ere, –pulī, –pulsus, drive on, incite, persuade.

imperātor, –ōris, *m.,* commander, general.

imperium, –ī, *n.,* command, power.

imperō, –āre, –āvī, –ātus, command, order, govern (*w. dat.*).

impetus, –ūs, *m.,* attack.

importō, –āre, –āvī, –ātus, import.

improbus, –a, –um, bad, shameless.

in, *prep. w. acc.,* into, to, against; *w. abl.,* in, on.

incendō, –ere, –cendī, –cēnsus, set on fire, burn.

incertus, –a, –um, uncertain.

incidō, –ere, –cidī, —, fall into *or* upon, happen.

incipiō, –ere, –cēpī, –ceptus, take to, begin.

incitō, –āre, –āvī, –ātus, urge on, arouse.

incolō, –ere, incoluī, incultus, dwell, inhabit.

incolumis, –e, unharmed.

indūcō, –ere, –dūxī, –ductus, lead in, induce.

ineō, –īre, –iī, –itus, enter upon; ratiōnem inīre, make a calculation.

īnfāns, –fantis, *m., f.,* infant.

īnfēlīcitās, –tātis, *f.,* unhappiness.

īnferior, īnferius, lower.

inimīcus, –a, –um, unfriendly, hostile; *as noun,* enemy.

inīquus, –a, –um, uneven, unfavorable, unjust.

iniūria, –ae, *f.,* wrong, injustice, injury.

inopia, –ae, *f.,* need, lack.

inquit, says he, said he.

īnsignis, –e, remarkable, notable.

īnstituō, –ere, –stituī, –stitūtus, establish, commence, train.

īnstō, –āre, īnstitī, ——, press on, threaten.

īnstruō, –ere, –strūxī, –strūctus, arrange, provide.

īnsula, –ae, *f.,* island.

integer, –gra, –grum, untouched, fresh.

intellegō, –ere, –lēxī, –lēctus, understand.

inter, *prep. w. acc.,* between, among.

intercipiō, –ere, –cēpī, –ceptus, intercept.

interclūdō, –ere, –clūsī, –clūsus, shut off, cut off.

interficiō, –ere, –fēcī, –fectus, kill.

interim, *adv.,* meanwhile.

intermittō, –ere, –mīsī, –missus, let go between, suspend, stop, cease.

inveniō, –īre, –vēnī, –ventus, come upon, find.

invideō, –ēre, –vīdī, –vīsus, be envious toward, envy.

iō, *interj.,* hurrah!

ipse, ipsa, ipsum, self.

īrācundia, –ae, *f.,* anger, temper.

is, ea, id, this, that; *as pron.,* he, she, it.

Isabella, –ae, *f.,* Isabella.

ita, *adv.,* so, in such a way, thus.

Italia, –ae, *f.,* Italy.

itaque, *adv.,* and so, therefore.

iter, itineris, *n.,* journey, road, march.

iterum, *adv.,* again, for the second time.

iubeō, –ēre, iussī, iussus, order, command.

iūdex, iūdicis, *m.,* judge, juror.

iūdicium, –ī, *n.,* trial, judgment.

iūdicō, –āre, –āvī, –ātus, judge, decide.

Iugurtha, –ae, *m.,* Jugurtha (*king of Numidia*).

Iūlia, –ae, *f.,* Julia.

Iūlius, –ī, *m.,* Julius.

iungo, –ere, iūnxī, iūnctus, join to (*w. dat.*).

iūnior, *adj.,* younger.

Iūnō, –ōnis, *f.,* Juno (*a goddess, wife of Jupiter*).

Iuppiter, Iovis, *m.,* Jupiter (*king of the gods*).

iūrō, –āre, –āvī, –ātus, swear.

iūs, iūris, *n.,* right, justice.

iūstē, justly.

iūstus, –a, –um, just.

Iuvenālis, –is, *m.,* Juvenal.

L

L., *abbreviation for* Lūcius.

labor, labī, lāpsus sum, slip, glide by

labor, –ōris, *m.*, work, trouble.

labōrō, –āre, –āvī, –ātus, labor, work, suffer.

Lacedaemoniī, –ōrum, *m.*, the Lacedaemonians, Spartans (*a people of southern Greece*).

lacrima, –ae, *f.*, tear.

Laecānia, –ae, *f.*, Laecania.

lancea, –ae, *f.*, spear.

lanterna, –ae, *f.*, lantern.

Lār, Laris, *m.*, *a household god.*

lassitūdō, –tūdinis, *f.*, weariness.

Latīnus, –a, –um, *adj.*, Latin, belonging to Latium; **Latīna** (lingua), the Latin language.

laudō, –āre, –āvī, –ātus, praise.

laus, laudis, *f.*, praise.

lava, –ae, *f.*, lava.

lectīca, –ae, *f.*, litter, sedan.

lēgātus, –ī, *m.*, envoy, lieutenant general.

legō, –ere, lēgī, lēctus, gather, choose, read.

Lentulus, –ī, *m.*, Lentulus.

levis, –e, light (*in weight*).

leviter, lightly.

levō, –āre, –āvī, –ātus, lift.

lēx, lēgis, *f.*, law.

liber, librī, *m.*, book.

līber, –era, –erum, free.

līberē, freely.

līberī, –ōrum, *m.*, children.

līberō, –āre, –āvī, –ātus, set free.

lībertās, –tātis, *f.*, freedom.

licet, –ēre, licuit, it is permitted.

lignum, –ī, *n.*, wood.

ligō, –āre, –āvī, –ātus, tie, bind.

lingua, –ae, *f.*, tongue, language.

littera, -ae, *f.*, a letter (*of the alphabet*); *pl.*, a letter (*epistle*), literature.

lītus, lītoris, *n.*, shore.

Līvius, –ī, *m.*, Livius.

locō, –āre, –āvī, –ātus, place, put, set.

locus, –ī, *m.* (*pl.*, **loca, locōrum,** *n.*), place.

longē, *adv.*, far away.

longus, –a, –um, long.

loquor, loquī, locūtus sum, talk, speak.

Lūcius, –ī, *m.*, Lucius.

lūdō, –ere, lūsī, lūsus, play.

lūdus, –ī, *m.*, game, school (*as a place for exercise*).

lūmen, lūminis, *n.*, light.

lupa, –ae, *f.*, she-wolf.

Lūsitānia, –ae, *f.*, Portugal.

lūx, lūcis, *f.*, light.

Lycōris, –idis, *f.*, Lycoris.

M

M., *abbreviation for* **Mārcus.**

magis, *adv.*, more; *superl.*, **maximē,** very, very greatly, especially.

magister, –trī, *m.*, teacher.

magnitūdō, –tūdinis, *f.*, greatness, size.

magnopere, *adv.*, greatly.

magnus, –a, –um, big, large, great; *comp.*, **maior, maius,** greater; *superl.*, **maximus,** –a, –um, greatest, very great.

maior, *see* **magnus.**

male, *adv.*, badly; *comp.*, **peius,** worse; *superl.*, **pessimē,** worst.

maleficium, –ī, *n.*, harm.

mālō, mālle, māluī, —, prefer.

malus, –a, –um, bad, evil; *comp.*, **peior, peius,** worse; *superl.*, **pessimus,** –a, –um, very bad, worst.

mandō, –āre, –āvī, –ātus, intrust.
Mandubiī, –ōrum, *m.*, the Mandubii.
maneō, –ēre, mānsī, mānsus, remain.
manus, –ūs, *f.*, hand, group, force.
Mārcus, –ī, *m.*, Marcus.
mare, maris, *n.*, sea.
Marīa, –ae, *f.*, Maria, Mary.
Marius, –ī, *m.*, Marius.
Mārs, Mārtis, *m.*, *god of war.*
māter, mātris, *f.*, mother.
māteria, –ae, *f.*, matter, timber.
mātrōna, –ae, *f.*, married woman, matron.
mātūrō, –āre, –āvī, –ātus, hasten.
mātūrus, –a, –um, ripe, early.
maximē, *see* magis.
maximus, –a, –um, *see* magnus.
Maximus, –ī, *m.*, Maximus.
medicus, –ī, *m.*, doctor.
Mediterrāneum (Mare), Mediterranean Sea.
medius, –a, –um, middle, middle of.
mel, mellis, *n.*, honey.
melior, *see* bonus.
memor, *gen.* memoris, *adj.*, mindful of, remembering (*w. gen.*).
memoria, –ae, *f.*, memory; memoriā tenēre, remember.
mēns, mentis, *f.*, mind.
mēnsis, –is, *m.*, month.
mercātor, –tōris, *m.*, trader, merchant.
Mercurius, –ī, *m.*, Mercury.
mereō, –ēre, meruī, meritus, deserve, earn.
merīdiānus, –a, –um, noon.
mēta, –ae, *f.*, goal, turning post (*in the Circus*).

mētior, mētīrī, mēnsus sum, measure, deal out.
meus, –a, –um, mine, my.
migrō, –āre, –āvī, –ātus, depart.
mīles, mīlitis, *m.*, soldier.
mīlitāris, –e, military.
mīlle, *pl.*, mīlia, thousand.
Minerva, –ae, *f.*, *goddess of wisdom.*
minimē, *see* minus.
minimus, –a, –um, *see* parvus.
minor, *see* parvus.
Minucius, –ī, *m.*, Minucius.
minus, *adv.*, less; *superl.*, minimē, least.
mīror, mīrārī, mīrātus sum, wonder, admire.
Mithridātēs, –is, *m.*, *king of Pontus* (*Asia Minor*).
Mithridāticus, –a, –um, Mithridatic, with Mithridates.
mittō, –ere, mīsī, missus, let go, send.
modus, –ī, *m.*, measure, limit, manner, kind.
moneō, –ēre, monuī, monitus, remind, warn.
mōns, montis, *m.*, mountain; summus mōns, the top of the mountain.
mōnstrō, –āre, –āvī, –ātus, point out, show.
mors, mortis, *f.*, death.
mortuus, –a, –um, dead.
mōs, mōris, *m.*, custom.
moveō, –ēre, mōvī, mōtus, move; castra movēre, break camp.
multitūdō, –tūdinis, *f.*, multitude, great number.
multum, *adv.*, much; *comp.*, plūs, more; *superl.*, plūrimum, most.

multus, -a, -um, much; *pl.*, many; *comp.*, **plūrēs, plūra,** more; *superl.*, **plūrimus, -a, -um,** most.

mŭniō, -īre, -īvī, -ītus, fortify, defend; **viam mūnīre,** build a road.

mūnus, mūneris, *n.*, duty, service, gift.

mŭrus, -ī, *m.*, wall.

mūtō, -āre, -āvī, -ātus, change.

N

nam, *conj.*, for.

nărrō, -āre, -āvī, -ātus, tell, relate.

născor, născī, nātus sum, be born.

Nāsīca, -ae, *m.*, Nasica.

nătūra, -ae, *f.*, nature.

nauta, -ae, *m.*, sailor.

năvigium, -ī, *n.*, boat.

năvigō, -āre, -āvī, -ātus, sail.

năvis, năvis, *f.*, ship.

nĕ, *conj.*, not, that not, lest; **nĕ ... quidem** (*emphatic word between*), not even.

-ne (*enclitic*), *introduces questions.*

nec, *see* neque.

necessārius, -a, -um, necessary.

necessitās, -tātis, *f.*, necessity.

neglegentia, -ae, *f.*, negligence.

negō, -āre, -āvī, -ātus, deny.

negōtium, -ī, *n.*, business.

nēmō, *dat.* nēminī, *acc.* nēminem (*no other forms*), no one.

nepōs, -ōtis, *m.*, grandson.

Neptūnus, -ī, *m.*, Neptune (*god of the sea*).

neque (*or* nec), and not, nor; **neque ... neque,** neither ... nor.

neuter, -tra, -trum, neither (*of two*).

niger, -gra, -grum, black.

nihil, nothing.

nisi, *conj.*, unless, except.

niveus, -a, -um, snow-white.

nōbilis, -e, distinguished, noble.

nōbīscum = cum nōbīs.

noceō, -ēre, nocuī, nocitus, do harm to.

nōlō, nōlle, nōluī, —, be unwilling, not wish.

nōmen, nōminis, *n.*, name.

nōn, *adv.*, not.

nōnus, -a, -um, ninth.

nōs, nostrum, we, *pl. of* ego.

nōscō, -ere, nōvī, nōtus, learn; *in perf. tenses,* I have learned, I know.

noster, -tra, -trum, our.

nōtus, -a, -um, known, familiar.

novem, nine.

novus, -a, -um, new, strange.

nox, noctis, *f.*, night.

nūllus, -a, -um, no, none, no one.

numerus, -ī, *m.*, number.

Numidia, -ae, *f.*, a country in Africa.

Numitor, -ōris, *m.*, Numitor.

numquam, *adv.*, never.

nunc, *adv.*, now.

nŭntiō, -āre, -āvī, -ātus, report, announce.

nūntius, -ī, *m.*, messenger.

nūper, *adv.*, recently.

O

Ō, *interj.*, O!

ob, *prep. w. acc.*, toward, on account of, for.

obiciō, -ere, -iēcī, -iectus, throw against, oppose.

oblīviō, -ōnis, *f.*, forgetfulness.

obsideō, -ēre, -sēdī, -sessus, besiege.

obtineō, -ēre, -tinuī, -tentus, obtain.

occāsiō, -ōnis, f., opportunity.

occīdō, -ere, -cīdī, -cīsus, kill.

occupō, -āre, -āvī, -ātus, seize.

occurrō, -ere, -currī, -cursus, run against, meet (w. dat.), occur.

Ōceanus, -ī, m., ocean (esp. the Atlantic Ocean).

octāvus, -a, -um, eighth.

octō, eight.

oculus, -ī, m., eye.

ōdī, ōdisse, ōsūrus, hate.

officium, -ī, n., duty.

ōh! interj., oh!

oho! interj., oho!

omnis, omne, all, every.

opera, -ae, f., work; meā operā, through my efforts.

oportet, -ēre, oportuit, it is fitting, ought.

oppidum, -ī, n., town.

oppōnō, -ere, -posuī, -positus, put against, oppose.

opprimō, -ere, -pressī, -pressus, overwhelm, surprise.

oppugnō, -āre, -āvī, -ātus, attack.

optimē, see bene.

optimus, see bonus.

opus, operis, n., work.

ōrāculum, -ī, n., oracle, prophecy.

ōrātiō, -ōnis, f., speech; ōrātiōnem habēre, deliver an oration.

ōrātor, -ōris, m., speaker, orator.

ōrdō, ōrdinis, m., order, rank; ex ōrdine, in turn.

Orgetorīx, -īgis, m., a Helvetian chieftain.

orior, orīrī, ortus sum, arise, rise.

ōrnāmentum, -ī, n., ornament, jewel.

ōrō, -āre, -āvī, -ātus, beg, ask; causās ōrāre, plead cases.

ostendō, -ere, ostendī, ostentus, (stretch out), show, display.

ōtium, -ī, n., leisure, rest.

P

P., abbreviation for Pūblius.

pācō, -āre, -āvī, -ātus, pacify, subdue.

paene, adv., almost.

pār, gen. paris, equal (w. dat.).

parātus, -a, -um, prepared, ready.

parcē, adv., sparingly.

parcō, -ere, pepercī, parsus, spare, save.

pāreō, -ēre, pāruī, pāritus, (appear), be obedient to, obey.

parō, -āre, -āvī, -ātus, get, get ready, prepare.

pars, partis, f., part, side.

parvus, -a, -um, small; comp., minor, minus, less; superl., minimus, -a, -um, least.

passus, -ūs, m., pace (about five feet); mīlle passūs, a mile.

pāstor, -ōris, m., shepherd.

pater, patris, m., father.

patior, patī, passus sum, suffer, endure.

patria, -ae, f., fatherland, country.

paucī, -ae, -a, few.

paulātim, adv., little by little.

paulō, adv., shortly, a little.

pauper, gen. pauperis, adj., poor.

pāx, pācis, f., peace.

pecūnia, -ae, f., money.

pecus, pecoris, n., cattle.

pedester, tris, -tre, adj., infantry.

peior, peius, see malus.

pellō, –ere, **pepulī**, **pulsus**, drive, defeat.

Penātēs, –ium, *m.*, *household gods*.

pendō, –ere, **pependī**, **pēnsus**, hang, weigh, pay.

per, *prep. w. acc.*, through, by.

perdūcō, –ere, –dūxī, –ductus, lead through, extend.

perficiō, –ere, –fēcī, –fectus, finish.

perīculum, –ī, *n.*, danger, trial.

perītus, –a, –um, skilled, experienced.

permaneō, –ēre, –mānsī, –mānsus, stay to the end, remain.

permittō, –ere, –mīsī, –missus, let go through, allow, intrust (*w. dat.*).

permoveō, –ēre, –mōvī, –mōtus, move throughout *or* deeply, induce.

permūtātiō, –ōnis, *f.*, exchange.

perpetuus, –a, –um, constant.

persōna, –ae, *f.*, character, person.

persuādeō, –ēre, –suāsī, –suāsus, persuade (*w. dat.*).

perterreō, –ēre, –terruī, –territus, frighten thoroughly, alarm.

pertineō, –ēre, –tinuī, –tentus, (*w.* **ad**), extend to, pertain to.

perveniō, –īre, –vēnī, –ventus, come through, arrive.

pēs, **pedis**, *m.*, foot; **pedibus**, on foot.

pessimus, –a, –um, *see* **malus**.

petō, –ere, **petīvī**, **petītus**, seek, ask.

pingō, –ere, **pīnxī**, **pictus**, paint, embroider.

pīrāta, –ae, *m.*, pirate.

pius, –a, –um, dutiful, loyal.

placeō, –ēre, **placuī**, **placitus**, be pleasing to.

plānus, –a, –um, level, plane.

plēbs, **plēbis**, *f.*, the people, the common people.

plēnus, –a, –um, full.

plicō, –āre, –āvī, –ātus, fold.

Plīnius, –ī, *m.*, Pliny (*a Roman author*).

plūrēs, **plūra**, more, *see* **multus**.

plūrimus, *see* **multus**.

plūs, *see* **multum**, **multus**.

poena, –ae, *f.*, penalty, punishment; **poenam dare**, pay the penalty.

pompa, –ae, *f.*, parade.

Pompeius, –ī, *m.*, Pompey.

pōnō, –ere, **posuī**, **positus**, put, place, set; **castra pōnere**, pitch camp.

pōns, **pontis**, *m.*, bridge.

pontifex, –ficis, *m.*, priest.

Pontus, –ī, *m.*, *the region south of the Black Sea*.

populus, –ī, *m.*, people; *pl.*, peoples, nations.

Porsena, –ae, *m.*, Porsena.

porta, –ae, *f.*, gate; **porta Capēna**, *a gate in the wall of Rome*.

portō, –āre, –āvī, –ātus, carry.

possum, **posse**, **potuī**, ——, can, be able (*w. infin.*).

post, *adv. and prep. w. acc.*, behind (*of place*); after (*of time*).

posteā, *adv.*, afterwards.

postquam, *conj.*, after.

potestās, –tātis, *f.*, power, authority, chance.

potior, **potīrī**, **potītus sum**, gain possession of (*w. abl.*).

prae, *prep. w. abl.*, before, in front of.

praecēdō, –ere, –cessī, –cessus, go before, surpass.

praeceps, *gen.* praecipitis, *adj.*, headlong, steep.

praecipiō, –ere, –cēpī, –ceptus, order, instruct, advise.

praeda, –ae, *f.*, booty, prey.

praedicō, –āre, –āvī, –ātus, declare, proclaim.

praeficiō, –ere, –fēcī, –fectus, put in charge of (*w. acc. and dat.*).

praemittō, –ere, –mīsī, –missus, send ahead.

praemium, –ī, *n.*, reward.

praesēns, *gen.* praesentis, *adj.*, present, in person.

praesidium, –ī, *n.*, garrison, guard, protection.

praestō, –āre, –stitī, –stitus, stand before, excel.

praesum, –esse, –fuī, –futūrus, be in charge of (*w. dat.*).

praetextus, –a, –um, woven in front, bordered; toga praetexta, *a cloak with a purple border, worn by children.*

prehendō, –ere, –hendī, –hēnsus, grasp, take hold of.

premō, –ere, pressī, pressus, press, press hard, oppress.

pretium, –ī, *n.*, price.

prīmus, –a, –um, first.

prīnceps, –cipis, *m.*, first man, chief, leader.

prō, *prep. w. abl.*, in front of, before, for.

probō, –āre, –āvī, –ātus, test, prove, approve.

Proca, –ae, *m.*, Proca.

prōcēdō, –ere, –cessī, –cessus, go forth, advance.

prōdūcō, –ere, –dūxī, –ductus, lead forth *or* out, prolong.

proelium, –ī, *n.*, battle.

proficīscor, proficīscī, profectus sum, start, set out.

prōgredior, prōgredī, prōgressus sum, step forward, advance.

prohibeō, –ēre, –hibuī, –hibitus, prevent, keep from.

prōiciō, –ere, –iēcī, –iectus, throw forward.

prōmittō, –ere, –mīsī, –missus, promise.

properō, –āre, –āvī, –ātus, hasten.

propinquus, –a, –um, near.

prōpōnō, –ere, –posuī, –positus, set forth, present, offer.

proprius, –a, –um, one's own, fitting.

propter, *prep. w. acc.*, on account of.

prōvideō, –ēre, –vīdī, –vīsus, foresee, provide.

prōvincia, –ae, *f.*, province.

proximus, –a, –um, nearest, next (*w. dat.*).

pūblicus, –a, –um, public.

Pūblius, –ī, *m.*, Publius.

puella, –ae, *f.*, girl.

puer, puerī, *m.*, boy.

pugna, –ae, *f.*, battle.

pugnō, –āre, –āvī, –ātus, fight.

pulcher, –chra, –chrum, beautiful.

Pūnicus, –a, –um, Punic, Carthaginian.

putō, –āre, –āvī, –ātus, think.

Pyrrhus, –ī, *m.*, *king of Epirus.*

Q

Q., *abbreviation for* Quintus.

quadrīgae, –ārum, *f.*, a four-horse team, a chariot.

quadringentī, –ae, –a, four hundred.

quaerō, –ere, quaesīvī, quaesītus, seek, inquire.

quaestor, –ōris, *m.*, quaestor (*a Roman official*).

quālis, –e, what kind of, such as.

quam, *conj.*, than; *w. superl.*, as . . . as possible.

quantus, –a, –um, how great, as (great as).

quārē, why.

quārtus, –a, –um, fourth.

quattuor, four.

–que (*always joined to second word*), and.

quī, quae, quod, *relat. pron.*, who, which, what, that.

quī, quae, quod, *interrog. adj.*, what.

quia, *conj.*, because.

quīdam, quaedam, quiddam, a certain one.

quidem (*placed after the word emphasized*), certainly, to be sure.

quiēs, quiētis, *f.*, rest, sleep.

quīndecim, fifteen.

quīnque, five.

quīntus, –a, –um, fifth.

Quīntus, –ī, *m.*, Quintus.

quis, quid, *interrog. pron.*, who, what.

quis, quid, *indef. pron.*, any.

quisquis, quidquid, whoever, whatever, what.

quod, *conj.*, because.

quondam, *adv.*, once (upon a time).

quoque, *adv.*, also.

quot, how many.

R

raeda, –ae, *f.*, four-wheeled carriage, omnibus.

rapidē, swiftly.

rapidus, –a, –um, swift.

rapiō, –ere, rapuī, raptus, seize, carry off.

ratiō, –ōnis, *f.*, account, plan, manner, reason.

recēns, *gen.* recentis, *adj.*, fresh, new, recent.

recipiō, –ere, –cēpī, –ceptus, take back, receive; sē recipere, retreat.

rēctē, rightly.

reddō, –ere, reddidī, redditus, give back, deliver.

redeō, redīre, rediī, reditus, go back.

redigō, –ere, redēgī, redāctus, drive *or* bring back, reduce.

redimō, –ere, redēmī, redēmptus, buy back, ransom.

redūcō, –ere, –dūxī, –ductus, lead back, bring back.

referō, referre, rettulī, relātus, bring back, report, give back.

reficiō, –ere, –fēcī, –fectus, repair.

rēgālis, –e, regal, kinglike.

rēgīna, –ae, *f.*, queen.

regiō, –ōnis, *f.*, district, region.

rēgnum, –ī, *n.*, royal power, kingdom.

regō, –ere, rēxī, rēctus, rule, guide.

regredior, regredī, regressus sum, go back.

Rēgulus, –ī, *m.*, Regulus.

reiciō, –ere, –iēcī, –iectus, throw back.

relinquō, –ere, –līquī, –līctus, leave (behind), abandon.

reliquus, –a, –um, remaining, rest (of).

remaneō, –ēre, –mānsī, –mānsūrus, remain behind, remain.

remedium, -ī, *n.*, remedy.

remittō, -ere, -mīsī, -missus, relax, send back.

removeō, -ēre, -mōvī, -mōtus, move back, remove, withdraw.

Remus, -ī, *m.*, Remus.

reor, rērī, ratus sum, think, calculate.

repellō, -ere, reppulī, repulsus, drive back, repulse.

rēs, reī, *f.*, thing, matter, affair; rēs frūmentāria, grain supplies; rēs mīlitāris, military affairs, art of war; rēs pūblica, public affairs, government.

reservō, -āre, -āvī, -ātus, save up, reserve.

resistō, -ere, restitī, —, stand against, resist.

respondeō, -ēre, -spondī, -spōnsus, answer.

restō, -āre, restitī, —, remain.

retineō, -ēre, -tinuī, -tentus, hold back, restrain, keep.

revertō, -ere, -vertī, -versus, return (*sometimes deponent*).

revocō, -āre, -āvī, -ātus, recall, call back.

rēx, rēgis, *m.*, king.

Rhēa, -ae, *f.*, Rhea.

Rhēnus, -ī, *m.*, the Rhine river.

rīdeō, -ēre, rīsī, rīsus, laugh (at).

rogō, -āre, -āvī, -ātus, ask.

Rōma, -ae, *f.*, Rome.

Rōmānus, -a, -um, Roman; Rōmānus, -ī, *m.*, a Roman.

Rōmulus, -ī, *m.*, Romulus.

Rubicō, -ōnis, *m.*, the Rubicon (*a river in Italy*).

rumpō, -ere, rūpī, ruptus, break, destroy.

rūrsus, *adv.*, again.

S

Sabidius, -ī, *m.*, Sabidius.

Sabīnus, -ī, *m.*, Sabinus.

sacer, -cra, -crum, sacred.

saepe, *adv.*, often.

salūs, salūtis, *f.*, health, safety, greeting.

salvus, -a, -um, unhurt, saved.

sapientia, -ae, *f.*, wisdom.

satis, *adv. and indecl. adj.*, enough.

satisfaciō, -ere, -fēcī, -factus, satisfy.

Sāturnālia, -ium, *n.*, *a festival in honor of the god Saturn*.

Sāturnus, -ī, *m.*, Saturn.

scēptrum, -ī, *n.*, scepter.

sciō, -īre, scīvī, scītus, know.

Scīpiō, -ōnis, *m.*, Scipio.

scrībō, -ere, scrīpsī, scrīptus, write.

sēcrētō, *adv.*, secretly.

sēcum = cum sē.

secundus, -a, -um, second.

sed, *conj.*, but.

sedeō, -ēre, sēdī, sessus, sit.

sēdēs, -is, *f.*, dwelling place.

sēditiō, -ōnis, *f.*, discord.

sēmita, -ae, *f.*, path.

semper, *adv.*, always.

senātor, -ōris, *m.*, senator.

senātus, -ūs, *m.*, senate.

senex, senis, *m.*, old man.

sententia, -ae, *f.*, feeling, opinion, motto.

sentiō, -īre, sēnsī, sēnsus, feel, realize.

septem, seven.

septimus, -a, -um, seventh.

sepulchrum, -ī, *n.*, tomb.

sequor, sequī, secūtus sum, follow, pursue.

sermō, -ōnis, *m.*, talk, conversation.

serviō, -īre, -īvī, -ītus, serve (*w. dat.*).

servitūs, -tūtis, *f.*, slavery.

servō, -āre, -āvī, -ātus, save, guard, preserve.

servus, -ī, *m.*, slave.

sescentī, -ae, -a, six hundred.

sex, six.

sextus, -a, -um, sixth; **sextus decimus**, sixteenth.

sī, *conj.*, if.

Sicilia, -ae, *f.*, Sicily.

signum, -ī, *n.*, sign, standard, signal.

silentium, -ī, *n.*, silence.

silva, -ae, *f.*, forest, woods.

Silvia, -ae, *f.*, Silvia.

Silvius, -ī, *m.*, Silvius.

similis, -e, like.

simulō, -āre, -āvī, -ātus, pretend.

sine, *prep. w. abl.*, without.

singulāris, -e, single, unusual.

singulī, -ae, -a, *pl. only*, one at a time.

sinister, -tra, -trum, left (*hand*).

sinō, sinere, sīvī, situs, let, permit.

Sīon, Zion.

socius, -ī, *m.*, comrade, ally.

sōl, sōlis, *m.*, sun.

sōlus, -a, -um, alone, sole, only.

solvō, -ere, solvī, solūtus, loose, pay.

somnus, -ī, *m.*, sleep.

soror, -ōris, *f.*, sister.

Spartacus, -ī, *m.*, Spartacus.

spatium, -ī, *n.*, space, time, distance, " lap " (*in a race*).

speciēs, speciēī, *f.*, appearance, pretense, kind.

spectō, -āre, -āvī, -ātus, look at, face.

spērō, -āre, -āvī, -ātus, hope (for).

spēs, speī, *f.*, hope.

spīna, -ae, *f.*, spina (*a low wall in the Circus, around which the track ran*).

spīrō, -āre, -āvī, -ātus, breathe.

statua, -ae, *f.*, statue.

statuō, -ere, statuī, statūtus, place, establish, determine.

statūra, -ae, *f.*, stature.

stō, stāre, stetī, status, stand.

stringō, -ere, strīnxī, strictus, draw tight, graze.

studium, -ī, *n.*, eagerness, interest, zeal; *pl.*, studies.

stupidus, -a, -um, stupid.

sub, *prep.*, under, close to, at the foot of (*w. acc. after verbs of motion; w. abl. after verbs of rest or position*).

subigō, -ere, -ēgī, -āctus, subdue.

subitō, *adv.*, suddenly.

sublevō, -āre, -āvī, -ātus, lift up from beneath, hold up.

submittō, -ere, -mīsī, -missus, (send from under), dispatch.

succēdō, -ere, -cessī, -cessus, come up, succeed.

suī, *reflexive pron.*, of himself, herself, itself, themselves.

Sulla, -ae, *m.*, Sulla.

sum, esse, fuī, futūrus, be, exist.

summus, -a, -um, highest, top of.

sūmō, -ere, sūmpsī, sūmptus, take, assume.

super, *prep. w. acc.*, over, above.

superbus, -a, -um, haughty.

superō, –āre, –āvī, –ātus, overcome, excel.

supersum, –esse, –fuī, –futūrus, be left over.

superus, –a, –um, on high, above.

supplex, *gen.* supplicis, *adj.*, (kneeling), suppliant, beseeching.

supplicium, –ī, *n.*, punishment, torture.

surgō, –ere, surrēxī, surrēctus, rise.

suscipiō, –ere, –cēpī, –ceptus, take up, undertake.

sustineō, –ēre, –tinuī, –tentus, hold up *or* back, maintain, endure.

suus, –a, –um, *reflexive adj.*, his, her, its, their; his own, her own, *etc.*

T

tālis, –e, such.

tam, *adv.*, so.

tamen, *adv.*, still, nevertheless.

tandem, *adv.*, at last.

tangō, –ere, tetigī, tāctus, touch.

tantum, *adv.*, only.

tantus, –a, –um, so great.

tardē, slowly.

tardus, –a, –um, slow, late.

Tarentīnī, –ōrum, *m.*, the Tarentines, inhabitants of Tarentum.

Tarentum, –ī, *n.*, a city in Italy.

Tarquiniī, –ōrum, *m.*, the Tarquins (*kings at Rome*).

tegō, –ere, tēxī, tēctus, cover, conceal.

tēlum, –ī, *n.*, missile, weapon.

temperō, –āre, –āvī, –ātus, regulate, refrain from (*w. abl.*).

tempestās, –tātis, *f.*, season, storm.

templum, –ī, *n.*, temple.

temptō, –āre, –āvī, –ātus, test, try, attempt.

tempus, temporis, *n.*, time.

tendō, –ere, tetendī, tentus, stretch.

teneō, –ēre, tenuī, tentus, hold, keep; memoriā tenēre, remember.

terminus, –ī, *m.*, end, boundary.

terra, –ae, *f.*, land, earth, country.

terreō, –ēre, terruī, territus, terrify, frighten.

tertius, –a, –um, third.

testis, testis, *m.*, witness.

Teutonēs, –um, *m.*, the Teutons (*a people of Germany*).

texō, –ere, texuī, textus, weave.

Thāis, –idis, *f.*, Thais.

Ti., *abbreviation for* Tiberius.

Tiberis, –is, *m.*, the Tiber (*a river of Italy*).

Tiberius, –ī, *m.*, Tiberius.

timeō, –ēre, timuī, —, fear, be afraid.

timidus, –a, –um, fearful, afraid.

timor, –ōris, *m.*, fear.

Titūrius, –ī, *m.*, Titurius.

Titus, –ī, *m.*, Titus.

toga, –ae, *f.*, toga, cloak.

tolerō, –āre, –āvī, –ātus, endure.

tollō, –ere, sustulī, sublātus, raise, remove.

torqueō, –ēre, torsī, tortus, twist, torture.

tōtus, –a, –um, whole.

trādō, –ere, –didī, –ditus, give *or* hand over, deliver.

trādūcō, –ere, –dūxī, –ductus, lead across.

trahō, –ere, trāxī, trāctus, draw, drag.

trāiciō, –ere, –iēcī, –iectus, throw across, pierce.

trānō, –āre, –āvī, –ātus, swim across.

trāns, *prep. w. acc.*, across.

trānseō, –īre, –iī, –itus, cross.

trānsportō, –āre, –āvī, –ātus, carry over, transport.

trecentī, –ae, –a, three hundred.

trēs, tria, three.

tribūnus, –ī, *m.*, tribune (*a Roman official*).

tribuō, –ere, tribuī, tribūtus, bestow, grant.

trīgintā, thirty.

triplex, *gen.* triplicis, *adj.*, threefold

triumphō, –āre, –āvī, –ātus, triumph.

triumphus, –ī, *m.*, triumph.

tū, tuī, you.

tum, *adv.*, then.

turbō, –āre, –āvī, –ātus, disturb, agitate.

turris, turris, *f.*, tower.

tuus, –a, –um, your, yours (*referring to one person*).

U

ubi, *adv.*, where (*place*); when (*time*).

ūllus, –a, –um, any.

ulterior, ulterius, farther.

ultimus, –a, –um, last, farthest.

ultrā, *adv.*, beyond, any more.

unda, –ae, *f.*, wave.

ūnus, –a, –um, one.

urbs, urbis, *f.*, city.

ut, *conj.*, in order that, that, so that; as (*w. indic.*)

ūtilis, –e, useful.

ūtor, ūtī, ūsus sum, use, make use of (*w. abl.*).

uxor, –ōris, *f.*, wife.

V

vacō, –āre, –āvī, –ātus, be free, be uninhabited.

valeō, –ēre, valuī, valitūrus, be strong, be well, be powerful.

vāllum, –ī, *n.*, wall.

varius, –a, –um, changing, varying, various.

vāstō, –āre, –āvī, –ātus, lay waste, ravage.

vehō, –ere, vexī, vectus, convey, carry.

veniō, –īre, vēnī, ventus, come.

Venus, –eris, *f.*, *goddess of love and beauty*.

verberō, –āre, –āvī, –ātus, beat, strike.

verbum, –ī, *n.*, word; verba facere, speak, make a speech.

Vercingetorīx, –rīgis, *m.*, *a Gallic chieftain*.

vērō, *adv.*, in truth, but.

vertō, –ere, vertī, versus, turn.

vērus, –a, –um, true.

vesper, –erī, *m.*, evening.

Vesta, –ae, *f.*, *a goddess*.

Vestālis, –e, Vestal, of Vesta.

vester, –tra, –trum, your, yours (*referring to two or more persons*).

vestis, –is, *f.*, clothing, garment.

via, –ae, *f.*, way, road, street; viam mūnīre, build a road.

victōria, –ae, *f.*, victory.

vīcus, –ī, *m.*, village.

videō, –ēre, vīdī, vīsus, see; *passive*, seem, be seen.

vigilantia, –ae, *f.*, vigilance.

vigilia, -ae, *f.*, guard, watchfulness.
vīgintī, twenty.
vīlla, -ae, *f.*, farmhouse, country home.
vincō, -ere, vīcī, victus, conquer.
vindicō, -āre, -āvī, -ātus, avenge.
vīnum, -ī, *n.*, wine.
violō, -āre, -āvī, -ātus, treat with violence, profane.
vir, virī, *m.*, man, hero.
virgō, -inis, *f.*, virgin, maiden.
virīlis, -e, of a man, manly.
virītim, *adv.*, man by man, individually.
virtūs, -tūtis, *f.*, manliness, courage.
vīs, —, *f.*, force, violence; *pl.*, vīrēs, -ium, strength.
vispillo, -ōnis, *m.*, undertaker.
vīta, -ae, *f.*, life.
vīvō, -ere, vīxī, vīctus, live.

vīvus, -a, -um, alive, living.
vix, *adv.*, scarcely, with difficulty.
vocō, -āre, -āvī, -ātus, call, summon.
volō, velle, voluī, —, want, be willing, wish.
volvō, -ere, volvī, volūtus, roll; *passive*, tumble.
vōmer, -eris, *m.*, plowshare.
vōs, vestrum, *pl. of* tū.
voveō, -ēre, vōvī, vōtus, vow, promise.
vōx, vōcis, *f.*, voice, remark.
Vulcānus, -ī, *m.*, Vulcan (*god of fire*).
vulnerō, -āre, -āvī, -ātus, wound.
vulnus, vulneris, *n.*, wound.

Z

Zama, -ae, *f.*, *a town in Africa.*

ENGLISH – LATIN VOCABULARY

A

abandon, relinquō, –ere, –līquī, –līctus.

able (be), possum, posse, potuī, —.

about, dē, *w. abl.;* circum, *w. acc.*

absent (be), absum, abesse, āfuī, āfutūrus.

abundance, cōpia, –ae, *f.*

accept, accipiō, –ere, –cēpī, –ceptus.

account : on account of, ob, *w. acc.*

accuse, accūsō, –āre, –āvī, –ātus.

across, trāns, *w. acc.*

admire, mīror, –ārī, –ātus sum.

advance, prōcēdō, –ere, –cessī, –cessus; prōgredior, –gredī, –gressus sum.

advice, cōnsilium, –ī, *n.*

affair, rēs, reī, *f.*

afflict, afficiō, –ere, –fēcī, –fectus.

afraid (be), timeō, –ēre, timuī, —.

after, *use abl. abs.;* post (*prep. w. acc.*); postquam (*conj.*).

afterwards, posteā (*adv.*).

against, contrā, *w. acc.*

aid, auxilium, –ī, *n.*

alive, vīvus, –a, –um.

all, omnis, –e.

allow, permittō, –ere, –mīsī, –missus; patior, patī, passus sum.

ally, socius, –ī, *m.*

alone, sōlus, –a, –um.

already, iam.

also, etiam.

although, *use particip. or abl. abs.*

always, semper.

America, America, –ae, *f.*

among, inter, *w. acc.*

and, et, –que.

Anna, Anna, –ae, *f.*

announce, nūntiō, –āre, –āvī, –ātus.

answer, respondeō, –ēre, –spondī, –spōnsus.

any, ūllus, –a, –um; **any one, anything**, aliquis, aliquid; quis, quid (*after* sī).

approach, accēdō, –ere, –cessī, –cessus (*w.* ad).

approve, probō, –āre, –āvī, –ātus.

arms, arma, –ōrum, *n.*

army, exercitus, –ūs, *m.*

around, circum, *w. acc.*

arouse, incitō, –āre, –āvī, –ātus.

arrive, perveniō, –īre, –vēnī, –ventus.

as, *use abl. abs.;* **so as to**, ut (*neg.* nē).

ask, rogō, –āre, –āvī, –ātus; quaerō, –ere, –sīvī, –sītus.

assault : take by assault, expugnō, –āre, –āvī, –ātus.

assemble, conveniō, –īre, –vēnī, –ventus.

at (near), ad, *w. acc.; abl. of time or place.*

author, auctor, auctōris, *m.*

authority, auctōritās, –tātis, *f.*

await, exspectō, –āre, –āvī, –ātus.

away (be), absum, –esse, āfuī, āfutūrus.

B

bad, malus, –a, –um.

battle, pugna, –ae, *f.*; proelium, –ī, *n.*

be, sum, esse, fuī, futūrus.

beautiful, pulcher, –chra, –chrum.

because, *use particip. or abl. abs.;* quod, quia.

become, fīō, fierī, factus sum.

before, prae, *w. abl.;* ante, *w. acc.*

beg, ōrō, –āre, –āvī, –ātus; petō, –ere, petīvī, petītus.

begin, incipiō, –ere, –cēpī, –ceptus; **begin battle**, proelium committō, –ere, –mīsī, –missus.

behind, post, *w. acc.*

behold, cōnspiciō, –ere, –spexī, –spectus.

believe, crēdō, –ere, crēdidī, crēditus (*w. dat.*).

best, optimus, –a, –um.

better, melior, melius.

between, inter, *w. acc.*

bind, ligō, –āre, –āvī, –ātus.

boat, nāvis, nāvis, *f.*

body, corpus, corporis, *n.*

book, liber, librī, *m.*

booty, praeda, –ae, *f.*

born (be), nāscor, nāscī, nātus sum.

boundary, terminus, –ī, *m.*; fīnis, fīnis, *m.*

boy, puer, puerī, *m.*

brave, fortis, –e; **bravely**, fortiter.

break, frangō, –ere, frēgī, frāctus; rumpō, –ere, rūpī, ruptus; **break camp**, castra moveō, –ēre, mōvī, mōtus.

breathe, spīrō, –āre, –āvī, –ātus.

bring, ferō, ferre, tulī, lātus; **bring about**, efficiō, –ere, –fēcī, –fectus; **bring back**, redūcō, –ere, –dūxī,

–ductus; referō, –ferre, rettulī, relātus.

brother, frāter, frātris, *m.*

but, sed.

buy, emō, –ere, ēmī, ēmptus.

by, ā, ab, *w. abl.*

C

Caesar, Caesar, Caesaris, *m.*

call, vocō, –āre, –āvī, –ātus; **call together**, convocō.

camp, castra, –ōrum, *n.*; **break camp**, castra moveō, –ēre, mōvī, mōtus; **pitch camp**, castra pōnō, –ere, posuī, positus.

can, possum, posse, potuī, —.

capture, capiō, –ere, cēpī, captus.

care, cūra, –ae, *f.*

carefully, cum cūrā.

carry, portō, –āre, –āvī, –ātus; ferō, ferre, tulī, lātus; **carry on war**, bellum gerō, –ere, gessī, gestus.

cart, carrus, –ī, *m.*

catch sight of, cōnspiciō, –ere, –spexī, –spectus.

cattle, pecus, pecoris, *n.*

cause, causa, –ae, *f.*

certain, certus, –a, –um; **certainly**, certē; **a certain (one)**, quīdam, quaedam, quiddam.

chance, cāsus, –ūs, *m.*

changing, varius, –a, –um.

charge, crīmen, crīminis, *n.*; **be in charge of**, praesum, –esse, –fuī, –futūrus; **put in charge of**, praeficiō, –ere, –fēcī, –fectus.

children, līberī, –ōrum, *m.*

citizen, cīvis, cīvis, *m.*

climb, ascendō, –ere, ascendī, ascēnsus.

close, claudō, –ere, clausī, clausus.
close together, crēber, –bra, –brum.
collect, cōnferō, –ferre, –tulī, collātus; cōgō, –ere, coēgī, coāctus.
colonist, colōnus, –ī, m.
come, veniō, –īre, vēnī, ventus; **come together**, conveniō.
command, imperō, –āre, –āvī, –ātus (w. dat.); iubeō, –ēre, iussī, iussus; **be in command of**, praesum, –esse, –fuī, –futūrus (w. dat.).
commence, incipiō, –ere, –cēpī, –ceptus.
commit, committō, –ere, –mīsī, –missus.
compel, cōgō, –ere, coēgī, coāctus.
complete, cōnficiō, –ere, –fēcī, –fectus.
condemn, damnō, –āre, –āvī, –ātus.
confess, fateor, –ērī, fassus sum.
confident (be), cōnfīdō, –ere, –fīsus sum.
confide, have confidence in, cōnfīdō (w. dat.).
conquer, vincō, –ere, vīcī, victus.
constant, perpetuus, –a, –um.
consult, cōnsulō, –ere, –suluī, –sultus.
convenient, commodus, –a, –um.
convey, vehō, –ere, vexī, vectus.
country, patria, –ae, f.
courage, animus, –ī, m.; virtūs, –tūtis, f.
cruel, crūdēlis, –e.
cry out, clāmō, –āre, –āvī, –ātus.
cut, caedō, –ere, cecīdī, caesus.

D

danger, perīculum, –ī, n.
daughter, fīlia, –ae, f.

day, diēs, diēī, m.
death, mors, mortis, f.
deceive, fallō, –ere, fefellī, falsus.
deed, factum, –ī, n.
deep, altus, –a, –um.
(deeply) move, permoveō, –ēre, –mōvī, –mōtus.
defeat, pellō, –ere, pepulī, pulsus; vincō, –ere, vīcī, victus.
defend, dēfendō, –ere, –fendī, –fēnsus.
deliver, reddō, –ere, –didī, –ditus; trādō, –ere, –didī, –ditus.
demand, exigō, –ere, exēgī, exāctus.
depart, excēdō, –ere, –cessī, –cessus; discēdō, –ere, –cessī, –cessus.
desert, dēserō, –ere, –seruī, –sertus; relinquō, –ere, –līquī, –līctus.
deserve, mereō, –ēre, meruī, meritus.
destroy, exstinguō, –ere, –stīnxī, –stīnctus.
determine, statuō, –ere, statuī, statūtus; cōnstituō, –ere, –stituī, –stitūtus.
difficult, difficilis, –e.
diligence, dīligentia, –ae, f.
dismiss, dīmittō, –ere, –mīsī, –missus.
dispatch, submittō, –ere, –mīsī, –missus.
display, ostendō, –ere, –tendī, –tentus.
distinguished, ēgregius, –a, –um.
distribute, distribuō, –ere, –tribuī, –tribūtus.
divide, dīvidō, –ere, –vīsī, –vīsus.
do, faciō, –ere, fēcī, factus; agō, –ere, ēgī, āctus; **do harm to**, noceō, –ēre, nocuī, nocitus (w. dat.).

down from, dē, *w. abl.*
drag, trahō, –ere, trāxī, trāctus.
drive, agō, –ere, ēgī, āctus; **drive back**, repellō, –ere, reppulī, repulsus.
dutiful, pius, –a, –um.
duty, officium, –ī, *n.*

E

eagerness, studium, –ī, *n.*
early, mātūrus, –a, –um.
earn, mereō, –ēre, meruī, meritus.
earth, terra, –ae, *f.*
easy, facilis, –e.
eight, octō.
eighth, octāvus, –a, –um.
either . . . or, aut . . . aut.
employ, adhibeō, –ēre, –hibuī, –hibitus.
end, fīnis, fīnis, *m.*
endure, sustineō, –ēre, –tinuī, –tentus.
enemy, inimīcus, –ī, *m.* (*personal*); hostis, –is, *m.* (*national*).
enforce, cōnfirmō, –āre, –āvī, –ātus.
enlist, cōnscrībō, –ere, –scrīpsī, –scrīptus.
enough, satis.
entire, tōtus, –a, –um.
envoy, lēgātus, –ī, *m.*
envy, invideō, –ēre, –vīdī, –vīsus (*w. dat.*).
escape, ēvādō, –ere, –vāsī, –vāsus.
establish, cōnfirmō, –āre, –āvī, –ātus.
Europe, Eurōpa, –ae, *f.*
even, etiam.
every, omnis, –e; **everything**, omne *or* omnia.
evil, malus, –a, –um.
example, exemplum, –ī, *n.*

excel, superō, –āre, –āvī, –ātus; praestō, –āre, praestitī, –stitus (*w. dat.*).
expect, exspectō, –āre, –āvī, –ātus.
explore, explōrō, –āre, –āvī, –ātus.
extend, pertineō, –ēre, –tinuī, –tentus (*w. ad*).

F

face, faciēs, faciēī, *f.*
fall, cadō, –ere, cecidī, cāsus; **fall in**, incidō, –ere, –cidī, —.
fame, fāma, –ae, *f.*
familiar, nōtus, –a, –um.
family, familia, –ae, *f.*
famous, clārus, –a, –um.
farmer, agricola, –ae, *m.*
farthest, ultimus, –a, –um.
father, pater, patris, *m.*
fear (*v.*), timeō, –ēre, timuī, —; (*noun*), timor, –ōris, *m.*
feed, alō, –ere, aluī, alitus.
few, paucī, –ae, –a.
field, ager, agrī, *m.*
fifth, quīntus, –a, –um.
fight, pugnō, –āre, –āvī, –ātus.
fill, **fill up**, compleō, –ēre, –plēvī, –plētus.
find, inveniō, –īre, –vēnī, –ventus.
finish, perficiō, –ere, –fēcī, –fectus.
firm, firmus, –a, –um.
first, prīmus, –a, –um.
fit, aptus, –a, –um.
five, quīnque.
flee, fugiō, –ere, fūgī, fugitūrus.
flight, fuga, –ae, *f.*; **put to flight**, in fugam dō, dare, dedī, datus.
flow, fluō, –ere, flūxī, flūxus.
fold, plicō, –āre, –āvī, –ātus.
foot, pēs, pedis, *m.*; **on foot**, pedibus.

for (*conj.*), nam; (*prep.*), prō, *w. abl.*; **for the sake of**, causā *or* grātiā (*preceded by gen.*).
force, manus, –ūs, *f.*; vīs, —, *f.*
forces (troops), cōpiae, –ārum, *f.*
forest, silva, –ae, *f.*
form, fingō, –ere, fīnxī, fictus.
fortify, mūniō, –īre, –īvī, –ītus.
fortune, fortūna, –ae, *f.*
four, quattuor.
fourth, quārtus, –a, –um.
free (*adj.*), līber, –era, –erum; (*v.*), līberō, –āre, –āvī, –ātus.
freedom, lībertās, lībertātis, *f.*
fresh, integer, –gra, –grum.
friend, amīcus, –ī, *m.*
friendly, amīcus, –a, –um; familiāris, –e.
friendship, amīcitia, –ae, *f.*
frighten, terreō, –ēre, –uī, –itus; **frighten thoroughly**, perterreō.
from, **out from**, ē, ex, *w. abl.*; **down from**, dē, *w. abl.*; **away from**, ā, ab, *w. abl.*
front: **in front of**, prō, *w. abl.*
further, amplius.

G

Galba, Galba, –ae, *m.*
garrison, praesidium, –ī, *n.*
gate, porta, –ae, *f.*
Gaul, Gallia, –ae, *f.*; **a Gaul**, Gallus, –ī, *m.*
general, dux, ducis, *m.*
Germans, Germānī, –ōrum, *m.*
get, **get ready**, parō, –āre, –āvī, –ātus; **get together**, comparō.
gift, mūnus, mūneris, *n.*
girl, puella, –ae, *f.*
give, dōnō, –āre, –āvī, –ātus; dō, dare, dedī, datus; **give up**, trādō, –ere, –didī, –ditus; **give back**, reddō, –ere, –didī, –ditus; **give thanks to**, grātiās agō, –ere, ēgī, āctus (*w. dat.*).
glorious, clārus, –a, –um.
glory, glōria, –ae, *f.*
go, eō, īre, iī, itus; **go away**, discēdō, –ere, –cessī, –cessus; **go back**, redeō, –īre, –iī, –itus; **go out**, exeō.
god, deus, –ī, *m.*
good, bonus, –a, –um.
grain, frūmentum, –ī, *n.*
grant, tribuō, –ere, –uī, –ūtus; dōnō, –āre, –āvī, –ātus; dō, dare, dedī, datus; permittō, –ere, –mīsī, –missus.
grasp, prehendō, –ere, –hendī, –hēnsus.
grateful, grātus, –a, –um; **be** *or* **feel grateful**, grātiam habeō, –ēre, –uī, –itus.
graze, stringō, –ere, strīnxī, strictus.
great, magnus, –a, –um; **so great**, tantus, –a, –um; **how great**, quantus, –a, –um.
guard (*noun*), vigilia, –ae, *f.*; praesidium, –ī, *n.*; (*v.*), servō, –āre, –āvī, –ātus; dēfendō, –ere, –fendī, –fēnsus.

H

hand, manus, –ūs, *f.*
hang, pendō, –ere, pependī, pēnsus.
happen, accidō, –ere, –cidī, —.
hard, dūrus, –a, –um; gravis, –e.
harm, **do harm to**, noceō, –ēre, –uī, nocitus (*w. dat.*).
harmony, concordia, –ae, *f.*
harsh, dūrus, –a, –um.

hasten, mātūrō, –āre, –āvī, –ātus; properō, –āre, –āvī, –ātus.

have, habeō, –ēre, –uī, –itus; **have confidence in**, cōnfīdō, –ere, –fīsus sum (*w. dat.*).

he, is; hic; ille; *often not expressed.*

head, caput, capitis, *n.*

hear, audiō, –īre, –īvī, –ītus.

heart, cor, cordis, *n.*

heavy, gravis, –e.

help, auxilium, –ī, *n.*

her (*poss.*), eius; (*reflex.*), suus, –a, –um.

hero, vir, virī, *m.*

hesitate, dubitō, –āre, –āvī, –ātus.

high, altus, –a, –um.

himself (*reflex.*), suī; (*intens.*), ipse.

hinder, impediō, –īre, –īvī, –ītus.

his (*poss.*), eius; **his own** (*reflex.*), suus, –a, –um.

hold, **hold back**, retineō, –ēre, –tinuī, –tentus.

home, domus, –ūs, *f.*

honor, honor, honōris, *m.*

hope (*v.*), spērō, –āre, –āvī, –ātus; (*noun*), spēs, speī, *f.*

horse, equus, –ī, *m.*

hostile, inimīcus, –a, –um.

house, domus, –ūs, *f.*

how, quō modō.

how great, quantus, –a, –um.

human, hūmānus, –a, –um.

humble, humilis, –e.

hundred, centum.

I

I, ego, meī; *often not expressed.*

if, sī.

in, in, *w. abl.;* **in order to**, ut (*w. subjunctive*).

inasmuch as, *expressed by particip.*

increase, augeō, –ēre, auxī, auctus.

influence, addūcō, –ere, –dūxī, –ductus.

inform, (eum) certiōrem faciō, –ere, fēcī, factus.

inhabit, habitō, –āre, –āvī, –ātus; incolō, –ere, –coluī, –cultus.

injury, iniūria, –ae, *f.*

inquire, quaerō, –ere, quaesīvī, quaesītus.

instruction, disciplīna, –ae, *f.*

intercept, intercipiō, –ere, –cēpī, –ceptus.

interest, studium, –ī, *n.*

into, in, *w. acc.*

intrust, mandō, –āre, –āvī, –ātus; committō, –ere, –mīsī, –missus.

invent, fingō, –ere, fīnxī, fictus.

island, īnsula, –ae, *f.*

it, id; hoc; illud; *often not expressed.*

Italy, Italia, –ae, *f.*

its (*poss.*), eius; (*reflex.*), suus, –a, –um.

itself (*reflex.*), suī (*see* **452**).

J

join, iungō, –ere, iūnxī, iūnctus.

journey, iter, itineris, *n.*

judge, arbitror, –ārī, –ātus sum; reor, rērī, ratus sum; exīstimō, –āre, –āvī, –ātus.

jump, **jump down**, dēsiliō, –īre, –siluī, –sultus.

just, aequus, –a, –um; iūstus, –a, –um.

K

keen, ācer, ācris, ācre.

keep, teneō, –ēre, –uī, tentus; retineō, –ēre, –uī, –tentus; **keep from**, prohibeō, –ēre, –uī, –itus.

kill, interficiō, –ere, –fēcī, –fectus; caedō, –ere, cecīdī, caesus.

kind, genus, generis, *n.*

king, rēx, rēgis, *m.*

kingdom, rēgnum, –ī, *n.*

know, *perfect tenses of* nōscō, –ere, nōvī, nōtus, *or of* cognōscō, –ere, –nōvī, –nitus; sciō, –īre, scīvī, scītus.

L

labor, labōrō, –āre, –āvī, –ātus.

land, terra, –ae, *f.*; **native land**, patria, –ae, *f.*

language, lingua, –ae, *f.*

large, magnus, –a, –um.

last, extrēmus, –a, –um.

late, tardus, –a, –um.

lay aside, dēpōnō, –ere, –posuī, –positus.

lay waste, vāstō, –āre, –āvī, –ātus.

lead, dūcō, –ere, dūxī, ductus; **lead across** *or* **over**, trādūcō; **lead back**, redūcō; **lead forth** *or* **out**, prōdūcō.

leader, dux, ducis, *m.*; prīnceps, prīncipis, *m.*

learn, nōscō, –ere, nōvī, nōtus; cognōscō, –ere, –nōvī, –nitus; discō, –ere, didicī, —.

leave (**behind**), relinquō, –ere, –līquī, –līctus; **be left**, supersum, –esse, –fuī, –futūrus.

leisure, ōtium, –ī, *n.*

letter (*of alphabet*), littera, –ae, *f.*; (*epistle*), litterae, –ārum, *f.*

level, plānus, –a, –um.

liberty, lībertās, –tātis, *f.*

lieutenant general, lēgātus, –ī, *m.*

life, vīta, –ae, *f.*

light (*noun*), lūmen, lūminis, *n.*; (*adj.*), levis, –e; **lightly**, leviter.

like, similis, –e.

likeness, imāgō, imāginis, *f.*

little, parvus, –a, –um.

live (**a life**), agō, –ere, ēgī, āctus; **dwell**, habitō, –āre, –āvī, –ātus; incolō, –ere, –coluī, –cultus.

long, longus, –a, –um; **no longer**, nōn iam.

look at, spectō, –āre, –āvī, –ātus.

loose, solvō, –ere, solvī, solūtus.

lose, āmittō, –ere, –mīsī, –missus.

love, amō, –āre, –āvī, –ātus.

lower, īnferior, īnferius.

M

maintain, sustineō, –ēre, –uī, –tentus.

make, faciō, –ere, fēcī, factus.

man, vir, virī, *m.*; homō, hominis, *m.*; **old man**, senex, senis, *m.*

manage, gerō, –ere, gessī, gestus; administrō, –āre, –āvī, –ātus.

manner, modus, –ī, *m.*

many, multī, –ae, –a.

march, iter, itineris, *n.*

Marcus, Mārcus, –ī, *m.*

Marius, Marius, –ī, *m.*

master, dominus, –ī, *m.*

meet, occurrō, –ere, –currī, –cursus.

memory, memoria, –ae, *f.*

merchant, mercātor, –ōris, *m.*

messenger, nūntius, –ī, *m.*

middle of, medius, –a, –um.

mind, animus, –ī, *m.*

money, pecūnia, –ae, *f.*

mother, māter, mātris, *f.*

motto, sententia, –ae, *f.*

mountain, mōns, montis, *m.*

move, moveō, -ēre, mōvī, mōtus;
move deeply, permoveō.
much, multus, -a, -um.
my, meus, -a, -um; **myself** (*re-flex*.), meī; (*intens*.), ipse, ipsa, ipsum.

N

name, nōmen, nōminis, *n*.
nation, gēns, gentis, *f*.
native land, patria, -ae, *f*.
nature, nātūra, -ae, *f*.
near, ad, *w. acc*.
necessary, necessārius, -a, -um.
neighboring, fīnitimus, -a, -um.
neither (*adj*.), neuter, -tra, -trum.
neither . . . nor (*conj*.), neque . . . neque.
new, novus, -a, -um.
next, proximus, -a, -um.
nine, novem.
no (*adj*.), nūllus, -a, -um; **no longer** (*adv*.), nōn iam; **no one** (*pron*.), nēmō, *dat*. nēminī, *m*.
noble, nōbilis, -e.
nor, neque.
not, nōn.
notable, clārus, -a, -um.
notice, animadvertō, -ere, -vertī, -versus.
nothing, nihil, *indecl*., *n*.
now, nunc.
number, numerus, -ī, *m*.

O

obedient (be), pāreō, -ēre, -uī, pāritus (*w. dat*.).
obey, pāreō.
obtain, obtineō, -ēre, -uī, -tentus.
of (concerning), dē, *w. abl*.
offer, dēferō, -ferre, -tulī, -lātus.

old man, senex, senis, *m*.
on, in, *w. abl.;* **on account of**, ob, *w. acc*.
one, ūnus, -a, -um; **one at a time, one by one**, singulī, -ae, -a.; **any one**, aliquis *or* quis; **one . . . the other**, alter . . . alter.
opinion, sententia, -ae, *f*.
or, aut.
order (*v*.), iubeō, -ēre, iussī, iussus; imperō, -āre, -āvī, -ātus (*w. dat*.); (*noun*), ōrdō, ōrdinis, *m*.; **in order to**, ut.
other, alius, -a, -ud; **the other (of two)**, alter, -era, -erum.
ought, dēbeō, -ēre, -uī, -itus.
our, noster, -tra, -trum.
ourselves (*intens*.), ipsī.
out of, ē, ex, *w. abl*.
over, trāns.
own, proprius, -a, -um; **his own**, *see* **his** (*reflex*.).

P

paint, pingō, -ere, pīnxī, pictus.
part, pars, partis, *f*.
pay, solvō, -ere, solvī, solūtus; pendō, -ere, pependī, pēnsus.
peace, pāx, pācis, *f*.
people, populus, -ī, *m*.
permit, permittō, -ere, -mīsī, -missus.
persuade, impellō, -ere, -pulī, -pulsus.
pitch camp, castra pōnō, -ere, posuī, positus.
place (*noun*), locus, -ī, *m*. (*pl*.), loca, -ōrum, *n*.; (*v*.), pōnō, -ere, posuī, positus.
plan, cōnsilium, -ī, *n*.
please, be pleasing to, placeō, -ēre, placuī, placitus (*w. dat*.).

pleasing, grātus, –a, –um.

point out, mōnstrō, –āre, –āvī, –ātus.

power, potestās, –tātis, *f.*; imperium, –ī, *n.*

powerful (be), valeō, –ēre, valuī, valitūrus.

prepare, parō, –āre, –āvī, –ātus.

present (be), adsum, –esse, –fuī, –futūrus.

present, dōnō, –āre, –āvī, –ātus.

preserve, cōnservō, –āre, –āvī, –ātus.

press, **press hard**, premō, –ere, pressī, pressus.

pretense, speciēs, speciēī, *f.*

prevent, prohibeō, –ēre, –uī, –itus.

price, pretium, –ī, *n.*

prisoner, captīvus, –ī, *m.*

promise, voveō, –ēre, vōvī, vōtus.

prove, probō, –āre, –āvī, –ātus.

public, pūblicus, –a, –um.

punishment, poena, –ae, *f.*; supplicium, –ī, *n.*

pursue, premō, –ere, pressī, pressus.

put, pōnō, –ere, posuī, positus; **put to flight**, in fugam dō, dare, dedī, datus; **put out**, exstinguō, –ere, –stīnxī, –stīnctus; **put in charge of**, praeficiō, –ere, –fēcī, –fectus.

Q

quick, celer, celeris, celere.

quickly, celeriter.

R

race, genus, generis, *n.*

rank, ōrdō, ōrdinis, *m.*

ransom, redimō, –ere, –ēmī, –ēmptus.

rather, *expressed by comparative.*

read, legō, –ere, lēgī, lēctus.

ready, parātus, –a, –um; **get ready**, parō, –āre, –āvī, –ātus.

realize, sentiō, –īre, sēnsī, sēnsus.

reason, causa, –ae, *f.*; ratiō, –ōnis, *f.*

receive, accipiō, –ere, –cēpī, –ceptus.

refrain, temperō, –āre, –āvī, –ātus (*w.* ab).

region, regiō, –ōnis, *f.*

reinforcements, auxilia, –ōrum, *n.*

remain, maneō, –ēre, mānsī, mānsus.

remarkable, ēgregius, –a, –um; clārus, –a, –um.

remember, memoriā teneō, –ēre, –uī, tentus.

remove, removeō, –ēre, –mōvī, –mōtus.

report (*noun*), fāma, –ae, *f.*; (*v.*), nūntiō, –āre, –āvī, –ātus; referō, –ferre, rettulī, relātus.

repulse, repellō, –ere, reppulī, repulsus.

reserve, reservō, –āre, –āvī, –ātus.

rest (of), reliquus, –a, –um.

rest, quiēs, quiētis, *f.*

retreat, cēdō, –ere, cessī, cessus; sē recipiō, –ere, –cēpī, –ceptus.

reward, praemium, –ī, *n.*

right, iūs, iūris, *n.*

river, flūmen, flūminis, *n.*

road, via, –ae, *f.*; iter, itineris, *n.*

roll, volvō, –ere, volvī, volūtus.

Roman, Rōmānus, –a, –um; **a Roman**, Rōmānus, –ī, *m.*

rout, fundō, –ere, fūdī, fūsus.

run, currō, –ere, cucurrī, cursus.

S

sacred, sacer, –cra, –crum.
safety, salūs, –ūtis, *f.*
sail, nāvigō, –āre, –āvī, –ātus.
sailor, nauta, –ae, *m.*
sake of, for the, causā *or* grātiā (*w. gen. preceding*).
same, īdem, eadem, idem.
save, servō, –āre, –āvī, –ātus; cōnservō, –āre, –āvī, –ātus.
say, dīcō, –ere, dīxī, dictus.
sea, mare, maris, *n.*
see, videō, –ēre, vīdī, vīsus.
seek, petō, –ere, petīvī, petītus.
seem, videor, –ērī, vīsus sum.
seize, capiō, –ere, cēpī, captus; occupō, –āre, –āvī, –ātus.
select, dēligō, –ere, –lēgī, –lēctus.
self (*intens.*), ipse, ipsa, ipsum.
senate, senātus, –ūs, *m.*
send, mittō, –ere, mīsī, missus; **send away**, dīmittō; **send back**, remittō; **send ahead**, praemittō.
set, pōnō, –ere, posuī, positus; prōpōnō; **set out**, proficīscor, proficīscī, profectus sum.
settler, colōnus, –ī, *m.*
seven, septem.
seventh, septimus, –a, –um.
severe, gravis, –e.
shape, fōrma, –ae, *f.*
sharply, ācriter.
she, ea; haec; illa; *often not expressed.*
ship, nāvis, nāvis, *f.*
shout (*v.*), clāmō, –āre, –āvī, –ātus; (*noun*), clāmor, –ōris, *m.*
show, mōnstrō, –āre, –āvī, –ātus.
sight: catch sight of, cōnspiciō, –ere, –spexī, –spectus.
sign, signal, signum, –ī, *n.*

similar, similis, –e.
since, *use abl. abs.;* quod (*conj.*).
sister, soror, sorōris, *f.*
sit, sedeō, –ēre, sēdī, sessus.
size, magnitūdō, –tūdinis, *f.*
skill, ars, artis, *f.*
slave, servus, –ī, *m.*
slowly, tardē.
small, parvus, –a, –um.
so, ita; **so great**, tantus, –a, –um.
so as to, ut; **so as not to**, nē, *w. subj.*
soldier, mīles, mīlitis, *m.*
solid, firmus, –a, –um.
someone, something, aliquis, aliquid.
son, fīlius, –ī, *m.*
speak, loquor, loquī, locūtus sum.
speech, ōrātiō, –ōnis, *f.*
speed, celeritās, –tātis, *f.*
spend (**years**), agō, –ere, ēgī, āctus.
spirit, animus, –ī, *m.*
stand, stō, –āre, stetī, status.
state, cīvitās, –tātis, *f.*
steep, praeceps, *gen.* praecipitis.
stick, haereō, –ēre, haesī, haesus.
stop, cōnsistō, –ere, –stitī, –stitus.
storm, tempestās, –tātis, *f.*
strange, novus, –a, –um.
street, via, –ae, *f.*
stretch, tendō, –ere, tetendī, tentus.
strong, firmus, –a, –um; fortis, –e; **be strong**, valeō, –ēre, valuī, valitūrus.
struggle, contendō, –ere, –tendī, –tentus.
studies, studia, –ōrum, *n.*
such (**great**), tantus, –a, –um; **in such a way**, ita.
suffer, patior, patī, passus sum.
suitable, commodus, –a, –um.

summer, aestās, –tātis, *f.*
summon, vocō, –āre, –āvī, –ātus.
supply, cōpia, –ae, *f.*
surprise, opprimō, –ere, –pressī, –pressus.
surround, circumveniō, –īre, –vēnī, –ventus.
swear, iūrō, –āre, –āvī, –ātus.
swift, celer, celeris, celere; rapidus, –a, –um.
swiftly, celeriter, rapidē.
swiftness, celeritās, –tātis, *f.*

T

take, capiō, –ere, cēpī, captus; **take by assault**, expugnō, –āre, –āvī, –ātus.
tall, altus, –a, –um.
teach, doceō, –ēre, –uī, doctus.
teacher, magister, –trī, *m.*
tell, dīcō, –ere, dīxī, dictus.
ten, decem.
tenth, decimus, –a, –um.
terms (of peace), condiciō, –ōnis, *f.*
terrify, terreō, –ēre, –uī, –itus.
territory, fīnēs, –ium, *m. pl.*
than, quam.
thank, grātiās agō, –ere, ēgī, āctus (*w. dat.*).
that (*demonst.*), ille, illa, illud; is, ea, id; **that of yours**, iste, ista, istud.
that (*relat.*), quī, quae, quod.
that, in order that, so that (*conj.*), ut; **that . . . not**, nē (*purpose*), ut . . . nōn (*result*).
their (*poss.*), eōrum, eārum, eōrum; (*reflex.*), suus, –a, –um.
themselves (*reflex.*), suī; (*intens.*), ipsī, –ae, –a.
there (*in that place*), ibi.

they, eī, eae, ea; illī, illae, illa; *often not expressed.*
thing, rēs, reī, *f.*; *often not expressed.*
think, putō, –āre, –āvī, –ātus; exīstimō, –āre, –āvī, –ātus; reor, rērī, ratus sum; arbitror, –ārī, –ātus sum.
this (*demonst.*), hic, haec, hoc; is, ea, id.
thoroughly frighten, perterreō, –ēre, –uī, –itus.
thousand, mīlle.
threaten, īnstō, –āre, īnstitī, —.
three, trēs, tria.
through, per, *w. acc.*
throw, iaciō, –ere, iēcī, iactus; **throw out**, ēiciō, –ere, ēiēcī, ēiectus.
thrust out, ēiciō, –ere, ēiēcī, ēiectus.
tie, ligō, –āre, –āvī, –ātus.
till, colō, –ere, –uī, cultus.
timber, māteria, –ae, *f.*
time, tempus, –oris, *n.*; **one at a time**, singulī, –ae, –a.
to, ad, *w. acc.*; (*purpose*), ut.
tongue, lingua, –ae, *f.*
too, *expressed by comparative.*
top (of), summus, –a, –um.
touch, tangō, –ere, tetigī, tāctus.
town, oppidum, –ī, *n.*
train, exerceō, –ēre, –uī, –itus, īnstituō, –ere, –stituī, –stitūtus.
transport, trānsportō, –āre, –āvī, –ātus.
troops, cōpiae, –ārum, *f. pl.*
true, vērus, –a, –um.
try, experior, –īrī, –pertus sum; temptō, –āre, –āvī, –ātus.
two, duo, duae, duo.
twofold, duplex, *gen.* duplicis.

U

under, sub, *w. acc. or abl.*
understand, intellegō, –ere, –lēxī, –lēctus.
undertake, suscipiō, –ere, –cēpī, –ceptus.
unfold, explicō, –āre, –āvī, –ātus.
uninhabited (be), vacō, –āre, –āvī, –ātus.
unjustly, cum iniūriā.
unlike, dissimilis, –e.
unwilling (be), nōlō, nōlle, nōluī, —.
urge on, incitō, –āre, –āvī, –ātus.
useful, ūtilis, –e.
use up, cōnsūmō, –ere, –sūmpsī, –sūmptus.

V

varying, varius, –a, –um.
very, *expressed by superlative;* **very carefully**, magnā cūrā.
victory, victōria, –ae, *f.*
voice, vōx, vōcis, *f.*
vow, voveō, –ēre, vōvī, vōtus.

W

wage war, bellum gerō, –ere, gessī, gestus.
wagon, carrus, –ī, *m.*
walk, gradior, gradī, gressus sum.
want, volō, velle, voluī, —.
war, bellum, –ī, *n.*
warn, moneō, –ēre, –uī, –itus.
waste (lay), vāstō, –āre, –āvī, –ātus.
water, aqua, –ae, *f.*
wave, unda, –ae, *f.*
way, via, –ae, *f.*

we, nōs; *often not expressed.*
weapons, arma, –ōrum, *n.*
well, bene.
what, (*pron.*), quis, quid; (*adj.*), quī, quae, quod.
when, ubi, cum; *often expressed by particip. or abl. abs.*
where, ubi.
which, quī, quae, quod.
while, dum, cum; *often expressed by particip.*
who (*rel. pron.*), quī, quae, quod; (*interrog. pron.*), quis, quid.
whole, tōtus, –a, –um.
why, cūr.
winter, hiems, hiemis, *f.*
wish, volō, velle, voluī, —.
wish not, nōlō, nōlle, nōluī, —.
with, cum, *w. abl.; sometimes abl. alone.*
witness, testis, testis, *m.*
wonder, mīror, –ārī, –ātus sum.
woods, silva, –ae, *f.*
word, verbum, –ī, *n.*
work (*v.*), labōrō, –āre, –āvī, –ātus; (*noun*), opus, operis, *n.*; labor, –ōris, *m.*
worthy, dignus, –a, –um.
wound, vulnus, vulneris, *n.*
write, scrībō, –ere, scrīpsī, scrīptus.
wrong, iniūria, –ae, *f.*

Y

year, annus, –ī, *m.*
you, tū (*sing.*); vōs (*pl.*); *often not expressed.*
your, tuus, –a, –um; vester, –tra, –trum.

INDEX

(The numbers refer to sections unless otherwise stated.)

www.ingramcontent.com/pod-product-compliance
Lightning Source LLC
Chambersburg PA
CBHW032037050726
47590CB00001B/35